Making European Space

'This is a fine contribution to the literature on European public policy and planning. It develops a critical approach to the European integration project, as this political idea is being translated into conceptions of the spatial organisation of the European territory and into resultant policy initiatives. Grounded in the new relational and multiscalar geography and in recent debates in planning theory, Richardson and Jensen provide a robust analysis of the power of dynamics of contemporary European spatial policy initiatives.'

Professor Patsy Healey, University of Newcastle, UK

'*Making European Space* exemplifies a new and exciting kind of planning research. By emphasizing power, Ole Jensen and Tim Richardson convincingly demonstrate how the emerging planning discourse in Europe – presented by its proponents as neutral and rational – is really frozen politics that effectively supports the spaces, infrastructures and mobilities which the powers that be want for Europe. Read this book if you wish to understand current European spatial planning and politics.'

Professor Bent Flyvbjerg, Aalborg University, Denmark

Making European Space explores how future visions of Europe's physical space are being decisively shaped by transnational politics and power struggles, which are being played out in new multi-level arenas of governance across the European Union. At stake are big ideas about mobility and friction, about relations between core and peripheral regions, and about the future of Europe's cities and countryside. The book builds a critical narrative of the emergence of a new discourse of Europe as 'monotopia', revealing a very real project to shape European space in line with visions of high speed, frictionless mobility, the transgression of borders, and the creation of city networks. The narrative explores in depth how the particular ideas of mobility and space which underpin this discourse are being constructed in policy making, and reflects on the legitimacy of these policy processes. In particular, it shows how spatial ideas are becoming embedded in the everyday practices of the social and political organisation of space, in ways that make a frictionless Europe seem natural, and part of a common European territorial identity.

Ole B. Jensen is Associate Professor in the Department of Development and Planning, Aalborg University, Denmark.

Tim Richardson is Senior Lecturer in the Department of Town and Regional Planning, University of Sheffield, and Visiting Professor in European Spatial Policy at Aalborg University.

Making European Space

Mobility, power and territorial identity

Ole B. Jensen and Tim Richardson

LONDON AND NEW YORK

First published 2004
by Routledge
11 New Fetter Lane, London EC4P 4EE

Simultaneously published in the USA and Canada
by Routledge
29 West 35th Street, New York, NY 10001

Routledge is an imprint of the Taylor & Francis Group

Typeset in Galliard
by Keystroke, Jacaranda Lodge, Wolverhampton
Printed and bound in Great Britain
by TJ International Ltd, Padstow, Cornwall

British Library Cataloguing in Publication Data
A cataloge record for this book is available from the British Library

Library of Congress Cataloging in Publication Data
A catalog record for this book has been requested

ISBN 0-415-29192-5 (hbk)
ISBN 0-415-29193-3 (pbk)

Contents

Illustrations

The authors and publisher have made every effort to contact and acknowledge copyright holders, but if any errors have been made we would be happy to correct them at a later printing.

Colour plates

Figures

Maps

Boxes

Tables

Preface

At a time when international conflict powerfully reminds us of the fragility of the project of European integration, and when the constitution of the European Union (EU) is being reformulated to cope with its rapid imminent growth, it seems more important than ever to reflect on the meaning of *Europe*. Missing from the multiple narratives of Europe is a critical analysis of the relationship of this contested European project with the *spaces* of Europe. What does the political and economic project of European integration mean for its cities, its environment and for its territory? In this book, we argue that a core dimension of the European project is the making of a single European space – *a monotopia* – and that this spatial agenda is becoming more explicit, and more coherent, with the advent of a new field of European spatial policy, which is embedding new ideas about relationships across space in a multi-level, transnational field of activity. So far there has been little critical scrutiny of this policy field, and relatively little debate about its meaning for space. We hope that this book will help in fuelling such a debate.

In the 1980s, a new discourse of European space emerged, combining ideas about mobility and transport with the political integration of Europe, and the completion of the Single Market. In the construction of this discourse, new modes of thought, forms of knowledge and practices emerged, which significantly shaped the EU policy agenda, and created the conditions for trans-European networks to become a priority focus of EU policy in the 1990s; this has progressed into the making of a strategic vision of European space (the European Spatial Development Perspective). Such initiatives are part of a rethinking of the EU's involvement in the making of European space, and are adding an explicit spatial dimension to its social, economic and political agenda, with consequences for the content of policy, programmes of action and governance structures.

In this book we explore how these new modes of policy thinking, institutional structures and practices are being constructed, in a spatialisation of governmental ideas as a new discourse of EU spatial policy is constructed. We reveal a complex milieu of power struggles and contested meanings extending across Europe and reaching from local to transnational policy arenas. The objectives of the book are to crystallise and critically examine the key policy ideas emerging in this new field of European spatial planning, and to explore the arguments surrounding policy themes such as polycentric development, sustainability, mobility and peripherality.

The narrative which we invite the reader to explore seeks to open up perspectives on the making of European space within the policy processes and institutions of the EU, and more particularly seeks to show how a particular discourse of monotopic Europe is embedding a hegemonic vision of EU space. For us, the term monotopia captures the idea of a one-dimensional (mono) discourse of space and territory (topia/topos). It is our aim here to reveal the discourse of 'Europe as monotopia' as an organising set of ideas that looks upon the European Union territory within a single overarching rationality of making a 'one space', made possible by seamless networks enabling frictionless mobility.

There is a vast literature analysing the nature of the EU, from geographical, political, economic and legal perspectives among others. There is a much smaller concentration of work on the ways in which the activities of the EU impinge on its physical spaces – on Europe's cities, its remotely scattered rural communities, its highways and airports, its mountains and seas. This book sets out to examine just that. But uniquely, it brings critical perspectives from sociology to bear in considering how Europe as a set of new transnational policy spaces is making a difference to Europe as a myriad of lived, experienced, meaningful, crucial spaces. It sheds light on the obscure policy making activities that focus on local places from a dizzying vantage point of scale.

There is of course a huge research field yet to be opened up, analysing the relationships between lived spaces and EU policies. Here, anthropological/ethnographic perspectives are beginning to give shape to this gap, and the potential field of inquiry which it suggests. Localised perspectives, such as those used by John Gray (Gray, 2000), help in exploring how the production of lived spaces such as rural landscapes, mirrors EU policy. Others explore the inside of the EU policy process, analysing the conscious attempts to reproduce 'Europeanness' among policy makers and citizens (e.g. Shore, 2000). But there is much more to be done to link ethnographic analysis of EU policy making with ethnographic analysis of the spaces which the policies touch. Here we stay firmly on Shore's side of things, recognising that in future it would be rewarding to visit the other side of this unexplored territory, and certainly keeping in mind that everyday space 'exists' beyond the policy processes and even beyond their capacity for policy capture or reach. Understanding more about the interweaving of policy discourse with our continuous making and remaking of everyday lived space seems an attractive and necessary challenge.

We hope that this book will contribute to the work of those who have sought to apply Foucault's ideas on governmentality to urban studies, for instance in analysing neo-liberal modes of city government (like Nikolas Rose, Thomas Osborne and Engin F. Isin). Inspired by Maarten Hajer (1995, 2000), we see the reproduction and institutionalisation of policy discourse as an analytical key, and inspired by Edward W. Soja we see the necessity to spatialise this analysis.

The idea of this book has matured since the beginning of our collaboration in 1999. Since 1994 we have individually built up a solid research capacity on the topic of European spatial policy (two PhD dissertations and a number of collaborative articles and papers). The book draws from case studies on European Union spatial planning (the European Spatial Development Perspective, the North Sea mega-region, the trans-European transport network, the Øresund cross-border region), based on primary research carried out by the authors, and supplemented by drawing from the rapidly growing research literature. It aims to be theoretically informed and critical rather than descriptive, and to appeal to a broad international audience, both in its scope of analysis and its potential readership.

We hope to encourage debate among policy makers, academics, researchers and students about this new and important policy field in the making, which deserves much more attention from planners, geographers, political scientists and sociologists than it is currently getting.

Ole B. Jensen and Tim Richardson
June 2003

Acknowledgements

We have many to thank for supporting the progress of this book. Certainly, it would not have been written without the support of our friends and families, to whom we dedicate this work. We received many helpful and constructive comments on drafts of chapters from Patsy Healey, John Urry, Henrik Halkier, Andreas Faludi, Edward W. Soja, Maarten Hajer and Bent Flyvbjerg. During the work phase on the book, we also benefited from discussions with Kai Böhme, Flemming Thornæs and Deike Peters, among many others. At the institutional level we would like to thank the Department of Town and Regional Planning, Sheffield University, and the Department of Development and Planning, Aalborg University, for supporting the inter-departmental venture that this collaboration forms part of. We also owe thanks to the Department of Development and Planning, Aalborg University for hosting Tim Richardson as a Visiting Professor. In terms of technical assistance we would like to thank Ania Jørgensen for helping with graphics. Finally, we would like to express our gratitude to Ib Jørgensen and Gordon Dabinett for their inspiration, and for showing the value of critical research into EU spatial planning.

1.1 A construction site of European democracy? Parthenon, Athens, 2002.

Part One
Introducing the Construction Sites of European Space

Here, we set out the idea of a discourse of monotopia, and introduce the policy spaces within which this new spatial policy discourse is being constructed, contested and reproduced. We move on to thinking about the nature of the 'European project' and the meaning of contemporary political integration, drawing out issues for spatial policy making. We then present the theoretical and conceptual framework for our empirical analysis, which draws together sociological and geographical theories (a 'cultural sociology of space') and a discourse analytical perspective.

Chapter 1

Introduction

> But let us get back to Europe's great engineering projects and the political significance of this initial programme of European infrastructural development. The whole point of all this development – the building of bridges and roadways, the digging of tunnels, the laying of railways and highways on expropriated land – is *to make the territory more dynamic*, in order to increase the transit speed of people and goods. That great 'static vehicle' constituted by the road and railway networks promotes the acceleration of the small 'dynamic vehicles' that use them, allowing whole convoys to glide smoothly; and, pretty soon, resistance to the forward motion of mobile vehicles, shown, from time immemorial, by a nation's geographical depth, will disappear. But so will all topographical asperities, those hills and steep valleys that were the pride, the splendour, of the regions traversed, being ironed out. And the (sole) winner will be the outrageously outsized metropolitan agglomeration capable of absorbing, on its own, most of the power of the nations of Europe, along with a whole country's productive output.
>
> (Virilio, 1997: 79–80, italics in original)

> Transnational policy discourses frame various social and physical realities, make some futures conceivable while others are suggested to be irrelevant. They come with a particular idea of rational action and present particular 'identity-offers'.
>
> (Hajer, 2000: 142)

Mobility and monotopia

Imagining the spatiality of possible futures is an endeavour as old as the territorial appropriation of space and place. In this book we shall encounter a particular vision for the future of the European Union territory. We shall address how ideas of territorial governance across national boundaries are linked both to the notions of an 'ever closer union' of the peoples of Europe, and to the increasing seamless flow of goods, people, capital and services. It is a story uncovering how the ambitions and dreams of European integration are based on a particular view of space and place which we frame as monotopia. It is also a tale of how such underlying rationales are linked to new ways of thinking about the place called Europe and its spatial ordering. By this we mean the social and political organisation of space within the European Union.

In an etymological sense the word 'utopia' has as its original connotation literally 'no place'. However, at least since the thinking of Thomas More (More, 1561) the concept has also come to mean the inaccessible or never achievable goals of humankind's dreams and ambitions. Closely linked to the dream of possible future worlds associated with Utopian Socialist thinkers, the notion of utopia gained an intellectual and political currency as the best of all places – being 'no place', however, in the 'real world'. The utopian imagination faces its opposite in the notion of 'dystopia' – the worst of all places. However, imagining the fall of humankind into uncanny and beastly disorder seemed to be less difficult to envision through the ages, from the agonising torture depicted in the medieval paintings of Pieter Breughel, to the post-modern dystopian urbanism of Ridley Scott's *Blade Runner.* Between utopia and dystopia is captured the tension of alternative possible futures of humankind – blessed or doomed.

The notion of ordering the territory of the EU according to a set of spatial imaginations or visions for the future can be interpreted as utopia or dystopia – a dream of a transnational space of equal opportunity, material growth, happiness and blessing, or the disorder of a regressive space of exclusion, of 'Fortress Europe' with its internal hierarchy of prosperous elites and its doomed outcasts. However, probing deeper into the spatial visions and imaginations underlying the new policies of European integration we would argue that a third kind of vision surfaces – of a space of *monotopia.* By this we mean an organised, ordered and totalised space of zero-friction and seamless logistic flows. In this book we will argue that, though the word 'monotopia' will not be found in any European plan, policy document or political speech, this idea of monotopic Europe lies at the heart of the new ways of looking at European territory. We will argue that a rationality of monotopia exists, and that it is inextricably linked with a governmentality of Europe, expressed in a will to order space, to create a seamless and integrated space within the context of the European project, which is being pursued through the emerging field of European spatial policy. The future of places and people across Europe seems closely linked to the possibility of monotopia.

A vision of monotopic Europe centres on the idea of a 'zero-friction society' (Flyvbjerg *et al.*, 2003; Hajer, 1999) based on an increasing harmonisation of mobilities of people, goods and information, leading to a new dimension of ambivalence. Within such a uniform space of flows we would argue that there may still exist 'pockets of resistance', contestation and counter practices. However, as European integration seems increasingly to be organised around the principle of spatial governance within a frame of seamless mobility, we would surmise that such Foucauldian counterpractices of 'heterotopia' are threatened with annihilation by the push towards a new European space of uniform flow. In this book we will explore this will to order European space by tracing its effect on the treatment of three distinct themes in policy making: the urban, the environment and the question of territorial identity. Along the way we will elaborate on what monotopia means for the urban development of its cities and regions, for its environment and for the territorial dimensions of identity.

Cities are increasingly seen as nodes in global networks of flows of capital and information. The EU articulates a vision of cities as urban nodes in this context of global competition. Such visioning is built on knowledge-intensive entrepreneurial cities, raising fundamental concerns about how Europe can become a space of urban competition, yet somehow ensure that the benefits of economic growth are evenly distributed and that regions, particularly those on the periphery, do not become losers in this globalised competition. The EU's spatial vision thus attempts the difficult task of reconciling competition with balanced spatial development, balancing the interests of core cities with those of peripheral regions, and re-orienting the urban towards a polycentric form.

We will argue that a precondition for a successful venture into this new highly competitive transnational space, and a central element of the monotopic discourse, is a hierarchical ordering which places the environment as subsidiary to the logics of material growth and market expansion. The European single market can only succeed if it can compete economically with its major competitors in the economic triad – North America and Asia. At stake in this globalised economic competition are biodiversity, environmental carrying capacity and landscapes of cultural heritage. The environmental dimension of the new European spatial policy discourse, attempting to deal with this fundamental tension, adopts an accommodationist vocabulary of ecological modernisation, which holds that economic growth and environmental protection can go hand in hand.

With thoughts about Europe framed by a vocabulary of monotopia, the attention of policy makers and planners is turned 'naturally' towards the harmonisation of flows of goods, services, capital and working power. But it also suggests a re-thinking of the meaning of Europe in terms of its territorial identity. So questions of territorial belonging, inclusion and exclusion in a new seamless space of European flows lead to a new imaginary of the EU, and thus to the question of territorial identity. By inserting the question of European identity into the frame of monotopic Europe we face new questions of where to go, and where to stay.

Our approach to the vision of monotopic Europe, and to issues as apparently diverse as the urban, the environment and the question of identity, is to keep focused on a single idea which cuts through them all – and which makes monotopia possible – attaining the vision of frictionless mobility. We will explore how the core issue of physical movement has become central to a policy discourse that can sustain the idea that the European vision 'works' for its core cities, its peripheral regions, its environment and its citizens. We will argue that the reorganisation of European space is inescapably about re-ordering mobility, placing cities, environment and identities in a new perspective of transnational flow and mobility.

Our investigation of the new discourse of monotopic Europe is therefore structured around these key issues of the urban, the environment, and the question of identity, explored with a constant awareness of the contested meaning of mobilities, at scales from the local to the transnational.

Contested spaces

Landmark case studies in planning have dramatically revealed the deep rooted, complex and hotly contested struggles that go on to shape the places we inhabit in everyday life (e.g. Flyvbjerg, 1998). However, it can come as something of a surprise, for professionals and politicians engaged in these localised planning struggles, to find that 'their' neighbourhoods or towns may feature on larger maps, and may feature in obscure debates which use unfamiliar language and take place between actors previously unknown to them. Cities may become 'nodes' in urban networks, mountain ranges and stretches of sea may become 'missing links' in international infrastructure networks, where the human scale seems to be lost completely, and where local knowledge seems no longer to fit. Once it is realised that these maps exist, of course, it may seem important to appear on them: for 'our town' to be recognised as a 'node' in a proposed network of some sort, say, rather than be lost in the unknown (and unimportant?) shadow spaces in between. Battles over space and place in Europe are no longer only fought in the trenches, or in the (relatively) accessible arenas of local politics. These days they are also fought in obscure policy spaces, away from the public gaze, and across a complex terrain that even those in the struggle may not fully comprehend. And in the last decade a new field of battle has been created: European space itself is the subject of a fledgling policy field which seeks to create a vision for its future, and to impose order on actions within it.

The emergence of a common EU approach to spatial policy raises a series of fundamental questions about the ways that places across Europe, in particular its cities and regions, will grow and connect with each other. Visions underlying this approach carry important ideas about how this future development should take place. All of this has implications for economies, environments and societies across Europe, both in terms of neighbourhoods and local markets and in terms of a European citizenship and single market. At the heart of this new field of activity are ideas that seek to reconstruct the fabric and infrastructure of Europe which will shape how we live, travel and work. Ideas about relationships between mobility and urban space are at the heart of these new spatial visions.

Mobility has become a defining feature of contemporary Europe. The four freedoms at the heart of the European Treaties are based on movement: of people, goods, capital and services. It could be argued that Europe is as much about movement as it is about place, as the European project seeks to break down the barriers to free movement: the great distances between the core cities and the peripheral dispersed communities, the natural barriers which are not crossed by high speed roads and railways, and the national borders across which transport systems do not mesh. These relations in space are framed in a new European lexicon which embodies, yet at the same time attempts to resolve, the great polarities of European space – between core and periphery, between urban and rural – through a new language of harmony and balanced development.

But European spatial planning is planning in and for Europe (Böhme, 1999a): it is partly a concerted attempt to impose a coherent European spatial vision on future development within the member states; and partly an attempt to achieve spatial co-ordination across the wide range of policies, regulations and instruments which implement EU economic and social objectives. These include the Structural Funds and the Cohesion Fund, the trans-European communications and transport networks, environmental policy and agricultural policy. Previously, the spatial impacts of many of these policies and programmes have been overlooked in their implementation and evaluation (Davies, 1994). So partly what is at stake is the way in which policies backed by very large amounts of money will be targeted.

Through spatial policy processes across Europe, a new discourse of European spatial development is taking shape, with the definition of a new policy language, new knowledge forms and new policy options. The purpose of this book is to carry out a critical analysis of this emerging field, focusing particularly on the power relations at work. We will encounter a series of policy spaces that we see as the construction sites of new policy discourses. In these spaces, canonical policy documents have been prepared which serve as vehicles for the expression of a new discourse of European space, capturing and framing the changing relations between society and space.

These activities are increasingly shaping planning interventions at all scales across Europe, raising further questions about the democratic nature of what is going on: Who is shaping policy? Which decisions are affected and who makes these decisions? Are citizens or stakeholder groups empowered to participate in these processes? Who might be the winners and losers in this reshaping of European space?

Introducing policy spaces

Our central aim is to crystallise and critically examine the key policy ideas emerging in the new field of European spatial planning, and to explore the arguments and power struggles surrounding the core policy themes. Throughout, we will focus on the issue of mobility, and its implications for the urban, the environment and territorial identity. These are emerging as challenges at every scale of governance and in every location across the EU. Our selection of cases allows scrutiny of the construction sites of policy discourse and its institutionalisation, and the difference this makes to places. We should emphasise that these are not comparative geographically defined cases. That is not our aim. Taken together, they are used to open up windows on the broad policy spaces that are touched by European spatial ideas, on their history and activity at different spatial scales from the city to the continental. They illustrate early steps in the emergence of a complex multi-level policy field.

Although the first steps towards a European spatial planning policy were taken by the Council of Europe in the 1960s, recent progress towards a coherent European spatial vision has advanced more rapidly within the more restricted membership of the EU. Our selected cases – the trans-European transport network (TEN-T); the European Spatial Development Perspective (ESDP) prepared by the Committee on Spatial Development for the European Union; the INTERREG IIC North Sea NorVISION Programme, prepared by the North Sea Region Spatial Vision Working Group (VWG) for the North Sea EU mega-region; and plans for the future development of the Øresund region, across the national boundaries of Sweden and Denmark – focus primarily on the EU, located within a wider Europe in the changing context of rapid and imminent enlargement. The wider perspective, beyond the EU, is provided by reference to the Council of Europe's work on a common spatial approach for the entire continent of Europe.

TEN-T[1] became one of the major early practical initiatives of European spatial integration, and stands as a signpost towards a field of European spatial policy (Giannakourou, 1996). In the mid 1990s agreement was reached by the EU on Guidelines for the development of a transport network which would reach into every corner of Europe, extending its physical contact across EU external borders into regions to the north, south and east. The TEN-T vision was truly global: an integrated network of modern high-speed roads, railways and other infrastructure crossing the European continent, filling the missing links between national transport systems, and applying state of the art information technology to the operation of the network. Increasing competitiveness, cohesion and economic growth, creating jobs and reducing peripherality: benefits were expected to flow in these key areas of the 1992 process. Important Commission documents, from the Maastricht Treaty to the key 1993 Delors White Paper, entwined European integration, the single market and transport infrastructure, fuelling the seemingly unstoppable momentum of the trans-European transport network. After more than a decade of policy development, the vision remains clear:

> Following the entry into force of the Maastricht Treaty in 1993, the Commission put forward a comprehensive global framework for the development of trans-European networks. This was the first time since the Roman era that Europe had started to think about transport systems going beyond national frontiers.
>
> (Preface by Commissioner Loyola de Palacio in CEC, 2003b)

and

> Freedom of movement for people and goods depends not just on the opening of transport markets but also on physical infrastructures. By promoting the construction of infrastructures that cross borders and connect national networks, the trans-European transport network accelerates the establishment of the internal market, links peripheral regions to the heart of the European Union and opens Europe to neighbouring countries.
>
> (Preface by Commissioner Loyola de Palacio in CEC, 2003b)

However, as we will see, the Commission has become increasingly concerned that the TEN-T is not being implemented quickly enough. The 2001 White Paper on Transport (CEC, 2001c), and the recently launched review of TEN-T policy, continue the trend of framing the problem of implementation around the lack of investment by member states, and identifying the need for appropriate transnational financial instruments.

While TEN-T policy has been practical – aimed at the delivery of a tangible infrastructure programme – and at the heart of the EU integration agenda, the broader scene of spatial policy has followed a hazier path at the margins of policy. The European Spatial Development Perspective (ESDP) (CSD, 1999) represents a key landmark in a decade-long attempt to make way for a future policy field of European spatial planning, through Commission initiatives and the work of the Committee on Spatial Development (CSD) (Jensen and Jørgensen, 2000; Jensen *et al.*, 1996b; Williams, 1996a). The ESDP's ambitious agenda is to provide a strategic spatial framework which could draw together many other EU initiatives with spatial impacts (such as TEN-T, the Structural Funds, agriculture and environmental policy), and to create a spatial vision which could shape the spatial planning activities within and between member states. This vision is based on harmonious, balanced development. Achieving this cannot be regarded a small task: the ESDP's spatial vision deals with one of the largest and economically strongest regions in the world, covering the territory of the EU as it stood in 1999 with its more than 370 million inhabitants covering an area of 3.2 million km^2 and an annual gross domestic product (GDP) of 6.8 trillion ECU (CSD, 1999: 8). Furthermore, the ESDP's visions reach further and specificially address the spatial dimensions of the forthcoming enlargment of the EU. After working through a series of drafts (to which we will return later), the final version of the ESDP, which enshrines this EU spatial vision, was adopted by the informal meeting of ministers responsible for spatial planning in the EU in Potsdam on 10–11 May 1999. The many issues raised by the creation of the ESDP as a new biblical text for European space, and the subsequent attempts to apply it, are central to our inquiry.

But to properly contextualise our analysis of spatial framing within the EU, and to indicate the breadth of spatial vision that is apparent in the minds of politicians, policy makers and international institutions, we will extend our scope to encompass continental Europe as a whole. In 2000, a set of *Guiding principles for sustainable spatial development of the European continent* was adopted in

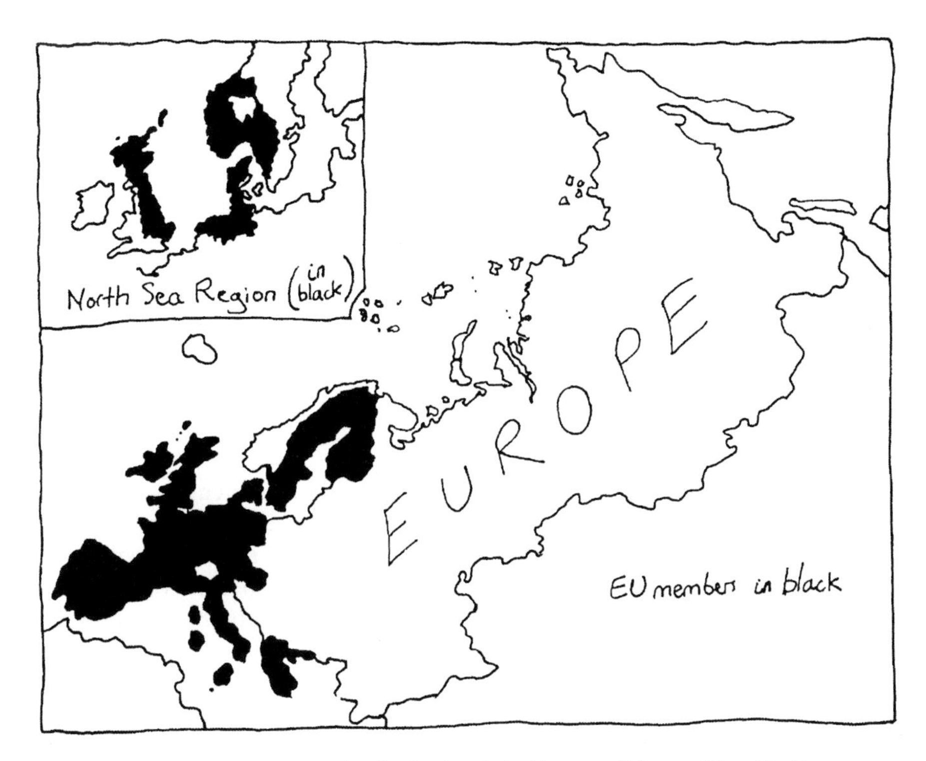

1.2 Nested spatial visions: the North Sea Region (inset), the European Union, and the wider Europe.

Hanover by the Council of Europe (CEMAT, 2000). As if to put the EU in its place, these Guiding Principles refer to the EU as being simply one of several 'large European regions' (CEMAT, 2000: 5)! Indeed, the Council of Europe membership of 45 countries represents the EU member states, but also gives voice to the interests of the 10 accession countries, as well as those unlikely to become EU members in the foreseeable future (Figure 1.2).

It is in the frameworks of the new EU mega-regions where European spatial planning, as a transnational activity, is being realised more quickly than anywhere else. As an example of the fast growing world of action programmes that are under development in the slipstream of the ESDP, we will focus on events in one of these INTERREG regions – one of the new transnational laboratories where mega-visions of European space are being tested and applied. The North Sea Region comprises regions from the UK, the Netherlands, Sweden, Denmark, Norway and Germany bordering the North Sea (Figure 1.2 inset). The North Sea has its own spatial vision, known as NorVISION, which sets out an agenda for the future development of this space. Here, we will explore the implications of attempting to develop spatial approaches across national boundaries, and building new institutional frameworks that might make this possible. We will look into one of the melting pots where top down and bottom up interests meet and are mediated.

But how are places across Europe responding to these framing practices? How are actors in cities and regions locating their activities in this new policy field, and what difference does it make? In turning our attention to cities and regions, we will focus on the Øresund region – a recent construction which binds together Denmark's capital city with a remote rural part of Sweden, made possible by a mega infrastructure project which creates the first direct physical road and rail link between Scandinavia and the rest of the EU. The Øresund case allows our focus on scale and mobility to be taken further as we see how ideas, places and institutions take on different lives at different scales.

The theoretical approach

Our aim is to build a theoretically informed critique which engages with the complexities and inner workings of policy making processes, and at the same time is concerned with how spaces are constructed within them. This is quite different from an approach which concerns itself primarily with the politics of European integration. It is essential, as far as we are concerned, to critically discuss the meaning of all this policy making for the Europe that lies beyond policy space. What sort of Europe – in spatial terms – is being constructed to lie at the heart of the new spatial visions?

The perspective we use to probe at this question we term a cultural sociology of space. To build this perspective, we draw from a variety of theoretical sources from critical geography to sociology, to argue for an understanding of the spatiality of social life that embraces meanings and material practices. The approach hinges on the dialectical relations between material practices and the symbolic meanings that social agents attach to their spatial environment. We can build bridges, but bridges have different meanings, especially when they can bind new regions, cross borders, form key links in international networks, or simply allow a person to get to work in a previously inaccessible location. Relations between society and space, then, need to be conceptualised in terms of their practical 'workings' and their symbolic 'meaning', played out at spatial scales from the body to the global. This leads to the emphasis we place on the 'politics of scale'. We place mobility at the foreground of our analysis, since it is movement within and between spaces that increasingly shapes socio-spatial relationships.

We apply discourse theory to create a framework for this analysis, which also provides the structure for the book. Our approach views spatial planning and policy making as an arena of constant struggle over meanings and values in society, played out in day-to-day micro-level practices. We are therefore very interested in what happens at the fine-grain level of policy making, where big ideas are reproduced through the everyday planning activities such as writing policy documents, using various tools to analyse impacts on space, and preparing maps to show how certain policy ideas might be applied. We are therefore interested in the creation of a new policy language (both visual and textual), and in the practices which help to legitimise this new language, and to reproduce it across the policy spaces of Europe (and beyond them). We are concerned with both informal and formal practices, because it seems clear that much of what is happening in this new field takes place in the face of a lack of legal competence to act, and relies on voluntary co-operation, or other subtle activities. In doing this we are interested in revealing the underlying power rationalities: in showing how certain ways of framing space come to be shaped through power struggles over the meanings that are being captured.

Our analysis, then, is firmly located among emerging research focusing on discourse and power relations in planning and policy making, and in particular research that 'takes values and power seriously' (Flyvbjerg, 2001: 162–165). We hope that our use of theory shows how power relations are shaping planning and policy making in a way that reveals some of the risks and dangers of current configurations of power and knowledge in Europe, and provides a basis for action to counter these risks. It is not our intention to make detailed recommendations for action, since the first intention of our theoretical approach is to unsettle the taken-for-granted, and to fuel critical debate. We prefer to reflect on how a basis for action can be established, rather than suggest precisely what should be done. It is here that we see the key contribution from critical social science. We do not attempt to provide an 'answer', since we see no 'answers' to politics and power struggles. We cannot expect theory to solve the problem of power, only to help us to understand how we can operate in the face of power. However, we are convinced that critical analysis of this type is a necessary contribution to understanding spatial policy making in a way that can open up new perspectives on what can be done.

Structure

Part One of the book contains a general introduction (this chapter), followed by two conceptual chapters which explore linkages between spatial policy and European integration, and then set out our analytical approach. So far in this introductory chapter we have given a brief overview of the key issues concerning European spatial policy, and set out the objectives, structure and argument of the book. We have also briefly introduced the policy spaces and the theoretical approaches that give shape to our analysis. Chapter 2 then discusses the potential contribution of the new field of EU spatial policy to European integration. It raises a series of challenging questions about the reconfiguration of regional and national governance and planning, with the advent of transnational spatial policy making and planning. It argues for closer attention to the spatial dimensions of European integration. Chapter 3 sets out more fully the theoretical approach used in the book, termed the cultural sociology of space, and a discourse analytical framework used to operationalise the approach. We discuss theories of spatial representation, and particularly emphasise the significance of the study of flows and mobilities in understanding socio-spatial relations. We then set out our approach to exploring attempts to represent European spaces in policy making, using a theoretical and analytical framework dealing with the double dimensions of discourse and space. The conceptual framework deals with how language and spatial practices are shaped by power-rationalities, giving a structure which is followed in the remaining sections of the book, as we reconstruct the emergence of a new spatial policy discourse of monotopia.

Part Two begins the empirical analysis of the policy discourse. This analysis is thematic, and the two chapters address the language and images which articulate the new discourse of European space. By analysing the cases presented in the introduction, Chapter 4 explores the new common lexicon of European spatial planning. The focus is on how particular spatial relations are captured in language. A new language of European space is revealed, centred on key terms such as polycentricity, mobility, sustainable development, balanced competitiveness, core and periphery. The analysis focuses on the contested and socially constructed nature of these terms and examines the reproduction of this language through policy documents and networks. Chapter 5 considers how the new policy language is accompanied by a new visual imagery of European space. New images and maps not only represent spaces as part of a discursive practice, they also express new demands for spatial knowledge. The chapter also deals with new visual technologies and the way they are applied in new forms of spatial representation labelled 'infographics'. The power of infographics to give new meanings to European space and identity is discussed.

In Part Three we turn to spatial practices. Here we deal with the practices, institutions, governance structures and questions of implementation relating to the policy field. In Chapter 6 the institutional design and forms of governance surrounding the new spatial policy field are analysed. Attention is given to the emergence of new transnational governance structures and institutional forms, and in particular the power structures embedded in the practices of comitology and 'second order governance' (a concept drawn from the work of Joseph Weiler). This chapter addresses the issue of contested governance and identifies a democratic deficit in European spatial policy making. In Chapter 7 we analyse how the new spatial policy discourse has given birth to new transnational approaches to spatial analysis, and the idea of a European field of spatial knowledge. Such spatial analysis and knowledge forms are demarcated by boundaries between legitimate and illegitimate knowledge, which we argue are vital in institutionalising European spatial planning as a 'rational, science-based policy field', and in excluding certain challenging forms of knowledge, such as radical environmental considerations or indicators of social equity. Chapter 8 seeks to identify the actual importance of the new policy discourse to spatial policy making at different scales. It explores how planning agencies in member states, from national to regional levels, and other actors, take the policy discourse into their own practices. The meaning and role of the EU Structural Funds, predominantly through the INTERREG programme, add crucially to this picture by enabling the formation of new networks and institutions of transnational planning. The importance of these new modes of transnational planning activity and institution building to European integration is explored in detail in the cases of the North Sea Region and the Øresund region.

In Part Four of the book we turn to power, rationalities and knowledge. Here, the underlying rationalities of the monotopic spatial policy discourse are presented and the wider implications for European integration are discussed. In excavating the rationalities underlying the new spatial policy discourse, the dialectical relations between the 'spaces of place' and 'spaces of flow' (as conceptualised by Manual Castells) are traced in the European spatial policy field. In Chapter 9, the new policy discourse is seen to be predominantly based on a rationality of mobility, accessibility, connectivity and global competitive flows (a Europe of flows, in the terms of Maarten Hajer). The discourse of a Europe of flows is seen to be articulated against a competing notion of a Europe of places. Chapter 10 takes the unpacking of the underlying rationalities further by identifying the tensions and contradictions evolved around the three central objectives of growth, equity and environment (forming the 'magic' policy triangle which serves as the guiding light of European spatial planning). The empirical examples clearly illustrate not only the lack of coherence between these objectives, but also their contested nature as divergent social actors and institutions compete to determine the meaning and conditioning effects of European spatial policy discourse. This chapter identifies the meaning of the discourse of 'monotopic Europe' and its relationship to the structuring themes of the urban, the environment and the question of territorial identity as it comes to the fore in the policy concepts of mobility and polycentricity. The last step, in Chapter 11, is to draw together the consistencies and inconsistencies of the discursive practices which form the new policy field. This synthesis of the book's critical investigation focuses on the power agendas and the different rationalities at work in the new policy field. Finally the question of the potential meaning of the new discourse to European integration policies is re-addressed. The book concludes that the outcomes of these new contested, multi-level processes of Making European Space reflect the increasing importance of mobility and competition, with consequent threats to environmental and social justice. We discuss how these outcomes may make a spatialised contribution to the formation of a European identity, which leads us to reflect on the possibilities for action and resistance in the face of this powerful and currently hegemonic discourse.

Chapter 2

European integration and the emergence of European spatial policy

> Space, the shaping of space and the objects located in this space co-determine identity at local, regional, national and even European level. The authors of the ESDP have been toying with a type of 'cultural' response to the great European project: the economic and monetary integration which should produce a 'level playing field', a space within which the conditions for the economic operation of economic subjects are no longer very different.
>
> (Dutch National Spatial Planning Agency, 2000: 127)

> A day will come when you France, you Russia, you Italy, you England, you Germany all you nations of the continent, without losing your distinct qualities shall dissolve in a higher unity and constitute the European brotherhood . . . A day will come when people will see . . . the United States of Europe.
>
> (Victor Hugo, Opening address to the Peace Congress, Paris, 21 August 1849)

Introduction

This chapter explains why the new field of European spatial policy is becoming an important dimension of European integration. It raises a series of challenging questions about the reconfiguration of regional and national governance and planning, with the advent of a new level of transnational spatial policy and planning. It argues for a critical examination of the spatial dimensions of European integration.

It is not the intention here to explain the nature and workings of the EU institutions in great detail. There is a vast and rapidly growing literature on this subject. However, it is necessary to provide some context for the case study by introducing the institutional environment within which the trans-European transport network and European spatial policy have developed. Some important aspects of the institutional relations are identified, which provide the setting for policy making, and which open up important perspectives on understanding the specificity of the dynamics between discourse, power, knowledge and rationality.

We will refer to this broad field of policy making as European 'spatial policy', even though it often goes under the self-proclaimed label of European spatial 'planning'. Our principal reason for this is that the idea of planning is itself a contested one – partly since the EU has no formal competency in this area, and key documents such as the European Spatial Development Perspective are clearly not labelled as 'plans'. Indeed, the very question of the possibility of planning at the level of the EU is at the heart of our inquiry. But we prefer to explore this question by taking a cross-sectoral perspective where policy, rather than planning, is the usual frame of reference. Needless to say, we will use the term planning when we find this specific language use in documents, literature and other sources. The idea of policy also helps to emphasise the diffuse and politicised nature of this complex field of activity.

The 'idea of Europe': peace, prosperity and supranationalism

As a starting point for our analysis of the relationship between European integration and spatial policy we want briefly to address some of the main conceptual foundations of the 'European project' in general. This will be done by listening to some of the 'voices' that have articulated, at key moments in its history, the quintessential ideas underpinning the European project. Brought together, these voices should leave no doubt about the contested nature of this project, and of its multidimensional rather than singular nature. Looking at the political and philosophical underpinning of the EU leaves a sense of 'the idea of Europe' as being not one coherent idea, but of many layers and interests, since:

> The concept of Europe is not some eternal core idea or a seed which we find back in history and whose development we then trace through the ages. Rather it is the story of several conceptual fragments that have become linked at various points to the idea of Europe and which are then articulated and re-articulated through the following periods. The five main fragments in the dominant discourses on Europe were: the role of Europe as a geographical concept, the concept of liberty, Europe as Christendom, the balance of power and European Civilization.
>
> (Wæver, 1997: 285)

Needless to say, different aspects of this multilayered narrative could be foregrounded. However, there is widespread consensus about the post-war quest for peace and stability as one of the main drivers for European integration. This quest for peace has been heralded by many sides in the political spectrum. Thus in the socialist based critique of fascism set out in the 'Ventotene manifesto' of 1941, Spinelli and Rossi argued for an 'abolition of the division of Europe into national, sovereign states' (Spinelli and Rossi, 1941: 5), making way for a federal Europe based on the political peace-driven interests of the working class. However, the notion of peace as the main driver of post-war integration has also been expressed from within the political establishment, perhaps most notably by the French Foreign Minister Robert Schuman. In what later came to be known as the 'Schuman declaration' of 9 May 1950, the preconditions for peace in Europe were pinned on the linking of Germany and France in a mutual commitment:

> The French Government proposes to take action immediately on one limited but decisive point . . . to place Franco-German production of coal and steel under a common High Authority, within the framework of an organization open to the participation of the other countries of Europe . . . The solidarity in production thus established will make it plain that any war between France and Germany becomes not merely unthinkable, but materially impossible.
>
> (Schuman, 1950: 14)

In essence this marriage of the economic and peace rationales in the emerging European post-war cooperation was 'moving the war into the bureaucracy'. This notion of peace through economic co-operation and interaction is at the core of the theory of neo-functionalist 'spill over' (Nugent, 1999). Some even argue that the whole point about the European project which is apparently exclusively concerned with economic integration and political institution building, is that it is *de facto* bound up with the creation of an 'imagined community' and a common European culture and identity (Shore, 2000). Obviously arguments over whether peace is the driving force of the economy, or vice versa, can be pursued into infinity. Here, however, our main point is that the driving rationale of European integration is located within the realm of the economic sphere: 'Building Europe' was perceived primarily in terms of dismantling barriers to the free movement of capital, goods, services and labour, and this was a task for economists and lawyers (Shore, 2000: 42).

Being the 'cradle of the nation state' (Therborn, 1995), any extension of co-operation in Europe will be intimately bound up with the changing role of the nation state. Needless to say we do not have space here to recount the many dimensions of the changing context of the nation state, particularly in the face of globalisation, though it is clear that responding to a globalising economy has become one of the main drivers for integration, and that member states see their economic prosperity as being tied to the success of the Single Market (Rumford, 2002). As Manual Castells has put it: 'European integration is, at the same time, a reaction to the process of globalisation and its most advanced expression' (Castells, 1998: 318). The role of the nation state in the process of post-war European integration has placed basic questions of political legitimacy, sovereignty and social identity at the centre of the debate. Thus technical sounding debates between federalism and anti-federalism address more than an institutional issue: they reveal more profound questions of social identity and belonging. The voices in favour of maintaining the integrity of the nation states have been heard from diverse sources: both from the former French President De Gaulle and from the strong anti-European voice of the former British Prime Minister Margaret Thatcher. To De Gaulle's mind there was only one building block of Europe, and that was the nation state: 'What are the realities of Europe? What are the pillars on which it can be built? The fact is that they are states . . . the only entities which have the right to issue orders and to be obeyed' (De Gaulle, 1971).

Thatcher's rhetoric, centred on the defence of the 'organic' community, also brought the nation states forward as the untouchable foundation stones of European integration. In a famous speech to the College of Europe in Bruges, Thatcher argued for Europe to become a 'family of nations' (Thatcher, 1988) above all else. In a direct reply to this speech Jacques Delors, then European Commission President, went to the same location a year later, and gave his federalist interpretation of European integration:

> There is no conspiracy against the nation state. Nobody is being asked to renounce legitimate patriotism. I want not only to unite people, as Jean Monnet did, but also to bring nations together. As the Community develops, as our governments emphasize the need for a people's Europe, is it heresy to hope that all Europeans could feel that they belong to a Community which they see as a second homeland?
>
> (Delors, 1989)

We see Delors as one of the recent major political architects of European space. As Commission President during the key early stages of policy development, Delors was a champion of TEN-T, devoting an entire chapter to it in his 1993 White Paper on *Growth, Competitiveness and Employment*. Endo (1999) notes that relations were close between Jacques Delors and Karel Van Miert, Transport Commissioner, who was described as his protégé, suggesting one reason why transport occupies such a politically significant role within the EU's sphere of action and influence, as well as being a dominant Directorate within the Commission.[1] Furthermore, as Commission President, Delors endorsed the ESDP process by participating in the Turin meeting of ministers responsible for spatial planning as early as 1990.

As Delors fought against the twin spectres of nationalism and Thatcherite Euro-scepticism he drew explicitly on one of the European project's most important pro-federalist voices and founding fathers, Jean Monnet. From Monnet's perspective, a European state would emerge through long-term and incremental steps towards integration (Shore, 2000: 42), although his rhetoric takes the same point of departure as the peace rationale:

> European unity is the most important event in the West since the war, not because it is a new great power, but because the new institutional method it introduces is permanently modifying relations between nations and men. Human nature does not change, but when nations and men accept the same rule and the same institutions

> to make sure that they are applied, their behavior towards each other changes. This is the process of civilization itself.
>
> (Monnet, 1962)

In the second article of the Treaty of European Union, we find the core rationale of the European project as it has developed from the discourses of the 'founding fathers' of European integration to the contemporary fusion of economic and political goals:

> The Community shall have as its task . . . to promote a harmonious and balanced development of economic activities, sustainable and non-inflationary growth respecting the environment, a high degree of convergence of economic performance, a high level of employment and of social protection, the raising of the standard of living and quality of life, and economic and social cohesion and solidarity among member states.
>
> (EC Council, 1992)

In his analysis of the historic development of the Community, Weiler finds three distinct principal ideals, that sum up our small collection of 'voices around the European idea' very nicely (Weiler, 1999: 244–252):

1. Peace (e.g. as we find it articulated in the Schuman declaration);
2. Prosperity (e.g. as we find it articulated in the Treaty of European Union);
3. Supranationalism (here meaning the Enlightenment liberalist agenda of taming the nation states' excesses without the abolition of the nation states).

In a rather disillusioned comment on the merits of these ideals, Weiler ends his analysis by stating that the EU has ceased to be a vehicle for these foundational ideals, since it has evolved into a contingent being which has left behind its normative beginnings, sharing the 'fashionable post-modern twist to modernist anxiety' (Weiler, 1999: 261).

Spatial policy issues and problem framing

The process of European integration, within the context of a globalised economy, raises major spatial challenges for the EU, which is placed in the difficult position of competing as a global trading power, whilst simultaneously securing balanced development across the disparate regions that comprise European space. Given the significance of the economic dimensions of the European project, it is not surprising that the twin discourses of European integration and the single market together have a strong effect in shaping EU policy making across many sectors, including spatial policy. As Giannakourou argues:

> If the needs of the European integration process seem to have added a European level of spatial planning policy to that of the national states, it is the economic and institutional properties and dilemmas of this same integration process that circumscribe the conceptual identity and the normative value of the emerging policy . . . the central question becomes what the conceptual and ideological identity of a European spatial planning policy can be under a market-oriented integration system.
>
> (Giannakourou, 1996: 602)

If we are to understand how spatial policy relates to these economic and political imperatives, it becomes necessary to begin by considering the nature of the European economy: a fragmented economy in search of integration, which reproduces the regional disparities of many of its constituent nations at a transnational scale. A prosperous core stands in stark contrast with its periphery, meaning that further concentration is an inevitable tendency, and redistribution of the benefits of the single market, and 'balance' between regions are, not surprisingly, key policy aims. The effects of globalisation, and the political action of creating a single European economic bloc have many implications: for the capacity of cities, regions and nations to restructure their economies in the face of the collapse of traditional industries; for the decisions made by businesses locating and organising their activities; as a result for labour markets; for the organisation of urban space and the location of new land uses; for mobility and the requirements for infrastructure provision; and consequently for the environment. Here we are particularly interested in these latter issues, placing a critical focus on the implications for spatial organisation of cities and mobility, for the environment, and for the more subtle questions of identity, which are all closely interwoven.

The political and economic discourses of European integration create very specific demands on mobility, necessitating what Maarten Hajer, following Castells, has described as a discourse of a Europe of flows (Hajer, 2000). This discourse is characterised by the development of technologies such as Just in Time logistics, which have enabled a more footloose approach to economic development, reliant on the fast, low-cost movement of goods by road. The increasing demand for personal mobility is also characteristic of this discourse. The challenge is for infrastructure networks to enable such frictionless mobility, a challenge which has featured prominently in the EU policy agenda, reflecting political struggles over the framing of future mobility and spatial organisation (see Box 2.1). The resulting TEN-T programme is a clear strategy for the restructuring of European space according to the integrationist vision, as a patchwork of national networks is transformed into a pan-European system, which identifies links, nodes and corridors of European significance. Transport and telecommunications networks are together seen as 'strategic carriers of the rapid and deep transformation of Europe's sociopolitical features' (Banister *et al.*, 1995b: 335).

Box 2.1 **Framing spatial problems**

The development of the trans-European transport network (TEN-T) and the focus on 'missing links' vividly illustrates how the policy discourse of European space expresses future 'imaginary landscapes', as well as becoming a vehicle for new forms of transnational policy making. TEN-T originated in the 1980s as a transport and communications policy, but figures prominently in the ESDP as a key component of delivering its spatial (and economic) agenda. The vision of a Europe without constraint on the physical movement of goods and people is a representation of a symbolic space of integration and cohesion. In order to achieve such a 'frictionless' space, the policy discourse frames the problem of friction in relation to traditional ways of thinking about transport systems, constrained by national boundaries. The language of 'missing links' and 'missing networks', originating in lobbying reports of the European Round Table of Industrialists (ERT, 1984, 1991a, b), therefore became a means of articulating the critical gaps and institutional barriers to completion of the European infrastructure jigsaw, and the need for transnational activity to deliver appropriate solutions. Framing the problem in this way generates a need for new spatial practices which respond to the new 'problems' by transcending nation state boundaries and physical barriers such as mountain ranges and stretches of water. They also play a part in generating a new politics of scale by re-articulating the territory of Europe as a transnational polycentric space connected by a single long-distance, seamless transport network.

A new framework for EU spatial policy

Having set out some of the core spatial tensions, we now outline the ways in which the European Union has sought to develop a coherent spatial policy response. In Chapter 1 we introduced the policy cases that form the focus of our analysis. Here we will briefly outline how these cases fit into the new field of European spatial policy: how they can be understood as elements of a larger narrative of an unfolding policy field. We do this by providing glimpses into these different spaces, different policy arenas, at critical moments in policy making, which are spread across time and place. This should help the reader to make sense of our subsequent attempts to illustrate the analytical potential of linking space and discourse by returning to analysis of this policy field.

So far, we have concentrated on infrastructure networks, which have been one of the EU's primary spatial concerns. Infrastructure has a special significance in the progress of European spatial policy because the concept of trans-European infrastructure networks became embedded in European policy, Treaties, budgets and programmes long before a spatial vision for the EU had even been drafted. But the spatial restructuring resulting from TEN-T will have profound implications beyond its identified political and economic objectives: as TEN-T transgresses national boundaries physically, reinforcing the new strategy of inclusion in Europe, it will simultaneously create new potentials for mobility and patterns of proximity, peripherality and exclusion, both within Europe, and between Europe and its neighbours. The implementation of TEN-T therefore creates a stark spatial development agenda for Europe, which is perhaps the single most difficult challenge in achieving a vision of balanced, sustainable spatial development. Spatial policy, like it or not, has been forced to adopt the TEN-T, to swallow whole a programme which threatens to undermine its basic intentions.

Towards integrated spatial policy: the ESDP

Since the late 1980s, principally under the auspices of its Directorate General for Regional Policy (previously named DGXVI, and later DG Regio), the European Commission has analysed and charted the spatial and territorial development of the Community with increasing scrutiny. The nature of this engagement has changed dramatically from its early interest in restructuring the Regional Development Fund to facilitate the redistribution of benefits under its cohesion policy, towards a more integrative cross-sectoral spatial agenda.

The ESDP attempts to provide a framework for simplifying co-ordination of transnational planning between member states, but also anticipates in the longer term a broader EU level of planning activity. It intends to encompass urban systems, infrastructure and knowledge, natural and cultural heritage and territorial perspectives, synthesised at the EU level. It is also intended that the ESDP will form part of a cascade of spatial policy making and implementation from the EU to the local level. The whole business of creating this document is to express a 'shared vision of the European territory' (CSD, 1998a: 3). Its *raison d'être* is an intervention in a development characterised by competition between regions and cities in order to secure a better balance between competition and cooperation. This has to be done in order to safeguard an 'optimum level of competitiveness' (CSD, 1998a: 2). The ESDP advocates a new scale of spatial planning and as such a new 'vision' of the European Union's territory.

The ESDP sets out a vision for the future of European space, which we will critically analyse throughout this book. It pursues a particular form of sustainable spatial development, centred on a polycentric urban system, linked by transnational infrastructure networks, and with a focus on the development of economic growth zones. As we will argue in the following chapters, the ESDP expresses a market- and competition-oriented spatial policy (Jensen, 1997: 48), which makes transparent a number of major economic, social and environmental tensions, and raises questions about the possible winners and losers.

Implementing EU spatial policy

The new field of EU spatial policy is not legally based on the Treaties of the European Union. The EU therefore has no formal competence for implementing spatial policy, and no powers to make its policies binding on member states, which makes the ESDP distinctive. It is carefully framed as serving as a basis for voluntary actions, setting out policy options, and even avoiding (after heated debate) the use of proposal maps. It's title of 'perspective', rather than 'plan' or 'policy', suggests its indicative status. However, in spite of this apparent lack of teeth, the thinking and vision-making in the ESDP is increasingly guiding European funding and influencing planning activity across Europe. This particularly applies to the INTERREG programme, which since the mid-1990s has proven to be the de facto mechanism for implementation of the emerging ESDP's transnational spatial policy thinking. Alongside EU initiatives like INTERREG, member states are increasingly integrating the ESDP's language and framing of spatial relations and policy options into planning strategies at national, regional and local levels in a more subtle process of Europeanisation of planning systems (to which we shall return in Chapter 8).

Spatial politics and the contested nature of European spatial planning

Once a policy domain was formed, it was evident that institutional design, agenda setting, policy making and implementation should be subject to pressures based on divergent interests across European space operating at different spatial scales. Here we do no more than hint at some of these pressures. That the attempt to build a common discourse of EU space is exposed to conflicting views and agendas should come as no surprise. During the decade-long gestation process, many spatial interests have been articulated. The most significant of these is that of the prosperous core 'pentagon' area, which is reflected in the ESDP process (Rusca, 1998; Faludi, 1997). More recently Faludi has argued that this core region should even become the subject of a separate ESDP (Faludi, 1999), because of its special position as an economically prosperous urbanised zone. Beyond the core, there is further divergence between southern and northern European views of the ESDP. Thus Rusca identifies the southern attitude as one of specific concern for the cultural heritage and identity of places (Rusca, 1998). This divergence has often been attributed to differences in planning and administrative culture between north and south. This might be the case, but a more realist account is the prospect of financial benefits linked for instance to Structural Fund initiatives that will be linked to the ESDP framework. Introducing a spatial dimension into the Structural Funds, as a result of the influence of the ESDP, could shift the basis of funding from socio-economic difficulties to a more spatialised agenda. This could lead to a reduction in overall EU funding to southern regions, a fear that is further nurtured by the prospect of entry of the relatively poorer newcomers into the European Union:

> the linkages among regional policies and spatial planning at European level will have to be discussed more seriously and peacefully. The traditional cohesion approach of regional policy will tend to allocate more and more economic resources to the future enlargement areas of the European Union. A more comprehensive concept of cohesion will have to be elaborated for the European territory.
>
> (Rusca, 1998)

The position of these accession countries is also difficult. They are currently excluded from the territory embraced by the ESDP, which is limited to the European Union. This omission was highlighted as a weakness by Czech and Slovak representatives at the launch of the ESDP consultation process. The interests of the countries of Central and Eastern Europe in a common pan-European spatial perspective are expressed more fully in a parallel process, managed by the European Conference of Ministers Responsible for Spatial Planning (CEMAT, 1999), which raises a number of challenges to the ESDP's spatial strategy – particularly its weak treatment of rural areas. Indeed the CEMAT document views the ESDP as representing the contribution of the fifteen EU member states to the development of the pan-European spatial strategy (CEMAT, 1999: vii). Elsewhere, some analysts are beginning to articulate specific Nordic interests in the ESDP, opposing the urbanised centre-periphery thinking which is seen as maintaining the economic strength of the 'pentagon' core region, and neglecting the Nordic countries' peripheral status (Böhme, 1998). For example the ESDP states that the European Union is a highly urbanised continent, yet as Böhme counters, less than 20 per cent of European space is urban. Böhme concludes that 'It [the ESDP] considers towns as the "one and only" development motor of the Union and does not pay attention to examples in which non-urban areas create benefit' (Böhme, 1998).

Böhme has even gone as far as foreseeing a possible Nordic ESDP, based not only on the contemporary similarities between these countries (i.e. strong regional and local government planning) but also on the historical legacy from the Kalmar Union (Böhme, 1998, 1999b; Gray, 2000). Alongside these regional interests the integration of the objectives and normative positions of the many different levels of government, and other actors, will be important in shaping the European spatial approach. It seems important, then, that academics should seek to understand the effects of power relations and normative agendas on the emerging planning framework. These power struggles are complex and take place in many arenas at different spatial scales and administrative levels, but the terrain includes (Dabinett and Richardson, 1999):

- between EU institutions: contested power struggles between the Commission, Council of Ministers, Parliament, and other institutions such as the Committee for the Regions (Richardson, J., 1996);
- within EU institutions: struggles between Commissioners, Directorates, Member States, regions (Shore, 2000);

- interests operating at the EU level to influence the overall direction of EU integration, e.g. environmental and industrial lobbies;
- within each sectoral policy area a set of interests contests policy making and implementation. For example: Structural Funds and agriculture (Scott, 1995); transport; environmental policy; competition policy; telecommunications (Andersen and Eliassen, 1993; Greenwood *et al.*, 1992).

These examples of scalar interests are intended simply to illustrate the significance of the underlying tensions and power struggles that give shape to the field of EU spatial policy. We will return to the substantive questions of urban bias and peripherality below.

New forms of governance

Having introduced the path towards a new policy discourse of European space, and highlighted some of the key conflicts that run through its policy making arenas, it is now important to turn to the institutional setting of the EU that forms the terrain for this policy making activity. In particular, we will examine the dynamic and volatile nature of this elaborate institutional network. Across the EU, governance structures are in a state of flux, with new forms of policy making emerging within and across member states. The process of Europeanisation is manifested – in the arena of spatial policy at least – in the introduction of new institutional structures and processes that work at new scales and transgress national boundaries, creating new possibilities for action. As a result, policy making takes place in an increasingly complex environment where it becomes increasingly difficult to locate single centres of decision-making, or of power. Castells has argued that one of the hallmarks of contemporary policy making is a new organisational configuration where networks supplement the traditional hierarchical bureaucracies. In his analysis of the 'Network Society', Castells identifies the EU as a 'network state' which is characterised by the 'sharing of authority (that is, in the last resort, the capacity to impose legitimised violence) along a network' (Castells, 1998: 332). As we will see, this particular network character is clearly manifested in the structures and activities of the new field of European spatial policy. The scope and nature of these changes are profound, and as we will argue are closely related to the manifestation of many of the central concerns of this book. In order to help understand these new modes of policy making, we introduce two concepts: *multi-level governance* and *infranationalism*.

Multi-level governance

According to the multi-level governance approach, EU policy is produced by a complex web of institutions at various levels, from the subnational to the supranational. In the multi-level governance model the European Commission is seen as a very powerful agenda setter compared to the nation states. Furthermore, agenda setting and decision making is now a shared and contested activity, between the Commission, the European Council, the Council of Ministers and the European Parliament, rather than being monopolised by one actor (Marks *et al.*, 1996: 280). This leads to a situation where multiple interest groups and lobbies mobilise and seek to influence policy initiation.

The most obvious sign that the multi-level governance model is making a difference to EU decision-making is found in the increasing number of constraints that nation states have had to operate under since the introduction of the Single European Act (Marks *et al.*, 1996: 282). Qualified majority voting between member states in the European Council, and the co-decision procedures between the European Parliament and the European Council, are two examples where limits have been established on the ways that member states can shape policy, locating their influence within a wider set of relations, and sharing power with other institutions.

The question of implementation is given particular prominence in the multi-level governance perspective. It is under this heading that the phenomenon of 'comitology' is key. This is the term used to describe the 'cascade of subcommittees' (Marks *et al.*, 1996: 282) established and controlled by the Commission, through which detailed policy is developed and implemented. The significance of comitology, central to a multi-level governance view of policy making, would be hard to explain from a state-centric view of policy making, and opens up a more nuanced view of the EU policy process. Interestingly, the showcase example of comitology as multi-level governance used by Marks *et al.* is the field of cohesion policy, which is very relevant to the delivery of spatial policy.

The multi-level governance model does not pose a clear and explicit challenge to member states. Instead, it suggests a more subtle process through which they are 'being melded gently into a multi-level polity' which leads, among other things, to multiple points of access for interests and a privileging of technical expertise matching the dominant style of EU policy making (Marks *et al.*, 1996: 282).

Infranationalism

Weiler (1999) coins the concept of *infranationalism* alongside *internationalism* and *supranationalism* as alternative modes of EU governance. Apart from the impossibility of covering all theories of European integration and policy making in one model (which is neither Weiler's nor our contention) the model reflects the reality that in some spheres EU governance is international, in others it is supranational, and in yet others it is infranational (Weiler, 1999: 272).

Weiler argues that infranationalism is the hallmark of the last decade of EU policy making and integration (Weiler, 1999: 98). This is so since increasingly large sectors of Community norm creation, according to Weiler, are carried out at the level of meso-governance (ibid.). This means that the actors involved are 'middle-range officials' of both the EU and the member states, who work closely with a variety of private and semi-public bodies, in ways that epitomise the 'comitology approach' to EU policy making.

In our analysis of the EU spatial policy discourse we will encounter all three of Weiler's modes of governance. That we find all these modes of governance 'in play' does not mean, however, that we cannot identify one as the most relevant category. Williams and Jørgensen have argued that the supranational mode of policy making operates at a scale that was not appropriate for the implementation of the ESDP (Williams and Jørgensen, 1998: 3). We would further argue that supranationalism does not provide an adequate description of the place of spatial policy (and the ESDP) in EU governance, or of its institutional capacity. Instead, we emphasise the infranational dimension, which will be revealed in our analysis of the ongoing policy processes as being of central importance.

Infranationalism in the EU has been defined as the 'second-order governance' involving commissions, directorates, committees, government departments, and other related structures (Weiler, 1999). Ways of working tend to be characterised by medium-to-low levels of institutionalisation, have the character of a network, practice an informal style and, last but not least, have a low actor – and event-visibility and process-transparency (see Table 2.1). Seen from a constitutional point of view, infranationalism is neither constitutional nor unconstitutional, as it is simply outside the constitution (Weiler, 1999: 98). Infranational working threatens a weakening of political control and increased autonomy being given to the administrative level, implying less control by the Member States and increased managerialism and reliance on expertise. In short:

> Infranationalism, because of its managerial, functional and technocratic bias, operates outside parliamentary channels, outside party politics. There is nothing sinister or conspiratorial in infranationalism, but its processes typically lack transparency and may have low procedural and legal guarantees. . . . Infranationalism is about transnational interests groups, governance without (State) government, empowerment beyond national boundaries, and the like. . . . In general, the classic instruments of control and public accountability are ill-suited to the practices of infranationalism.
>
> (Weiler, 1999: 284–285)

In an analysis of the EU spatial policy discourse as it materialises in the INTERREG programme for the North Sea Region, Williams and Jørgensen identify the following characteristics of infranational governance: a managerial and technocratic reliance on expertise, a mode of operation outside political assemblies, and a search for legitimation by results rather than processes (Williams and Jørgensen, 1998: 4). Applying the same conceptual tool to another EU mega-region under the INTERREG programme, Jørgensen and Nielsen find that in the Baltic Sea Region there is clearly a situation in which the international co-operation between

Arena	International	Supranational	Infranational
Disciplinary background of observers	International relations	Law (typically public law)	Policy studies; sociology
Typical issues of governance	Fundamental system rules; issues with immediate political and electoral resonance; international 'high politics'; issues outside Treaty	The primary legislative agenda of the Community; enabling legislation; principal harmonisation measures	Implementing and executive measures; standard setting
Principal players	Member states	Union/Community and member states	[Union/Community is policy making context]
Principal actors	Governments (Cabinets-Executive Branch)	Governments; Community institutions; Commission; Council; Parliament	Second level organs of governance (Commission; Directorate; Committee; Govt. Departments etc.); certain corporate and social-industrial NGOs
Level of institutionalisation	Low to medium	High	Medium to low
Mode of political process	Diplomatic negotiation	Legislative process; bargaining	Administrative process; networking
Type/style of intercourse	Informal procedures; low level of process rules	Formal procedures; high level of process rules	Informal procedures; low level of process rules
Visibility/ transparency	High actor and event visibility. Low transparency of processes	Medium to low actor and event visibility and medium to low transparency of process	Low actor and event visibility and low transparency of process

Table 2.1 Internationalism, supranationalism, and infranationalism: static (structural) elements.

Source: Weiler, 1999: 275.

member states is being paralleled by the practices of infranational governance (Jørgensen and Nielsen, 1997: 8). This leads the authors to conclude that: 'It may be surmised that these transnational committees and sub-committees will act as Superstate committees functioning in relatively 'closed rooms' without a substantial linkage to the national structures of agency and influence within regional policy and spatial planning' (Jørgensen and Nielsen, 1997: 9).

The multi-level governance model, together with the infranational mode of governance, helps in illuminating important dimensions of EU policy making. Together, insights are provided into the workings of institutional power plays that are not immediately visible at the 'surface' of the EU. Needless to say, the EU also works in supranational and more state-centric ways, but being restricted to these approaches would in our view be to submit to an unnecessary analytical 'blind spot'.

Towards a new European architecture?

In EU spatial policy, such conflicts have become engrained: a particular vision of European space is contained within the policy discourse – a vision which is contested and interest-based, and which is grounded in specific rationalities, or in the words of Chris Shore, 'the new European architecture is based on an altogether more diffuse, anarchic and unaccountable system of power in which no single member state or national culture is dominant or controls the direction of the EU and its machinery' (Shore, 2000: 215).

When the European project is considered over the timescale from the 1950s to today, the early stages of the construction processes were nationally oriented regarding spatial policies. Even though the regional policy had its institutional foundation in 1975 (the European Regional Development Fund, ERDF), it was not until the early 1980s that regional policy gained momentum. With the reform of the ERDF in 1984, the spatial dimension was given a global orientation with the introduction of two types of areas: the less developed regions and the industrial areas in decline (Giannakourou, 1996: 599). The next landmark in the spatialisation of EU politics was the Single European Act of 1986. The Internal Market was of course an important factor shaping the socio-spatial relation, but the Treaty's theme of social and economic cohesion was also important. The Treaty expresses the internal contradiction of balanced spatial development combined with economic growth under sustainable conditions. This tension between liberalism and state interventionism forms the underlying ideological dilemma of the whole European discourse (Giannakourou, 1996: 602). The European spatial policy discourse is thus embedded in a rather unique spatial strategy:

> The emerging European spatial strategy is 'concerted' (its options resulting from consensus among member-states and through a 'bottom-up' approach), 'selective' (dealing only with territorial issues which have to be talked about at the European

> level), 'flexible' (designed for different contexts and depending on the voluntarism of the public or private sector for its implementation), and 'consistent' (promoting the symbiosis of the various Community policies instead of a strict discrimination). The central idea underpinning the new European planning rhetoric is that of a more general reorientation of the traditional spatial fairness concept in the new context provided by the competition principles of a spatial integration process that is market-oriented.
>
> (Giannakourou, 1996: 603)

In this analysis Giannakourou pinpoints three driving concepts in the discourse of 'justice'. First, the concept of 'competitive spatial justice', promising the levelling of spatial imbalances through the redistribution of competitiveness among European areas. Second, a concept of 'diversified spatial justice' tolerating discrimination of goals, instruments and actors for the handling of divergent problems. Finally, a concept of 'pluralist spatial justice' appealing both to public and private stakeholders to contribute to the redistribution of spatial prosperity (Giannakourou, 1996: 603). Together these three theoretical pillars are an expression of a specific notion of 'spatial fairness' (we shall return to the debate of 'spatial justice' in Chapter 11) that involves the paradox of invoking a welfare principle in order to ensure global competitiveness (Giannakourou, 1996: 604). Thus Giannakourou finds a break with the traditional universal and legally formal approach to spatial justice (i.e. the right to equal treatment of all territories) towards a novel rationale of the diverse and unequal as a result of a more complex and unpredictable world. In other words a 'Transition from a unitary and substantive rationale of fairness towards a pluralist and procedural one' (Giannakourou, 1996: 605).

A corresponding transition can be found in the institutional context of government decision making, as essential and formal legislation is increasingly replaced by non-binding recommendations, declarations annexed to treaties and various forms of interpretative communications, all encapsulated by the term 'soft law' (Giannakourou, 1996: 606). Such 'soft law' corresponds with the emerging practice of European spatial policy, and with the notions of multi-level governance and infranationalism. This trend seems to be shaped by two factors:

> The first is the replacement of the traditional hierarchical, vertical and centralized form of state spatial action by a voluntary, cooperative and horizontal model of coordinated European or transnational spatial options. The second is the replacement of substantive rules by procedural, prospective and general frames of reference and action expressive of information, proposed standards of good practice and recommendations rather than legally enforceable objectives and means of action.
>
> (Giannakourou, 1996: 606–607)

This amounts to saying that the decision-making process is moving away from 'positive' co-ordination, relying on hierarchical and homogeneous national spatial standards, towards a 'negative' action co-ordination based on information exchange, non-binding principles and encouragement of voluntary and decentralised spatial planning (Giannakourou, 1996: 607). This is part of a general trend in Western democracies undergoing a dialectics of 'explosion and implosion of politics' (Pedersen, 1994). *Explosion* in the way that politics has moved out and away from the traditional representative institutions and into various new institutional settings of corporate bodies and semi-private organisations. A movement which has in a way meant an ephemeralisation of political responsibility making the democratic control of these new institutional settings even harder than before. Thus the *implosion* of politics, as the political spheres close in on themselves or implode in their various forms.

Much has obviously happened to erode the historic idea of the defence of nation state sovereignty, as we today face a situation of closer and deeper co-operation between member states, 'forcing' them to cede more and more power to the EU. However many analysts agree that whilst the EU may have taken over competencies and powers from the nation state, this has neither led to the abolition of the nation state nor to the construction of a whole-hearted federal structure. Instead, something new and in-between these well established categories is being established (Nugent, 1999; Weiler, 1999). The institutional system of the EU has in its current shape properties of a 'state-like politico-administrative system', which has a rather unique constitutional set-up (Wessels, 1996: 20–21). Unlike traditional international organisations, the EU has an institutional setting where policies to a large degree are made independently of national governments. This implies that sovereign states have to deal with political actors which are outside their immediate control (Wessels, 1996: 21).

Such an institutional set-up makes it very difficult to identify the decision makers in the system. This problem has been accentuated by the increasing tendency towards majority voting in the European Council. The constitutional model of the EU is changing as a part of the ongoing integration process. At least three models can be identified in order to frame the discussion of EU integration: the intergovernmental model, the federal model of the 'United States of Europe and the co-operative federal model of a 'merged Europe'. The intergovernmental model is characterized by national sovereignty of member states and a 'pooling of sovereignties' (Wessels, 1996: 23). The federal model of the 'United States of Europe' would imply a rearrangement of the present institutional framework. Nevertheless, it seems to be the ideal of many Eurocrats and EU level politicians in the current debate. In such a model the Commission would have the status of government and the historical European nation state would be substituted to the 'European Federation'. This model would probably be more efficient when it comes to making fast decisions. Finally the co-operative model of a 'merged Europe' would be based on the concept of dual legitimacy, i.e. that of the member state and the Commission. In such a model the areas of competence would be less clear since national and Community areas of competence would be mixed. The current situation can be described as a 'fusion model' of European institutionalisation (Wessels and Rometsch, 1996: 360). This means that the institutional processes of European integration are neither fully federal nor (any longer) intergovernmental:

> Thus the development towards a 'federal system' seems to be unlikely; nor can we observe a turning back to an 'intergovernmental model'; more likely seems to be a further degree of institutional fusion and a higher procedural complexity in the upcoming future from which there is no easy way out. However an institutional 'de-Europeanization' will not take place; there are no signs of a withdrawal from the system but more of an institutional learning and re-equilibrium.
>
> (Wessels and Rometsch, 1996: 365)

Such a development will most likely be of 'advantage' to those within the bureaucracy resulting from the institutionalisation processes of European integration policy. This tendency, combined with an increasing 'atomisation' of the decision-making process in the EU, makes it impossible to control the internal co-ordination process through a central body (Wessels and Rometsch, 1996: 332) leading to growing 'in-transparency' (Wessels and Rometsch, 1996: 360). Seen alone, the politico-administrative system is certainly not a static system. An extensive growth is taking place in decision making by the Council and the Commission. And despite much debate over the principle of subsidiarity we are facing a situation where:

> Competences for operating public policies have increasingly been transferred upwards to the level of the European Union by new treaties, treaty reforms such as the Single European Act and the Maastricht Treaty on European Union, incremental adaptions using Art. 235 EEC and legal 'mutations' by ECJ [European Court of Justice]. . . . We are confronted with a 'messy' and ambiguous vertical fusion of national and EU competences and even more with a highly differentiated 'mixture' of public instruments located on several levels.
>
> (Wessels, 1996: 34)

In terms of its institutional, juridical and spatial dimensions some analysts have argued that the EU constitutes nothing less than the first 'truly postmodern international political form' (Ruggie, 1993: 140). So what we find is a rather 'messy and ambiguous' fusion of competences (Wessels, 1996: 34), leading some theorists to proclaim an accelerated unbundling of territoriality, towards a post-modern political space where 'the single-point perspective and singular sovereignty of independent statehood are being displaced by multiple and overlapping sovereignties' (Anderson, J., 1996: 143). In fact Jørgensen concludes that the ESDP may be contributing to such a situation in which there is no longer any fixed viewpoint (Jørgensen, 1998:19).

Much more could be said about the European project and the competing models for describing it. However it is sufficient to underline here the diverse character of this project and to emphasise its contested nature.

The European institutions and inter-institutional politics

Having sketched out a conceptual framework for EU governance, based on its multi-level nature and predominantly infranational mode of working, it is now appropriate to set out the institutional fabric of the EU with these critical perspectives in mind. We will therefore introduce the key institutional structures, before moving on to a discussion of the informal ways of working and inter-institutional practices that characterise the policy domains within which European spatial policy has been shaped. The central question we are asking here is, given the highly complex nature of EU policy making, how does the EU organise itself?

As a part of a rather unique form of supranational government, possessing juridical authority (unlike other supranational bodies such as the Council of Europe), the formal EU institutions are of major importance (Williams, 1996b: 30–54). The most important institutions are the European Commission, the Council of Ministers, the European Council, the Council of Permanent Representatives and the European Parliament. Two other significant institutions are the Economic and Social Committee that provides institutional representation for the 'social partners' of employers and employees, and the relatively recently constitued Committee of the Regions (CoR). Finally, European law is enforced by the European Court of Justice, which formally has authority over national courts, even though they have not all been equally keen to accept this fact: the German Court has notably expressed its opposition (Weiler *et al.*, 1995: 8).

Here we will mention some important features of these institutions, as well as introducing the Committee for Spatial Development (CSD) – which has overseen the preparation of the ESDP – and the INTERREG Programme, which has been a crucial EU instrument in the application of transnational spatial policy.

The Council of Ministers

The Council of Ministers is the supreme legislative authority of the EU, and it consists of one member from each EU member state, with the actual membership depending on the specific subject on the agenda. The General Council consists of the ministers of foreign affairs. The Council is a shifting institutional framework which brings together representatives of the EU member states on a range of sectoral issues. Transport ministers, for example, come together as the Transport Council, while ministers responsible for the environment, regional policy, agriculture, and so on, meet separately. The European Council meets twice each year.

The President, who is the appropriate minister from the member state holding the rotating EU presidency, convenes meetings of the Council. Transport ministers holding the presidency at key stages of the policy process play an important role, alongside the Transport Commissioner, in ensuring progress.

At present there is no spatial policy council, which is why the meetings between the ministers responsible of spatial planning and development have the status of being 'informal'. Normally the Council acts only on the basis of proposals from the Commission, and it cannot initiate proposals itself. In practice, the Councils are able to request the Commission to undertake any study and submit to it appropriate proposals for action. So the relation between the Commission and the Council is encapsulated in the saying that: 'The Commission proposes, and the Council disposes'. The various voting procedures are rather complex, but can roughly be described as unanimity, simple majority voting and qualified majority voting. The Presidency of the Council of Ministers is held on a 6-month rotation between the member states. The European Council is the term applied to the EU's summit meetings, which are attended by the heads of governments and foreign ministers. The Council of Permanent Representatives (COREPER) is the permanent representation maintained by the member states' governments in Brussels.

Being the EU's legislative authority, the Council of Ministers is an important arena for policy making. It is the arena within which member states, with their conflicting agendas and priorities, seek common positions. This clearly raises difficulties on controversial policy areas. Commission proposals, such as those for TENs, before being considered by the Council of Ministers, are scrutinised by COREPER. It is within COREPER that negotiation takes place between different governments to try and establish texts which can be agreed by the Council of Ministers. The Council has a reputation for lack of transparency, and the Commission has attempted to open up its various structures, in particular by bringing documentation into the public domain. This has, however, not been very successful, and information is generally more accessible to those established in Brussels, who understand the relevant processes. It is perhaps for these reasons that the Council can appear to be more unified than the other EU institutions. Its very real internal differences are often obscured by lack of transparency, as well as by its need to act in a unified way within the EU inter-institutional arenas. For example, whilst it is clear that the member states held different positions on exactly how policy on TEN-T should develop, we will argue in the following chapters that it is the Council acting as a unified body which is critical to the outcome of the policy process, rather than the actions of individual member states.

The European Commission

The Commission can be seen as the executive part of the government, or its civil service (in pursuit of Article 211 of the Amsterdam Treaty). Its twenty members

(Commissioners) are appointed by the member states. The Commission serves a 5-year term of office, and technically its members must be approved by the European Parliament, and can be held to account and even sacked by it. As well as carrying out its bureaucratic role of initiating policy measures, and implementing legislation, the Commission is a political player, with a leadership which acts as guardian of the European treaties. The Commissioners, supported by their personal Cabinets, play a prominent role in policy development.

The bureaucratic structure of the Commission is formed by a series of Directorates-General (DGs), supported by a number of specialist services. Of particular interest to spatial policy making are the Directorates-General for Regional Policy; Energy and Transport; and Environment. The Commission staff numbers around 27,000 civil servants. Because of its small size, it suffers (like the Parliament) from a lack of in-depth expertise in many technical areas. On many areas of detail, both Commission and Parliament may lack the resources to develop their positions, whilst the Council is able to draw on the resources of civil servants from the various governments to provide expert input.

The organisational structure of the European Commission illustrates very clearly the interests and power relations at work. Among more than twenty general Directorates promoting economic growth and trying to make Europe competitive in the global arena, only one (Regional Policy DG) 'takes care of the losers', understood as the regions that cannot keep up with the accelerating pace of economic competition (Masser *et al.*, 1992: 107). Regional Policy DG is particularly interesting since it is the institutional home of the spatial policy documents, and hosts the Committee on Spatial Development (CSD). Energy and Transport DG is the lead Directorate on TEN-T.

Within the Commission, small groups of bureaucrats work on policy development. Staff in the different DGs work informally together, for example creating working groups on the Strategic Environmental Assessment of TEN-T. The Commission's open door policy means that lobbyists are able to build and maintain close communication with bureaucrats. Spatial policy making at the EU level necessarily involves concerted integrated working between the various Directorates of the European Commission responsible for regional policy, transport, environment and agriculture. The Commission works closely with the European Council and the European Parliament in a hotly contested lobbying environment to move forward the policy field whilst reconciling or mediating between conflicting positions and interests.

Besides its formal institutional role, the Commission with its staff of civil servants plays an important informal role of safeguarding the 'European idea' and ethos, its *esprit de corps* (Shore, 2000).

The European Parliament

The European Parliament is the only directly elected and democratic body of the EU (it has held direct elections since 1979). Elections are held at 5-year intervals. The seat of the Parliament is in Strasbourg, and its secretariat is located in Luxembourg. The political work of Members of the European Parliament (MEPs) is done in cross-national party groupings. The Parliament maintains a total of seventeen standing committees, and (in 2003) six temporary committees, one of the most interesting in this context being the Committee on Regional Policy, Transport and Tourism (RETT), which in 1999 was formed from the separate committees for transport and regional policy. This wide-ranging committee is responsible for matters including regional policy, regional planning and urban policy, and the common transport policy, including TEN-T. The Parliament's role in decision making has strengthened under the co-decision process. Previously, for example, in the early years of TEN-T development a relationship existed where the Council adopted policies proposed by the Commission. As the first TEN-T proposals took shape, the Parliament's role was almost as a lobby, rather than as a decision-making partner.

The 626 members of the European Parliament are the only directly elected, and therefore directly accountable, politicians among the EU institutions. The presence of seven different cross-national political groupings, drawing their members from over 100 national political parties, means that any position is contingent on securing enough political support from other groups to survive a vote in full session. It is the Parliament that, perhaps more than any other institution, is subject to great pressure from outside interests. MEPs are lobbied by local and regional authorities, and from specialist interest groups. As will become clear, the Parliament's position needs to balance these often-conflicting pressures. A further problem for the Parliament is that it lacks its own bureaucracy, and so often lacks the expertise to support its engagement in debates on complex technical issues. This partly explains why MEPs are open to outside interests who may provide expertise in various forms. In the case of TEN-T, for example, environmental and transport lobby groups worked in close proximity to MEPs, providing information in documents lobbying the Parliament on the position it should adopt.

Inter-institutional relations

The key point here is that each of the core EU institutions plays an integral part in policy and decision-making, but that each institution cannot be seen simply as a homogenous body. Different interests are at work within each institution as well as between them. Broader discourses give shape to conflicts and debates within institutions, and individual bureaucrats and politicians must negotiate their way through a complex array of competing ideas, values and 'assumed' knowledges about what 'should' be done. What is also significant is the absence of any formal inter-institutional space where the Parliament, Commission and Council can come together, and engage in debate and decision-making. Much debate across institutional boundaries, negotiation, and even decision-making ultimately continues through a variety of informal processes and political conflict.

Transport policy is one of the areas that has historically been a source of major conflict between the EU institutions. For example, in the 1970s and 1980s, to the frustration of the Parliament, there had been relatively little progress towards a common transport policy due to lack of action by the Council. Williams (Williams, 1996a: 67) describes this as 'one of the greatest failures of the EU'. However, the Parliament lacked any formal powers to intervene. In 1980 its Transport Committee called for a transport infrastructure plan for the EU. In 1984, it went so far as to seek a ruling in the European Court of Justice against the Council for failing to fulfil the Treaty of Rome by not adopting a common transport policy. The Council argued in its defence that lack of agreement between members had prevented progress, but the Court's findings were that it had in fact been negligent.

The Committee of the Regions (CoR)

Other institutions play a part in policy development. The Committee of the Regions (CoR) acts as both a decision-making structure for regions, and a source of interest representation in its own right. The diversity of regional and local authorities within the CoR makes this particular institutional setting a field of various (and sometimes divergent) interests. Wiehler and Stumm conclude that its work has resulted in the political upgrading of the regions at European level (Wiehler and Stumm, 1995: 247). This may conform to the European Parliament's demands first of all, but cannot conceal the difficulty that most of the regions represented in the CoR are said to lack a democratically legitimised substructure. For example, in TEN-T policy making, the Committee was used as a channel for regional interests to assert their various needs to be on the TEN-T map, which basically meant that many regional infrastructure projects were adopted as part of the network.

The Committee on Spatial Development (CSD)

The CSD is a relatively new body under the European Commission. It has only existed since 1991, and is not formally constituted under the Maastricht Treaty (Williams, 1996a: 48). The CSD is an intergovernmental forum of senior officials from the ministries responsible for spatial planning. The CSD has responsibility for the preparation of the ESDP, as well as for implementing the co-operation network of spatial research institutes (ESPON). In spite of its informal status, the CSD has been one of the most central EU bodies, when it comes to the articulation of the European spatial policy discourse: 'Although not able to adopt EU legislation as a formal council could, they [the CSD] have proved to be a significant driving force in the formulation of EU spatial policy' (Williams, 1996a: 87).

The CSD has the unique status of being a transnational network of civil servants looking at European space from a new transnational perspective. It has thus become an institution that neither national nor EU politicians have full control over. This is not the least due to its 'infranational' character:

> So far the work of the CSD has taken place in the proverbial back rooms. Only a handful of cognoscenti has been able to follow it, making use of such personal contacts with members of the CSD as they might have. This is perhaps the greatest challenge for the CSD: how to generate support outside the inner circle of civil servants and their fellow travellers.
>
> (Faludi *et al.*, 2000: 129)

The CSD in its original shape has been abolished, but there is still work being done in a comitology-like process, with civil cervants seeking to continue the ESDP process. We will look more closely at this latest development in Chapter 6.

The Structural Funds – money to back up action

The EU Structural Funds play a major part in regional development policy. There are three elements to the Structural Funds: the European Development Fund (ERDF), the European Social Fund (ESF) and the European Agriculture Guidance and Guarantee Fund (EAGGF). Both the ERDF and the ESF have funded many urban projects. The INTERREG programme (under ERDF) was originally developed in order to break down the barriers made by the nation states to Community actions at a regional level (Veggeland, 1996: 74). The first programme, INTERREG I, was targeted at cross-border regional co-operation. The INTERREG II was then expanded towards co-operation between regions without common borders. INTERREG IIC (1994–2000) enabled cross-border transnational planning initiatives between national and European levels, working within the context of transnational regions subsumed under the ESDP framework. The current strand of INTERREG III with relevance to spatial policy is the new and economically stronger INTERREG IIIB, which runs from 2000–2006. The programme explicitly states that recommendations made in the ESDP must be taken into account, and encourages the drawing up of 'spatial visions' at the transnational level. The philosophy behind the INTERREG is articulated by the Environment DG like this:

> The initiative lies at the heart of unity in Europe. It aims to establish closer cooperation between regions that are separated by national boundaries but share

> common economic interests. These areas often suffer further isolation through being far from the centres of economic activity and political decision-making.
>
> (Community Initiatives, CEC, Environment DG, 1994, in Veggeland, 1996: 75–76)

What should be noticed first is that it is the economic interests that are central in this co-operation. Next, this formulation implicitly acknowledges a core-periphery image of European space. Since cross-border activity is stressed even more in INTERREG II, this could be seen as a strengthening of 'region-building' by means of stronger institutionalised cross-border co-operation (Veggeland, 1996: 78). The INTERREG programme must therefore be considered as one of the central institutional frameworks for regional and urban spatial development in Europe. The link between the ESDP and the INTERREG IIC programme is very clear in the minds of the CSD:

> Basically, the objective of the ESDP is not to make new policies for the Union. It is rather to make a catalogue of supplementary policy ideas and proposals as seen from a spatial development point of view. Implementation of these policies will have to take place at different levels: national, transnational, Community and Europe-wide. . . . INTERREG IIC has to do with the transnational level, and there is a very strong connection between INTERREG IIC and the ESDP.
>
> (Derek Martin, member of the CSD and Co-ordinator of International Affairs at the Dutch National Spatial Planning Agency, in Jensen *et al.*, 1996a: 21)

This assessment corresponds with the thoughts of the Principal Administrator of unit A3 within Regional Policy DG, Henriette Bastrup-Birk. She underlined that the INTERREG IIC initiative should constitute the test-bed for practical measures relating directly to the objectives and approaches anchored in the ESDP (Jensen *et al.*, 1996a: 18). The same point of view has been expressed by the Committee of the Regions:

> The INTERREG IIC initiative should maintain where desirable, from the viewpoint of local and regional authorities, parallels with the development of the European Spatial Development Perspective (ESDP), which will be finalized during the course of 1997. In this context, the INTERREG IIC initiative should, the CoR believes, provide a vision for the territorial areas within which the actions of the initiative can be strategically implemented. Local and regional authorities must have a strong role in creating such a vision and helping to bring to the fore their priorities for spatial development. An important role for the European Commission must therefore be the creation of a synergy between the top-down and bottom-up perspectives.
>
> (CoR, 1997: 3–4)

In other words, the European spatial policy discourse relies heavily on EU regional policy for its institutional and economic leverage.

Concluding remarks

Policy development at the EU level does not take place in a clearly identifiable arena. With no single body controlling decision making, policy takes shape through a complex inter-institutional process which is not immediately transparent to the observer. Over the past decade, significant changes have taken place in the relations between the key institutions – the Commission, the Council of Ministers and the Parliament – with marked effects on the policy process. The positions of each of the key EU institutions, the array of other interests which seek to shape the path of policy development, and the relations between them, have not been fixed. Relations remain contingent and highly transient, reflecting the volatile state of institutional relations at the EU level, the high level of lobbying and, of course, the controversial nature of the policy ideas at stake.

In terms of our three guiding themes (the urban, the environment, and territorial identity) and their threading motif of mobility, we want to put forward some preliminary points to be drawn from this discussion, which will be further elaborated as we chase the meanings and workings of the monotopic discourse through the representations, practices and power-rationalities in the chapters to come.

The urban theme is captured in the way that mobility and cities are linked into a narrative of urban nodes, within a web of high quality infrastructure. By adding a transnational level to the perception of cities and networks within the EU territory, the institutional architecture of Europe adds a new dimension to its political integration. Transgressing the nation state boundaries in a new transnational urban system opens up opportunities and prosperity for the successful cities (the cities of centrality and nodal status in the transnational web). However, the discourse of monotopic Europe then leaves us with difficult questions: which cities and regions get seen as the 'urban motors', and which cities are left as backwater spaces, or are framed as lagging or backwards-looking? Are the central urban growth regions of the 'Blue Banana' (stretching from southeast England to North Italy) or the reconfigured 'Pentagon' (embracing London, Hamburg, Paris, Munich and Milan) becoming a new imaginary geography of Europe which supplements (or substitutes for) the nation state? Are we to think of the EU in terms of a new Europe of urban mega-regions?

As regards the framing of the environment within the institutional architecture of the EU, we most clearly see the connection between the environment and mobility in the efforts to produce a seamless transnational infrastructure of flows, as in the case of the TEN-T. The political integration of the EU is closely linked to the possibility for goods, services and people to move with as little friction as possible. But the environment is affected too. This is indicated by the increasing stress put upon the ecology of Europe, as policies favouring mobility seem likely to lead to even more traffic in EU territory. This leads to the question of whether European integration through increased mobility overrides concerns for environmental carrying capacity. And further, whether the new spatial dimension to the political integration process feeds into a policy tension (or incoherence), as the environmental dimension of EU policy seems to be more and more at odds with the general thrust of EU policy.

The third theme, the question of how these developments in spatial policy may have implications for territorial identity, is embedded within the institutional structure of the EU. It becomes an issue of how to institutionalise, articulate and practice a common understanding of Europeanness. What we find is a nurturing of the link between mobility and identity, as the hard and soft political dimensions of European integration offer new mental frames for imagining belonging. The spatial policy discourse of monotopic Europe is in this sense a new transnational vocabulary and mindset, reconfiguring what it means to live in a particular city, region, or nation state within EU territory.

We will turn next to a theoretical framework which will help in analysing the construction of the new EU spatial policy discourse. Bringing a discourse perspective to bear on the ideas, policy infrastructures and power relations shaping the spatial dimensions of the European project seems likely to add new layers to our understanding of the governance of European space.

Chapter 3
Linking discourse and space

> What various forms of rationality claim to be their necessary existence, has a history which we can determine completely and recover from the tapestry of contingency.
>
> (Foucault, 1989: 252)

> Conceptions of space – which are central to any ontology – are part and parcel of notions of reality. Much more than simply a world view, this sense of space, one's 'spatiality', is a fundamental component of one's relationship to the world.
>
> (Shields, 1991: 31)

> Spaces, then, may be constructed in different ways by different people, through power struggles and conflicts of interest. This idea that spaces are socially constructed, and that many spaces may co-exist within the same physical space is an important one. It suggests the need to analyse how discourses and strategies of inclusion and exclusion are connected with particular spaces.
>
> (Flyvbjerg and Richardson, 2002: 56)

Introduction

In this chapter we set out a framework which has helped us to explore how spatialities are 'constructed' in European policy and planning discourses. In other words, we are interested in what happens when policy makers, politicians and lobbyists struggle over ideas about space. By this, we mean how conflicts emerge not just over whether a particular highway should be built, and whether it should be constructed through a particular natural habitat or local community, but how the *ways* in which such difficult decisions take place become contested. What do we need to know to be able to balance the benefits of development against the inevitable impacts? Here, 'facts' about the economic benefits of a new road to a peripheral region, or of the damage to vulnerable habitats that will result from its construction, become the terrain of struggle. The ways in which such facts are generated – using tools like economic and environmental assessments – become crucial in determining what sorts of things should be measured, what level of impact is 'significant', and what dimensions of space 'count' in decision-making. And all of this is subject to the influence of powerful interests.

Our aim in this chapter, then, is to introduce a framework for the analysis of spatial policy discourses that deals not only with discourse (with the ideas, language and practices of policy, the knowledge that provides its legitimacy), but also with a clear focus on the framing of space (spatialities) in policy making. We believe that this approach, combining the double dimensions of discourse and space, makes a significant contribution to reflections surrounding the more general resurgence of space in current debates in the social sciences.

We begin by outlining a general theoretical framework of space and spatiality – a *cultural sociology of space* in our terminology. In line with calls for a new spatially conscious sociology (Sayer, 2000), we draw from a variety of theoretical sources, from critical geography to politics and sociology, to argue for a practice- and culture-oriented understanding of the construction of spatialities that create the conditions for everyday life.

It is important to locate our work carefully here within this 'spatial turn'. Certainly, we recognise the importance of attention to lived space by geographers as being a necessary dimension to critical social science research. We have been particularly inspired by the work of Edward W. Soja, a strong advocate of the need to supplement the commonly held meagre, reductionist understandings of space with an examination of lived spaces (Soja, 1996, 2000). And we agree with Soja's calls for 'a critical re-reading of the presuppositional work on space, knowledge and power by Henri Lefebvre and Michel Foucault' (Soja, 1997).

However our task here is to analyse policy making processes, and this requires a shift of perspective. Inspired by the concerns of Foucault and Lefebvre with space and power, we are interested in examining how lived spaces, and possible spaces, get represented in policy processes. With this in mind, we aim to analyse how European space is constructed in policy knowledge, language and images, and we are extremely interested in the practices which reproduce these constructions, or representations, of space. We do not set out to explore lived European space – this would be a very different, and very interesting project! We do see the need for a perspective which usefully reminds us that representations of space in policy making can only be limited, partial and contingent views of what lived spaces are actually like. Our search for a conceptual framework is therefore shaped by these needs.

Along with Soja, David Harvey is one of the geographers who has explored an explicitly spatialised perspective on the relations between power and society. Harvey, another of our main sources of inspiration, adds a notion of dialectical relations between discourse and space, which is helpful in bringing a sharp analytical edge to this line of enquiry.

We then turn to three critical elements of a cultural sociology of space. The first of these is the role of socio-spatial relations in the construction of a territorial dimension of identity. The second is the significance of the study of flows and mobilities in understanding socio-spatial relations. Here, we have found the work of Castells and Urry to be particularly helpful in conceptualising the huge contemporary significance of mobility to the organisation of society. Finally, Brenner helps us to consider how mobility, and the organisation of space, must be considered across spatial scales from the local to the global, if we are to understand how Europe is being constructed.

To analyse complex relations in this cultural sociology of space, we turn to discourse, and in particular we draw from Foucault's work on power-knowledge and governmentality, to build a conceptual framework dealing with how language and spatial practices are shaped by power-rationalities. In Foucault's work, and in Lefebvre's, we see lived space as being in a dialectical relationship with discourse. Discourses produce lived spaces, and actions within lived spaces in turn shape discourses. If discourse is necessary for attaching meaning to things in everyday life (as much as in policy making, which is just one of those things that can happen in everyday life), then analysis of discourse is inseparable from the analysis of space. In fact, analysis of space requires analysis of discourse if we are to understand how spaces come to be as they are, how people exist and act within them, and how our ideas and ways of thinking are affected by what happens in spaces. The framework we draw together from these elements, which we elaborate below, is used to structure the analysis in the remaining sections of the book.

Towards a cultural sociology of space

The fundamental assumption of a cultural sociology of space is that analysis must deal with the dialectical relations between socio-spatial practices and the symbolic and cultural meanings that social agents attach to their environments (these two spheres are separated analytically, not as an ontological statement). That is to say, we need to conceptualise socio-spatial relations in terms of their practical 'workings' and their symbolic 'meanings'. This dialectical perspective means that the spatiality of social life is thus simultaneously understood as a field of action and as a basis for action (Lefebvre, 1974/1991: 73, 191). We enrich this analysis by incorporating the perspectives of the politics of identity, scale and mobility.

Socio-spatial/material practices

The first dimension of the cultural sociology of space deals with the coercive and enabling effects of socio-spatial relations on social practices. The emphasis is not only on the material dimension of human agency but also on the significance of power. Harvey stresses that social relations are always spatial and exist within a certain produced framework of spatialities, and that this framework consists of institutions understood as 'produced spaces of a more or less durable sort' (Harvey, 1996).

Such spatialised institutions range from territories of control and surveillance to domains of organisation and administration, creating institutional environments within which symbolised spaces are produced and attributed meanings. In line with the dialectical framework specific places must furthermore be conceptualised in relational terms. Lefebvre, among others, has recognised the importance of the production of space through spatial practices:

> Spatial practice thus simultaneously defines: places – the relationship of local and global; the representation of that relationship; actions and signs; the trivialised spaces of everyday life; and, in opposition to these last, spaces made special by symbolic means as desirable or undesirable, benevolent or malevolent, sanctioned or forbidden to particular groups.
>
> (Lefebvre, 1974: 288)

Turning more specifically to the ways that material practices play a part in the production of spaces, Foucault in particular was very interested in how domains of organisation and administration operate through the power relations embedded in local practices, through the 'apparently humble and mundane mechanisms which appear to make it possible to govern' (Miller and Rose, 1993: 83). These local practices included 'techniques of notation, computation and calculation; procedures of examination and assessment; the invention of devices such as surveys and representational forms such as tables . . . the inauguration of professional specialisms and vocabularies' (Miller and Rose, 1993: 83).

This insight suggests the importance of close attention to the fine grain of the policy process. The focus is turned towards how commonly used techniques of analysis construct particular forms of knowledge, providing legitimacy for particular spatial strategies whilst marginalising other ways of understanding policy problems. The tools and frameworks of policy making may mask such conflicts, but inevitably they are marked by them.

In these terms, we might conceptualise the emerging field of European spatial policy discourse as an attempt to produce a new framework of spatialities – of regions within member states, transnational mega-regions, and the EU as a spatial entity – which disrupts the traditional territorial order, and destabilises spatialities within European member states. The new transnational orientation creates new territories of control, expressed through the new transnational spatial vision of polycentricity and mobility. It necessitates new territories of surveillance, manifested in the need for enhanced spatial analysis focusing on new problems at new spatial scales. Significantly much of this analysis is focused on flows between European regions. These new territories are given life by a variety of more or less formal administrative arrangements and symbolic investments.

Symbolic meanings

The second (analytical) dimension of the cultural sociology of space addresses how meaning is attached to the spatiality of social life. In other words, it deals with the question of how representations, symbols and discourses frame the cultural meaning of socio-spatiality. By means of a process of 'social spatialisation' social agents appropriate and give meaning to spaces through socio-spatial practices and identification processes (Shields, 1991: 7, 31). Social agents 'appropriate' space in terms of ascribing cultural and symbolic attributes to their environment whilst their spatial practices are simultaneously enabled or restricted by the very quality of this spatiality. A discursive representation of space prescribes a domain of 'meaningful' actions and thus finally provides a regulatory power mechanism for the selection of appropriate and meaningful utterances and actions. In the words of Lefebvre we are exploring the 'representations of space', that is the:

> . . . conceptualized space, the space of scientists, planners, urbanists, technocratic subdividers and social engineers, as of a certain type of artist with a scientific bent – all of whom identify what is lived and what is perceived with what is conceived. . . . This is the dominant space in any society . . . representations of space are shot through with a knowledge (savoir) – i.e. a mixture of understanding (connaissance) and ideology – which is always relative and in the process of change.
>
> (Lefebvre, 1974/1991: 38–39, 41)

Again, it is possible to see social spatialisation as a major activity in the new field of European spatial policy, as physical spaces are attributed new meanings. In the new transnational spatial visions, cities, ports and airports may be represented as key nodes in transnational networks. This process of attributing meaning is contested between actors from the local to the European level, given what is at stake in terms of the perceived link between connectedness and economic competitiveness. Regions may be represented as core, peripheral, urban or rural, as well as successful or lagging, in the new European geography. And local roads and railways may be represented as segments of international high-speed transport corridors.

The politicial sociology of identity

The cultural sociology of space, with its double focus on material practices and symbolic meanings coins the question of belonging and the construction of identity as a matter of material as well as cognitive processes:

> The experience of identity remains a combination of fragmentation and symbolic levelling that derives from the media and, simultaneously, the unending search for authenticity which is as dependent on *material artifacts*, institutions, and localized space as it is on cognitive processes of self-integration.
>
> (Gottdeiner, 1995: 242, our emphasis)

Here we view social identity as a process of constructing meaning on the basis of pre-given cultural attributes (Castells, 1997). But, even though social identities can be originated or 'induced' from dominant institutions (e.g. the EU), they will, in the words of Castells, only become identities in so far as social agents internalise them in a process of individuation. This is important both in the context of the debate over 'Europeanness' but also in the context of 'globalisation', and suggests the need to broaden the debate over the nature of EU spatial policy. Thus 'the construction of identities uses building materials from history, from geography, from biology, from productive and reproductive institutions, from collective memory and from personal fantasies, from power apparatuses and religious revelations' (Castells, 1997: 7).

The spatial location of social action is, according to Castells, vital for processes of socio-spatial identification at all spatial scales from the neighbourhood to the transnational and the global. In order for such an identity to come about, a process of social mobilisation is necessary. Policy discourses of European space, then, can be said to do more than carry with them visions and ideas for the transnational functional co-ordination of activities in space. The ESDP, for example, can be seen as both articulating a functional network of regions and nation states in a competitive global region, as well as injecting a spatial dimension into the discourse of political integration in Europe, and thus potentially spatialising the less tangible notion of a European identity.

The political sociology of scale

The next (analytical) dimension of a cultural sociology of space addresses scaling: the ways that spatial practices and the construction of symbolic meanings take place at particular, and possibly politically defined, spatial scales. A key dimension of this framework is its focus on the construction of spatial visions in different arenas at very different spatial scales. This practice of 'scaling' should never be seen as a power-neutral affair. The 'politics of scale' (Brenner, 1998) suggests that scaling means framing, and framing is the main tool in shaping agendas and thereby setting up the arena for potential decisions. Locations at different scales are 'nested places' to be understood in relational terms (Allen *et al.*, 1998). That is to say that cities, regions and mega-regions are never isolated islands, but are interdependent on their contextual relations at these various spatial scales.

Scaling should not be understood as an ontological statement on the profound nature of fixed hierarchies of places. What it means is rather to notice the power relations and workings of a 'politics of scale'. Such politics of scale makes a cultural analysis of space sensitive to the ways in which, for example, social agents relate to spaces and places in terms of identification, and to how power relations at different scales (and across them) can be understood as either enabling or constraining action, as they represent:

> a range of discourses in which the meaning and identity of political actors are referred to a particular place, a portion of a real space, whether it be a neighbourhood, a city, region, or national territory, and where as a result a certain degree of political closure is effected or at least reinforced.
>
> (Low, 1997: 225)

In other words, social agents make use of more or less fixed notions of a spatial hierarchy of nested places in order to navigate their own reality, but also in the construction of 'realities' of place. In principle this range of scaling extends from the body ('the geography closest in') to the global:

> The continual production and reproduction of scale expresses the social as much as the geographical contest to establish boundaries between different places, locations and sites of experience. The making of place implies the production of scale in so far as places are made different from each other: scale is the criterion of difference not so much between places as between different kinds of places.
>
> (Smith, 1993: 99)

In the context of European spatial policy, this amounts to noticing these discursive practices of scaling and 're-scaling', from the nested territories of cities and urban regions to the nation state, the new transnational regions, the EU and the wider continent of Europe. European spatial policy discourses constructed in these multi-level arenas are not only expressions of a new politics of scale, they are framed in the context of globalisation, and so explicitly articulate a global-local dialectic, manifested in the interaction of multiple and complex localised practices crossing time and space (Harvey, 1996).

The political sociology of mobility

As a further critical dimension in the cultural sociology of space, flows and mobilities are highly significant in understanding socio-spatial relations in society. The new mobility forms transforming the spatiality of social life are important contributors to uneven geographical development, 'producing difference' at various spatial scales (Harvey, 2000: 75–83). Indeed it is important that we intertwine our critical investigations of scale and mobility. The problem of uneven development in the face of globalisation creates a critical problem in framing policy discourses carrying the idea of balanced development. According to Castells the complex dynamics of globalisation can be understood as a dialectical tension between two forms of 'spatial logic', or forms of rationality (Castells, 1996: 378). In line with the work of, for example, Hajer (2000) and Urry (2000), Castells sees mobility as the key to understanding these relations. The essence of his conceptualisation is therefore a dialectical tension between the historically rooted local spatial organisation of human experience (the *space of places*) versus the global flow of goods, signs, people and electronic impulses (the *space of flows*) (Castells, 1996: 412, 423). In the words of Lefebvre:

> The local (or the 'punctual', in the sense of determined by a particular 'point') does not disappear, for it is never absorbed by the regional, national or even world wide level. The national and regional levels take innumerable 'places'; national space embraces the regions; and world space does not merely subsume national spaces (for the time being at least) but precipitates the formation of new national spaces through a remarkable process of fission.
>
> (Lefebvre, 1974/1991: 88)

That is to say that spaces and places are not isolated and bounded entities, but are material and symbolic constructions that work as meaningful and practical settings for social action because of their relations to other spaces and places (Allen *et al.*, 1998). In other words 'A place is a site of relations of one entity to another and it therefore contains "the other" precisely because no entity can exist in isolation' (Harvey, 1996: 261).

According to Castells' analysis, the relationship between the space of places and the space of flows is not predetermined in its outcome. Thus it becomes an empirical question how this simultaneous globalisation and localisation is played out in the specific environments studied, in our case the nested visions and representations of the spatiality of Europe. So a critical analysis of the representations of space which form the new field of European spatial policy reveals them as attempts to frame spaces in line with a particular ideology of European space, which we will argue asserts a new space of flows against a space of places. Furthermore, the representation of space articulated within policy discourses of European space is bearing on this tension. A tension that, according to Castells, is the hallmark of our time:

> because function and power in our societies are organized in the space of flows, the structural domination of its logic essentially alters the meaning and dynamic of places. Experience, by being related to places, becomes abstracted from power, and meaning is increasingly separated from knowledge. It follows a structural schizophrenia between two spatial logics that threaten to break down communication channels in society. . . . Unless cultural and physical bridges are deliberately built between these two forms of space, we may be heading toward life in parallel universes whose times cannot meet because they are warped into differential dimensions of a social hyperspace.
>
> (Castells, 1996: 428)

Urry (2000) also points to a deeper understanding of these different social forms of spatial mobilities as a vital dimension of the cultural sociology of space. His work suggests an understanding of places as both sites of co-presence and flows:

> Places can be loosely understood therefore as multiplex, as a set of spaces where ranges of relational networks and flows coalesce, interconnect and fragment. Any such place can be viewed as the particular nexus between, on the one hand, propinquity characterised by intensely thick co-present interaction, and on the other hand, fast flowing webs and networks stretched corporeally, virtually and imaginatively across distances.
>
> (Urry, 2000: 140)

Framing mobilities

Mobility, as we have noted, has become a recent concern of sociology, but there remains a need for more work to define the field of enquiry. In order to locate our own interests, we now put forward a framework for analysing possible spatialities of mobility as a contribution to a cultural sociology of space. By spatialities of mobility, we mean the way that particular sets of relations between spatial practices and symbolic meanings combine to produce specific rationalities which support particular forms of mobility, and require (or resist) certain interventions in physical space. So, in an analysis of the significance of certain constructions of mobility in shaping European space, it seems to us that we need to focus on (at least) the following forms of mobility: the dynamics of movement between spaces across transport infrastructure; the frictionless desire in the nodal spaces of infrastructure networks; and the consumption of space by infrastructure. These are spatialities which contain divergent (and contested) constructions of mobility and space, and have either become characteristic elements of spatial policy discourse, or have been voiced as counterdiscourse. We will use these perspectives to analyse how spatial policy discourse contains and reproduces certain constructions of these spatialities, whilst neutralising, marginalising or excluding others.

Managing the dynamics of movement between spaces: infrastructure and mobility

Systems of infrastructure like motorways, railways, telecommunications and other networks facilitate mobility across and between spaces. These networks are an important spatiality of mobility because their development is bound up closely with the development of spatial relations in society. The spatial effects of infrastructure networks are shaped by the hegemonic strategies of geo-politics and market forces, yet they are also increasingly contested in a field of cultural political engagement. The uncertain development of infrastructure networks has become one facet of the struggle between the spatiality of alternative futures (Foucault, 1989; Graham and Marvin, 2001). The central place of mobility and infrastructure in the reproduction of capitalist society has been explored variously (by, among others, Deleuze and Guattari, 1988; Harvey, 1982; Swyngedouw, 1993). In neo-marxist and post-structuralist readings, infrastructure development is managed by the state as part of a process of territorial organisation. Infrastructure development brings liberation from existing spatial barriers, and 'time-space compression' occurs as barriers of distance are removed (Harvey, 1982, 1985; Janelle, 1969). Movement across space becomes a strategic necessity for the functioning of markets and the state itself, and therefore mobility becomes a governed activity.

In this way, enhancing mobility becomes a 'necessary element in the struggle for maintaining, changing or consolidating social power' (Swyngedouw, 1993). However, as Swyngedouw realises, the liberation of mobility, which assists the development of a globalised economy, merely reconstitutes boundaries, and creates new patterns of exclusion among changing sub-groups in society. A link is thus drawn between the macro level of strategic infrastructure planning, and the micro level of activities and perceptions in everyday life. The outcome of the progressive removal of barriers to mobility through the introduction of new infrastructure leads, however, to the reconstruction of barriers rather than to their removal. The planning of infrastructure networks is therefore a potentially powerful tool in shaping the social world, affecting issues of equity and exclusion by changing the conditions and possibilities for mobility.

Seen from this perspective, a programme such as TEN-T aims to reorganise the dynamics between spaces, cities and regions, and to reframe the possibilities for transnational mobility. The core vision embodies the Europe of flows, relying on integrated networks, the reduction of peripherality, and the related polycentric spatial strategy. Within the policy process, the risks to this spatial vision of uneven development and unacceptable environmental impacts appear as difficulties which needed to be resolved, rather than as embodying intrinsic contradictions as perhaps suggested by Harvey and others.

Frictionless nodal spaces

Hajer has discussed how nodal spaces of mobility – railway stations, airports and transport interchanges, for example – are frequently designed as 'mono cultural zero friction enclaves' (Hajer, 1999). He suggests that these spaces function in a disciplined way, as machines for movement, designed to move people smoothly between one form of transport and another. As illustration, Hajer cites Calatrava's multi-modal station at the 1998 Lisbon EXPO, with its almost religious celebration of mobility and movement, of 'frictionless speed'. His critique is that even though attention is paid to the policy turn towards integrated transport, there is no cultural sensitivity: 'What is the meaning of the mobility that is being celebrated? Where do people go? Where do they come from? What is the meaning of their movement?' (Hajer, 1999). Elsewhere, Castells has similarly discussed the functional design of Barcelona airport: 'in the middle of the cold beauty of this airport passengers have to face their terrible truth: they are alone, in the middle of the space of flows . . . they are suspended in the emptiness of transition. They are, literally, in the hands of Iberia Airlines' (Castells, 1996), as they enter the 'non-places' of super-modernity (Augé, 1995). Rem Koolhaas theorises this design of spaces of frictionless movement as architecture's engagement with the process of delocalisation (Koolhaas, 1995).

As transport policy turns towards integration of modes, and towards a reassertion of the role of public transport, the tendency is to pursue the functional model. The objectives concern how quickly, and smoothly, travellers can complete their transitions between buses, cars, trains and planes. Cultural interests are overlooked in this friction-free utopianism (Richardson and Jensen, 2001). Instead of taking advantage of the new possibilities for meaningful interaction which are provided in the grand interchanges of late capitalism, the agenda of efficient traveller flow handling dominates. By focusing his analysis on the transport node, Hajer addresses the role of architects, planners and urban designers in attending to a particular static component of the network of mobile spaces: the nodal spaces which travellers enter at fixed points on their journeys. Certainly the transport node provides opportunities for these professions of space to engage with questions of public domain and friction. But the spaces of mobility require further analysis, and Hajer's arguments hold relevance for other spaces of mobility where friction and public domain may be at stake.

Integral to the networks of mobility which structure the ESDP is the identification and development of key transport nodes, such as major airports and high speed rail terminals. Such sites have been heavily contested as regions and other economic interests struggle to ensure that they are strategically placed on the new map of Europe. For many Europeans, passing through these nodes as they enter and leave high speed trains and planes is the quintessential experience of the new spaces of European mobility.

Infrastructure 'consuming' space

If infrastructure plays a central but contested role in the development of spatial relations in society, and in creating, breaching and redrawing boundaries, then it also plays a more direct role in re-shaping the concrete spaces where it is constructed. The hegemonic strategy of constantly improving and expanding infrastructure networks has resulted in myriad locally contested spaces, where new roads, airports or high-speed railway lines are proposed and constructed. These projects directly supplant urban and rural communities, habitats and landscapes, 'slicing up' the urban spaces (Lefebvre, 1974/1991) and so contributing to the trend of 'splintering urbanism' (Graham and Marvin, 2001). Thus we use the term infrastructure consuming space to reflect the social construction of infrastructure as environmental and social threat.

Perhaps the most apparent aspect of the cultural politics of mobility in the 1990s has been the way that proposals for new infrastructure projects have become foci of organised opposition. As the transport agenda has shifted, so these spaces of protest have broadened from road construction to target other types of infrastructure projects, such as the Betuwe rail freight line in the Netherlands, which is planned to cut through a number of ecologically important sites, or neighbourhood level opposition when disused railway lines – which have been reclaimed as cycle and pedestrian paths, or wildlife corridors – are turned to new transport uses such as tramways. In urban areas particularly, these concerns have sometimes been expressed differently, in a backlash against the loss of public domain to spaces of mobility. A growing social movement seeks to symbolically reclaim streets from the car, through non-violent direct action. For a brief time, spaces of mobility have been forced back into the public domain as roads have been blocked and street parties and theatre have taken over. Sometimes cars have been burned, and tarmac torn up to plant trees.

The longstanding hegemony of infrastructure over other forms of space, protected by deeply embedded policy knowledge, is appearing increasingly fragile in many European countries. Increasingly, the interests which have for many years been associated with infrastructure development, are shifting ground, moving into debates about improving network efficiency, rather than adding more road space. So the struggles over specific roads and other infrastructure projects – either where new proposals threaten habitats or communities, or where the tide is turning and they may be threatened by the inevitable logic of their own construction – are deeply affected by the cultural politics of the moment (Vigar, 2001). Of course, elsewhere the cultural politics of infrastructure and mobility may vary greatly. In the countries of Central Europe seeking accession to the European Union, for example, transport and communications infrastructure development is a core condition for entry, and personal mobility is a highly valued commodity in post-Communist states – as it has been for a long time in the 'West'. In spite of these debates we will see how, in terms of European spatial policy making, the potentially destabilising spatial construction of infrastructure consuming space has had little apparent impact. These spatial constructions of the striation of space by new infrastructure have been largely excluded from the policy debate, from the evaluation frameworks used to support decision-making, and from the policy discourse itself.

Framing mobilities – summing up

The exclusion of spatial constructions relating to the damaging consumption of space by transport networks has been critical to policy progress, but runs against a current policy turn, in some member states at least, away from high levels of infrastructure spending, particularly on roads. The development of infrastructure according to the particular spatial vision of a Europe of flows seems likely to bring about profound spatial economic, social and environmental effects. Across Europe, proposals for local projects forming parts of the TEN-T have become a focus for political action from the regional to the international level. In France direct action has been staged against the construction of the southern extension of the TGV network. In the Netherlands, demonstrations have taken place on the runway at Schiphol airport. In the Basque regions high speed trains have been stopped in their tracks by activists. All of these actions, targeting proposed regional infrastructure projects, are linked. Their aim, through opposing local projects, is to assert that high speed infrastructure, as an instrument of the single market, is fundamentally damaging. These protests do not set out any alternative proposals at the level of managing the dynamics between spaces. The discourses of environmental reform and opposition fail to make competing alternative demands for mobility in European space, their focus being placed more clearly on resisting the threat of destruction of local ecologies and the homogenisation of local cultures. However, the policy discourse has systematically neutralised and excluded such destabilising knowledges, fuelled by the overwhelming will to integration. Juxtaposing these different and incompatible frames of mobility is helpful in illustrating how the discourse of environmental opposition failed to construct a message which made sense within the rationality of the policy process, so that it remained outside and beyond – an 'other' way of understanding, against which the policy discourse could shape and define itself.

Albertsen and Diken (2001) have analysed how these symbolic meanings of different mobilities are expressed and justified in ways that help to show how these alternative spatialities can exist or compete. They argue that in general people engaged in public discussion refer to different 'regimes of justification' in order to legitimise their arguments and thus at the end of the day support their statements with their own internal criteria of validity and internal consistency. In a sense, we could perceive such regimes of justification as a dimension of the power-rationality forms underpinning spatial policy discourse. However, of interest here is the way Albertsen and Diken relate such regimes to the actual theme of physical mobility. They argue that different regimes create different and conflicting justifications of mobility (Albertsen and Diken, 2001: 17).

From this perspective, strategies and visions for mobility in European space are clearly framed within a market and industrial regime, focusing on the deployment of new technologies to reduce friction, resulting in the shrinking of Europe in pursuit of the single internal market, and simultaneously becoming an increasingly strong competitor in the global marketplace. However, the aims of political integration also relate to the core values of freedom of movement, enshrined in the Union's Treaties, and so mobility as inspiration appeals to individuals across Europe to expand their spatial horizons, as barriers to free movement are removed. Albertsen and Diken's idea of mobility as opinion is also increasingly critical of this paradigm of Europe's future, referring to elites who depend increasingly on being in many places to achieve influence. In opposition to this coalition is a strengthening discourse which constructs 'zero friction Europe' as being antithetic to communities, and to civil society. The disruption of territory by the construction of high-speed infrastructure projects, for example, is constructed as a threat to local communities in marginal places such as border areas. And the process of planning such infrastructure programmes is seen as anti-democratic, and as being strongly influenced by powerful industrial lobbies.

This tentative framework of mobilities highlights how mobility (and spatial practices in general) is intrinsically related to power-rationalities of contested interest, and to power struggles over the possibilities of alternative discourses securing hegemony. This idea of alternative, contested constructions of mobility raises the need for a framework that we can use to unpack and analyse struggles over their representation in (or exclusion from) hegemonic policy discourses.

Drawing together a cultural sociology of space

Drawing together these dimensions of material practices, symbolic meanings, and political sociologies of identity, scale and mobility has several important consequences. First, as Harvey expresses it, representations of space not only arise from social practices, they also 'work back' as regulations on those forms of practice (Harvey, 1996: 212), thus creating a complex socio-spatial dialectics. In other words, the spatial visions contained in the new policy discourses of European space not only express future 'imaginary landscapes', they also 'work' in terms of being vehicles for new forms of transnational policy making.

Second, this approach to the relation between space and discourse also implies that power is central. As Beauregard reminds us (Beauregard, 1995: 60), the city does not present itself but is rather represented by means of power relations expressed in strategies, discourses and institutional settings. European space can also be understood in these terms. Thus we subscribe to the numerous conceptualisations of planning as an expression of a 'will to order' (among others see Boyer, 1983; Diken, 1998; Flyvbjerg, 1998; Sennett, 1990; Wilson, 1992). The creation of a new field of European spatial policy can be understood as an expression of a 'will to order' European space, with its emphasis on ideas such as cohesion and balance, which articulate the idea of a harmonised Europe.

Third, and as a direct consequence of seeing spatial policy making as the 'will to order', the concept of knowledge and the social relations governing the various claims to valid knowledge are central to the analysis. As Perry reminds us, we should think of planning and policy making as a spatial and strategic discourse rather than as a science or knowledge of space (Perry, 1995: 237). Thus the question becomes what epistemologies govern the 'knowledge policy' in operation. In the words of Harvey, 'Discursive struggles over representation are . . . as fiercely fought and just as fundamental to the activities of place construction as bricks and mortar' (Harvey, 1996).

This leads to a view of policy making and planning as more than a rhetorical activity. It can be seen as 'world making' (Fischler, 1995). Not in the sense that plans and visions automatically determine a material and spatial outcome, but in the sense that their words, signs and symbols frame the thinking of social agents as well as being the outcome of the historical and contextual conditions under which they are articulated: 'while sets of meanings of the social imaginary are conceptualized in symbolic languages, these meanings are materialized and become real in all sorts of spatial and social practices, from urban design to housing policy' (Zukin, 1998: 629).

In other words, social agents 'appropriate' space through socio-spatial practices and identification processes. One of the ways that places are given a specific meaning is through the creation of 'place images' which imply simplification, stereotyping and labelling (Shields, 1991). Brought together collectively, a number of place images forms a 'place myth' (Shields, 1991). Again, the place images constructed within EU spatial policy discourse can be seen as attempts to realise new transnational place myths of European space.

The basic proposition here is that socio-spatial relations work by means of their coercive or enabling capacities for spatial practices. Furthermore these relations convey meaning to social agents via multiple representations, symbols and discourses. Thus on the one hand socio-spatial relations express possibilities and limitations to social actions within the built environment, and on the other hand the meaning and valuation of these relations are constantly negotiated and re-negotiated on the basis of social imageries and cultural values. This dialectical tension also captures a politics of scale in the sense that socio-spatial practices and meanings produce and re-produce spatialities at scales from the body to the global, as witnessed in, for example, new forms of transnational socio-spatial mobility.

In summing up this part of the theoretical framework, we would argue for the importance of a deeper understanding of how relationships between physical space and social life are played out in a dialectical relationship between spatial/material practices and symbolic meanings. Furthermore, this is shaped by power struggles at multiple spatial scales, as the new politics of scale gives shape to a contested field of spatial practice. Mobility, and the politics of mobility, are central to the power-laden relations between society and space in Europe today.

Analysing spatial policy discourse

From the construction of a cultural sociology of space, we now move on to discuss how a discourse analytical framework can allow the symbols, meanings and practices shaping space to be researchable. The particular challenge is to establish a framework which operationalises an analysis of both the cultural and material dimensions of a cultural sociology of space, in a way which would be useful in researching spatial policy making. Following an increasingly popular path emerging within planning and policy research inspired by Hajer among others, we have explored how a focus on how discourses get fought over and embedded in particular institutional settings can actually be operationalised in research. Our distinctive approach is to use a discourse analytical framework that focuses on how different modes of communication and actions frame and represent spaces on the basis of certain relations between power and rationality (see Jensen, 1997, 1999; Richardson, T., 1996, 2000b). This particular approach to discourse analysis, with an analytical interest reaching beyond language and text, is well equipped to deal with spatiality because of its explicit incorporation of a dimension of socio-spatial practices, embracing materiality, representation and imagination (Harvey, 1996). The essence of such an approach is that it explores the performativity of discourse: how social structures create conditions for thought, communication and action, and how different configurations of power and rationality shape, and are shaped by, policy processes. Analysing language, and analysing practices, become complementary ways of revealing these struggles for control over meaning in policy making and implementation.

In the light of what we see as a need to bridge the gap between linguistic discourse and socio-spatial practices, we adopt an approach to discourse, drawing from Foucault (e.g. Foucault, 1979, 1990), and Hajer, which embraces material practices (Jensen, 1997; Richardson and Jensen, 2003). Here a spatial policy discourse is defined as an entity of repeatable linguistic articulations, socio-spatial material practices and power-rationality configurations. Accordingly, our analysis of discourse as representations is divided into three (analytical) spheres: *language*, *practice* and *power-rationality*. Thus a discourse can be understood as expressing a particular conceptualisation of reality and knowledge that attempts to gain hegemony. This 'will to knowledge' attempts to embed and naturalise particular values and ways of seeing and understanding the world, so that they become taken for granted and slip from critical gaze. It is thus an institutionalisation and fusion of articulation processes and practice forms, which generates new forms of knowledge and rationality, and frames what are considered to be legitimate social actions. This approach is quite different from examining how rhetorical 'discourse' is reproduced in practice. Instead the analysis focuses on how ideas within a policy discourse are manifested and reproduced in policy languages and in policy practices, and to try and understand the relations between power and rationality as a new discourse emerges in a contested policy space, and possibly attains hegemonic status.

The potential of Foucault's work in developing a more nuanced socio-spatial theory has clearly been recognised by critical geographers (e.g. Philo, 1987; Sibley, 1995), though there is disagreement over whether the full import of Foucault's work has been properly addressed by many of those in the spatial disciplines. The Foucauldian approach links space with the operation of discourses and power (discussed by, among others, Casey, 1996; Flynn, 1993; Lyon, 1993; Marks, 1995), which seems particularly helpful in understanding the spatial implications of policy making, and in operationalising a cultural sociology of space. Foucault's critique, in *Discipline and Punish*, of Jeremy Bentham's panopticon stands as perhaps the archetypal example of this approach (Foucault, 1979, discussed in e.g. Lyon, 1993: 655–656 and Marks, 1995: 75).

This insight suggests the need to analyse how particular spatial strategies, policies and practices may bring about – deliberately or inadvertently – various forms of inclusion and exclusion, control and resistance in lived spaces. This means focusing on how certain types of urban, rural or mobile spaces are constructed within the policy process. This deliberate spatialisation is akin to Shields' concept of social spatialisation (Shields, 1991). Shields' use of 'social spatialisation' is helpful in conceptualising the link between policy discourse and space, where social agents appropriate and give meaning to spaces through socio-spatial practices and identification processes (Shields, 1991). EU spatial policy discourse, and local discourses of competing cities and regions express these social dynamics.

We attempt to situate the analysis of European spatial policy both historically, within long policy processes, and in terms of the power relations and institutional dynamics that have shaped the form and content of a suite of policy documents, and which will continue to shape its implementation. So we are not attempting a static linguistic analysis but a more dynamic analysis of discourse which embraces power-rationality, and institutionalisation through material and spatial practices. This is partly an immanent analysis, drawing from the ESDP's own terms of reference, enriched through our own empirical research on aspects of the policy process, and partly drawing from broader theoretical debates and research to inform our critique. In line with Foucault, we subscribe to the point of view that the discourse analyst must do the 'hard work' of operationalising the theoretical concepts in such a way that they 'fit' the empirical research question.

Policy discourse, then, is understood as a complex body of values, thoughts and practices – which includes communicative acts and scientific knowledge alongside unspoken actions, lay knowledge and power relations. The approach calls for critical inquiry into the rationalities at work in policy making. Policy is constructed on a field of power struggles between different interests, where knowledge and truth are contested, and the rationality of policy making itself is exposed as a focus of conflict. This is what Flyvbjerg has called *realrationalität*, or 'real-life' rationality (Flyvbjerg, 1998). This type of analysis is likely to 'disrupt taken-for-granted knowledge and point to the contingent power relations which create spaces for particular assertions to operate as absolute truths' (Pavlich, 1995), where particular thoughts, ideas, knowledges and practices become accepted, marginalised or silenced. The all-pervasive nature of power, with its productive as well as destructive potential, is recognised.

How might this approach be useful in analysing the treatment of issues such as mobility and urban development in the emerging field of European spatial policy? First, the socio-political context of spatial policy is provided by a constellation of discourses, some in harmony, some in competition. Each of these discourses is grounded in a particular set of contested values, expressed through its own language and practice. Spatial policy processes at all levels are pursued within this field of discursive conflict, which shapes the relations of power and knowledge, and affects the fine grain of policy making. In the construction of policy processes, ground rules are set out for the creation of knowledge, by processing certain data using particular methodologies. At this stage spatiality is framed and agenda setting takes place. The specific ideas, practices and solutions that are possible in policy making at any particular time and place are conditioned. This is what we might understand as the construction of rationality of the policy process. This rationality defines the relationship between technical and lay knowledges, politics and communication, which will establish the legitimacy of policy. The ESDP policy process can be understood as just one of many transient and recurring arenas of conflict between these competing discourses. Gradually, a hegemonic spatial policy discourse may emerge, formed and reformed through many successive policy processes, reflecting the values, thoughts, languages and practices of successful discourses of development, and marked by unresolved conflicts.

The point then is to analyse the field of European spatial policy as one in which specific policy documents express the balance of power at critical moments. The documents are placed within a wider political process, their form and content shaped by power struggles:

> EU spatial planning is being developed in a complex institutional framework, and will be shaped by major tensions and power relations. It is important then that we do not try to understand this emergence of an EU spatial planning framework as a purely comprehensive scientific rational process, or the benign convergence of national planning systems. It bends to an agenda, and to forces, which contest the future path of development of Europe, and so is likely to have at its core the currently hegemonic ideologies of the single market and political integration, but will also reflect other debates about cohesion and environment.
>
> (Dabinett and Richardson, 1999: 228)

So, the process of creating a new field of EU spatial policy is not reducible to a technical exercise. It is implicitly normative and ideological – about politics and power. It seems important, then, that we should attempt to understand the effects of power relations and normative agendas (discussed in Chapter 2) on the emerging spatial policy framework.

We use the discourse analytical framework as an operational and analytical tool for probing at the ways in which spaces, places and mobilities are represented strategically in policy discourses in order to bring about certain changes of socio-spatial relations and prevent others. Following this approach, policy discourses can be explored in terms of their reproduction in *languages* and *practices*, to reveal their underlying *power-rationalities* (see Box 3.1). We now discuss each of these dimensions of policy discourse in turn, illustrating their application to the field of European spatial policy.

Box 3.1 **Operationalising discourse analysis**

Mapping languages
Metaphors, symbols, key words
'Conceptual history' and conceptual changes
New concepts (neologisms)
Inter-textuality
Language style (common sense, expert etc.)
Genre and style (linguistic and expressive conventions)
Cartography, graphics, maps ('infographics')

Mapping practices
Agents – who's in, and who's out?
Institutions (formal as well as informal)
Contextualisation and eventualisation (events)
Mapping resources (agent and institutional resources)
Mapping conflicts
Who is 'constructing' truth and knowledge claims?

Mapping power-rationalities
Conceptualisations of truth criteria and knowledge forms
Criteria of knowledge validity
How are truth and knowledge claims 'constructed'?
Mapping interests in the field
Mapping dominant values and norms
Mapping the relations between power and knowledge

Language and representation

According to our approach to discourse analysis, the first step is to explore how particular ideas, actions, institutions, physical artefacts, attributes or relations are represented in the language and imagery of policy documents. In the plethora of new European spatial policy processes, a series of documents charts the progress and shifts in policymaking, the emergence of new ideas, the entwining of strategies, policies and actions. Key documents are fragments of different knowledge framing processes. Thus different ways of framing 'space' set up different requirements for 'spatial knowledge' to be gathered and analysed in particular ways, to feed and support different spatial representations.

For example, the core ESDP vision is expressed in what might be termed a new language of European spatial relations. It centres on a policy triangle of economic and social cohesion, sustainable development and balanced competitiveness. These objectives are to be pursued through the development of a balanced and polycentric urban system, new partnerships between urban and rural areas; securing parity of access to infrastructure and knowledge; and sustainable development, prudent management and protection of nature and cultural heritage (CSD, 1999: 11). Each of these terms carries particular meanings, but at the same time leaves room for interpretation, having been first coined and shaped in a gestation process of policy development.

The concept of the polycentric urban system, for example, took shape through a series of European Commission studies and reports in the 1990s. Europe 2000+ (CEC, 1994a) developed the notion of socio-spatial 'polycentricity' and growth. In the face of global economic competition, the goal of creating a more equal economic and social development within the EU's cities is envisioned through the establishment of integrated systems of agglomerations and common actions between large urban centres (CEC, 1994a: 19). This has led to a notion of a 'polycentric urban system', a notion that is both very central to the discourse but also very vague and polyvalent in itself. The approach builds on the existing densely urbanised and historically strong settlement pattern as the legacy upon which any spatial policy for the urban system must build. The polycentric urban system is seen as a necessary response to environmental, social and traffic problems of increasing urban growth, by enabling horizontal integration and spreading specialisation to a number of urban centres. The ESDP strategies for creating a new polycentric European space include the emergence of 'urban networks', including new integration scenarios for cross-border regions in particular (CSD, 1999: 65). Co-operation between cities across borders may not only imply functional and economic advantages, but may also facilitate the vision of a Europe where national borders are criss-crossed by a new urban policy of inter-city co-operation.

Another example of the new language of European space is the notion of 'dynamic global economy integration zones' (CSD, 1999: 20). As an antidote to the traditional growth core of Europe (known as the 'blue banana') the ESDP envisions that such zones should be created in other regions to imitate and duplicate the prosperous core (CSD, 1999: 20). This is in spite of severe problems with traffic congestion in the core, which the ESDP recognises undermine its sustainability objectives. For weaker regions, outside the proposed zones, the approach is to widen the economic base and carry out economic restructuring (CSD, 1999: 22).

However, the question of representation is not one of words alone. We also perceive images in the broadest sense to be part of the 'language' and vocabulary used to frame European spatial development – a sort of 'textual mapping'. Here we will argue for an inclusion of maps, pictures and other visual representations into the conceptualisation of discourse.

Conceptualising the meaning of images and metaphors

Images are understood as elements of an emerging transnational spatial policy discourse, and so are analysed in the context of contestation over meanings, played out in policy debates, in documentation and in other practices of spatial planning. Images used together with textual references and discussions form a persuasive component of spatial policy discourse. We therefore analyse these contested representations of space to reveal the underlying power-rationalities, leading to insights into the ways that such images are playing an increasingly important role in foregrounding certain ways of thinking about European space and mobility whilst bracketing others.

But how can we 'break the code' in terms of analysing such images? We are all familiar with the more or less realistic territorial representations that we call maps. From the geography schoolbooks picturing the nation state territory to the iconic diagram of the London tube we have learned to deal with such visual representations of space and place in our daily lives. But what is a map more precisely? A map can be understood as a cultural text (Harley, 1996: 432), meaning that one has to engage in an interpretative activity in terms of its analysis. The cultural significance of maps lies in their ability to capture and frame ideas about space, and carry them from one mind to another, in a field of discursive struggles over meaning and interpretation. Mapping and imaging are therefore techniques of power in that they capture and frame certain ideas, relations, realities and potentials whilst excluding others. In doing this, they also mask the interests that bring them into being (Wood, 1993: 95):

> It is, of course, an illusion: there is nothing natural about a map. It is a cultural artefact, a cumulation of choices made among choices every one of which reveals a value: not the world, but a slice of a piece of the world; not nature but a slant on it; not innocent, but loaded with intentions and purposes; not directly, but through a glass; not straight, but mediated by words and other signs; not, in a word, as it is, but in . . . code.
>
> (Wood, 1993: 108)

As Latour (1990) argues, mapping means 'drawing things together' in the sense that diverse semantic fields immediately can be brought into contact. In this way maps act as a focusing device (Wood, 1993: 117). In the words of Dematteis, as they 'connect together a quantity of "superficial" evidence, they mark changes and problems, suggest hypotheses, challenge consolidated images' (Dematteis, 2000: 71). This is partly because the process of map making involves activities of selection, omission, simplification, classification, creation of hierarchies and symbolisation (Harley, 1996: 437). Furthermore de-constructing the map also means an epistemological shift from a strict reality-representation link towards seeing maps as inherently power laden (Harley, 1996). Thus the 'cartographic rules' in a sense resemble the Foucauldian 'epistemes' (Foucault, 1969) with certain rules of representation. But they also act as rhetorical devices.

Mapping is thus also a communicative event in the sense that we are dealing with both author subjects and institutions as well as audiences. But space can also be represented in ways which rely more on the use of metaphor than representation, where the graphical qualities of the image do not rely on an attempt to represent physical space in anything more than a notional manner. We need to think about how such spatial images combine visual graphics and concepts, and that these concepts are often metaphorical in their core. The essence of metaphor is understanding and experiencing one kind of thing in terms of another (Lakoff and Johnson, 1980: 5). Within social theory there is a very widespread use of metaphors for consciously and analytically describing social phenomena in terms of machines, living systems, legal orders, war, market places, games, theatres, and discourses (Rigney, 2001). However, social theory may also import metaphors in a less reflective way, and thus make use of such 'thinking devices' without really critically appreciating them (Urry, 2000). Thus spatial metaphors play a critical role in the formation of human knowledge, action and imagination and provide a quasi-logical framework of associations (Williams, 1996a: 95). So the metaphors form a vital part of the 'spatial imaginary' and refer to the processes of social spatialisation (Shields, 1991: 7).

The spatial metaphors analysed here are in fact famous for their colourful and associative capacities. Notions of 'blue bananas', 'bunches of grapes' and 'golden triangles' (Williams, 1993), are ways of imposing certain qualities of these metaphors and excluding others and are thus an expression of a European spatial rhetoric (Williams, 1996a). According to such a perspective the images work by providing principles of spatial organisation that stick in planners' minds, enticing them to act, and assisting public dialogue (Faludi, 1996: 97). The London Green Belt, the Copenhagen Finger Plan, and the Dutch Green Heart are all examples of this 'framing with images' (Faludi, 1996) where a spatial policy discourse makes use of powerful metaphors. Many people have never seen the original images which first articulated these concepts, but they retain some sense of the vision which lies behind them, capturing core values and spatial relations. Metaphors such as the blue banana carry powerful messages about the organisation of European space and economy as they become policy icons which take on a life beyond their graphic origin.

Summing up, we are arguing for a critical focus on language, maps, images and spatial metaphors as vital elements in the discursive framing of European space. In widening the 'vocabulary' of analysis from text to include graphical representations we aim to deepen our understanding of how spatial policy discourses work in power laden and rhetorical modes. In this way, we may bring to empirical analysis of spatial policy discourses some basic insights into the deep embeddedness of images and maps in textual representations, illustrating the powerful urge for 'being on the map'.

Practices

Analysing key policy documents captures the representation of space in language and images, and reveals some of the power relations that contest these representations. This is, however, a partial analysis that needs to be placed within the context of a live policy process, where different interests compete for hegemony over the shape of policy, and where different spatial visions are contested. Spaces and places do not present themselves as such, but are rather represented by means of power relations expressed in strategies, discourses and institutional settings. Although some of this is inherent in the texts and imagery of policy documents, what is required is a broader view of the policy process that focuses on institutions, actions and practices.

So, in the multi-level processes of European spatial policy making, multidimensional conflicts inevitably arise, from the internal power struggles of the EU spatial policy community to the conflicts between regions and other interests who have a stake in the spatial visions and in the implementation of policy.

Alongside the new spatial practices relating to the ESDP's comitology (discussed in Chapter 2), the question of implementation of the ESDP's policies has led to a further set of interesting practices. The first of these has been an emphasis on practical actions which are beyond the control of member states. Given the lack of legally binding status, it is not surprising that many of the possible actions identified within the ESDP focus on the transnational level (CSD, 1999: 35), thus avoiding the resistance of member states.

A further set of spatial practices relates to the reproduction of the new spatial policy discourse. In the words of Andreas Faludi, the success of the ESDP (for example) must be measured in terms of its ability to 'shape the minds' of social agents (Faludi, 2001). As the emerging discourse becomes institutionalised in new spatial practices, including those of spatial analysis, the construction of knowledge forms and fields of knowledge results in boundaries being established between valid and in-valid, reasonable and unreasonable forms of knowledge. Such boundaries are vital in institutionalising European spatial planning as a 'rational, science-based policy field', and at the same time they act as powerful instruments in the process of marginalising and excluding other forms of knowledge (e.g. radical environmental considerations or indicators of social equality). As an example of this 'knowledge policy' the 'Study Programme on European Spatial Development' (SPESP, 2000) should be emphasised. Apart from stressing a need for more comparable data and more solid knowledge of the spatial development of the European territory, the SPESP introduces an interesting new concept that illustrates the power-knowledge dimension. Thus in pursuit of a deeper spatial understanding, the process must be supplemented with 'infography', to which we return in Chapter 5 (SPESP, 2000: 13).

Power rationalities

Discourses frame and represent spaces and places, and thus express a specific power-rationality configuration. In the 'classic' sociological tradition, rationality is understood as the underlying structure of values and norms that governs social actions (Weber, 1978). However, rationality is inseparable from power (Flyvbjerg, 1998). Construed in a productive way, power is here seen as the foundation for social action as well as potential control and coercion (Foucault, 1990). Thus different rationalities – with their distinctive horizons of values and norms that guide social actions – are implicitly acts of power in that they are attempts to govern what sort of social actions are to be carried out, and what are not.

We move towards power-rationality, a fairly abstract concept, by first analysing language and practice. This allows us, step by step, to identify the core ideas at stake in shaping places, in making European space, by tracing first their articulation and then their institutionalisation. As this book unfolds, we will use this approach to show how a particular configuration of power-rationality, which we identify as a will to create a monotopic European space, has become a hegemonic idea which fundamentally shapes the EU spatial policy discourse.

If discourse is everything, maybe it's a brick!

A frequently expressed concern with this type of social constructionist approach is that it appears to deny that things have any actual existence. To us this seems to miss the point. Mouffe and Laclau pin the misperception down quite effectively:

> The fact that every object is constituted as an object of discourse has nothing to do with whether there is a world external to thought, or with the realism/idealism opposition. An earthquake or the falling of a brick is an event that certainly exists, in the sense that it occurs here and now, independently of my will. But whether their specificity as objects is constructed in terms of 'natural phenomena' or 'expressions of the wrath of God', depends on the structuring of a discursive field. What is denied is not that such objects exist externally to thought, but the rather different assertion that they could constitute themselves as objects outside any discursive condition of emergence.
>
> (Laclau and Mouffe, 1985: 108)

So it is how we attach meaning and significance to things that is discursive, and it seems difficult to imagine how to think, communicate or act without doing this.

Linking discourse and space – concluding remarks

The aim of this chapter has been to set out an approach to thinking spatially about spatial policy discourses. This might seem unnecessary or redundant, but it is part of our critical agenda to suggest an alternative to the frequently a-spatial policy analysis of spatial policy discourses. This rests on the assumption that discourses might be seen as social constructions but also that policy discourses dealing with representations of space must be understood in relation to their spatial 'object'. This is in no way an inclination to a simple correspondence notion of discourse and 'reality'. Rather, we see the importance of understanding discourses of space against the background of a cultural sociology of space that offers a meta-theoretical understanding of the relation between social life and its material surroundings.

Developed from the insights provided by Foucault's work, and drawing from Harvey, it is possible to set out a set of basic dialectical insights which are helpful in bridging discourse and space (adapted from Harvey, 1996: 111–113):

- The discursive activity of 'mapping space' is a fundamental prerequisite to the structuring of any kind of knowledge.
- Mapping is a discursive activity that incorporates power. The power to map the world in the one way rather than the other is a crucial tool in political struggles.
- Social relations are always spatial and exist within a certain produced framework of spatialities.
- Material practices transform the spaces of experience from which all knowledge of spatiality is derived.
- Institutions are produced spaces of a more or less durable sort . . . they are territorialisations – territories of control and surveillance, terrains of jurisdiction, and domains of organisation and administration.
- The imaginary (thoughts, fantasies, and desires) is a fertile source of all sorts of possible spatial worlds that can prefigure – albeit incoherently – all manner of different discourses, power relations, social relations, institutional structures and material practices.

Harvey provides us with an important way forwards in applying the Soja-inspired notion of critical spatial analysis. Furthermore, it is an understanding that seeks to remain open to the contingency of the material and symbolic dimensions of social practice.

Summing up on the separate cultural-sociological and discursive elements of our conceptual framework, one should bear in mind that this separation results from analytical necessity, and that discourse and space at the ontological level of everyday life are obviously not separable. Having said this, we think that understanding the relationship between physical space and social life in its dialectic relationship between spatial/material practices and symbolic meanings is essential to critical spatial analysis. As all spatial scales from the body to the global are in play, the analysis should furthermore be sensitive to how a politics of scale gives shape to a contested field of spatial practice.

These socio-spatial relations are conceptualised in a particular language with distinct forms of representation. They are set into action by social agents and their material practices within complex new institutional settings. A new field of action is created guiding values, norms and rationales, at the end of the day expressing the exercise of power in order to set the agenda for spatial policy in the EU. These themes and issues should be born closely in mind when it comes to analysing the construction of the environment, the urban system and the meaning of territorial identity within the policy process.

4.1 The Øresund bridge.

Part Two
Analysing the Discourse of Monotopia

In this part of the book we begin our empirical anaysis by focusing on the forms of representation (the words and images) that articulate the powerful spatial ideas shaping Europe. We find a new vocabulary of space and mobility, which uses iconic images to capture and distil critical ideas about European space. We attempt to identify how these spatial ideas will impact on the construction of territorial identity. We argue that the policy language and iconic representations of European space seek to articulate an apparently unified vision of European spatial development, but that they also cannot help but reproduce serious uncertainties, conflicts and tensions at the heart of the discourse. This is partly because of the presence of deep-seated and continuing power struggles over the content of the spatial agenda, but also because the dominant spatial discourse carries with it uncomfortable realities, which cannot be easily smoothed over.

Chapter 4
Languages of European space

> No scientific discipline exists without first inventing a visual and written language which allows it to break with its confusing past.
>
> (Latour, 1990)

> Prior to the meetings of the CSD in October [1997] the Irish delegation had screened the basic documents for 'single-word terms' and 'word groupings', coming up with a list of about 150, which was dubbed the 'ESDP dictionary'.
>
> (Faludi and Waterhout, 2002: 100)

Introduction: the power of language

As we explained in Chapter 3, the articulation of policy ideas in language is the starting point for our analysis of policy discourse. In this chapter, then, we explore the new common lexicon of European spatial policy, focusing on how particular spatial relations are captured and framed in language. A new policy language of space and mobility is revealed, centred on key terms such as polycentricity, mobility, sustainable development, balanced competitiveness, core and periphery. The analysis focuses on the contested and constructed nature of these terms and examines the reproduction of this language through policy documents and networks. We structure this analysis by exploring how the new language of European space expressed in the ESDP reconfigures understandings of mobility, the urban, the environment and territorial identity.

We then consider how this new language is reproduced across a new intertextual field, making possible multi-level spatial narratives which locate places (cities, regions) in EU space, and frame their visions in this Europeanised mode of expression. We illustrate how in multi-level policy processes across Europe, a series of documents mirrors the progress and shifts in policy language: the emergence of new spatial ideas, the entwining of strategies, policies and actions. We analyse key documents that we acknowledge to be fragments of different knowledge framing processes. We explore how different framings of 'space' set up different requirements for spatial 'knowledge' to be gathered and analysed in particular ways, to feed and support different spatial representations.

The ESDP: landmark text in an intertextual field

It is important to begin by setting the context for the ESDP as a canonical text: a document which ostensibly does nothing more than set out policy options, but which has attained the status of being a standard reference across spatial policy and planning throughout the EU from national to local scales. An 'informal' policy document whose ideas and language have become critical points of reference in a multiscale reframing of spatial concerns across Europe.

The decade long ESDP process has seen the commitment of a large amount of human resources over a long period (Jensen *et al.*, 1996a: 16). In the 1990s, through Commission initiatives and the work of the infra-national CSD, the EU progressed a series of initiatives on spatial co-operation in Europe. Progress was marked by the DGXVI-led explorations of European spatial trends and concepts, and the publication of key policy documents setting out spatial analysis and policy issues at the scale of the EU (*Europe 2000* (CEC, 1991) and *Europe 2000+* (CEC, 1994a), and the *Compendium of studies of spatial planning systems and policies in the member states* (CEC, 1997)). In these analytic and visionary preparatory documents can be found explicit evidence of an intertextual connection of plans and visions for the EU, which are all part of the discursive construction of a new spatial policy and planning field. This work has been buttressed by increasing transnational actions by member states, for example in co-operation over international infrastructure links, and by the increasing political support for transnational planning in the EU institutions, particularly within the Committee of the Regions (Williams, 1996a).

Through these activities, the aim has gradually broadened and become more ambitious: to provide a strategic spatial framework which could draw together many other EU initiatives with spatial impacts (such as trans-European networks, agriculture and environment policy), and to create a spatial vision which could shape the spatial planning activities within and between member states.

The ESDP was initially published as a First Official Draft at the informal meeting of the EU ministers responsible for spatial planning in Noordwijk on 9–10 June 1997 (CSD, 1997), and was presented one year later as a Complete Draft at the meeting in Glasgow on 8 June 1998 (CSD, 1998a). The drafting process has been the vehicle for elite consultation at the EU level and within member states on the future direction of spatial planning in Europe (Williams, 1999). Compromises were necessary as the content of a series of drafts and working documents presented to the informal meeting of ministers responsible for spatial planning was debated, and a final document was prepared which could be adopted by the meeting of ministers.[1]

The EU's overall spatial framework and vision is now enshrined in the European Spatial Development Perspective (the ESDP: CSD, 1999), adopted by the informal meeting of ministers responsible for spatial planning in the EU in Potsdam on 10–11 May 1999. The Potsdam document stands as a key landmark text in the emergence of a new policy discourse. When the suite of transnational spatial policy documents is consulted, one gains a very fine impression of the construction of a policy discourse which gains strength and legitimacy through comprehensive intertextual referencing.

A new language of European space

The specific policy goals of the ESDP were initially established at the informal meeting of ministers responsible for spatial planning in Leipzig in 1994. The 'Leipzig Principles' (CSD, 1994), a policy triangle of economic and social cohesion, sustainable development and balanced competitiveness, still govern the notion of a spatial vision for the European territory. The draft ESDP clearly states that 'these three constitute the objectives of spatial planning in Europe' (CSD, 1998a: 72). The final version sets out the following objectives (CSD, 1999: 11):

- development of a balanced and polycentric city system and a new urban-rural partnership;
- securing parity of access to infrastructure and knowledge; and
- sustainable development, prudent management and protection of nature and cultural heritage.

Although the importance of the objectives of sustainability and accessibility is highlighted in the ESDP, the rationale of economic competitiveness is dominant and influences the way the other two are given meaning (Davoudi, 1999). This can be seen, for example, in the way that the notion of a balanced regional development is linked to the issue of global economic competitiveness (CSD, 1999: 20). The powerful core region of Europe (originally framed as the 'blue banana', and more recently as the pentagon) is framed as a model for other EU regions. This is to be achieved by the new concept of 'dynamic global economy integration zones' (CSD, 1999: 20), which should imitate and duplicate the prosperous core. For weaker regions, outside the proposed new dynamic zones, the ESDP's approach is to widen the economic base and carry out economic re-structuring (CSD, 1999: 22). Box 4.1 shows some of the ESDP's core policy options, placing these zones within a wider framework of a polycentric urban system, urban-rural integration, transnational co-operation, and the binding together of these systems with an increasingly accessible trans-European transport network.

A new language of European mobility

The ESDP clearly enshrines a language of 'frictionless mobility', mirroring the policy language which has characterised the process leading to the establishment of the TEN-T, and which is the hallmark of the EU's transport policy. In this section we explore the interplay between the 'official' mobility policy of the European Union, as it has developed across these policy arenas influenced both by powerful pressure groups and internal political struggles, to show how the

Box 4.1 **Extract from the ESDP: core policy options**

Strengthening of several larger zones of global economic integration in the EU, equipped with high-quality, global functions and services, including the peripheral areas, through transnational spatial development strategies

Strengthening a polycentric and more balanced system of metropolitan city regions, city clusters and city networks through closer co-operation between structural policy and the policy on the Trans-European Networks (TEN-T) and improvements of the links between international/national and regional/local transport networks

Promoting integrated spatial development strategies for city clusters in Member States, within the framework of transnational and cross-border co-operation, including corresponding rural areas and their small cities and towns.

Strengthening co-operation on particular topics in the field of spatial development through cross-border and transnational networks

Promoting co-operation at regional, cross-border and transnational level; with towns and cities in the countries of Northern, Central and Eastern Europe and the Mediterranean region; strengthening North-South links in Central and Eastern Europe and West-East links in Northern Europe.

Source: CSD, 1999

language which plays such a powerful role in shaping spatial thought has been carefully and deliberately constructed in the face of intense power struggles.

Bottlenecks, missing links and networks

Early references to the need for a trans-European transport network can be found in lobbying material produced by the European Round Table of Industrialists (ERT). The ERT has been described as 'the spiritual progenitor of the 1992 process [of European integration, which culminated in the Maastricht Treaty], and the single most powerful business group in Europe' (Gardner, 1991: 48). In 1985, the ERT produced their proposal 'Agenda for action – Europe 1990', which became a blueprint for the White Paper which launched the 1992 process just 5 months later. Their working group on infrastructure, at the formative stages of TEN-T policy, was chaired by Umberto Agnelli from Fiat, with Bosch, Daimler Benz, Petrofina, Pirelli, Total, Volvo amongst the membership. In early documents ('Missing Links', ERT,

1984) can be found strong advocacy for TEN-T. In later documents, the ERT proposed not only physical infrastructure, but a shift in the mindset of politicians and policy-makers: 'to think and rethink existing networks in specifically European spatial and economic terms' (ERT, 1991b). The emphasis was very much on removing obstacles, and establishing new frameworks for implementation. Overall, the ERT set a dual agenda: claiming the need both for hard infrastructure, and for dynamic frameworks and methods to secure their implementation. To achieve this, they posited new concepts and languages of space, framing the ideas of missing links, and missing networks. Although missing links referred to physical infrastructure deficiencies, often across national borders, missing networks referred to deficiencies in the institutional frameworks needed to deliver transnational infrastructure. The focus on missing links has dominated EU transport policy, often rearticulated as bottlenecks in national and international transport systems which reflect the lack of a European scale of thinking (see Box 4.2). In Box 4.3, we show how one of the sites framed as a missing link – the lack of a road crossing of the Pyreneean mountains – was constructed in very different ways by different interests.

Box 4.2 **The framing of bottlenecks in EU transport policy**

In border areas, the present infrastructure networks still reflect the narrow national views (sometimes going back to the nineteenth century), which influenced their construction. Wattrelos in France, which is not connected to the Belgian motorway network passing only a few metres away, is a good example of the dysfunctions that can arise. Between Germany and France, the towns of Kehl and Strasbourg are still linked only by a low-capacity single track over the narrow bridge which crosses the Rhine. In the Pyrenees a single track crosses the border to link the national double-track systems. However, it is not only at borders that problems are to be found. In Bordeaux a double-track bridge which is well over a century old has to be used by TGVs, regional trains and freight trains alike to travel from northern Europe to Spain, the Pyrenees or the Toulouse region. Similarly, on the roads and motorways, the lack of bridges means that the meeting of local and interregional or international flows creates the notorious Bordeaux bottleneck. Little has been done in terms of traffic management and user information on these routes. Other famous bottlenecks include the one due to the delay in the construction of the Lanaye Lock, preventing the linking of the Meuse and the Rhine, and the ones on certain sections of the Danube (e.g. Straubing–Vilshofen).

Source: EU White Paper on Transport (CEC, 2001c)

Box 4.3 **What does it 'mean' to fill a 'missing link'?**

The articulation of space within the policy process was considered for one remote valley in the Pyrenees. The construction of the Somport tunnel, and its connecting motorways, is planned to link France and Spain across the Pyrenees. The route is articulated within the policy process as a 'missing link', a space of strategic political importance for physical integration and economic development. The Pyrenean mountain chain represents in this construction, a natural barrier to the completion of TEN-T, crossed by this key link.

An alternative construction has been promoted by the European environmental movement. The Vallée d'Aspes, a mountain valley through which the route passes, is one of the last surviving habitats in Europe of the brown bear. The threats to the ecology of the area posed by the infrastructure project have been used to build a high profile international campaign, which has drawn activists from across Europe to this remote valley. One hope is that procedures such as Strategic Environmental Assessment will be able to integrate such concerns into decision-making, although, for the many reasons analysed in this study (see Chapter 7), this seems unlikely. The construction of the Somport area as internationally important ecological habitat seems unlikely to impinge in any significant way on the Brussels policy process.

A second alternative construction is of the area as a traditional hill farming community. The local community has campaigned vigorously against the infrastructure projects, in defence of its own culture and heritage. This local voice has been a lonely one, which has failed to attract the attentions of either EU politicians and policy makers, or international environmental NGOs. The one exception is A SEED, an NGO which acts as a network of local groups, and explicitly links environmental and developmental issues, in the context of the single market. Within campaign literature produced by A SEED, a small international platform has been created for this construction of a local cultural space endangered with first physical fragmentation followed by cultural homogenisation.

A fourth possible construction of the area affected by the route might have been that of one of Europe's last wilderness areas – the high mountains of the Pyrenees – being destroyed by infrastructure. This construction has not been articulated, having no place in the EU policy language, or in the very specific ecological and cultural concerns of those actively opposing the project.

Infrastructure for competitiveness: accessibility and efficiency

The question of mobility has long been a vexed issue within the EU. Developing a common transport policy has been difficult, and subject to deeply entrenched disputes between member states (Whitelegg, 1992). What is indisputable, however, is that EU transport policy has always placed increasing mobility at its heart. Achieving 'sustainable mobility' was a key transport policy theme in the early 1990s, but within the ESDP the policy language has shifted, to place mobility within a spatial perspective. It is this attempt to articulate a spatialisation of mobility within the ESDP that opens up more clearly the complexity and conflicts which arise in thinking about sustainable mobility at the level of the EU. While the rhetoric of the ESDP returns frequently to the theme of mobility, the problem of mobility is framed in two ways: first, particularly for regions on the periphery, as a problem of *accessibility*, and second, particularly for the core regions, as one of *efficiency*.

The ESDP states that improvements to accessibility are regarded as a critical priority in the development of the polycentric urban system, and furthermore as preconditional in enabling European cities and regions to pursue economic development within an overall spatial strategy of harmonisation (Box 4.1). Thus the notion of frictionless mobility and the cities as nodes in a polycentric spatial development model are two sides of the same coin:

> Urban centres and metropolises need to be efficiently linked to one another, to their respective hinterland and to the world economy. Efficient transport and adequate access to telecommunications are a basic prerequisite for strengthening the competitive situation of peripheral and less favoured regions and hence for the social and economic cohesion of the EU. Transport and telecommunication opportunities are important factors in promoting polycentric development. . . . Spatial differences in the EU cannot be reduced without a fundamental improvement of transport infrastructure and services to and within the regions where lack of access to transport and communications infrastructure restricts economic development.
>
> (CSD, 1999: 25)

Within the ESDP, continuing an emphasis in earlier landmark EU documents such as the Maastricht treaty and the Delors White Paper, the primary policy response is clear: the construction of TEN-T to remove barriers to communication and facilitate economic convergence and competition. TEN-T is identified as the area of existing EU policy with most relevance to the ESDP process in terms of spatial development impacts and financial implications (CSD, 1999: 14), though clearly, this policy originated in the Commission's transport Directorate. Indeed, the development of TEN-T is regarded as crucial to the economic and social aims of the ESDP as well as potentially contributing to its environmental objective. Furthermore, specific policy options, such as the 'dynamic zones of economic integration', are particularly dependent on infrastructure development. It is stated that policy measures in such areas, include the deployment of the Structural Funds, should focus on providing a 'highly efficient infrastructure at transnational, national and regional level' (CSD, 1999: 21). Significantly, the ESDP states that prioritisation of development of the major arteries and corridors of TEN-T will not suffice. It is necessary to upgrade the regional transport networks which will feed into TEN-T, if economic benefits are to be secured.

Here the ESDP repeats the blurring of earlier Commission policy documents (Richardson, 1995). Europe 2000+ (CEC, 1994a), placing TEN-T at the centre of a pan-European spatial planning framework, identified the problematic double role of assisting the creation of the single market whilst enabling balanced development of the Community as a whole. Significantly, it was recognised that TEN-T creates a tension between these core territorial issues. While global competitiveness requires 'continuation, even acceleration of the implementation of large-scale TENs', this is accompanied by the risk 'of an increase in the imbalances in the Union', stemming from the 'strengthening of the centre to the detriment of the periphery' (among other factors) (CEC, 1994a). The question of harmonious, or balanced, development is linked with competitiveness. Ensuring spatial competitiveness between regions within the EU depends on 'avoiding the unacceptable risks and costs of widening disparities' between regions. Balanced development, in turn, is seen as reliant upon decreasing the competitive disadvantage of peripheral regions. Achieving both of these objectives relies on avoiding the centralising impacts associated with TEN-T. So, TEN-T is clearly identified as threatening to drive a wedge between European global competitiveness and internal spatial competitiveness. Richardson (1995) has argued that the EU discourse manages to avoid the difficult policy implications of this dilemma by relying on a series of unproven assumptions about the effects of infrastructure development, allowing the impression that TEN-T can achieve such divergent and contradictory policy objectives (summarised in Box 4.4). Here we can see the manifestation and interaction of the twin core discourses of European development: a powerful argument for integration representing the market, which has, through its own logic, precipitated the creation of an alternative or counter-discourse, representing the interests of the regions.

It appears that there is a strong tension between the two, which runs throughout the EU's spatial policy. So, whilst the ESDP repeats these concerns about 'pump' effects (where new high-speed infrastructure removes resources from structurally weaker and peripheral regions) and 'tunnel' effects (where such areas are crossed without being connected) (CSD, 1999: 26), all of the policy options identified pursue the general aim of improving accessibility as an unproblematic generic response. The ESDP's analysis of the problem of accessibility in the EU is straightforward:

> Good accessibility of European regions improves not only their competitive position but also the competitiveness of Europe as a whole. . . . Islands, border areas and

Box 4.4 **Six assumptions in the logic of integration**

Assumption 1: regional competitiveness and balance are the same thing

The Commission's strategy for cohesion is based on market competition between regions. The role for TEN-T is to facilitate more of a level playing field for inter-regional competition. The conditions for economic development are, however, many and varied. Even if TEN-T provides a framework for equitable accessiblity, other conditions will not necessarily be harmonised. Implementation of TEN-T may therefore raise the competitive stakes in disadvantaged regions. Competition creates winners and losers, and the outcome is not bound to be the even development of regional economies.

Assumption 2: that there is a causal link between infrastructure provision and economic development

The relationship between infrastructure provision and economic development is becoming one of the more vexed questions in transport planning. The link has long been assumed in policy making, but research has yet to establish causality. This policy blindspot is increasingly being challenged (e.g. RCEP, 1994, EIB, 1994, SACTRA, 1999), with calls for a more critical analysis of infrastructure needs – identifying where infrastructure is a constraint on development rather than seeing it as a simple solution to economic depression: 'transport investment is likely to have its greatest impact where remote areas have advantages which cannot be fully exploited due to transport costs' (Nash, 1995).

Assumption 3: centre/periphery distribution of economic benefits

Linked with this is increasing awareness of the centralising effects of infrastructure, which can undermine the hoped for benefits to disadvantaged regions: 'to the extent that transport investments impact on the location of production and distribution facilities, that effect tends to be centralising' (Nash, 1995). Europe 2000+ fails to explain how this problem can be addressed.

Assumption 4: TEN-T and peripherality – even distribution of benefits within regions

The assumption of causality discussed above is related to a further assumption of accessibility. This is, that as TEN-T supports the development of peripheral economies, the consequent benefits will be evenly distributed within regions. The weakness of this position is illustrated by closer analysis of issues of accessibility (Vickerman *et al.*, 1995). This research firstly identifies the uneven distribution of accessibility within regions, caused by the presence (or otherwise) of strategic transport nodes and corridors. The conclusion from this work is that the impact of TEN-T will be unpredictable, but that it may increase disparities in accessibility through concentration and shadow effects. In other words, new strategic infrastructure improvements on the peripherality may, at the same time as it brings parts of remote regions closer to the centre, create zones of relative peripherality both in these remoter regions, and more generally.

TEN-T policy assumes that regional transport networks will provide efficient access to TEN-T, to avoid these problems. This relies on a reorientation of national and regional transport networks towards the nodes and corridors of TEN-T. Whilst appearing to bring overall regional benefits, TEN-T may result in new fine grain patterns of subregional peripherality, challenging the approach to peripherality adopted in Europe 2000+, and suggesting that the impact of TEN-T on peripherality will not be as clear in practice as it is made to appear in EC documentation.

Assumption 5: long distance movements on TEN-T will be cheap enough to allow effective competition between central and peripheral regions

Recent patterns of economic development have placed a heavy reliance on low transport costs of goods. In particular, the low cost of road freight has enabled industry to rationalise into a fewer number of centres, and for complex distribution networks to be established over large areas. This reliance on cheap transport is being increasingly challenged by two developments:

- arguments that costs incurred by users do not reflect the full social and environmental impacts of transport, supporting the extension of user charges through road pricing and taxation;
- serious concerns about the financial burden of TEN-T. The EC will provide only a small amount of the funding required: there is a high level of expectation that national governments, the private sector and other institutions will bear the costs of TEN-T projects. In at least a few EU member states, the level of government expenditure on public infrastructure is being revised downwards. The prospect of user charges is one policy option for generating the return that will be required to recoup this investment.

As public investment and free access are replaced by a new environment of partnership and pricing, it is difficult to see how expensive infrastructure networks can create the economic level playing fields required for equitable regional competition. As TEN-T seeks to reduce travel times between centre and periphery, it seems likely to increase the cost of movement of goods on these journeys. The effect of this may be disadvantageous to the competitiveness of regions on the periphery, relying on TEN-T for access to distant markets.[1]

continued

Assumption 6: peripherality is about being on the edge

In examining the argumentation surrounding peripherality, we should be aware that the term is politically charged. 'Peripherality' is seen as a valuable argument to be deployed in the quest for EC financial support. Ball (1995: 154) explained it thus: 'Perhaps, it is the opportunity for such (infrastructure) development that motivates some authorities into representing themselves as peripheral, despite constant attempts in other areas of image construction to put across precisely the opposite picture.' We should therefore be careful about claims made for peripherality, and measures proposed for reducing it.

Source: Richardson, 1995

[1] For example, possible measures in Germany to reduce transit traffic include the tripling of motorway charges (T&E Bulletin, no 39 June 1995).

> peripheral regions are generally less accessible than central regions and have to find specific solutions.
>
> (CSD, 1999: 69)

The examples of Sweden and Finland, where regional airports link to European gateways, are quoted. The consequent risks are explicitly recognised, that:

> improved accessibility will expand the hinterlands of the economically stronger areas . . . the newly accessible economies will have to compete against the large firms and the competitive services in these economically stronger areas . . . competition may well benefit the stronger regions more than the newly accessible weaker ones.
>
> (CSD, 1999: 70)

Yet the policy response to these uncertainties is no more than to suggest that such infrastructure improvements need to be seen alongside other sectoral policies and integrated strategies. A further European spatial trend recognised in the ESDP is the growth of development corridors, where new development concentrates along transnational and cross-border corridors in already relatively urbanised areas. The need is recognised for integrated transnational strategic planning (CSD, 1999: 71).

So, within the ESDP, mobility is framed as accessibility, and accessibility is framed in economic rather than social or environmental terms. This rhetorical construction appears to ignore the rather different ways that accessibility is being used in transport policy debates. In the UK, for example, accessibility has rapidly become a core focus of policy, but is concerned with quality of life and social inclusion as much as with economy. Here access to employment, services and leisure are considered to be important policy concerns.

The second core element of the discourse is efficiency. The problem of mobility framed here is the growth in road and air transport with resulting environmental and efficiency problems. The need to promote alternative modes is emphasised, but with several strong caveats:

> however this objective must be achieved without negative effects on the competitiveness of both the EU as a whole and its regions . . . [and] nevertheless, both road traffic for passengers and freight will remain of great importance, expecially for linking peripheral or sparsely populated regions.
>
> (CSD, 1999: 28)

Similarly, while the potential for high speed rail is recognised as a competitor to air travel in the denser regions: 'in sparsely populated peripheral regions, particularly in insular locations, regional air transport including short-haul services has to be given priority'(CSD, 1999: 28). Here once again arises a question of the extent of harmony between EU and national policy discourse. Drawing again from the UK example, where policy discourse has shifted towards demand management and integration, efficiency of networks is certainly an increasingly important objective. However, in the UK, policy shifted away from road building in the 1990s, whilst road building remained the major component of overall spending on TEN-T. Another example of the contradictory effects of the general mobility policy of efficiency can be drawn from the Danish case of the fixed link over the 'Great Belt'. After one year of operation, the number of cars crossing the bridge exceeded the most optimistic forecasts made by the proponents of the bridge, undermining the official Danish policy of reducing car traffic. Elsewhere, in the accession countries, increasing road traffic levels – car ownership in particular – are positively welcomed as signs of freedom in the post-Soviet era. Indeed, the rhetoric of the ESDP suggests that growth in overall traffic movements will be the key to improving accessibility.

TEN-T itself was intended to allow 'higher efficiency, higher safety standards, improved services to customers, and less impact on the natural environment under economically viable conditions' (CEC, 1994b). However, the outline plans for each mode continued to develop separately, increasingly influenced by lobbying from regions and member states on the inclusion (or otherwise) of particular lines on the maps. The series of revised plans for each transport mode came to form a central focus to the development of policy, and have been adopted in the drafting of the ESDP, yet they do not bear the hallmarks of an integrated approach to transport planning.

A new metaphor for mobility: The single European sky

The mobility dimension of monotopia has so far been explored as an articulation of surface mobility. However, the challenge from the transport sector to a more integrated spatial perspective is perhaps manifested even more starkly in the skies of Europe, which are to be metaphorically reduced to a 'Single European Sky' (DG TREN, 2000). The aim is to create an integrated airspace over the territory of the EU. What is on the agenda here is thus at the practical level the mending of the previous 'partitioning' of Europe's skies into layers. But it is also a practice which articulates the EU as one space, at multiple scales – a space of monotopia:

> A plane flying from the United Kingdom to France has to fly at two different altitudes: over British territory it flies at 24 500 feet and then has to drop to 19 500 feet when it enters French airspace.
>
> (CEC, 2001c: 36)

> Today, in the age of the single market and of the single currency, there is still no 'single sky' in Europe. The European Union suffers from over-fragmentation of its air traffic management systems, which adds to flight delays, wastes fuel and puts European airlines at a competitive disadvantage. It is therefore imperative to implement, by 2004, a series of specific proposals establishing Community legislation on air traffic and introducing effective co-operation both with the military authorities and with Eurocontrol.
>
> (CEC, 2001c: 17–18)

The proposals are linked to the predicted and planned future growth of air traffic within the EU. The apparently serious environmental concerns of such development are dealt with by simply referring to efficiency benefits and mitigating technological advances, but ignoring broader concerns relating to mobility trends, capacity or demand management, let alone broader spatial considerations: 'This reorganisation of Europe's sky must be accompanied by a policy to ensure that the inevitable expansion of airport capacity linked, in particular, with enlargement, remains strictly subject to new regulations to reduce noise and pollution caused by aircraft' (CEC, 2001c: 17–18).

So at the heart of the EU spatial vision are fundamental and unresolved difficulties over the role of road and air traffic. The EU's transport policy, running in parallel with spatial policy, strongly reasserts the central place of TEN-T, and of air travel, leaving a clear sense that the writers of EU spatial policy have been left with an unenviable task – of massaging a massive infrastructure programme and an unsustainable mobility scenario into a vision of sustainable spatial development. Meanwhile transport policy continues to press its unproblematic case for TEN-T: 'Nevertheless, whatever the delay to certain projects, support should continue to be given to the trans-European network, which is an important factor in European competitiveness and improves the links between the European Union's outlying regions and its central markets' (CEC 2001c, White Paper).

A new language of the urban

Alongside this reframing of flows and mobilities is a new language of *the urban*. It is a language in which the urban is framed by different rationalities, each striking a chord with different and often contradictory ways of seeing urban development. Some cities, urban agglomerations and regions are thus characterised by being transnational, whilst others are seen as nodes in polycentric urban networks, and yet others are characterised by their location in the traditional core/periphery dichotomy.

At the heart of the ESDP's spatial strategy is the polycentric urban system, which has taken shape through a series of Commission studies and reports in the 1990s. In Europe 2000 (CEC, 1991) the cities and urban spaces are conceptualised in a vocabulary of economic competition, with references to the underlying 'growth rationale' of the EU (CEC, 1993). The aspiration of combining growth with concerns for the environment is articulated (CEC, 1991: 111). In a context of global footloose economies, the future urban system is characterised as one of great potential for competitive cities which can create strategic visions and new 'urban identities' (CEC, 1991: 148). The main elements in a successful urban strategy are said to be: the ability to adapt the economic base to a new demand for specialised production, efficient transportation, infrastructure and communication links, a well educated workforce, good 'quality of life', local institutional capacity as well as an open attitude towards urban networking with other cities and regions (CEC, 1991: 148).

Europe 2000+ (CEC, 1994a) develops the notion of socio-spatial 'polycentricity' and growth. Global economic competition is said to represent a risk of increasing the Union's 'imbalances' further (CEC, 1994a: 16). Environmental concern is again addressed through a competition-oriented economic rationale, where environmental quality plays an increasingly important role in the attractiveness of specific territories (CEC, 1994a: 17). The goal of creating a more equal economic and social development within the EU's cities is envisioned through the establishment of integrated systems of agglomerations, and common actions between large urban centres (CEC, 1994a: 19). This leads to a notion of a 'polycentric urban system', a notion that is both very central to the discourse but also very vague and polyvalent in itself. The approach builds on the existing densely urbanised and historically strong settlement pattern of the core, which is the legacy upon which any spatial policy for the urban system must build. The polycentric urban system is seen as a necessary response to environmental, social and traffic problems of increasing urban growth. It is assumed that a polycentric urban system will operate on a horizontal level of integration, bringing benefits by spreading specialisation to a number of urban centres.

The ESDP suggests several ways of enhancing the notion of a new space of polycentric development. One strategy is the creation of 'urban networks'. By 'pooling resources' and co-operating in new fields of action, medium-sized and smaller cities may compensate for their relative lack of metropolitan qualities. These activities fit the picture of a new integration scenario for cross-border regions in particular (CSD, 1999: 65). Co-operation between cities across borders may not only imply functional and economic advantages, but may also facilitate the vision of a Europe where national borders are criss-crossed by a new urban policy of inter-city co-operation. Whilst far from the notions of 'new medieval territorialities' and the resurgence of the 'city state'(Anderson, J., 1996), such activities nevertheless suggest the emergence of cracks and holes in the established territoriality of the member states within the EU. However, the ESDP recognises that cities are involved in competition more often than co-operation: 'Competition for mobile investment between cities is becoming tougher. Not every town or city will find its new situation as advantageous as its present one. As a result towns and cities will need to adopt a new dynamic for developing their potential' (CSD, 1999: 21).

Thus a trans-European stage is set for inter-urban competition where the globalisation of the economy and the shift to post-Fordist and knowledge and service oriented economies calls for old industrial cities to diversify their economic base. However, such diversification should not be seen as a clinical exercise of urban managers, but as a serious struggle for economic survival that will not come about without social conflicts and major power struggles between the 'haves' and the 'have nots'. The direction of urban policy seems to be set in terms of increasing inter-urban competition. The ESDP, however, tries to articulate a vision of such inter-urban competition and economic restructuring in a euphemistic vocabulary of Cupertino: 'Cities and regions which know how to exploit their own economic opportunities and potential do so not at the cost of others but, on the contrary, can strengthen the world-wide competitive position of the EU. In this sense, competition is very positive' (CSD, 1999: 65).

The ESDP wants to facilitate a 'healthy' level of competition. That is to say, the document distances itself from a notion of 'competition using all available means' (CSD, 1999: 65). However, this is where the rationale of the vision seems to be self-contradictory at best, since the mild aspirations on behalf of healthy competition might not suffice in a world of increasing global inter-urban competition: 'In a Europe of competitive cities there is a tendency to ignore the fact that there are only so many international business travellers, or potential stations on high-speed lines, or opera houses to go round. Competition has losers as well as winners' (Newman and Thornley, 1996: 17). The risk of competition is of a range of adverse spatial consequences which the ESDP seeks to avoid, including: 'a widening of the gap between winner and loser cities, further decentralization of activities within urban areas and an erosion of rural settlement patterns' (Masser *et al.*, 1992: 116).

Dealing with the urban system, the problem of uncontrolled urban sprawl due to the pressure on the land for more residential accommodation is targeted under the rationale of the 'compact city' and 'land recycling' (CSD, 1999: 66). Characteristically the Potsdam document does not put much emphasis on the social dimension of the urban agenda. There is though a small paragraph on the problem of the increase in social exclusion within cities. Here the tendency of the middle classes and those well off to leave the old city centres in favour of suburban areas, and the concentration of poorer families and immigrants in inner cities and public sector housing estates is identified. However, the fight against social exclusion and ghettoisation is not exactly the hallmark of the ESDP. The overwhelming emphasis on economic development within the ESDP suggests that the EU's spatial strategy will be played out in competition between cities and regions, and between core and periphery. Social and environmental concerns seem less likely to benefit from these attempts at increasing the spatial coherence of EU policy.

Peripherality and the Nordic 'problem'

Within the policy rhetoric there is a confused blurring between the terms 'rural' and 'peripheral', which creates a puzzling idea of what the spatial vision really means for the (so far) less urbanised parts of the EU. This blurring, which may in fact mask an urbanisation agenda, is nicely pinned down in Böhme's analysis of the treatment of Nordic interests within the ESDP process (Böhme, 1999b). The ESDP regards rural regions which have failed to restructure as having:

> considerable economic problems, often due to their peripheral location. Besides a high percentage of agricultural employment, the structural weaknesses of these areas can have other causes, such as an extremely low population density; inaccessibility; climatic disadvantages; poor infrastructure; lack of structural development; outdated industrial structures and outdated agricultural production conditions.
>
> (CSD, 1999: 23)

As Böhme argues, from a Nordic perspective, 'it is astonishing that the ESDP document does not take into consideration periphery, where this cannot be equated with rural and agricultural areas' (Böhme, 1999b). The label of peripherality is also used to express the hinterland function of peripheral regions in relation to urban areas. The ESDP states that the problems faced by rural areas originate in urban areas: 'rural areas which are subject to new pressures, for example through economic growth and the expansion of neighbouring settlements of metropolises and larger cities and areas hit by the decline of agriculture, also have to face great problems' (CSD, 1999: 23). Here, Böhme refers to Mønnesland's work to point out the inappropriateness of the urban-rural relation, where 'travelling to "town" means journeys of up to half a day or more and sometimes involves air travel. Even trips to the nearest urban concentration point often imply longer travel times than one would need in more central parts of Europe to go from one capital to the next' (Mønnesland, 1995: 136). Böhme challenges the ESDP's urban bias, arguing that the polycentric model may be relevant in the central countries – Germany, the Benelux countries and perhaps France – but that it does not fit Nordic geography.

Because the ESDP regards urban areas as the sole development motors of the EU, the question is raised as to the implications for migration if non-urban areas are simply constructed as areas of agriculture, green tourism and environmental protection. The ESDP's central response to the 'problem' of peripherality is to improve the accessibility of peripheral regions, within an overall polycentric urban system, thereby removing the problem (Box 4.5). The analysis is straightforward: 'Good accessibility of European regions improves not only their competitive position but also the competitiveness of Europe as a whole. . . . Islands, border areas and peripheral regions are generally less accessible than central regions and have to find specific solutions' (CSD, 1999: 69).

The examples of Sweden and Finland, where regional airports link to European gateways, are quoted. The consequent risks are explicitly recognised, that: 'improved accessibility will expand the hinterlands of the economically stronger area . . . the newly accessible economies will have to compete against the large firms and the competitive services in these economically stronger areas . . . competition may well benefit the stronger regions more than the newly accessible weaker ones' (CSD, 1999: 69).

Previously, we have argued that EU discourse manages to avoid the difficult policy implications of this dilemma by making a specific knowledge claim about the effects of infrastructure development, based on the rhetorical proposition that infrastructure programmes can achieve such divergent policy objectives (Box 4.4). Thus, for example, TEN-T, and improved regional connections to it, provide the means for solving the problem of peripherality. This has serious implications for the future development of regional transport infrastructure networks, with implications for the deployment of Structural Funds. This is a clear site of future struggle. In many EU member states, widespread opposition to new infrastructure building has already brought strong challenges to national policy. Furthermore, a turn away from public support for big infrastructure is taking place across the EU. Specific proposals for the strengthening of regional infrastructure networks in peripheral regions across the continent raises the prospect of a series of bitter local conflicts. This problem with peripherality runs unresolved through the ESDP. The ESDP's overall message here seems to be that it is the periphery that needs to be developed, and this can be equated with a process of urbanisation.

Box 4.5 **Polycentric development model: a basis for better accessibility. Policy options**

24. Strengthening secondary transport networks and their links with trans-European transport networks (TENs), including development of efficient public transport systems.
25. Promotion of a spatially more balanced access to intercontinental transport of the EU by an adequate distribution of seaport and airports (global gateways), and an increase of their service level and improvement of links with their hinterland.
26. Improvement of transport links of peripheral and ultra-peripheral regions, both within the EU and with neighbouring third countries, taking into account air transport and the further development of corresponding infrastructure facilities.
27. Improvement of access to and use of telecommunication facilities and the design of tariffs in accordance with the provision of 'universal services' in sparsely populated areas.
28. Improvement of co-operation between transport policies at EU, national and regional level.
29. Introduction of territorial impact assessment as an instrument for spatial assessment of large infrastructure projects (especially in the transport sector).

Source: ESDP (CSD 1999)

Urban/rural relations

A further important dimension of the ESDP's framing of urban space is its treatment of urban-rural relations. We have already pointed to an urban bias in the policy discourse, but the reaction of rural interests such as the Nordic region to the draft ESDP has in fact raised challenges to, and brought about a shift in, its treatment of rurality. Urban-rural relations have been addressed since the early stages of the ESDP process (CSD, 1994). This relationship is strengthened in the final ESDP into an 'urban-rural partnership', in an attempt to deal with this criticism of urban bias (Box 4.6). Indeed the first objective of the ESDP becomes a combination of the development of a balanced and polycentric city system with the emergence of a new urban-rural partnership, in an attempt to overcome 'the outdated dualism between city and countryside' (CSD, 1999: 19). The way of achieving this is to move away from urban/rural separation and instead focus on functionally integrated regions to secure

Box 4.6 **Urban-rural partnership: policy options in the ESDP**

19. Maintenance of a basic supply of services and public transport in small and medium sized towns in rural areas, particularly those in decline.
20. Promotion of co-operation between towns and countryside aiming at strengthening functional regions.
21. Integrating the countryside surrounding large cities in spatial development strategies for urban regions, aiming at more efficient land use planning, paying special attention to the quality of life in the urban surroundings.
22. Promotion and support of partnership-based co-operation between small and medium sized towns at a national and transnational level through joint projects and the mutual exchange of experience.
23. Promotion of company networks between small and medium-sized enterprises in the towns and countryside.

Source: ESDP (CSD 1999)

> integrated treatment of the city and countryside as a functional spatial entity with diverse relationships and interdependencies. A sharp distinction between city and countryside within a region ignores in most cases the fact that only regions can form labour, information and communications markets. The region is therefore the appropriate level for action and implementation.
>
> (CSD, 1999: 23)

In this new relationship the regional level emerges within the ESDP as an increasingly important locus of rurality in Europe. Yet within this construction, the importance of small and medium-sized towns in rural regions is stressed: 'in rural "problem" regions only these towns are capable of offering infrastructure and services for economic activities in the region and easing access to the bigger labour markets. The towns in the rural areas, therefore, require particular attention in the preparation of integrated rural development strategies' (CSD, 1999: 23). Similarly, gateway cities will assist the development of peripheral regions.

Is there an institutional shift here – a move away from geographically distinct rural space towards a functional region? If so, this raises questions about the treatment of rural interests within the institutions and processes of regional spatial planning, as well as individual sectoral policy areas. In this regional shift, the place of a distinctive rurality is at risk. The construction of tools of analysis and instruments of implementation are therefore likely to be a site of contest, if rural policy knowledge is not to be subsumed into a regional approach, and measures are not to become more focused on cities and towns.

A new language of the environment

Alongside the new language of the urban is a new language of the environment. Here we find, perhaps unsurprisingly, notions of sustainable spatial development, where the environment is articulated as being integrated and interdependent with other policy goals of social cohesion and economic growth. However, this approach to environmental integration is part of a language of ecological modernisation, which relies on technological and institutional innovation to deal with environmental risks. Here we will explore how these risks were dealt with in the TEN-T policy process, setting out an argument that ecological modernisation successfully underpinned an accomodationist language of environmental integration which (as we will explore more fully in later chapters) was a weak construction which would not materially affect policy making.

However the discourse of a Europe of flows is challenged by increasing concern and resistance to the environmental impacts of frictionless mobility. This has been expressed at all levels from local to global, and a resurgence of concern has identified increasing road traffic as the most serious environmental trend in the European Union (CEC, 1996b, 1996e). The tensions within and between these discourses are clear. For example, the impacts of increasing personal mobility on the environment have been apparent in transport policy since at least the 1960s (Steering Group, 1963; Liniado, 1996), and are still apparent in the EU's concept of sustainable mobility.

Since the 1990s EU policy discourse has encountered resistance from an environmental counterdiscourse which it has responded to by explicitly integrating environmental dimensions into sectoral policy making. Article 2 of the Maastricht Treaty placed environmental compatibility as a basic principle in policy making, and an integral aspect of economic growth. In the early 1990s this was extended to the Union's Common Transport Policy (CTP) in Article 74. The CTP centred on the principle of sustainable mobility, which attempts to resolve the difficult tensions between increasing traffic growth and environmental impacts (Green Paper, CEC 1992, and White Paper, CEC 1993). Unfortunately, no clear definition of sustainable mobility was provided in the policy, fuelling scepticism among environmentalists as to whether sustainable mobility amounts to anything more than rhetoric. Elsewhere, the 1995 update of the EU's Fifth Environmental Action Programme identified priority measures in the transport sector, including demand-side management initiatives (internalising external costs and promoting integration between land-use and transport planning, and the use of telematics), and reducing imbalances between modes, in particular through the development of Strategic Environmental Assessment (SEA) for TEN-T – a theme we return to below (CEC, 1996a).

Understanding the potential environmental impact of TEN-T may be better understood by briefly considering how European transport trends are related to the single market. Cecchini argued that the single market will bring overall macro-economic benefits. The underlying vision is of an evenly developed Europe of economically competitive regions, where TEN-T provides efficient access to resources, labour and markets across the continent (Cecchini, 1988). However, critics have responded that these benefits are likely to be unevenly distributed (Begg, 1989; Grahl and Teague, 1990; Padoa-Schioppa, 1987). An alternative possibility, recognised by the Commission as a danger (CEC, 1994a), is of an increasingly centralised Europe where TEN-T exposes peripheral markets to rapid access and increased competition from the economically dominant centre (Whitelegg, 1992). These uncertainties about the re-distributive effects of the single market highlight a difficulty in establishing exactly what new patterns of mobility may be facilitated by TEN-T, and what the broader impacts may be. However, the trend which underlies both scenarios is a dramatic increase in mobility, and in particular in long distance movements of goods, as economies restructure to respond to the pan-European scale of activity: 'The internal market will cause considerable increases in the volume of traffic and related environmental damages. The main concern of the future Common Transport Policy must be to find a solution to the transport sector's conflicting economic and ecological objectives' (Bail, 1993). As a major infrastructure programme, TEN-T, a key element of the CTP, will potentially result in a range of serious environmental impacts. These include: disturbance to, or destruction of, protected landscapes and habitats, particularly in the environmentally sensitive zones of many of Europe's border regions; land take, barrier effects and new development pressures; increased atmospheric emissions of carbon dioxide and other pollutants from increasing traffic (particularly on roads); the disruption of local cultures in remote rural areas; increased energy consumption and noise pollution. Certainly TEN-T policy, a cornerstone of the CTP, appears difficult to reconcile with EC environmental policy (Whitelegg, 1992).

Commission studies state that since 1980, 'road transport of goods and passengers has increased by about 45 per cent and 41 per cent respectively. . . . In parallel, rail transport of goods has actually decreased.' Forecasts for road transport predict continued growth past 2000, whilst air passenger transport is likely to grow most dramatically, increasing by 182 per cent between 1990–2000 (CEC, 1996b). 'Transport demand and traffic in the Community are expected to increase significantly in the future, especially following the completion of the internal market' (CEC, 1996c: 7). This growth in mobility is recognised as having a range of environmental impacts. For example, the Commission's evaluation of progress towards CO_2 targets states that 'whereas energy related emissions in most sectors have levelled off . . . or substantially fallen . . . they are still rising in the transport sector (7% increase 1990–1993)'. Similarly for NOx, where the growth in car ownership and the sharp increase in road transport of goods offsets reductions in other sectors. The Commission expresses concern that, in spite of an emphasis on rail and combined transport in the TEN-T priority projects, there remains a general emphasis on EU financial support for road construction (CEC, 1996c: 33). A major challenge for TEN-T policy is how a network which is designed to increase the capacity of all modal transport systems, to meet the increased mobility demands of the single market, can achieve the modal transfer away from road which is critical to environmental protection.

The pivotal question, then, is whether environmental protection can be successfully integrated with economic growth within the development path of the European single market. Since the mid 1980s a discourse of ecological modernisation has emerged, based on the conviction that 'the ecological crisis can be overcome by technical and procedural innovation' (Hajer, 1996: 249). Policy integration of environmental risks is seen as a crucial element of ecological modernisation: 'rather than perceiving the goals of environmental protection to be a brake on development, ecological modernisation promotes the application of stringent environmental policy as a positive influence on economic efficiency and technological innovation' (Gouldson and Murphy, 1996). Gouldson and Murphy argue that the EU has progressed towards ecological modernisation in several ways: by adopting the belief that environment and economy can achieve synergy for further economic growth; by integrating environmental policy into other sectors; by exploring innovative policy measures; and by promoting new clean technologies. In this analysis, the EU is passing through an institutional learning phase. The main barrier to ecological modernisation in this analysis is that, whatever the EU's desire to instigate change, its strategic capacity to do so is limited, principally because of the resistance of member states to environmental reforms. We will return to these themes, exploring how the relations between mobility, urban development and environment are dealt with in the new European spatial policy discourse, and examining the success of ecological modernisation in providing answers to the challenges that are encountered.

Clearly the development of policy for TEN-T was not smooth – turbulence was caused by the rapidly increasing weight of the European environmental agenda. The conflict between the European integration process and the protection of the European environment has become one of the critical contemporary spatial issues, and TEN-T has become one of the arenas where this conflict is most apparent, most intractable, and potentially pyrrhic in outcome. By setting out this tension between global economic and environmental impacts of a single spatial idea (TEN-T) in some detail, we have hopefully clarified how spatial agendas are powerful articulations of the European project, with serious and contested implications for European space. In this wider context of spatial policy, we once again see a difficulty with the ESDP's core vision, centred on a golden policy triangle of economic and social cohesion, sustainable development and balanced competitiveness (CSD, 1999: 11). The challenge to the spatial policy process, then, is whether a form of urban-centred development which is heavily reliant on increasing mobility can deliver environmental sustainability. In the following chapters, we will see how such tensions are shaping policy and practice across the multi-level arenas of EU spatial policy making, examining in detail how the question of environmental integration is played out.

Intertextuality and multi-level narratives

In this section, we examine how the new policy language of European space is reproduced in policy processes at different spatial scales. We will see how core policy concerns of mobility, the urban and the environment discussed above are reconfigured in the light (or shadow) of the ESDP. In examining policy making in the new transnational arenas of spatial planning, we will also open up an important perspective on territorial identity, by illuminating how places appear (and are framed) differently in the context of a European spatial vision.

Though the ESDP has no binding power, it is explicitly intended to form part of a cascade of spatial policy and implementation from the EU to the local level, working towards a 'shared vision of the European territory' (CSD, 1998a: 3). The visions of the new EU transnational regions fit neatly into this intertextual field. Similarly in the notes of the NorVISION we find frequent reference to the ESDP, and to other regional visions such as the CADSES vision and the VASAB vision (CADSES, 2000; Ministers for Spatial Planning and Development, 1994). These documents are contributing to a new language of spatial planning and development at the same time as carrying the message from other documents in the same genre. Each document contributes to and legitimises a complex web of words, concepts and strategies that frames the future articulation of European spatial development for the social agents within this field. Similarly, the CEMAT Guiding Principles note its relation to the ESDP, to regional visions and strategies including those around the Baltic, and to its own Council of Europe documentation, including the Torremolinos Charter (Council of Europe, 1983).

Multi-level narrative: NorVISION

The NorVISION document deals with the strategic role and position of the transnational North Sea Region (NSR) in the new Europe. Its key vision statements are set out in Box 4.7. As in other transnational regions, the document analyses the NSR in the European context by means of an assessment of its strategic strengths and weaknesses. The document sets out a number of strategies and action proposals. At the beginning we get the message that the NSR should be conceptualised as a specific example of 'ESDP thinking' (VWG, 2000b: 1). In fact the NSR should be seen as one of the proposed 'dynamic zones of global economic integration' launched in the ESDP (CSD, 1999: 20). Furthermore, at a meeting of the Vision Working Group, the need to follow a polycentric approach, characterised by the 'bunch of grapes' metaphor, was identified as critical to the success

Box 4.7 **Vision statements in NorVISION**

1. A NSR well integrated into the development of the European Space and into the World Economy
2. A NSR with a balanced spatial structure
3. The NSR – a model for democratic and co-operative planning
4. A NSR which takes care of its natural resources and ecological equilibrium and its cultural heritage
5. Urban regions developing in an environment friendly way
6. Urban regions as motors of economic regional development
7. Urban regions which promote Social Integration
8. Urban regions are attractive places for their populations and visitors
9. Human activities which are in harmony with nature
10. Rural populations participate fully in economic and social progress

Source: VWG, 2000b

of the region's vision. The implication of this is a focus of attention on the development of networks of smaller towns (VWG, 2000b).

As in the ESDP the methodology is evolved around SWOT analysis, which is used to set out an image of a common identity, and common potentials and threats across the region. In terms of the identity question, the language embraces notions of nature, a strong regional identity, the North Sea itself, the North Sea climate, cultural landscapes, and the absence of any dominating mega-urban agglomeration in the NSR (VWG, 2000b: 4). On the opportunity side we find themes such as energy resources, tourism, a differentiated urban system, advanced research and skills capacities. On the negative side – the threats – we find sea and soil pollution, the rising sea level, coastal erosion, declining traditional sectors, social segregation within towns, urban sprawl, inner city decay and loss of the traditional economic bases for employment.

NorVISION re-articulates a number of 'basic values' found in the ESDP: freedom, democracy, equality, justice, solidarity, diversity, identity, welfare and respect for nature and cultural landscapes (VWG, 2000b: 7). This new vocabulary of 'inclusive politics', as we might term it, can be seen as a serious obligation towards increasing the transparency and participatory element of the vision-making process. Translated into policy themes, these basic values give shape to a new EU planning vocabulary articulated around keywords such as participation, spatial balance, economic and social cohesion, competitiveness, sustainability, flexibility, subsidiarity, market efficiency and ecological planning (VWG, 2000b: 7). The articulation of such 'basic values' expresses a sense of territorial identity where these values become the normative underpinnings or building blocks for a self-proclaimed new notion of Europeanness, played out in the activity of transnational region building.

By touching briefly on some of the difficult issues lying behind NorVISION's core statements, we can see how such spatial policy documents smoothly deal with very deep rooted – and increasingly transnational – conflicts. The first of the ten vision statements (VS 1) is an explicit expression of the 'fear' of not being linked to TEN-T. This concern can be put into its wider context by looking at the TEN-T proposals, and in particular the plans for a prioritised Nordic Triangle of high-speed road and rail links. There is a clearly perceived risk, from the perspective of the peripheral Nordic regions who are members of the NSR, that they are likely to be left in the shadow of the improved accessibility and development opportunities afforded by this infrastructure triangle linking the capitals Oslo, Stockholm and Copenhagen.

The Swedish/Danish growth project of creating a powerful new cross-border region on this triangle (the Øresund region), is mentioned as a further example of a major and important development hub that lies outside of the NSR (VWG, 2000b: 38). This is, to our minds, an interesting example of the complex inter-regional competition that such EU funding is de facto fuelling, by supporting neighbouring regions to develop competing spatial strategies. The Øresund region, regarded in NorVISION as a nearby competitor on the European scene of regional and urban competition, declares itself elsewhere as nothing less than 'a laboratory for a transnational city construction and a model for European integration' (City of Copenhagen and City of Malmoe, 1999: 16). Thus, we learn that a new cross-border region adjacent to the NSR perceives itself as the major hub in the North European space, making a serious challenge to the NorVISION strategy.

In tune with the ESDP, NorVISION places its urban regions as motors in regional development. As mentioned above, due to the relative 'lack' of metropolitan agglomerations within the NSR, the favoured spatial development strategy is based on urban networking (VWG, 2000b: 41).

At the end of the document is an annex setting out the draft guidelines for the INTERREG IIIB programme, confirming that NorVISION really is 'thought into' this frame. Furthermore, the comprehensive notes within the document give a very fine impression of how these various documents on European spatial planning and development constitute a discourse based on intertextual references. In the notes of NorVISION we thus find several references to documents such as the ESDP, the CADSES vision and the VASAB vision (CADSES, 2000; CSD, 1999; Ministers for Spatial Planning and Development, 1994). In other words, NorVISION is contributing to the creation of a new language of spatial policy at the same time as carrying the message from other documents in the same genre. At the end of the day it forms part of a complex web of words, concepts and strategies that frames the future articulation of European spatial development for the social agents within this particular field.

Multi-level narrative: ripples in European space – from ESDP to CEMAT

As we have argued throughout, the issue of scale is crucial. Seen as an expression of the 'politics of scale' the new spatial narratives are busily re-articulating space and territory from transnational levels of region building up to the 'big picture' of the whole EU territory. These logics of nested spatial narratives can be followed further into the global and transnational space transgressing the European Union. We illustrate this by turning to the spatial principles articulated by the Council of Europe.

It is immediately clear from the Council of Europe's CEMAT Guiding Principles that at the pan-European level, though many of the issues faced are similar to those of the EU which they embrace, they have different dimensions and manifestations. The approach taken is not to simply adopt and replicate the discourse emerging in the ESDP. The document points to the different challenges of planning for the wider continent of Europe, rather than for the EU, stressing a 'continental dimension' of spatial development that it regards as being as yet overlooked by the ESDP (CEMAT, 1999: 2). The document is very brief, and unlike the ESDP contains no detailed analysis or discussion. This elaboration is currently taking place through the continuing work of CEMAT. The key principles are set out in Box 4.8. These are amplified in the document in relation to different regional types: cultural landscapes, urban and rural areas, mountains, coastal and island regions, eurocorridors, flood plains and water meadows, redundant military and industrial sites, and border regions.

Overall, it is clear that the economic imperative driving the ESDP and NorVISION is repeated in the CEMAT Guiding Principles, though with a different emphasis reflecting the 'transitional' and 'underdeveloped' nature of many of the European countries currently outside the EU. Europe as a whole is framed as a trading block comparable to Mercosur, NAFTA and ASEAN. It specifies the primary direction of its external trade links – with Asia and the Middle East – and proposes 'new exchange corridors' in Russia, the countries bordering the Black Sea and Greece.

One of the apparent differences between the rhetoric of the CEMAT vision and the ESDP is the emphasis on the primary importance of social cohesion in the wider Europe, rather than foregrounding economic growth.[2] Alongside cohesion, sustainable spatial development is emphasised, where 'sustainable development is gradual development geared to human needs' (CEMAT, 1999: 3). Like the ESDP, however, the key challenge for spatial development is recognised as globalisation, and the need for intra-European east-west economic integration in response. So although the rhetoric of the CEMAT Guiding Principles, mirroring the ESDP, embraces balance, sustainability and cohesion, in pursuit of the 'magic' balance

Box 4.8 **Extract from the Guiding Principles: principles for a planning policy for sustainable development in Europe**

Promoting territorial cohesion through a more balanced social and economic development of regions and improved competitiveness

Encouraging development generated by urban functions and improving the relationship between town and countryside

Promoting more balanced accessibility

Developing access to information and knowledge

Reducing environmental damage

Enhancing and protecting natural resources and the natural heritage

Enhancing the cultural heritage as a factor for development

Developing energy resources while maintaining safety

Encouraging high quality, sustainable tourism

Limitation of the impact of natural disasters

Source: CEMAT, 2000

between growth-ecology-equity, the imperative of economic competitiveness again dominates, articulated forcefully in the more detailed discussion of themes and possible measures. So the main strategy of pursuing cohesion appears to be through territorial balance and competitiveness, where 'large scale disparities can be reduced by aiming at a higher level of competitiveness in regions lagging behind or undergoing economic restructuring' (CEMAT, 1999: 1). The key to balanced development is to be found through enhanced economic competitiveness.

Although there is common ground between the ESDP and the Guiding Principles in the problem framing of peripheral and underdeveloped regions, CEMAT also attaches a different significance to regions with a predominantly agricultural function. There is a tension between the emphasis on economic development through influencing locational choice in the face of globalisation, and an approach which recognises the virtues of, and need for, endogenous rural and regional development. The document warns that failure to implement adequate rural and agricultural policies could give rise to 'undesirable massive long-distance migration' (CEMAT, 1999: 16). The objective of balanced development specifically seeks to reduce migration and rural-urban movements.

Compared to the ESDP's urban bias, the CEMAT Guiding Principles are clearer in their emphasis on rural regions. However, the future of urban areas remains a priority. The document points to the rapid growth in cities which have been on the periphery of the EU, such as Lisbon, Dublin and Athens, as a result of economic integration. It argues that with EU enlargement capitals such as Prague, Bratislava, Bucharest and Budapest can form the major nodes in a polycentric system extending across the European continent.

We have shown how the ESDP places the need for enhanced mobility as a critical priority for securing economic development within an overall spatial strategy of harmonisation (CSD, 1999: 26). Mobility is once again of critical importance in the Guiding Principles, and is generally expressed in relation to the development of trans-European and pan-European transport corridors and networks, and in relation to the problem of accessibility. The framing of the 'problem' of poor accessibility as a major threat in an integrated economy is captured in the following extract from the working draft:

> Economic integration may have marginalisation effects on more disadvantaged regions, in particular those remote from significant agglomerations or located in badly accessible areas (mountains, islands, etc). This marginalisation effect can be accentuated by the differential in the relative efficiency of transport systems. Rarely served by motorways, having only small motorways at best, and being far away from the high speed stations, these areas in particular are at a disadvantage in terms of attracting activities which require good access to the high speed networks. And their image suffers as the symbols of modernity and new resources mount up in the better-served regions. This aggravates inequalities in development as the most profitable infrastructure investments expand. There is a 'vicious circle' for those areas of Europe which are at best characterised by slow development but which most often see this backwardness accentuated with the common symptoms of a cumulative process of underdevelopment: negative migration figures, accelerated ageing of the population, job losses, the flight from the land, etc.
>
> (CEMAT, 1999: 32)

The statement from ministers which accompanies the CEMAT Guiding Principles further highlights the importance of transport infrastructure to its spatial vision:

> we stress. . . . That the speedy development and implementation of the pan-European transport network (especially the 10 Pan-European Transport Corridors), is an indispensable prerequisite for good accessibility of large areas across the entire continent, has to be expedited, and point out that the agreements reached on the shape of the networks should, if necessary, be reviewed and augmented taking sustainable development and environmental aspects into account.
>
> (CEMAT, 2000)

Consequently, key measures in the Guiding Principles aim to improve accessibility and reduce the isolation of peripheral regions (CEMAT, 1999: 1). They include improving connections from rural areas to the main axes and centres of transportation through infrastructure improvements, eliminating missing links, and improvements to public transport services. A particular challenge is to ensure that secondary networks are in place to create access to the proposed pan-European transport corridors and other major corridors, which would otherwise create tunnel effects. For Central and Eastern European countries this also means improving transport networks so that they link smaller cities and towns to each other as well as to the major centres, resolving a legacy of the Soviet era.

Concluding remarks

In excavating the new policy language and illustrating its intertextuality, we have shown that the treatment of the environment and the urban are criss-crossed by the mobility agenda, producing a new narrative field and a new vocabulary for a single European space – a Europe of monotopia. The new spatial policy language articulates an apparently unified set of ideas, but we find two problems. The first is the existence of internal contradictions and tensions within the discourse. For example the language around cohesion and balanced competitiveness masks uncertainties about the likely impacts on core-periphery relations of the TEN-T. The second is the external mechanism of exclusion of certain issues and themes – such as alternative approaches to mobility.

Underlying the new policy language is a rationale of economic competitiveness, which remains a central driver in EU discourse. Europe is articulated as a space of flows: of frictionless mobility within a polycentric spatial form. Key terms in the policy language are polycentricity, efficiency, accessibility, and the ambiguous rhetorical device of a golden policy triangle of growth-ecology-equity.

However there exists a dilemma here which mirrors a deeper tension within the EU project. Within the Treaty of European Union, social and economic cohesion are subordinated to the aim of building an open market with free competition. As Giannakourou argues, there is 'no legal basis for the introduction of any measure which could lead to a distortion of competition in the field of spatial cohesion' under the Treaty (Giannakourou, 1996: 604). The importance of economic competitiveness can be seen in the linkage of the critical role of the spatial strategy with the aims of balanced regional development and global economic competitiveness. There is a strong urban bias here. Cities are constructed as the driving forces and 'motors' of regional economic development within an increasingly competition oriented space economy.

The overwhelming emphasis on economic development within the ESDP suggests that the EU's spatial strategy will be played out in competition between cities and regions, between urban and rural, between core and periphery, and along growth corridors, with the marginalisation of social and environmental concerns. It is in response to these risks of fracture and injustice that the EU's cohesion agenda has emerged. And it is here that we find the issue of territorial identity reflected in the new vocabulary. Springing from cohesion as a response to a territory in danger of breaking apart, the new language of territorial identity itself subtly articulates an idea of European unity. In the words of Chris Rumford, cohesion policy is more about the 'creation of a harmonized European economic space' than a redistributive agenda (Rumford, 2002: 179). Thus below the explicit notions of a single space of flows in terms of mobilities, goods, people and capital we find less tangible, but equally important, notions of the need for seeing Europe as 'one space', further eroding the previous hegemony of the member states. It is as if the European project requires a single space, and dealing with the adverse impacts of this project further reinforces the need for the creation of that single space. These twin mirrors of European policy, of growth and cohesion, of competition and balance, together require and reproduce monotopia.

Chapter 5

Being on the map

The new iconographies of power over European space

> Maps, stripped of all elements of fantasy and religious belief, as well as of any sign of the experiences involved in their production, had become abstract and strictly functional systems for the factual ordering of phenomena in space. The science of map projection, and techniques of cadastral surveying, made them mathematically rigorous depictions.
>
> (Harvey, 1989)

> When maps are drawn, emotions run high.
>
> (Dutch National Spatial Planning Agency, 2000)

> In years gone by, drawing lines on maps has led to war. Nowadays people draw lines on maps and it leads to Conciliation, which is pretty close to the same thing.
>
> (A Brussels bureaucrat, commenting on the preparation of the TEN-T proposals maps)

Introduction

This chapter examines how the new policy language is accompanied by a new set of visual images and maps of European space. These images and maps not only represent spaces as part of a discursive practice, as discussed in Chapter 3, they also express new demands for spatial knowledge. The chapter also deals with new technologies and the way they are applied in new forms of spatial representation labelled 'infographics'. The power of infographics to give new meanings to European space and identity is discussed. This chapter, then, explores how the representation of European space in images has played a part in building and reproducing policy discourses of European space. Landmark and less well known images of European spatial relations are discussed, from representations of trans-European infrastructure networks to the iconic 'bananas' and 'grapes', and through to the new science of infographics, which explicitly attempts to articulate new European spatial concepts such as polycentricity in image form. In doing this, we hope to draw together and build on some of the observations of previous critical research which have pointed to the significance of images in European spatial policy making (particularly Faludi, 2000a; Kunzmann, 1996; Williams, 1996a, b). Building on the conceptual framework set out in Chapter 3, exploring the different ways that spatial images can play a part in policy making, we analyse some of the major examples of European spatial policy images, focusing specifically on the use of proposals maps for TEN-T and successive drafts of the ESDP.

The themes of the urban, the environment and territorial identity, and their common thread of mobility, are linked in this chapter in the following way: issues of environmental risk and urban relations are covered in the narrative of images of accessibility and the TEN-T. Then the issue of identity is addressed by showing how the policy images start to be accompanied by other types of images which reproduce the core vision in a range of media for consumption by policy makers but also by stakeholders and citizens across Europe. We use the examples of images which articulate the promise of the Øresund, and the North Sea Region and North West Metropolitan Area, to illustrate this. Furthermore, we will include images and maps that have gained iconic status over the years as framing devices for the annihilation of 'missing links' and the quest for a zero friction European space, and the ideas of a polycentric urban system of 'grapes' versus an urban agglomeration scenario of development 'bananas'.

We discuss how, in the new spatial policy discourse, the imagery of European space is changing, as explicit maps of policy proposals are replaced by impressionist representations of policy ideas. We draw things together by suggesting that these images play a significant role in articulating the new policy discourse of European space.

Mapping European space

Shrinking Europe

One of the most striking examples of attempts to frame space in EU spatial policy can be found in the agenda-setting work of the industrial lobby and in particular the European Round Table of Industrialists. Here we explore how a critical policy problem for European integration – the absence of adequate infrastructure to support the completion of the single market – was first framed in agenda-setting lobbying using spatial metaphors such as 'missing links' and 'missing networks', and was subsequently re-articulated in the policy discourse of frictionless trans-European mobility in a more positive way: the solution of high speed infrastructure and a shrinking Europe.

Here we argue that iconic images of EU space have been decisively shaped by this lobbying (though as we will see, wider power struggles would attempt to reshape and control their meaning). Endo (1999) points to the ERT as one of the few pressure groups able to actually change EU policy. Having defined the infrastructure problem in terms of missing international infrastructure links discussed in the previous chapter, the ERT next sought to set the agenda for action in *Missing Networks – A European Challenge, proposals for the renewal of Europe's infrastructure* (ERT, 1991). The first level of action, based on the rethinking of spatial relations on a European scale, was to continue to deal with the problem of missing links. By 1991, however, the need for physical infrastructure improvements had extended eastwards, to encompass the new European orientation of the Central and Eastern European states, and had become more of a network view, as international corridors were identified.

The second level of action called for by the ERT was perhaps more far reaching in its scope. They called for a fundamental restructuring of institutions and practices in order to achieve the required pan-European transport perspective. The 1991 report goes beyond arguing for physical solutions – building new roads or railways – and states the need for new ways of conceptualising, decision making and financing trans-European networks. Here, then, was an explicit call for a EU policy response, rather than simply transnational infrastructure project implementation. Building on the imagery of *Missing Links*, in *Missing Networks*, the ERT proposed not only new physical infrastructure, but also a shift in the mindset of politicians and policy-makers: 'to think and rethink existing networks in specifically European spatial and economic terms' (ERT, 1991).

Inherent in these metaphors is the quest for frictionless mobility, in this case to be achieved by removing the physical and institutional barriers to free movement across Europe. The shift from a problem of friction to a solution of free mobility, traceable in the emerging policy discourse, is powerfully articulated through another important spatial metaphor: 'shrinking Europe'. The trans-European transport network contributes to an effect of shrinking European space by reducing journey times, and so reduces the barriers of time-space between European member states, regions, and cities. In *Missing Links*, the ERT graphically illustrated equivalent length journeys in the US and Europe, and identified the additional time delays caused in Europe by border crossings and inadequate infrastructure – the economic message was clear. The idea of a shrinking Europe has become a preoccupation of policy makers and analysts. Map 5.1 demonstrates how the benefits of TEN-T are communicated graphically in a Commission policy document, in the image of a shrinking EU space. The image is based on detailed analysis, but the overall effect is powerfully rhetorical. In Europe 2000+ (CEC, 1994a), a key Commission policy document setting out elements of its spatial vision, the image is accompanied by the text 'Planned improvements will . . . *effectively* bring regions closer together'.

The TEN-T proposals maps

We turn now to the use of proposal maps in European spatial policy making. Proposals maps have been highly controversial, and have attracted political

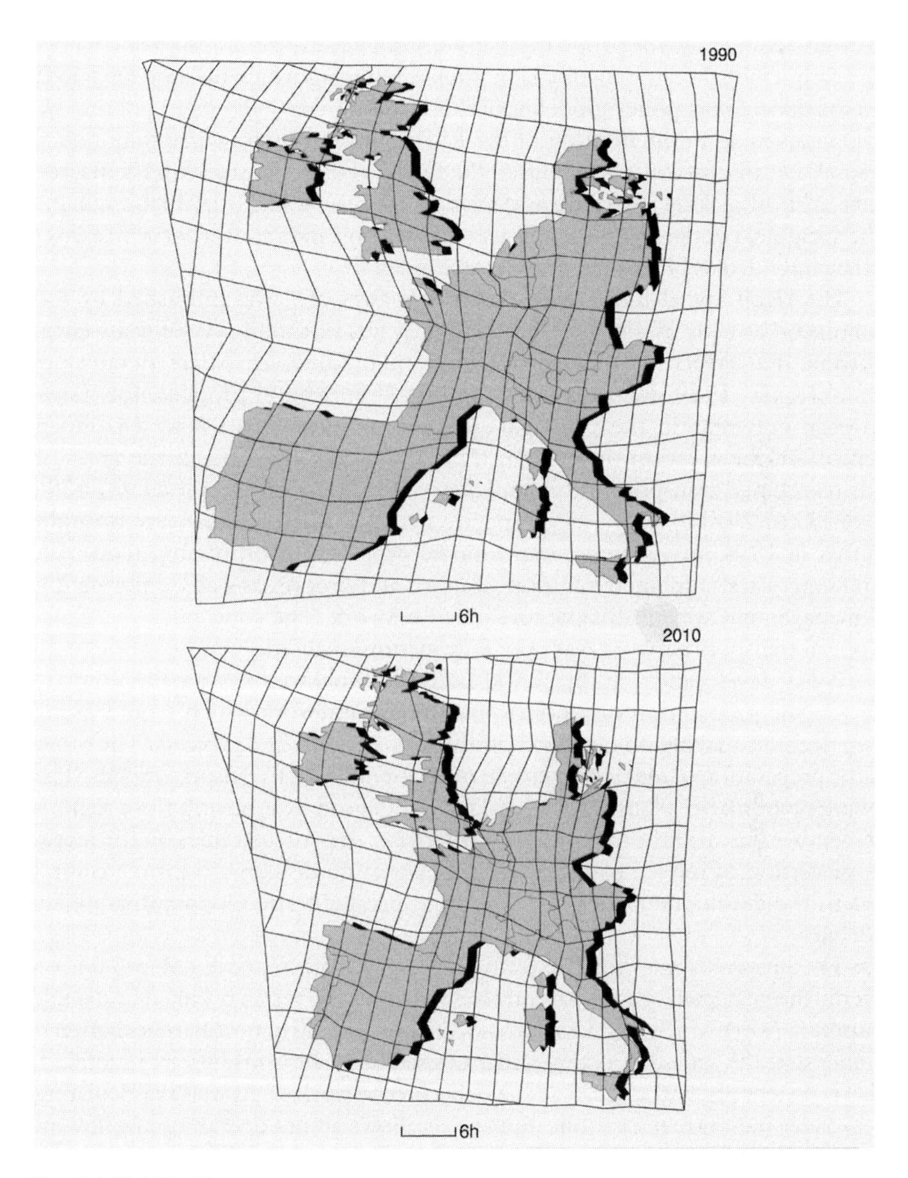

Map 5.1 Shrinking Europe.

Note: the map shows how distances are deformed in relation to the time taken to travel between regions by high-speed train. Planned improvements will, for a constant time scale (6 hours), effectively bring regions closer together.

Source: CEC, 1994a

struggles that have tended to mask the actual policy issues at stake. We illustrate this by discussing how the proposals maps for trans-European transport networks in the early 1990s became the focus of intense lobbying which became separated from the debate over policy guidelines. This is followed by a discussion of the use of proposals maps in the drafting of the ESDP, illustrating how mapping policy proposals became so controversial that the final ESDP dispensed with them altogether, instead making use of maps depicting the results of spatial analysis. Thus in the struggles over proposals maps, we can see contestation over their meaning: are they intended as blueprints or as 'target images'?

The High Speed Rail (HSR) network master plan was published by the Commission as early as 1990 (CEC, 1990). It was not until several years later, following the Treaty of European Union that Karel van Miert (Transport Commissioner, 1989–1995) set out the first Commission proposal for trans-European networks in the principal transport modes. This led to a Council Decision on the creation of separate trans-European networks in the areas of roads, combined transport and inland waterways (Council Decisions 93/628–630/EEC of 29/10/93). These separate network master plans were brought together in 1994 into a single, multi-modal proposal, incorporating road, rail, inland waterways, combined transport, seaports and airports, as well as information and management systems for the integrated network. The concept of the trans-European transport network was now fully institutionalised.

Policy development in the period after 1992 followed two parallel courses. One was the preparation of a policy/planning framework which would guide future decision-making on networks, individual corridors and projects. The other was the preparation of a series of outline plans for individual transport modes. The drawing up of master plans was increasingly influenced by lobbying from regions and member states on the inclusion (or otherwise) of particular lines on the maps. The succession of revised plans for each transport mode came to form a central focus to the development of policy, running parallel to development of policy guidelines.

The proposals map for the trans-European road network (Map 5.2) is a powerful image depicting an apparently homogenous EU territory linked by a single transport network which seamlessly crosses the borders and natural barriers between member states. A series of existing and proposed links and corridors are identified, which represent physical space in a reasonably precise manner. As well as articulating the broader message of a mobile Europe, it allows actors operating at different spatial scales and representing different interests to ask questions such as 'is our town on the map?', and 'will our commercial strategy be supported by the new infrastructure proposals'. In fact, the preparation of these maps reflected the playing out of EU, national and regional political, industrial and environmental interests. In the drawing up of this map, and the corresponding maps for other transport modes, several strategies can be identified. Perhaps the most apparent is the EU discourse of integration through the establishment of the networks. However the

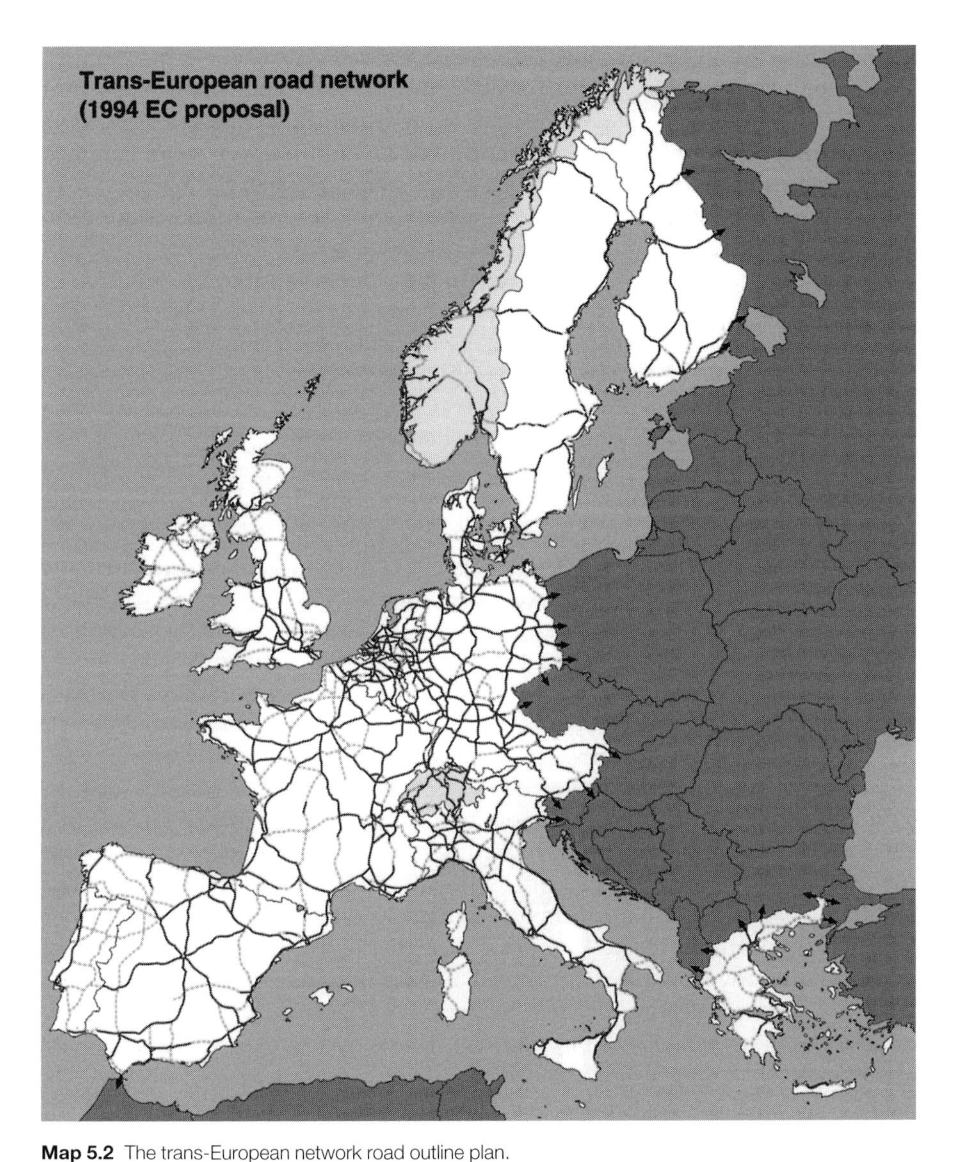

Map 5.2 The trans-European network road outline plan.

Source: CEC (1995) The trans-European Road, EC Directorate General for Transport, Brussels.

strategies of other actors did not fit so neatly into this harmonious view of European space. One example is the use of TEN-T by member states as a means of promoting their adopted national transport plans. The emerging maps can be interpreted as reflecting in large part the transport plans of individual member states, rather than a European view: 'where things went wrong in the first place was that the

Commission then got in touch with each member state and asked them what they wanted and of course all they did was dust down all their old national plans from the shelves and put them in' (Member of the European Parliament).

Later, regions and other local authorities would become more active in lobbying for the adoption of locally preferred schemes within the outline plans, but in the early 1990s member states carried out only limited consultations in developing their submissions to the Commission.

The infrastructure lobby maintained a powerful hold at the EU level, as the proposals from member states and other bodies were filtered and assembled into network outline plans. The membership of one of the key decision-making bodies illustrates the institutional power of this lobby. Proposals for the Trans-European Road Network (TERN), for example, were developed by the Motorway Working Group (MWG) of the Commission's Transport Infrastructure Committee. Membership of this Group includes representatives of the Commission, member states, the European Conference of Ministers of Transport, and significantly a number of private sector interests including the European Round Table (ERT), the Association des Constructeurs Européens d'Automobile (ACEA), and the International Road Transport Union (IRU) (CEC, 1992). The overwhelming dominance of transport interests, and the infrastructure lobby, and the absence of environmental interests can be seen. It is difficult to imagine that such a committee could produce anything other than a solid case for progressing TERN. The decision making process adopted by the MWG is unclear, although they transformed national infrastructure 'shopping lists' into international network proposals. However, environmental criteria were not integrated into decision making although they were identified, in broad terms, in policy documents (Bina *et al.*, 1995). The published proposals identify a network of corridors, but fail to set out the criteria used in their designation, leaving a strong impression that the debate within this key decision-making arena was largely political.

The importance of the European industrial lobby in the development of TERN was clearly recognised within the EU institutions, but was perhaps seen more as a positive influence in achieving a pan-European perspective, counter to some of the more parochial lobbying:

> We're building a single market for Europe, we need a single European transport system to go with it, that system must be sustainable. But it's got to be European, we can't have national networks superimposed on each other and bad interconnections. And they're the people building this stuff, and also they're the people using it.
>
> (European Commission official)

A feature of the preparation of outline plans was that, although the infrastructure lobby enjoyed a high level of access in decision-making, environmental organisations were never formally consulted. The Member States were expected by the

Commission to represent their respective environmental interests (Frommer, 1992: 10, and European Commission official's comments). Given the above, it is not surprising that any comprehensive planning which might have taken place in the preparation of the outline plans was overshadowed by multi-level lobbying and political bargaining. What was launched as a grand European vision risked becoming an assemblage of local pet projects: 'Oh yes. It was all terribly parochial, terribly parochial. I mean this isn't really European planning this is all about member states trying to get a bit of Commission money for things they were going to do anyway, and local authorities trying to jump on the bandwagon. That's really what was happening' (European Commission official). This high level of interest in TEN-T can be simply explained by the prospect of a new source of funding (the EU budget) for local or national projects at a time when finance was becoming difficult in the face of recession and increasing resistance to infrastructure development on environmental and social grounds. One interviewee explained this financial interest thus:

> And at that point ministers got involved, and said 'well these are some maps and we want to put a bypass on there'. And then people start smelling money, so you get everyone coming along. Local authorities, they fail to get money out of national government, they haven't got enough money in their own coffers, so they think they're going to get money out of the Community. So everyone comes along lobbying to get their little pet schemes onto the TEN and the result is that you end up with, not a tight limited set of routes of importance, but you end up with a whole load. Right, so rapidly this process started spiralling out of control. In addition, the southern member states were told that the maps for TENs would be used in some way as the basis for the allocation of cohesion funding. And that's big money. So of course they've bunged on everything they could find.
>
> (European Commission official)

The fine grain of TEN-T – the outline plans composed of individual projects – was being shaped politically. For some policy makers this politicisation of decision making was simply business as usual.

'No line on the map, no money' – on pork-barrelling and TEN-T as an institutional battlefield

A feature of the TEN-T policy process, then, was that even as policy was being developed, advocacy for the detailed projects which would comprise the networks was taking place. As the procedural arguments continued over issues such as environmental integration, simultaneous struggles were taking place over the content of policy: the adoption and prioritisation of projects, corridors and networks. In some cases, EU money was already being used to finance projects as well as to fund feasibility studies.

In early decision making, lobbying for the inclusion of individual projects in the lists annexed to the policy guidelines, and represented on the outline plans, had been important in shaping the emerging proposals. Following ratification of the Maastricht Treaty, TEN-T policy after 1994 came under the new process of co-decision between Council and Parliament (under Article 189b of the Treaty). In co-decision, the Commission prepared proposals on TEN-T, which became the subject of committee work and debates in both Council and Parliament. The Parliament responded to the proposal, and the Council in turn responded to the Parliament's position, setting out its own Common Position. This cycle was then repeated. The role of the Commission in this iterative process was to guide policy development in a way which moved towards a position which could be agreed by all parties. The Parliament quickly used this opportunity to voice their concern about the undemocratic nature of the early stages of the process, strongly condemning in particular the failure to involve the Parliament in the decision to prioritise certain critical corridors (see Chapter 6).[1] In co-decision, a new lobbying route was opened – through MEPs and the Parliamentary process. The later stages of drafting the policy guidelines under co-decision were marked by intense lobbying from regions for projects to be added to the network, as 'what was for the Commission a skeleton became all the veins and arteries as well' (European Commission official).

This 'pork-barrelling', as it was described by one interviewee, raised the concern that TEN-T, rather than delivering a European infrastructure plan, was being taken over by member states trying to obtain money for projects they were going to implement anyway, and local authorities trying to jump on the bandwagon, in a climate of uncertainty over continued public investment in infrastructure. There was clearly a perceived regional interest in getting projects onto the maps. TEN-T designation offered a new lever for releasing funding from the EU budget for local infrastructure projects. For example, in the UK's governments consultation on roads, which shaped its submission to the Commission on TEN-T, the regions complained when their local 'lines' were not adopted in the proposals map, because they felt 'no line on the map, no money' (European Commission official). The nature of the policy process was clearly shaped by this lobbying. Developing a 'rational' network from these diverse projects was a difficult task, as local political interests blurred the clear rationality of the original vision:

> This was one of the worst aspects of the process. It was frankly almost scandalous, the kind of pork-barrelling that was going on. There were ridiculous things. In the first reading you'll find for example two high speed train [proposals] from Amsterdam to Hanover. Those were the kind of amendments that we were having to put up with. It was a joke, which detracted from the more serious amendments.
>
> (European Commission official)

The end of pork-barreling?

These acknowledged problems with the initial designation of the TEN-T, and with the prioritisation of certain projects and corridors, were to be addressed in a revision of the policy guidelines. As a result, the Commission has engaged in a two-stage revision of the trans-European network guidelines (CEC, 2001c: 50–51). The first stage in 2001 carried out a limited adaptation of the existing guidelines (in line with Article 21 of the guidelines). This revision, which the Commission should have completed in 1999, was not foreseen as a further opportunity to add new infrastructure routes to the TEN-T map. Its intention was to concentrate on eliminating bottlenecks on routes already identified; completing the routes identified as priorities for absorbing the traffic flows generated by enlargement, particularly in frontier regions; and improving access to outlying areas. In this context, the list of priority corridors adopted by the Essen European Council is being updated, as called for on several occasions by Parliament and the Commission since 1997. This is starkly illustrated in the Commission's priorities argued in the 2001 Transport White Paper, which continue the concern with 'the saturation of the main arteries' and the remedial surgery of removing 'bottlenecks':

> Given the saturation of certain major arteries and the consequent pollution, it is essential for the European Union to complete the trans-European projects already decided. For this reason, the Commission intends to propose revision of the guidelines adopted by the Council and the European Parliament, which will remain limited until funding is secured for the current projects. In line with the conclusions adopted by the Gothenburg European Council, the Commission proposes to concentrate the revision of the Community guidelines on removing the bottlenecks in the railway network, completing the routes identified as the priorities for absorbing the traffic flows generated by enlargement, particularly in frontier regions, and improving access to outlying areas. To improve access to the trans-European network, development of the secondary network will remain a Structural Fund priority.
>
> (CEC, 2001c)

The 2001 White Paper proposes that the following projects will be added to the TENs priority list 'by way of illustration':

- a high-capacity railway route through the Pyrenees for freight;
- East European high-speed train/combined transport Paris–Stuttgart–Vienna;
- the Fehmarn bridge/tunnel between Germany and Denmark;
- the Galileo satellite navigation project;
- improvement of the navigability of the Danube between Straubing and Vilshofen;
- the Verona–Naples rail link, including the Bologna–Milan branch;
- the interoperability of the Iberian high-speed rail network.

Furthermore, it states that in 2004 the Commission will present a more extensive review of TEN-T, aimed in particular at introducing the concept of 'sea motorways', developing airport capacity, linking the outlying regions on the European continent more effectively and connecting the networks of the candidate countries to the networks of EU countries (CEC, 2001c: 18). What is overwhelmingly clear here is that the priority TEN-T projects continue to have a high level of political significance, and that the network is growing to reflect the enlargement of the EU to the east. The emerging spatial policy agenda has not yet had any apparent impact on the TEN-T policy path.

The ESDP from Noordwijk to Potsdam: a retreat from proposals to analysis

From this discussion of the early use of proposals maps in representing mobility dimensions of European space, we move forwards to the use of maps in the preparation of the European Spatial Development Perspective (ESDP). During the gestation process of the ESDP maps were often an issue to be discussed. In a working document from the CSD we thus find the notion of the ESDP maps as a unifying 'cartographic language': 'Experiences from the ESDP-process so far show that the elaboration of European maps of a strategic nature cannot be undertaken within a short time. . . . This work will be aiming to define a cartographic language common to all Member States and applicable to all relevant geographical scales' (CSD, 1998b:3).

Studying the actual maps in the ESDP process we find that there is a difference between the first draft version (the so-called Noordwijk document), the subsequent Glasgow draft document, and the final Potsdam document. The main point is that there is less and less political vision and leverage in the maps as we approach the Potsdam version (Jensen, 1999: 289; SPESP, 2000: 94). Faludi also notes the special attention given to maps in the ESDP gestation process: 'Maps were another problem. The CSD saw the drafts a month before the target date [of the Noordwijk document] and some delegations were not amused. It was decided to eliminate policy maps altogether' (Faludi, 2000b: 247).

Elsewhere, in a report assessing the impact of the ESDP on Regional Planning Guidance in England, the existing use of maps in regional planning is criticised, and a more 'European' and outward looking perception is called for:

> For diagrams to effectively represent a region in its wider UK and European contexts, they need to be more than simple 'geography maps' showing the location of the region. More thought needs to be given to how the functional linkages with other regions and key EU contexts such as INTERREG programme areas and projects can be represented. A starting point could be to include maps showing the position of the region in relation to any relevant transnational megaregions and INTERREG projects.
>
> (Shaw and Sykes, 2001: 63)

In a very well informed analysis of the ESDP gestation process, Faludi and Waterhout discuss the specific topic of maps in the ESDP process under the headline 'the problem of maps'. They suggest that up until the very last moment, maps were an issue of controversy (Faludi and Waterhout, 2002: 104). The maps turned out to be sites of contested representation, as the different member states focused on their own territories and their position relative to the others. Thus in the run up to the preparation of the Noordwijk version of the ESDP, the only maps provided were given a very careful proviso or 'Nota bene' stating that:

> This representation is only an illustration of certain spatial elements referred to in the text of the First Official Draft of the ESPD (sic), presented at the informal meeting of ministers responsible for spatial planning of the member states of the EU in Noordwijk, 9–10 June 1997. They do in no way reflect actual policy proposals and there is no guarantee that the elements displayed here are exhaustive or entirely accurate.
>
> (CSD, 1997)

According to Faludi and Waterhout such maps played a part in triggering the North-South conflict over the ESDP, allowing the southern Europeans to interpret the maps as reflecting a centre-periphery model which stigmatised the South European regions (Faludi and Waterhout, 2002: 107).

When we turn to look at the maps themselves, we find the Noordwijk map on 'Accessibility, infrastructure and transport' enclosed loose in the back of the draft ESDP. This map includes proposals for the trans-European networks, and identifies peripheral regions, population centres and congested corridors (Plate 1). This map is certainly about friction and accessibility, as it represents a vision of European territory in terms of flows and nodes. In this sense we could say that the periphery is framed in terms of immobility or lack of access. Overcoming this state of unequal accessibility relies on one of the core rationales of Regional Policy DG (formerly DGVXI), namely that of 'cohesion'. Furthermore, by imaging the cohesion problem in terms of mobility potentials and friction, the theme of European 'integration' becomes represented by cross-border movements.

All that remains in the final ESDP is a map of 'Accessibility', depicting 'within 3 hours travel time accessible EU population by combined transport mode (road, rail, air) in 1996 NUTS 3' (Plate 2). This is spatial analysis 'pure and simple'. It is used for problem framing where we find the previously mentioned key rationale of cohesion explicitly linked to the other basic rationale of economic competitiveness: 'Good accessibility of European regions improves not only their competitive position but also the competitiveness of Europe as a whole' (CSD, 1999: 69).

A narrative of the role of maps in the ESDP process can be found in a publication from the Dutch Planning Ministry (Dutch National Spatial Planning Agency, 2000). Starting from the basic question 'Am I well represented?' the report uncovers the fact that map making in the ESDP process was a rather sensitive business. The prime example of conflicts and tensions within this process that came out very clearly in relation to mapping was the 'North-South' conflict and its alleged foundation in different planning cultures:

> In some countries a map is a 'plan', a blueprint of how things should be. Other countries also have more indicative maps, not blue prints but 'target images', intended as a framework for the co-ordination of actions, not to be taken as literal reality. In the Netherlands, such 'target images' are a favoured means of 'getting everyone facing in the same direction' towards an often abstractly formulated long-term goal. This phenomenon is also familiar in Belgium, Denmark and Germany. In countries such as Spain, Portugal and, to a lesser extent Italy, maps are interpreted more as blueprints.
> (Dutch National Spatial Planning Agency, 2000: 47)

Map making is, however, not only an expression of power but also a communicative event. Maps, then, clearly have an 'ambivalent potential'. In the words of the Dutch National Spatial Planning Agency, once an image provides the visualisation needed to depict a dominant paradigm, it becomes a kind of policy icon (SPESP, 2000: 93). Thus some analysts see a progressive potential in the new practice of EU spatial policy map making. According to Kunzmann the cartographic exercises in the EU have the following advantages (Kunzmann, 1996: 144):

1. The process is more important that the plan – maps are facilitating a 'joint cross-cultural understanding of spatial development processes in Europe'.
2. Visualisation of spatial problems makes public and political communication much easier.
3. 'Symbols and spatial images play an underestimated role in spatial planning' – and reduces complexity.
4. Shortcomings or dissatisfaction with maps and concepts triggers off new research.

Thus maps can be seen as moments in the process of decision-making (Wood, 1993: 185). Among the benefits of the ESDP is its ability to provide 'a useful, visual identification of the spatial issues that confront the EU' (Chapman, 2000: 219).

Towards impressionism

A different role for images is in attaching significance to particular constructions of planning problems, and also in articulating the emerging politics of space. Here we are thinking of spatial images which may be more impressionistic in their form, and which rely on conveying ideas about space in a more metaphorical sense, without necessarily being tied to particular dimensions of physical space. The point of such images is that they are designed to carry an idea, an impression, rather than a specific policy proposal. The important feature of these images is that they are less precise in their attempts to represent space. They articulate spatial relations in the broadest sense, in a way which does not allow their meaning to be pinned to specific localities. We explore the increasing reliance on such images by first analysing images which took on iconic significance in framing particular issues and opportunities, and then moving on to discuss the new, increasingly coherent 'science' of consciously producing a vocabulary of images which reproduces key ideas in the new transnational spatial policy discourse. We move from single key images which stand as iconic representations of European space, capturing critical moments in policy debates, to more orchestrated activity which sets out to create the next generation of spatial icons.

The blue banana . . .

Probably the most well known of all these spatial images is the 'blue banana' (Plate 3). According to Williams this was in fact the metaphor that started the widespread use of metaphors in EU spatial policy discourse (Williams, 1996a). The metaphor refers to the economic and political core of Europe taking shape as a banana and running from the south east of England to the north of Italy. The image of the so-called 'blue banana' was originally published in a report made for the French Spatial Planning agency DATAR (Brunet, 1989) (Figure 19), where the economic core region of Europe was identified as the 'Dorsale Européenne', literally the 'backbone of Europe'. Thus we find also here a powerful image coupled to a metaphor that in its original form had organic connotations to the body. This image clearly juxtaposes this core zone with lacunae, which me might translate as shadow regions, and proposes a new southern growth region, the Nord du sud. This image was then adapted in Europe 2000, a policy document originating in the European Commission's Directorate Generale for Regional Development, to identify the existing economic core region and propose a new core region (the Nord du sud). There are a number of anecdotes and stories to explain why this 'backbone' became the 'blue banana'. For one thing it can be seen from the original source (Brunet, 1989) that the banana is not blue as it is actually hatched black in the original DATAR image. According to Faludi and Waterhout:

> It was quite accidentally that the dorsale got the name 'Blue Banana'. On a visit to DATAR, the French Planning Minister, Jacques Chérèque, saw a map of Europe with the dorsale printed in blue and asked: 'What is this blue banana for?'. A reporter from the weekly *Le Nouvel Observateur*, after overhearing this comment, published an article under the title La banane bleue, and the name stuck.
>
> (Faludi and Waterhout, 2002: 11)

Whatever the real reason for the naming of this particular spatial image, 'this metaphor creates a memorable image which simplifies and structures peoples' thinking about the spatial structure of Europe' (Williams, 1996a: 96).[2] Evidently the banana image is framed around a notion of core and periphery (Williams, 1996a), thus adding to the fact that it has been seen as highly controversial, especially politically (Dutch National Spatial Planning Agency, 2000: 25). This seems to be the case not least in relation to the South European countries. The Scandinavian countries have also noted their peripheral representation. As will become evident, this particular influential metaphor and image must be seen in relation to the follow-ups that tried to articulate visions and ideas of the European territory in explicit relation to the 'banana'. Thus, our analysis of this particular image implicitly carries on in the following sections.

. . . and the bunch of grapes

As an alternative to the Blue Banana we find the metaphor of a Europe of 'grapes' (Map 5.3). According to Williams (1996a) this was Germany's response to the banana, based on the its experience of post-war federalism. This metaphor conveys a polycentric rather than centralised image of Europe's urban and economic structure. The grape metaphor is described by its creator as articulating a 'Europe of sustainable regions' (Kunzmann, 1996), signalling the beginning of a discourse of sustainable spatial development. Waterhout sees the tension between the two images as representing the playing out of a 'one-dimensional view of Europe' versus a 'more subtle, diversified view of Europe' (Waterhout, 2001: 9). Accordingly the advantage of the 'grape' metaphor should be a willingness to take individual regional characteristics into consideration (ibid.).

Waterhout furthermore interprets the 'banana' and the 'grapes' as being two generically speaking different types of images. He argues that the former should be understood in descriptive terms, whereas the latter should be perceived in normative terms (Waterhout, 2001: 10). These two iconic images have played an important part in the shaping of the ESDP. Waterhout sees the ESDP as performing a narrative function in moving from the iniquitous centre-periphery model towards the more polycentric pattern of the grapes:

> In the ESDP the European territory is described in the vein of the blue banana, with a core and a periphery. However, the ESDP vision (only described verbally) reflects much more the idea of the European bunch of grapes, with several core zones. So, what the ESDP actually did is bridge the gap between the archetypes of European spatial conceptualisation: the blue banana and the European bunch of grapes and all the connotations that belong to them.
>
> (Waterhout, 2001: 16)

We would certainly not disagree on the perception of the 'banana' as one of great wealth and economic prosperity (and of congestion and internal unequal

ACCESSIBILITY, INFRASTRUCTURE AND TRANSPORT

Islas Canarias
Açores
Madeira
Guadeloupe
La Réunion
Guyanne (scale 50 %)
Martinique

Scale 1 : 12.000.000
0 250 500 km

NOTA BENE: This representation is only an illustration of certain spatial elements referred to in the text of the First Official Draft of the E.S.P.D., presented at the informal meeting of ministers responsible for spatial planning of the Member States of the European Union in Noordwijk, 9/10 june 1997. They do in no way reflect actual policy proposals and there is no guarantee that the elements displayed here are exhaustive or entirely accurate.

source: Eurostat, ESDP

main european networks
road network
conventional rail network
high speed rail network (existing and planned)

main traffic axes
mainly road congested corridor
congestion corridor for all transport modes
major airports (community connecting points)
major seaport (area)

multimodal transhipment terminals
road rail terminal
inland waterway terminal
sea terminal

accessibility
peripheral and remote area
ultra-peripheral area

size in thousands of inhabitants
+ than 10,000
+ than 5,000
2,000 to 5,000
1,000 to 2,000
500 to 1,000
200 to 500
100 to 200
50 to 100
- than 50

metropolitan region
international level agglomerations / cities
national level cities or large towns
regional level towns

Plate 1 Accessibility, infrastructure and transport in the draft ESDP (Noordwijk version).

Source: CSD, 1997.

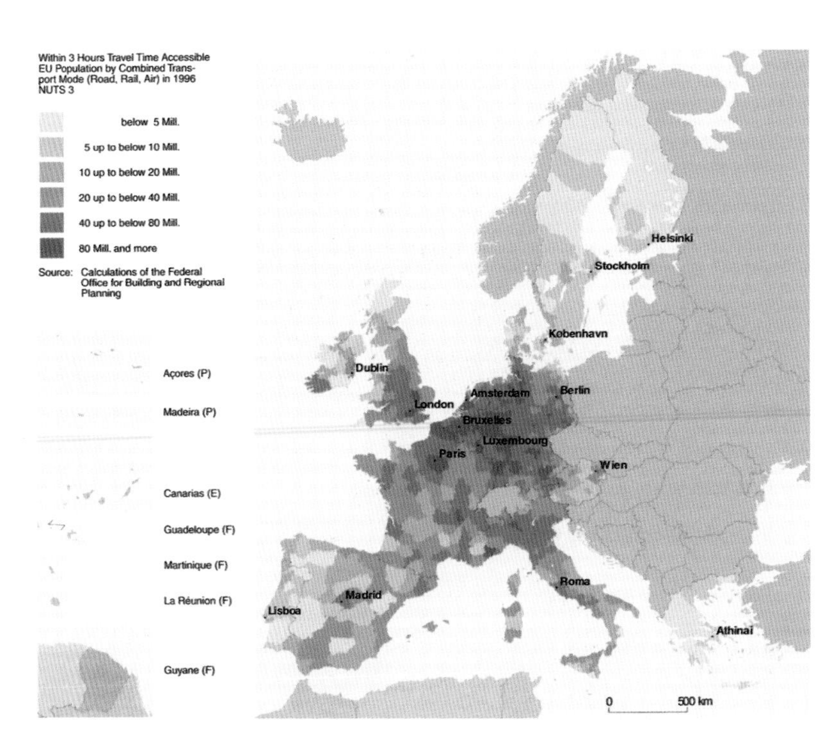

Plate 2 Accessibility in the final ESDP.

Source: CSD, 1999: 70.

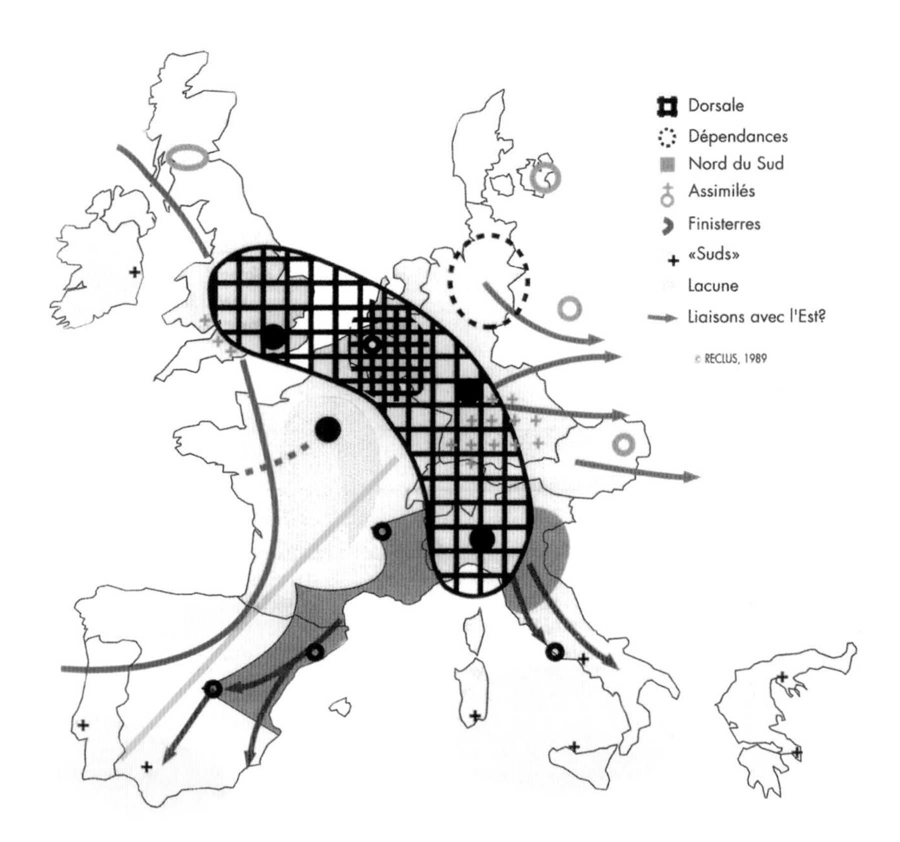

Plate 3 The 'Blue Banana'.

Source: Brunet, 1989. Reproduced by kind permission of DATAR.

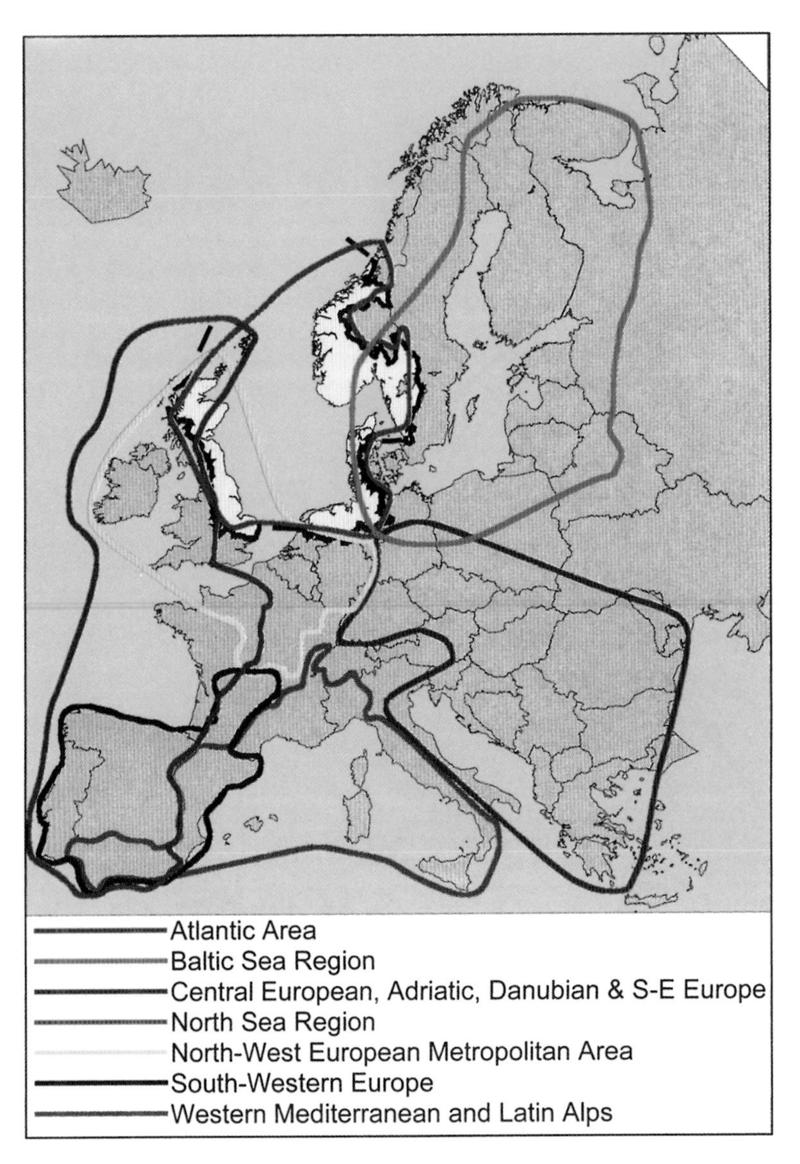

Plate 4 The North Sea INTERREG Region: part of a new transnational layer of vision-making.

Source: VWG, 2000b: 1.

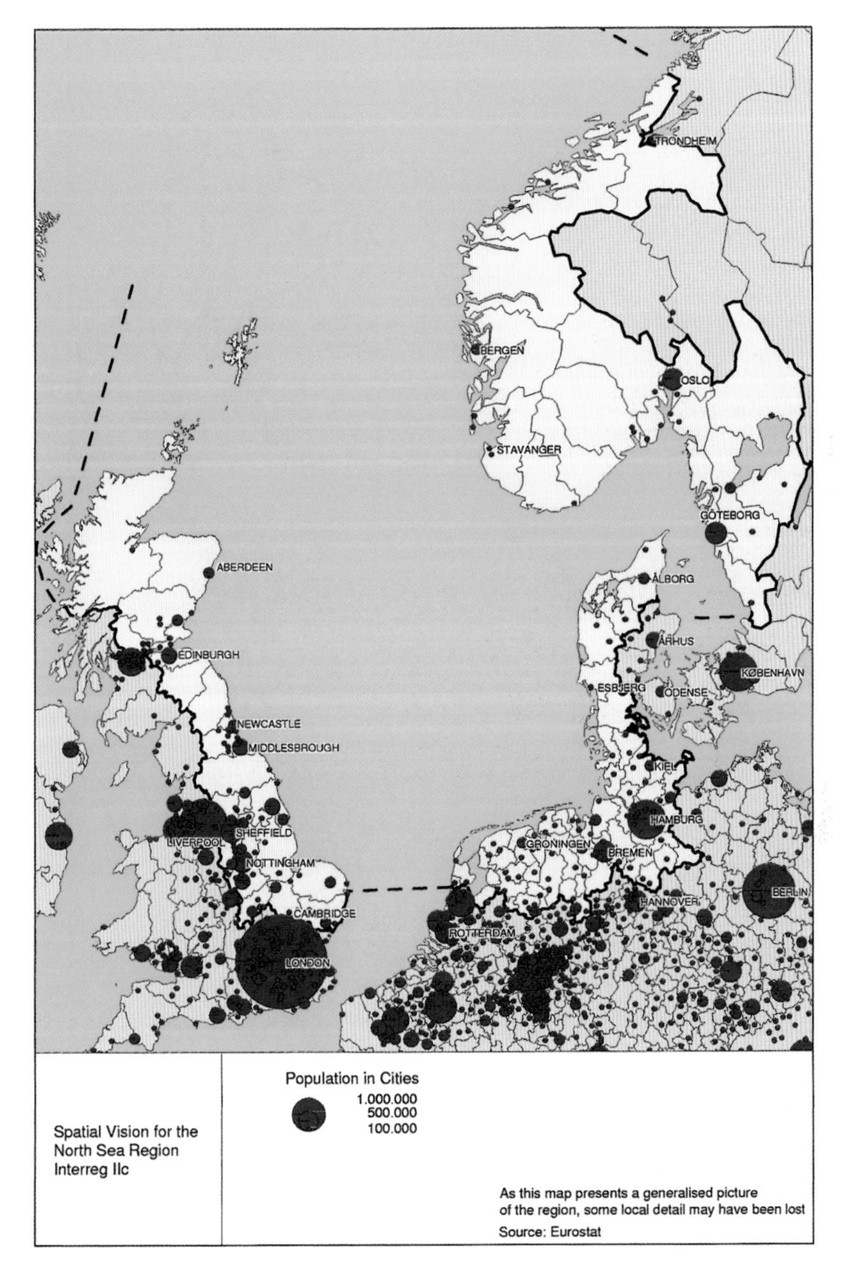

Plate 5 The urban system in the North Sea Region.

Source: VWG, 2000a: 14.

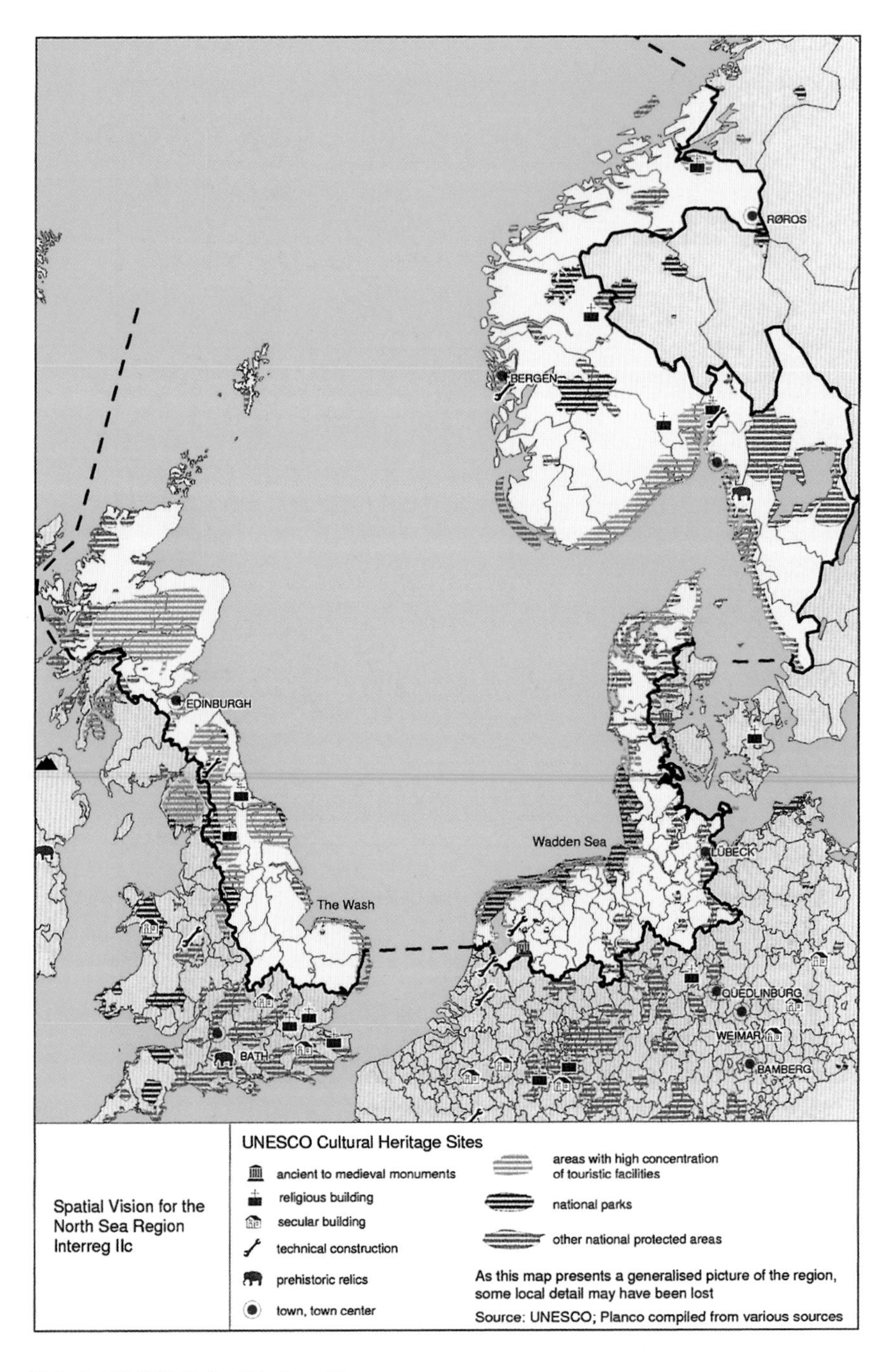

Plate 6 UNESCO Cultural Heritage Sites.

Source: VWG, 2000b: 19.

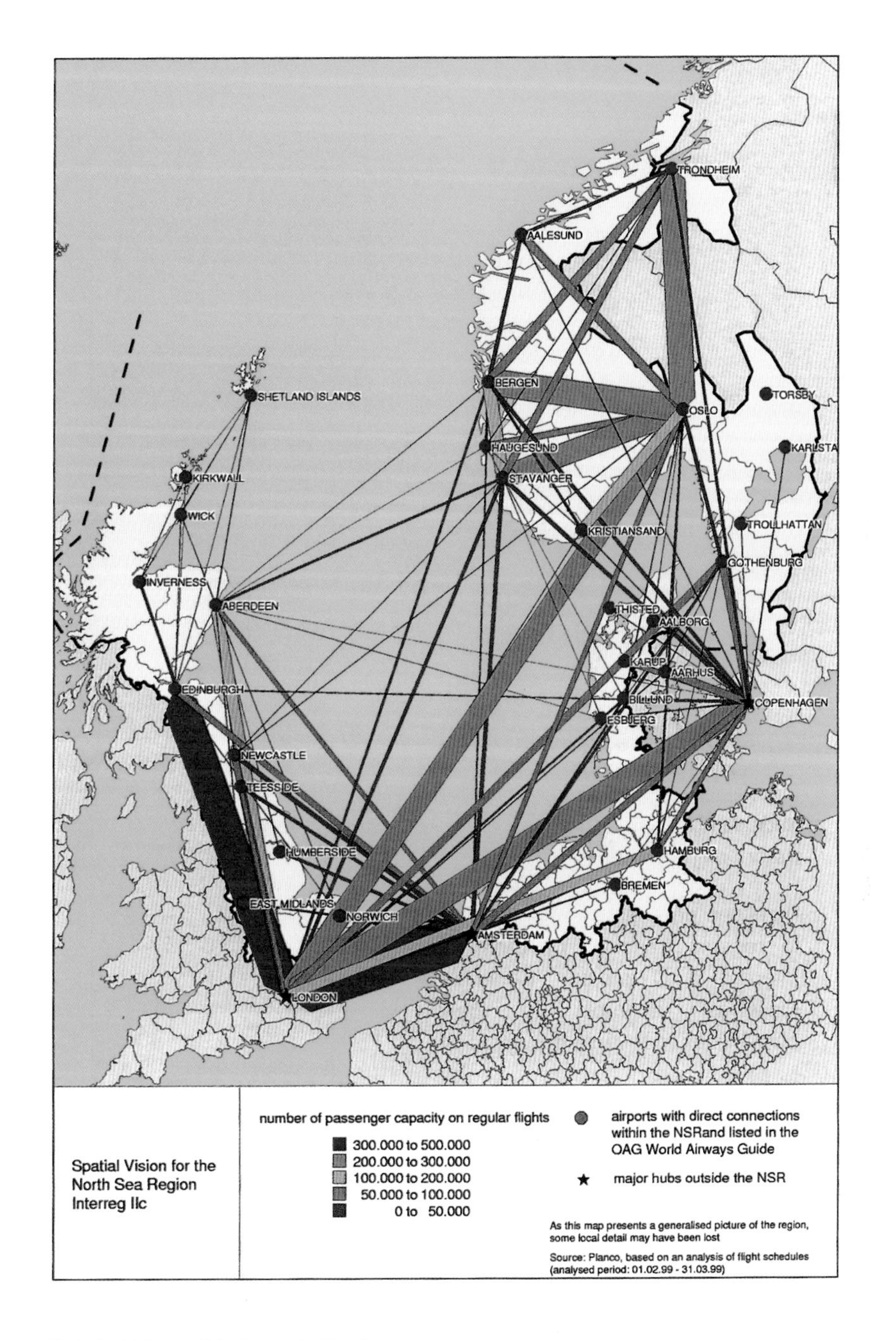

Plate 7 Air links within the North Sea Region.

Source: VWG 2000a: 25.

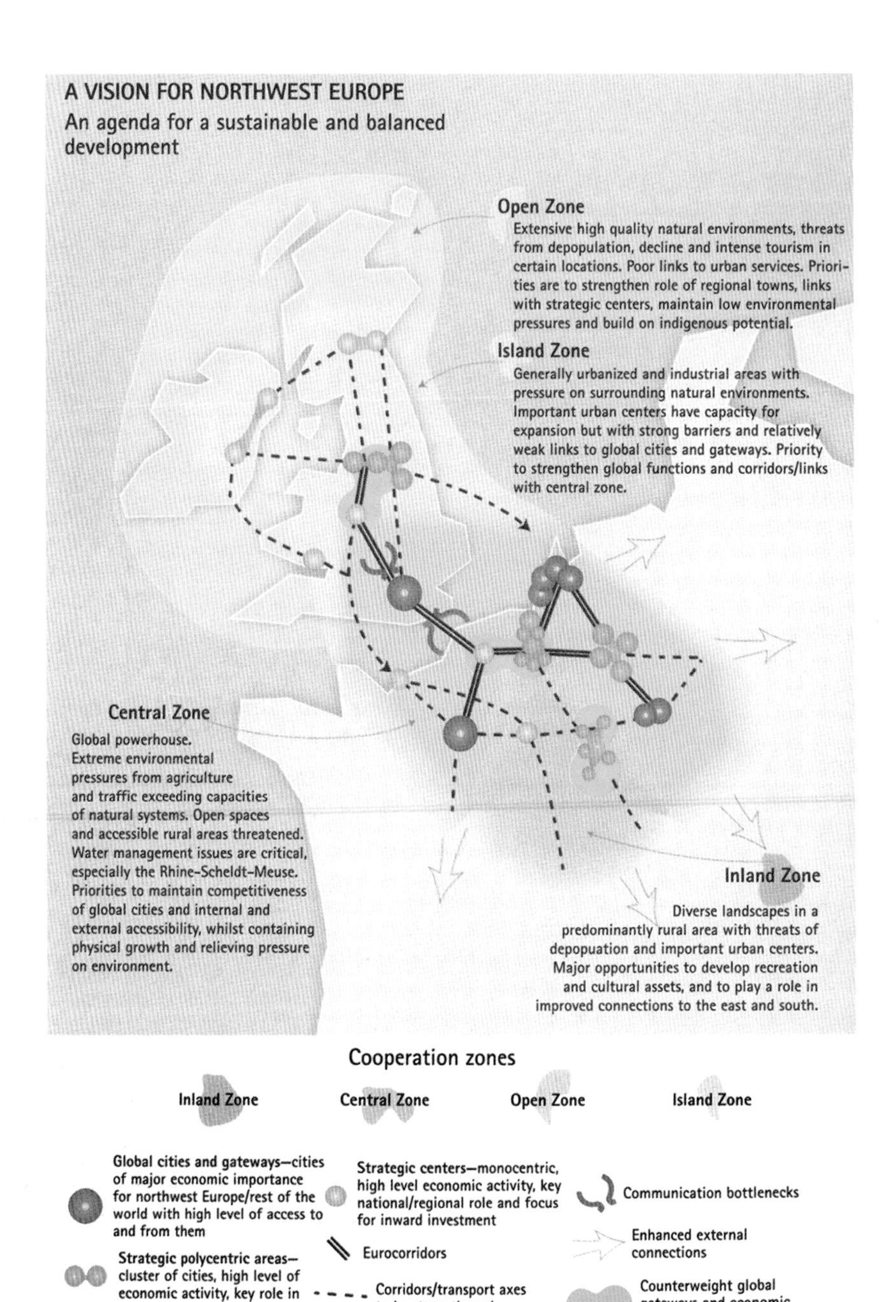

Plate 8 A vision for Northwest Europe.

Source: NWMA Spatial Vision Group, 2000: 30.

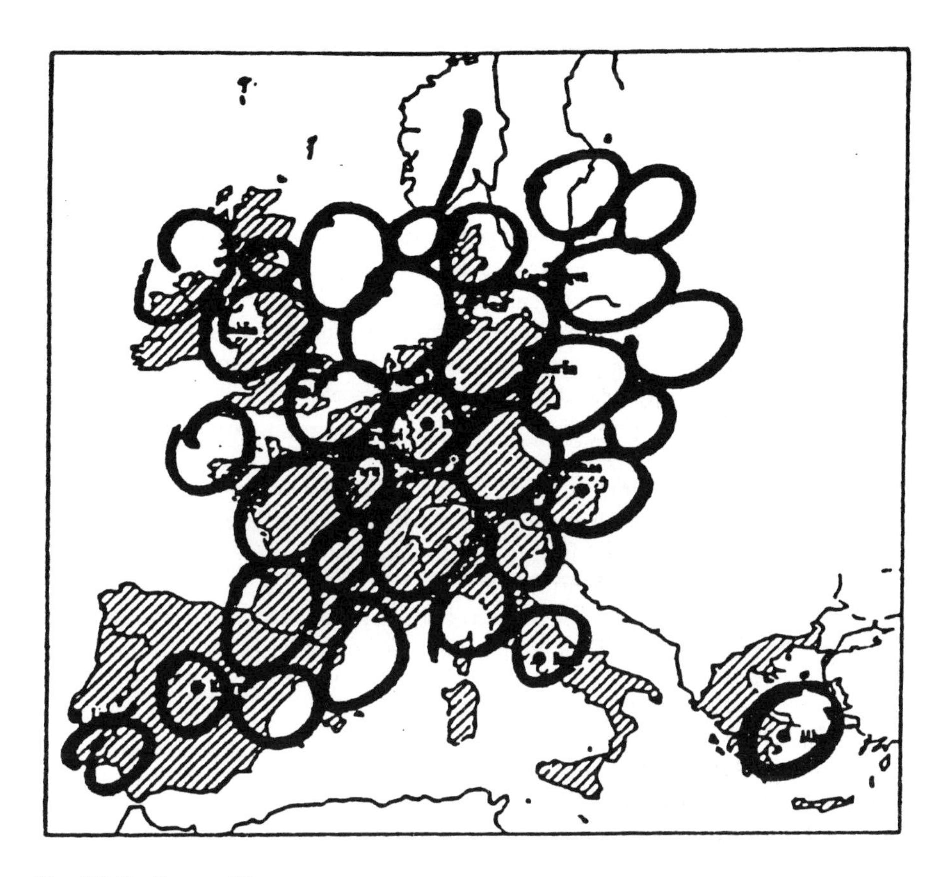

Map 5.3 The Europe of Grapes.

Source: Kunzmann and Wegener, 1991. Reproduced by kind permission of Kunzmann.

development). But this distinction is too simple since it ignores the normative way in which the blue banana was graphically presented. The blue banana represented the existing growth centre of the EU, but it was accompanied by the Nord du sud – a second banana centred on the Mediterranean arc of EU members, which articulated very strikingly a proposal for channelling future growth, into a second core region rather than across a more devolved network. This interpretation is of course open for contestation as one could see the 'grapes' as the antidote to the 'banana disease'. However, one needs only to look at the way that the 'banana' image is perceived in Scandinavia or in the southern European member states to realise that it is more than a cool factual statement of how things are. Furthermore, and to our minds even more seriously, understanding images and metaphors as 'descriptive' and thus purely objective is to miss the point of how spatial representations in words and images always carry the potential for normative understandings and power laden strategies. That these do not simply implement themselves instrumentally in the minds of the beholders should not mislead us into believing in their neutrality.

Williams also seems to argue in line with Waterhout, as he stresses that the images and metaphors should not be understood in deterministic ways:

> Metaphors such as these are not predictions, and certainly not predestination, though people sometimes talk in these terms. This is especially true of the blue banana, which is sometimes taken to imply that all other areas are doomed. They really should be regarded simply as ways of describing the spatial structure of Europe in a manner that can be easily grasped, which may help people who find it difficult to think in European terms to gain a sense of spatial positioning, and may also help with place marketing.
> (Williams, 1996a: 97)

Obviously the wording alone and the metaphorical quality of the spatial image may not exercise causal forces on the complex field of social agents within planning across Europe. However, having said this we would argue that these images do portray key spatial rationalities that are contested. The tension or relation between the images articulates the struggle between alternative spatial rationalities. These metaphors are linked as elements in a spatial narrative. They are not simply descriptive, but are semantic tools for sliding back and forth around this more or less tangible spatial imagination of Europe.

Taking the images downscale

From the spatial level of the EU we will now track some of the spatial images generated at a lower spatial scale, which draw upon the conceptualisation and framing set out in the ESDP. Returning to NorVISION (VWG, 2000b), we find a number of spatial images and representations that vividly illustrate a downscaling to the transnational level of the ESDP's reasoning, part of a new transnational layer of vision building made possible within the INTERREG regions (Plate 4).

The urban system, for example, is represented by a map showing the existing urban settlements in the transnational region (Plate 5). The framing of the urban as we find it in this map of the North Sea Region is interesting as it shows how the existing urban systems within the various subnational regions and countries can no longer be comprehended in isolation from their neighbours. The map seems to suggest that we are dealing with a less urbanised region, where the extent of urban agglomeration is different from, for example, its neighbouring region of the Northwestern Metropolitan Area (NWMA) – another INTERREG megaregion. The largest urban nodes in the NSR are comprised of the urban field of mid-England, and of the metropolitan area of Hamburg in Germany. Accordingly the network of small towns is quite dense in major parts of the NSR, and acts not only as important regional 'engines of growth' but also as 'communities with identity that extends beyond their retail and commercial role' (VWG, 2000b: 15).

Another central theme of the monotopic discourse is that of the environment, an issue represented and mapped in NorVISION by means of the UNESCO Cultural Heritage Sites map (Plate 6). From this representation it appears that mapping the environment is done with an eye to the tourism industry as well. So side-by-side with the mapping of protected areas, we find the areas with high concentrations of leisure and tourist facilities.

As with the spatial representation of the urban, from a mobility perspective the transnational region is placed within a larger network of nodes and flows in Europe. A strong spatial image of the North Sea Region and its place as a transnational region of flows is found in the map picturing regular air links in the region (Plate 7). This representation of air connections shows a fundamental aspect of this new transnational space: namely, that what used to be understood as a barrier to social interaction, the North Sea itself, is now articulated in the opposite manner, as a bridging space which integrates the region. Interestingly, this imagery of mobility in the NSR exemplifies how the downscaling of the ESDP can be used to re-imagine a unitary and homogeneous transnational space within the wider European territory.

Persuasive mobility and cross-border urbanism

Another European transnational region that can be understood in relation to the ESDP's framing, is the Danish-Swedish cross-border Øresund region. In Chapter 8 we will deal with this case in more detail. It is sufficient here to highlight the way the region is represented in spatial maps dealing with the twin themes of mobility and the urban.

Certain images have been used to help reproduce the idea of the Øresund region, and to encourage regional organisation and mobility. Here we find new representational practices, where the region is reconfigured as one mobility zone rather than as two zones separated by the barrier of the Øresund which until now has been the most difficult to transcend – the nation state border.

The picturing of the region as a unified transnational urban mobility region is only possible due to a larger infrastructure tying the region together. In other words, the fixed link across the Øresund serves the purpose of constructing the urban as one transnational metropolitan area and urban node (Map 5.4). However, it is important to note here that the bridge across the sound also fits the 'bigger picture' as it is one of the TEN-T priority projects contributing to the seamless territory of Europe.

A final example of mapping the transnational is to be found in the case of the North West European Metropolitan Region. An INTERREG project coined around one of the most urbanised areas in the EU territory – 'Europe's main

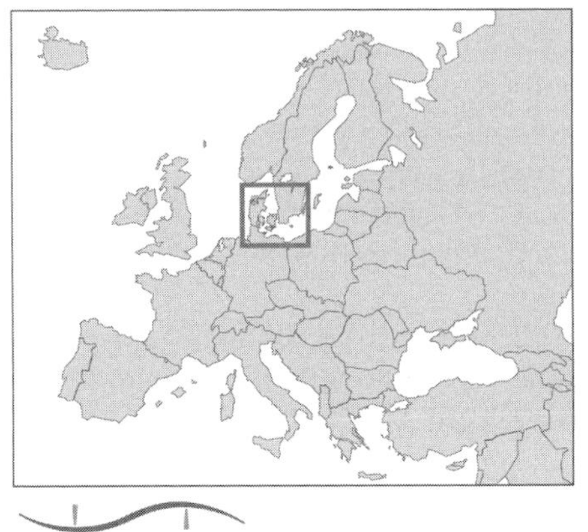

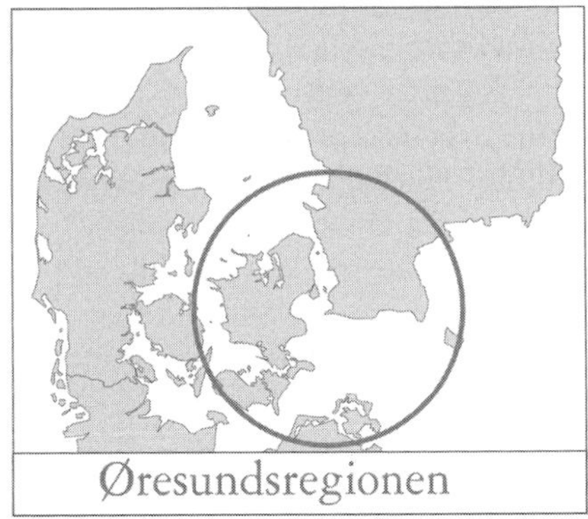

Map 5.4 The Øresund Region.

Source: Øresund Konsortiet

powerhouse' (Doucet, 2002: 61). Starting out as an INTERREG IIC project termed the Northwestern Metropolitan Area (NWMA) this project was continued as an INTERREG IIIB project titled North West Europe (NWE).

In parallel with the NSR project of NorVISON, NWE produced a spatial vision. However, noticeable differences occur as this vision in a very self-conscious manner proclaims to be more than a mere 'mini-ESDP' (Doucet, 2002: 70). As a direct consequence the vision not only produced a map of its territory, but it also produced a much more daring and outspoken normative projection than we would find in the NSR's spatial vision. So the Vision Working Group of the NWE produced a highly stylised map showing the core area of urban Europe and its division into four categories: Inland Zone, Central Zone, Open Zone, and Island Zone (Plate 8).

Interestingly the reason for the clearly non-urban labels of 'Open Zone' and 'Island Zone' was that the whole of the UK ended up being part of the INTERREG project. On closer inspection the map evidently embodies the more iconographic style developing as a new trend of policy map-making in the EU. It is operating with global cities, gateways and strategic polycentric areas linked by the network of mobility flows in the Eurocorridors. Furthermore, strategic centres with a monocentric structure are identified. Clearly the idea of an urban core and a rural periphery reflects not only the vision of urban centrality but also the identification of the 'Open Zone' as an 'extensive high quality environment', threatened by depopulation and poor links to urban service. Difficult as it may be to offer a homogenous vision for such a diverse transnational region, the map adopts a clear position when compared to the few (and indicative) maps in the final ESDP, and the more diffuse practice of infographics to which we now turn.

Infographics: the new science of spatial representation

The latest development of a new spatial vocabulary of concepts and images within the EU spatial policy discourse is being carried out under the aegis of the 'Study Programme on European Spatial Planning' (SPESP).[3] Apart from stressing a need for more comparable data and more solid knowledge of the spatial development of the European territory the document introduces an interesting new concept that illustrates the power-knowledge dimension. The rationale behind the SPESP is amongst other things to develop alternative graphic images based on the ESDP policy aims (SPESP, 2000: 93). Furthermore, the significance of being involved in the SPESP and ESPON is the opportunity to influence the struggle for redefining the structural fund targets and areas, especially with an eye to enlargement.

Thus in pursuit of a deeper spatial understanding the process must be supplemented with 'infography' (SPESP, 2000: 13). Behind this new concept lies a very explicit acknowledgement of the importance of spatial representations that has a deliberate twist away from 'realistic' description. In so recognising the rhetorical and powerful importance of spatial representations it is said that in recent years, numerous symbolic representations of the European territory have been created. Often they have presented mind-catching illustrations, which have served as powerful tools for both shaping attitudes and visualising policy aims. Some images even have become policy icons (SPESP, 2000: 13). Furthermore there is a large appendix with very colourful and rhetorical maps as an example for the future 'knowledge policy' within the SPESP and the ESDP.

According to the SPESP document the high level of national sensitivity towards how 'territorial policies' are communicated at European level led to this new approach to spatial images and map making (SPESP, 2000: 94). As the work mandate was to produce a 'collection of visualisations of European spatial policy using new alternative methods to represent the policy aims of the ESDP' the discipline of 'infographics' was born (SPESP, 2000: 94). In this sense the images should illustrate the corresponding political text of the ESDP, while explaining the ESDP policy in a more 'user-friendly manner' (SPESP, 2000: 95). So the issue was how policies can be communicated effectively, and honestly, to people (as the document says). Methodologically the new approach hinges on cartographic rationality combined with infographic creativity in order to fuse a rational and objective representation of reality with an artistically oriented procedure (SPESP, 2000: 95).

However, the new concept of 'infographics' indicates a conscious and deliberate framing of knowledge that challenges mere 'realistic' spatial representations based on scientific rationality as laid down by the Renaissance map with its focus on objectivity, practicability and functionality (Harvey, 1989: 245). Infographic framing can be seen as a rhetorical and creative way of reproducing the policy discourse in new forms of spatial representation, and as such is a vivid expression of the intimate link between the visual and the textual. Through such devices, the new spatial discourses give top priority to propositions that place cities as growth motors in an increasingly global world. The multiple references to the questions of identity, multiplicity and otherness appear merely as a legitimising vocabulary:

> Infographics could certainly be a powerful tool in conveying a territorial strategy in a world where the role of visual media is constantly increasing, though some care in the use of political images should however, be observed in view of the vagaries of 20th Century European history.
>
> (Bengs, 2002: 11)

Map 5.5 for example shows how, in the ESDP, infographics are used to articulate the core concepts of polycentricity and networks. These images represent European space in a very impressionistic way, where particular places are less important (in fact unidentifiable) than the ideas about the ways these spaces are organised in a polycentric development system. The message is one of balance and harmony, but also one of homogeneity. These new infographic practices in EU spatial policy making mark a clear shift towards less 'realistic' mapping, communicating broad visions rather than spatially accurate proposals, reflecting a wider trend in strategic spatial planning.

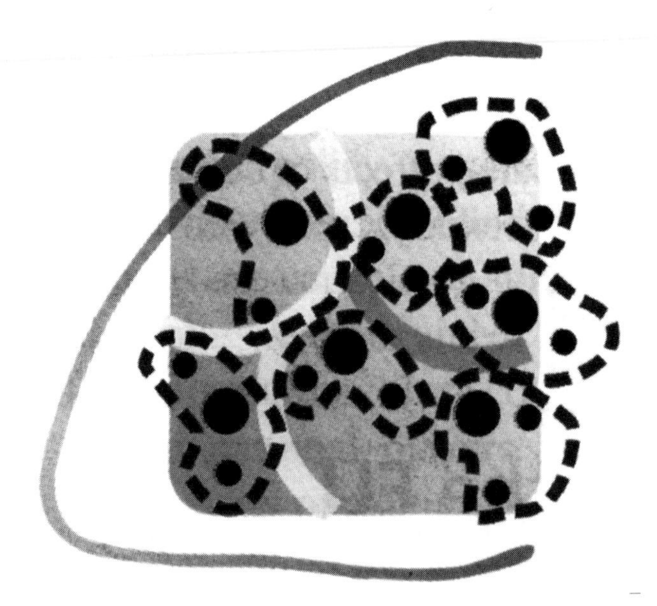

Map 5.5 Imagining polycentricity.

Source: CSD, 1999.

Being on the map: concluding remarks

The images analysed in this chapter show how different types of images can play different roles in policy making. We have seen how images are used to capture and frame moments in political struggles over policy ideas and institutional responses. Images can be used to press a case for a policy or institutional response, and to frame problems for policy attention.

In policy processes, images are commonly used to frame representations of 'what is out there' in particular ways which suggest certain responses. The image of a shrinking Europe (Map 5.1), for example, carries a powerful rhetorical force, which conceals the strategic power play behind its making, and presents a persuasive offer of seamless freedom of mobility (if, of course, the policy is implemented). This is an image that now appears 'of its time', as we enter a more cautious and unstable period where the European project, and the extent of integration in all its forms, are under renewed scrutiny. Images may also reflect consensus among a coalition of interests, or may communicate uncertainty, unresolved tensions, stalemate and compromise. The proposals map for the trans-European road network (Map 5.2) shows how an apparently unified image of networked mobility across European space is in fact the product of complex multi-level power struggles. The maps of infrastructure proposals found in the draft ESDP documents articulate the coherent discourse of a 'Europe of flows', but are once again shaped within a contested field of divergent spatial representations. Thus the image of flows is most striking in the draft ESDP (Plate 1) and is watered down in the analytical map of accessibility that appears in the final ESDP (Plate 2). Here we see how even the presence (or absence) of images can indicate something about the extent of consensus among policy actors.

The images of the banana (Plate 3) and the grapes (Map 5.3) together capture a much broader discursive struggle than seems apparent from an examination of their graphic form. Their juxtaposition symbolises a tension between centralised and decentralised urban development that recurs at various spatial scales and across spatial policy processes. The example of Denmark serves to illustrate this tension well, as national spatial policy was marked by a dispute between the decentralised 'star city sketch' versus the agglomeration-oriented notion of urban development along the motorway structure called the 'big H' (Jensen, 1999). Notwithstanding our earlier comments, Faludi and Waterhout see these iconic images of European space in a dialectical relation to each other (Faludi and Waterhout, 2002: 12). Williams even stresses the potential for the 'blue banana' image to become the backbone of a EU spatial planning doctrine (Williams, 1996a: 97).

As we moved downscale, we found other interesting ways of mapping European space. In the NorVISION document the key issues of mobility, the urban, and the environment were highlighted in a series of maps imagining and representing the transnational level in new ways, and thus adding to the multiple mappings of monotopic Europe.

In the case of the Øresund region (Map 5.4), we saw how a transnational region is materialising not only in terms of hard infrastructures, but also as a coherent unit within which people move in accordance with a new codified perception of the region. The fixed link across the Øresund serves the purpose of constructing the urban as one transnational metropolitan area and urban node putting the region into the 'bigger picture', as it is one of the TEN-T priority projects contributing to the monotopic and seamless territory of Europe.

From our analysis, we can identify several reasons why, as policy making progresses, images may change their nature and lose definition, become more indicative and impressionistic, or even disappear altogether. These reasons include the need for images to play a role in working towards consensus, where the precision of detailed maps of proposals is contested. The changing representation of accessibility from the early TENs proposals maps to the drafting ESDP illustrates this quite clearly. But they also include the need to find iconic images that can carry perhaps quite simple, but potentially epistemic, framings of space and spatial relations. The final images discussed in this paper are examples of this new form of spatial representation within the European spatial policy discourse. The way that polycentricity is imagined within the emerging field of 'infographics' (Map 5.5) is to our minds a powerful new field of spatial representation which we will most certainly see more of in the future. The work of the Study Programme in European Spatial Planning on images shows clearly that the new spatial policy discourse is concerned not only with being reproduced in words and concepts but also in visual terms. Interestingly, it appears that representing accessibility and mobility, which at the EU level is pinned heavily to the idea of networks, remains unresolved. Infographic endeavour has as yet failed to produce a new iconic image of mobility in European space comparable to the blue banana and the iconic policy metaphor of polycentricity.

Several points are to be drawn from this analysis. On the conceptual and theoretical side this firstly speaks in favour of widening the notion of spatial policy discourse beyond text. On the policy side the lesson to be learned, as Morley and Robins (1995: 189) have argued, is that in the new European Community, the matter of territorial coherence and integrity is paramount. Here infography has become useful in articulating relations and changes that can not be represented in traditional maps, where the albeit limited experience at the transnational level has shown that political agendas quickly overrun any attempts to debate policy issues. Each of these images focuses on aspects of spatial development in Europe, either as a deliberate expression of power and tactics or as a reflective conceptualisation of spaces and places. Furthermore, the role of metaphors is striking, and suggests that we should not only think of spatial policy images in terms of their visual qualities, as they are more often than not linked to a complex linguistic and metaphorical play of signification. Thus they 'carry meaning' by fusing words and pictures.

So we would argue that maps are not only to be seen as a 'planners tool'. As we learn from history, the discipline of cartography has (together with the other great discipline of 'spatial order': geography) played a major role in the process of nation building. Thus the new practices of map-making in the European Union may be seen in parallel with the political project of 'building Europe': 'The new Europe is being constructed on much the same symbolic terrain as the old nation-states of the last two centuries. Flags, anthems, passports, trophies, medals and maps are all icons for evoking the presence of the emergent state' (Shore, 2000: 50).

Maps and discursive images have clearly facilitated discussion, and have become part of the new vocabulary of European spatial policy. As such they may be regarded as a platform for enhanced mutual understanding (Tewdwr-Jones and Williams, 2001). However it is important to maintain a critical view of the use of these images. Refined images may carry particular meanings within a sophisticated but exclusive policy world. The images and the meanings conveyed by them may simply reproduce a hegemonic discourse, or they may be contested. Alternatively, they may remain more open to interpretation, and encourage a subtle and less clear re-imagining of Europe as a transnational space. In different ways, then, the top-down process of reproducing a spatially homogenising and integrating discourse, may be pursued through the deployment of analytical maps and iconographic images which together encourage the acceptance and adoption of new spatial agendas. What is clear is that images are part of the armoury of persuasion used by interest groups and policy makers operating in the multi-level arenas of European spatial planning. Images are clearly useful tools for persuading policy makers to notice certain things, politicians to understand in a particular way, and citizens to re-conceptualise their relationships with the space around them.

In summary, in the new policy language and images we have traced the existence of an intertextual field where ideas are contested, and a hegemonic language and associated imagery emerges, which neutralises and masks oppositions and uncertainties. This is the policy discourse of monotopia. It raises the question of how such a discourse could create the conditions for its own survival and reproduction, in ways that have become embedded, or institutionalised, in practice. This is the question we turn to next.

6.1 Rolling out the TEN-T.

Source: CEC, 1994c.

Part Three
Spatial Practices

In this section of the book, we explore how the discourse of monotopia is being reproduced across multi-level spatial policy processes. First we analyse the institutional design and new forms of governance, focusing in particular on the power relations within the practices of comitology and infranational governance, and consider the extent to which the EU's capacity to act is limited by its apparent lack of legal powers in the area of spatial policy. Next, we critically analyse the tools which are being created to make transnational spatial policy making possible. Here we see the quest for new tools to support a new transnational planning system, and consequently the construction of new types of knowledge which frame European space in novel ways. Then we consider more fully the nature of 'Europeanisation', as we reflect on how EU spatial policy ideas are being contested within existing national and new transnational policy arenas.

Chapter 6

Shaping a pan-European spatial planning system?

> Rien est possible sans les institutions: rien est possible sans les hommes.
>
> (Monnet, 1976)

> This all raises the critical issue of who owns the ESDP. Strictly, the answer remains that it is owned by the CSD. In Weiler's terms, therefore, it is owned by an infranational body not directly accountable to any formal institution either at member state or EU level, although its individual members are accountable to the governments they represent.
>
> (Williams, 2000: 363)

> The Commission stands for integration, and this puts it at loggerheads with member states. So the Commission has few friends, and the present groundswell of public opinion directed against European integration is certain to reinforce this antagonism built into the institutional architecture of the European Union.
>
> (Faludi, 2000b: 254)

Introduction

In this chapter we will explore how, within and around the policy process, fierce struggles have taken place over the construction of the institutions that would embed the visions, language and images of European space in new practices. These struggles have centred on sensitive issues, including the role and powers of the EU and the new transnational institutions to make and implement policy. Following our analytical framework, we are interested here in how the new policy language and imagery of European space is contested and reproduced across multi-level policy processes as it gives shape to a new field of practice. Thus we need to consider the nature of the policy processes: the different interests and the power dynamics within and between them, and crucially how these relations bear on the production of spatial knowledge within policy making. How do certain policy ideas or strategies become hegemonic in some processes but not in others? Although some of this is inherent in the language and imagery of policy documents, what is required is a broader view of the policy process that focuses on institutions and actions – in other words on spatial practices.

Drawing from the perspective of discourse theory, one expects to find the operation of interests and the consequent power relations bearing on the construction of institutions, and of institutional practices. The policy process is problematised as an arena of 'guerrilla warfare of power struggles' (Dyrberg, 1997: 104), rather than as a manifestation of top-down sovereignty.

It is when we start to look at the challenge of institutionalisation that we begin to see big differences between TEN-T and the ESDP on key questions. Here we focus on TEN-T in some depth as it seems to be doing its 'own thing'. The articulation of TEN-T policy is found to be continuing in isolation from the spatial policy process. The White Paper on Transport reinforces the emphasis on TEN-T, and makes very weak links to spatial planning at all, and no reference to the ESDP. However, the reverse is the case for the ESDP, which refers massively to TEN-T. One of the most strongly contested issues being played out across the policy arenas is the question of competency, and in particular the extent to which the ESDP process will give the EU any power in spatial planning, particularly since the field of EU spatial planning is not legally founded in the Treaties of the European Union. In its own terms the ESDP has no legal force, and is to be seen as a basis only for voluntary actions (CSD, 1999: 35). However a conflation in argumentation, which we need to tease apart in this chapter, seems to be that because the ESDP is not legally binding, and spatial planning is not specifically written into the Treaties, the EU has no legal competence in this field. From the case of TEN-T, we can clearly see that the question of competency is more complicated than this. Here, even though written into the Maastricht Treaty, serious problems of implementation have occurred, and one chapter of the White Paper on Transport, dealing with 'missing links', stands as a political commentary on these failings (CEC, 2001c). Clearly TEN-T illustrates both the complexity in the Treaty, but also the huge implementation problems.

So by highlighting this institutional question we uncover an immensely complex issue which dissolves the simple binary argumentation surrounding formal/informal decision-making capacity. We see this distinction as being unproductive, limiting understanding of how policy issues and practices can have real effects without being formalised. This places the spotlight on the issue of power as performativity rather than power as being legally legitimised and institutionalised. We develop this argument by exploring a number of cases seen as institutionalising practices of spatial policy discourse. The first case concerns the struggle to prioritise certain projects within TEN-T. Second, we address the issue of TEN-T and the competency argument. Third, the process of drafting the ESDP and its importance for the institutionalisation issue is looked into. Fourth, we address the case of INTERREG as yet another example of the practices that frame the question of a European spatial planning system.

Practice 1 – The Christophersen list: a struggle for decision power

First we will turn once more to the trans-European transport network, where we will focus on one of the most contested issues: how would certain international routes be prioritised, and where would the decision-making power lie over the development of these corridors?

A particular feature of the early stages of TEN-T policy development, following the 1993 Council decision to adopt outline maps of the different modal networks, was the creation of a group headed by Henning Christophersen (then Commission Vice-President), which would be responsible for identifying priority projects from the many routes identified in these draft network plans. The aim of this high-level working group was to eliminate obstacles to progress, and to 'facilitate rapid political agreement' on TEN-T (CEC, 1994b). Membership of this group was restricted to representatives of the (then) twelve heads of state, and the President of the European Investment Bank (EIB) (Sir Brian Unwin). The Christophersen Group developed a focus on the priority projects, holding seminars which involved 'in principle all interested partners: national and regional authorities, promoters, financial institutions, industrialists, users, etc' (CEC, 1994b: 51). The prioritised projects have become central in the TEN-T debate, benefiting from closer study of the international corridor context of individual projects, and being placed in the front line for Community financial support.

The Commission's White Paper (CEC, 1993) and member states' interests were the basis for the priority list, with environmental protection stated as one of eight criteria for selection. However:

> Projects should comply with the Union's legislation regarding the protection of the environment. However, it is difficult to identify any concrete way in which environmental concerns altered the outcome of the prioritisation, apart from a bias towards high speed rail in the prioritised list. However, this was apparently not for environmental reasons, but 'reflects primarily that work [of the Group] is more advanced in certain transport modes than in others'.
>
> (CEC, 1994b: 94)

It is also worth noting that whilst the development of motorway networks across Europe has proceeded rapidly in recent years, there are significant technical and financial problems in creating a rail network, including inter-operability between national systems, and the current crisis of investment in European railways. This may have influenced a stronger Community focus on rail networks. The treatment of environmental risks by the Christophersen group has been criticised as 'a formal rather than substantial inclusion of environment interests in the debate' (Bina *et al.*, 1995). The cost of the eleven original priority projects was estimated at

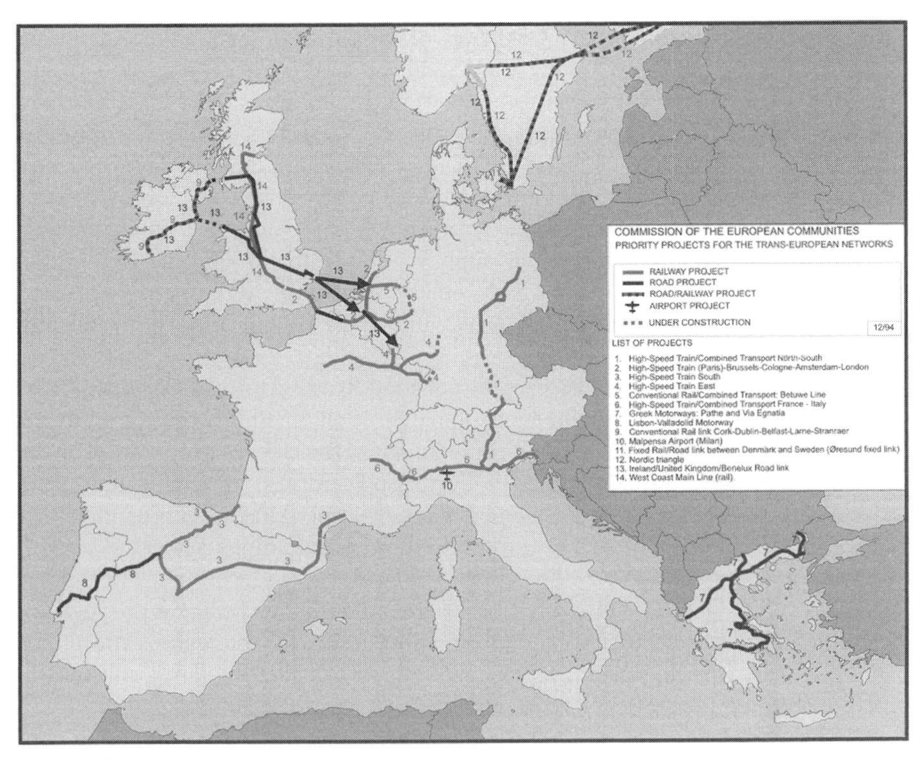

Map 6.1 Christophersen list of priority TEN-T projects.

ECU 68 billion over their lifetimes, requiring investment of ECU 4–6 billion per year. At the Essen Summit (December 1994) the Christophersen list was endorsed, and supplemented by a further three projects, reflecting in part the accession of Nordic nations, but also including the UK West Coast Main Line (rail), and the Ireland-UK-Benelux road link (Map 6.1).

The Council had used its powers to prioritise selected corridors for EU support shortly before the new institutional arrangements gave the Parliament co-decisional power over policy development. This action was to lead to a bitter dispute between Council and Parliament over control of the Christophersen list: 'and of course the new member states were having a slice of the action too, so it became a bit of a political carve up. And a political deal was done at Essen, and these projects were endorsed, whatever that means, the priority nature of these 14 projects was endorsed. And this was heads of state' (European Commission official). This difference was to lead to what has been described as a 'rather bloody co-decision and conciliation process'.

After 1994, the co-decision process provided the Parliament with new powers in decision-making over TEN-T, which it quickly used to voice concern about the undemocratic nature of the early stages of the process, strongly condemning in particular the failure to involve the Parliament in the Christophersen Group's work, or to provide information about its work. Inherent in the EP's position was the principle that TEN-T was properly within the competence of the Community, rather than being simply a concern of member states. Investment in infrastructure should therefore be tied to EU environmental conditions. They considered this to be fully compatible with subsidiarity, and a way of pursuing EU environmental and transport objectives. There was support for a formal role at the EU level in planning and implementing TEN-T. So the environmental amendments had become expressions of the tension between the Parliament and Member States (the Council).

As stated above, in the Parliament's Second Reading on 13 December 1995, the Parliament largely maintained its original position, including the commitment to SEA. The rapporteur, Wilhelm Piecyk, lamented the lack of co-operation by the Council of Ministers, and described its Common Position as 'miserable, unimpressive and provocative'. The Parliament's renewed position recommended 111 amendments to the Council's Common Position, maintaining its demand for SEA (European Parliament, 1995). The Commission, in response, continued its support for SEA (CEC, 1996d). However, other amendments, including a proposal for economic cost-benefit analysis and job creation studies for the regions affected by TEN-T, were not supported, on the grounds of subsidiarity. The position was that this should properly be the responsibility of Member States.

The Council again rejected the Parliament's amendments, triggering conciliation between Parliament and Council. This final stage in the development of policy guidelines became perhaps the most tangible arena of struggle for political power between the two institutions. In conciliation the stakes were high. The cost of not reaching agreement within the tight timetable for conciliation would have been to disrupt the legislative path of TEN-T, leading to a possible delay of several years. This was an unacceptable outcome for all parties, and consequently there was a shared commitment to finding a workable common position. However, the conciliation itself was anything but amicable, and resembled a naked power struggle rather than a consensus-seeking process.

Naked power

> So the whole conciliation meetings are just a kind of ballet. They're unreal. Absolutely unreal.
>
> (MEP)

In the conciliation process can be seen a flexing of the Parliament's muscles, as it asserts its new role in EU decision-making. The reaction was resistance from the Council (and therefore Member States) to this sharing of power. Tensions ran high, and resentment at the way the opposing parties had engaged in the process was expressed by interviewees from both institutions, and recorded in Parliamentary debates. MEPs roundly criticised the Council's attitude, feeling that it had not participated fully in the co-decision process: 'I would say to the Council that in future it is important that it works with Parliament rather than going off at a tangent and doing its own thing' (Brian Simpson MEP, reported in European Parliament, 1996).

Through most of the conciliation process, the Council was represented by fonctionnaires, and so there was no possibility for movement until the very end of the process. This was frustrating for the Parliament's delegation. The Commission supported the EP's amendments through these stages. But in the last 2 to 3 days their position shifted, and they tried to convince the Parliament to adopt the Council's position. The following quote from the MEP who represented the Parliament's Environment Committee in conciliation gives a flavour of the process and hints at the power relations at work. It concerns the way the article on SEA (Article 8) was treated in the last stages of conciliation:

> The worst meeting was the second formal meeting . . . which was held in the new Council of Ministers building across the road from the Parliament, which is a huge power building, a megalopolis, designed by Stalin and built by Mussolini. It's the most incredible big heavy granite and marble edifice with huge ceilings. And we kind of crept in looking like worms, and we were put in this enormous room with a big table half a mile long. After quite a long time of preparatory meetings in filed all these officials, three per country, and we had twelve of us from the Parliament, and two staff or something, and it was just like intimidation, total intimidation. And that was the point where they came up with another version [of Article 8], and we chucked that out as well, and we adjourned until three o'clock in the morning – we had started at about five o'clock in the afternoon. We adjourned, we were just in and out with little adjournments. And at three o'clock in the morning they came in and Neil [Kinnock] thought he had actually struck a deal, and he came in and made an impassioned speech for about an hour, and then the Italian [Transport] Minister made an impassioned speech for about an hour. And we didn't like it. We didn't think it was good enough. And about four thirty in the morning, ten to five it had got to, we just said no. And they all said 'right, all the compromises that have been made so far are off the table. Everything's off.' And they stormed out. And we thought 'shit we might have blown it here'.
>
> (MEP)

Another MEP captured the Council's attitude: 'They just felt "its nothing to do with you, you're just the Parliament. What the hell are you doing here?" Almost. This is from the bureaucrats as well. I don't mind being told by the minister that, but when I'm being told by bureaucrats from the member states' (MEP).

Two contested issues were at the heart of conciliation. As suggested above, both issues were about the power relations between Council and Parliament, as much as about their content. They were the treatment of the Christophersen priority list, and the inclusion of the article on SEA as a means of addressing environmental risks. A notable feature of the process was that it was heavily procedural, with no real opportunities for debating the issues at stake: 'it was this most horrendous nightmare of endurance, when you never really actually got round the table and shouted at each other' (MEP).

Who owns the Christophersen list?

The status of the Christophersen list had been a controversial issue throughout co-decision. In conciliation it became one of the crux issues. The original list of priority projects had been prepared under the aegis of the Council and Commission prior to co-decision, and the Parliament were keen to secure some decision-making power over these critical projects. Two issues were in dispute. First, whether priority projects should be agreed in co-decision, and therefore whether the list, agreed at the Essen Summit, needed to be validated by the Parliament. Second, and related to this, was whether the list actually placed any duty on member states to implement the priority projects, or whether it simply enabled the EU to take a proactive role in their development. These issues of decision-making control were hotly contested in conciliation.

At the heart of the arguments between the Council and Parliament over the Christophersen list was a dispute over the EU's proper role in national infrastructure planning and implementation. The Christophersen list was a mechanism for prioritising certain international corridors from the many TEN-T projects. These projects could be seen as important in an overall European context, but all also had special significance for their respective member states. For the Council, the matter of prioritisation was about implementation rather than policy, and so fell outside the co-decision process for the policy guidelines. This reading effectively meant that it was the member states, meeting in Council, that would agree the priority projects which would receive the lion's share of EU funding. The Parliament, however, saw the list as a crucial element of policy, and therefore of co-decision. However, Parliamentary involvement in prioritisation could be seen as giving the Parliament political power over which projects went ahead: an unprecedented role.

The Council's position was that according to Treaty Article 129d decisions regarding whether to build projects needed to be approved by Member States, rather than the European Parliament:

> You can't have the community forcing you to build a project, when it's actually going to pay ½ per cent towards the actual costs and you've got to pay the other 99½ per cent.
> (European Commission official)

> It was all about a power struggle on institutional matters about whether it was just going to be the 12 – or whatever – Essen projects . . . and whether any changes to

> the Essen system would have to come back to the Parliament to be agreed or whether they could be agreed by the Council of Ministers. And that became the whole stamping ground for the battle, all the stuff about whose power it was to decide. And that was a mega-stopper, because countries like France were basically saying we're not putting money into something that we're not deciding ourselves. And they started quoting clauses in Treaties and Articles and being legalistic and constitutional and stuff, and so 99 per cent of the stuff was this constitutional and legalistic mega-battle which was kind of all about power, and very important but immensely boring [laughs].
>
> (MEP)

So within conciliation, the interests of individual member states could be seen shaping the negotiations.

> Basically what happened was, at two o'clock in the morning Kinnock came in and beat them up for two hours and said 'you must stop being so stupid about this, we've got to get these guidelines through, you're never going to persuade the Council about this'. I mean you can see it from the point of view of member states, and there were quite a few others that were stronger than the UK on this point. They are not going to accept a community obligation to spend billions of their own money on their own projects. That's what it boiled down to.
>
> (European Commission official)

In the adopted policy guidelines, the priority projects are included in an annex. Different interpretations of this policy formulation exist. From the Parliament's perspective, the inclusion of the list is seen as a success, in that it brings the prioritisation of projects into the domain of co-decision. However, from other viewpoints, less weight is given to its inclusion:

> Well it's in here as a historical statement. It basically says it is noted that this list, that these projects, were endorsed at the European Council of Essen as being of a priority nature. But it doesn't stop anybody changing them, or make anybody do them. We were very careful to get legal advice on this. It is no obligation on member states to do any of these projects.
>
> (European Commission official)

The political nature of the agreed formula was clear: 'It was a presentational way of getting them off the hook . . . the Parliament were given a fig leaf. And some of them realised it was a fig leaf, and others pretended that they had got a victory' (European Commission official). Shortly after the conciliation process reached agreement, but before the guidelines were formally adopted, one event pointed to the different readings of the Christophersen outcome. At the Florence Summit, two member states, Spain and Portugal, sought to alter a joint project on the list from a motorway to a multi-modal project. The Parliament reacted angrily to the Council's action, pointing out that this should have been a matter for co-decision. The ambiguity of the outcome allowed both sides to claim success in the power struggles of conciliation, but events quickly exposed the lack of clarity: 'I think we don't see it as a victory for anybody frankly. . . . It was a political fudge at the end of the day and I think they all knew' (European Commission official).

Adding new links

Without doubt, the Christophersen list has been central to the EU's efforts to implement TEN-T since 1996, and has occupied a central position in the revision of the TEN-T policy guidelines. The first stage of this revision, set out in the chapter on 'bottlenecks' in the EU Transport White Paper, reveals new and renewed struggles over the contents of the Christophersen list – raising questions about how new member states and accession countries are represented in the locations and benefits of the priority projects.

Since the early days of the Christophersen list the priorities have shifted as new financial instruments, institutional set ups and strategies are being implemented. In the post-2001 situation especially a new financial instrument calls for attention. The following quote clearly shows how the priorities have shifted since 1996 in the light of poor implementation. First of all we see a proposed strengthening of the key financial instrument, doubling the EU contribution to the cost of certain projects. This is linked to particular projects that have faced difficulties in demonstrating 'trans-European added value'. This concept links back to the idea of community benefits discussed above, and shows the continuing difficulties faced in arguing a micro-economic case for the benefits of completing TEN-T from a European perspective.

> In this context, the list of 14 major priority projects adopted by the Essen European Council and included in the 1996 European Parliament and Council decision on the guidelines for the trans-European transport network must be amended. . . . and six or so new projects will be added (e.g. Galileo or the high-capacity railway route through the Pyrenees). To guarantee successful development of the trans-European network, a parallel proposal will be made to amend the funding rules to allow the Community to make a maximum contribution – up to 20% of the total cost – to cross-border railway projects crossing natural barriers but offering a meagre return yet demonstrable trans-European added value, such as the Lyon–Turin line already approved as a priority project by the Essen European Council. Projects to clear the bottlenecks still remaining on the borders with the candidate countries could qualify for the full 20%.
>
> (CEC, 2001c)

New institutional approaches to implementing TEN-T

For the time being, revision of TEN-T means concentrating on 'unblocking the main arteries'. Irrespective of the issue of priority infrastructure routes, the main problem is to solve the headache of funding, for which the White Paper makes concrete proposals, notably the pooling of funds.

What is envisaged here is a dramatic intervention in the way that member states manage their infrastructure investment. For example in the UK, major infrastructure projects are increasingly financed through private finance initiatives which leave operators to recoup the toll charges (e.g. the Skye Bridge and the Birmingham Northern Relief Road). The new proposals would mean a change of approach where toll revenues were put into a regional pot, which implies that the tolled infrastructure had to have already covered its own costs. This is a major weakness in the EU's proposals, since the UK Government's Private Finance Initiative approach, at least, is constructed as a way of financing project costs, and does not obviously yield extra revenue which might be directed towards a pool for funding other projects:

> Given the low level of funding from the national budgets and the limited possibilities of public/private partnerships, innovative solutions based on a pooling of the revenue from infrastructure charges are needed. To fund new infrastructure before it starts to generate the first operating revenue, it must be possible to constitute national or regional funds from the tolls or user charges collected over the entire area or on competing routes. The Community rules will be amended to open up the possibility of allocating part of the revenue from user charges to construction of the most environmentally-friendly infrastructure. Financing rail infrastructure in the Alps from taxation on heavy lorries is a textbook example of this approach, together with the charges imposed by Switzerland, particularly on lorries from the Community, to finance its major rail projects.
>
> (CEC, 2001c)

The 2001 EU White Paper on Transport is a powerfully political document, which sends out strong messages to member states and to other actors. According to this document:

> saturation on some major routes is partly the result of delays in completing trans-European network infrastructure. On the other hand, in outlying areas and enclaves where there is too little traffic to make new infrastructure viable, delays in providing infrastructure mean that these regions cannot be properly linked in. The 1994 Essen European Council identified a number of major priority projects which were subsequently incorporated into outline plans adopted by the Parliament and the Council, which provide a basis for EU co-financing of the trans-European transport network. The total cost was estimated at around EUR 400 billion at the time. This

> method of building up the trans-European network, as introduced by the Maastricht Treaty, has yet to yield all its fruits. Only a fifth of the infrastructure projects in the Community guidelines adopted by the Council and Parliament have so far been carried out. Some major projects have now been completed, such as Spata airport, the high-speed train from Brussels to Marseilles and the Øresund bridge-tunnel linking Denmark and Sweden. But in far too many cases, the national sections of networks are merely juxtaposed, meaning that they can only be made trans-European in the medium term. With enlargement, there is also the matter of connection with the priority infrastructure identified in the candidate countries ('corridors'), the cost of which was estimated at nearly EUR 100 billion in Agenda 2000. It has not been possible to meet these significant investment requirements by borrowing at Community level, as the Commission proposed in 1993. The lack of public and private capital needs to be overcome by innovative policies on infrastructure charging/funding. Public funding must be more selective and focus on the major projects necessary for improving the territorial cohesion of the Union as well as concentrating on investment which optimises infrastructure capacity and helps remove bottlenecks. Motorway density in countries such as Greece and Ireland was still far below the Community average in 1998. In the new context of sustainable development, Community co-financing should be redirected to give priority to rail, sea and inland waterway transport.
>
> (CEC, 2001c: 12–13)

From these examples we learn how power struggles shape the form of institutions, as the central struggle is the question of whether the member states or the EU should control decisions over major infrastructure projects. However, there is a further twist to the story of major infrastructure projects in the wake of the enlargement of the European Union.

Practice 2 – TEN-T and competency arguments

In the early stages of policy development, the infrastructure lobby maintained a powerful hold. The membership of one of the key decision-making bodies for TEN-T illustrates the institutional power of this lobby. Proposals for the Trans-European Road Network (TERN), for example, were developed by the Motorway Working Group (MWG) of the Commission's Transport Infrastructure Committee. Membership of this Group includes the Commission, member states, the European Conference of Ministers of Transport, and significantly a number of private sector interests including the European Round Table (ERT), the Association des Constructeurs Européens d'Automobile, and the International Road Transport Union (CEC, 1992). The Committee was overwhelmingly dominated by transport and infrastructure interests, with a notable absence of environmental interests. It is difficult to imagine that such a committee could produce anything other than a solid case for progressing TERN. The decision-making process adopted by the MWG is unclear, although they transformed national infrastructure 'shopping lists' into international network proposals. However, environmental criteria were not integrated into decision making although they were identified, in broad terms, in policy documents (Bina *et al.*, 1995). The published proposals identify a network of road corridors, but fail to set out the criteria used in their designation. It appears that the debate within this key decision-making arena was largely political. The institutional power of the infrastructure lobby demonstrated here through its strong presence in an infranational arena was further enhanced by ready access to top ranking EC and member state politicians.

The construction of TEN-T narrative can be seen as a key element in the emergence of a European spatial policy discourse. As Dick Williams has argued: 'In the context of spatial planning at the EU scale, TENs have an obvious resonance . . . the relationship between transport TENs and the development of EU spatial policy needs to be clear if the latter is to achieve general acceptance' (Williams, 1996a: 168). The lessons learned in the TEN-T policy process should therefore be directly relevant to the implementation of the ESDP.

For TEN-T, the lack of clarity over the EU's formal capability in infrastructure (and spatial) planning had dire effects on the possibility of any real planning taking place. The Commission, Council and Parliament struggled horizontally for control over decision making as part of broader inter-institutional struggles at the EU level. There was a further vertical struggle between the member states and the EU institutions, over the relations of power. The fields of these struggles embraced broad principles such as spatial planning, and specifics such as the treatment of economic and environmental risks. Ultimately the rationality of the new policy discourse itself was contested across this complex terrain, with the clear impacts on policy outputs discussed above. Running through these struggles was the central question of the EU's competence to intervene. Could the EU actually plan one of its largest programmes for physical development? The evidence above suggests that it could not.

In a Europe of subsidiarity, where Community actions must be justified in terms of value added, the idea of Community Benefits provided a valid rationale for Community intervention. However, this position was resisted by member states, who held that 'planning' national infrastructure projects – the components of TEN-T – had to be solely the competence of member states. There was concern that the EU should not have power over member states in the planning and implementation of such projects. One consequence of this impasse is the use of EU structural (and other) funds to secure spatial programs by the back door.

A further conclusion is that the power struggles which shaped the rationality of policy making precluded the possibility of any 'rational' or deliberative approach to determining an appropriate spatial planning framework. Power relations ruled the day in a way which excluded debate and reflection on what were seen as marginal or irrelevant issues. The reasoned basis for EU intervention in infrastructure planning was never the subject of critical debate within the policy process. A seemingly unproblematic rationality was constructed through discursive struggle which marginalised or excluded potentially destabilising challenges. Critical arguments were subsumed through the process of integration into weak evaluation frameworks. TEN-T policy debates never contained a question-mark, a pause for thought. Indeed the engagement of industrial interests, and later the EU institutions, was focused on speeding implementation, removing barriers to progress. The widespread acceptance of the need for TEN-T across the EU institutions meant that difficult questions had to be accommodated without compromising the overall project. This clearly suggests that very careful analysis of the emerging involvement of the EU in spatial planning will be required, to scrutinise these workings of power.

Furthermore, it is clear that inter-institutional issues at the EU level are likely to continue to problematise the EU's search for an appropriate level of competence in spatial planning. At least in this case, the co-decision process itself does not appear to have been a useful arena for supra-national planning.

Towards a European planning system?

In studies of the European Union, a recurrent question concerns its teleology. Is it moving towards a European superstate? Chris Shore identifies the evolutionary conception of the European project by the EU institutions, an idea of European integration as an 'unfinished project of social and political engineering', and characterised by a supranational idealism (Shore, 2000). He sets out two ways in which the EU has sought to legitimise its own project: the first by the 'Europeanisation of the masses', and the second by the more subtle process of creating the embryo of a European identity within its own institutions, which could act as a catalyst for diffusing the European idea. Similarly, in response to questions about whether European spatial planning is moving towards a super planning system, it is important to ask critical questions and not fall into the trap of supranational idealism or of denial. Shore argues that these dimensions of the teleological construction of the EU project 'all combine to obstruct critical and intellectually honest thinking about its institutional shortcomings' (Shore, 2000: 207). Within debates about European spatial policy, it is possible to discern a range of views on this question of teleology.

The first of these is the frequently encountered argument that there is no 'masterplan', no attempt to create a supra-national planning system. This argument is important in protecting the fragile new policy domain from claims that it is simply another manifestation of the EU seeking to usurp the powers of member states. In response to this argument, we point to the range of formal and informal capabilities which are available for the implementation of European spatial planning (and here we deliberately use the term 'implementation', as against 'application' which is favoured by those who argue that European spatial planning is not a quest for competence). Among these capabilities are legal powers provided under an ever increasing series of EU Directives (EIA, SEA, Birds, Habitats, Water Framework). Alongside these formal powers are a range of informal programmes expressly designed to encourage transnational planning activity, as well as the less visible tuning of other policy programmes and budgets to operate within the ESDP unbrella. It seems clear that many of the basic elements of European spatial planning are already in place, and it would seem unusual to claim that in this policy field the EU does not seek to establish powers, when it clearly does elsewhere. As Shore has argued, the Commission has long held a belief in the moral superiority of supranationalism as a more advanced system of governance. Why would this not apply to spatial policy? Here, two EU civil servants comment on the competency issue:

> Strategic spatial planning is usually understood as a field of action that clearly exceeds conventional land-use planning, and which covers the coordination of policies that have a direct impact on territorial development. By this definition, the Community clearly has a competence in spatial planning since it concerns the coordination of Community policies which affect the use, organization and structure of the EU territory.
>
> (Bastrup-Birk and Doucet, 1997: 312)

Practice 3 – Drafting the ESDP: principles of EU governance – democracy, transparency, subsidiarity

The role of the ESDP within the wider field of EU spatial policy can be seen as twofold: first, framing a common vocabulary of symbols and visions, part of the structuration of a new discourse of European spatial development; and, second, embedding new institutional forms and relations which reproduce the discourse across and beyond the European spatial policy arenas, and which may bring about the articulation of the discourse in European space, and in localities. Within this process, a new discourse of European space is being constructed and institutionalised. The ESDP document itself is not seen as containing the discourse, but as one manifestation of it. Further manifestations occur in the area of policy implementation, as the new spatial rhetoric is being institutionalised through the adoption of new practices in spatial analysis, knowledge building and policy measures.

The process of consultation in the member states during the ESDP process offers a window into what sort of transparency and participation notions are embedded in the discourse. According to Williams this series of seminars 'could be regarded as a form of public participation' contributing to the final version of the ESDP (Williams, 2000: 2). However, in a rather modified form of public participation:

> Considered as a programme of public participation in the ESDP process, the seminars cannot be said to have reached all who may in due course need to pay attention to the ESDP, but they did reach many people who would normally be outside normal EU policy processes and Brussels comitology. They were not simply intended as publicity sessions. The Commission wanted informed debate by participants with some understanding of the ESDP concept. . . . So, it could be said that a reasonable level of élite participation was achieved, which would stand well in comparison with other sectors of EU policy development.
>
> (Williams, 1999: 360–361)

Obviously, we cannot put special demands on this particular field of spatial policy, but it seems that relativising the level of participation here just side-tracks the issue. Thus the real issue is that the process of constructing the ESDP policy was indeed 'concerted' and demanded a special audience.

A further impression of the underlying tensions and power struggles that shape the ESDP can be found in the series of so-called 'transnational seminars', held during the ESDP consultation process. From April 1998 to February 1999, nine semi-public seminars were held by DG XVI, drawing upon inputs from experts, civil servants and politicians (Box 6.1).

At the opening seminar in April 1998 in Berlin, the ESDP was introduced (DG Regional Policy, 1998a). The politicians had a more 'high flying' vision than the planners, neatly expressed in the statement from the German Minister for Raumordnung, Bauwesen und Städtebau, Eduard Oswald. He saw the ESDP

Box 6.1 **The nine transnational seminars held during the preparation of the ESDP (places and themes)**

Berlin, April 1998: The ESDP: Towards a policy strategy for the European continent
Naples, May 1998: Transport, telecommunication and transeuropean networks
Lille, June 1998: Cities: perspectives for the European urban system
Thessalonika, July 1998: An integrated approach for water management
Manchester, September 1998: Knowledge as a development factor
Salamanca, October 1998: For a new rural-urban partnership
Gothenberg, October 1998: Environmentally sensitive areas
Vienna, November 1998: Co-operation on spatial planning in the context of the EU enlargement
Brussels, February 1999: The ESDP forum closing event

as part of the process of building European unity on the basis of common cultural basic values (Oswald, 1998: 3) – a most outspoken illustration of the identity theme. At the next seminar in Lille (France) opposing views were put forward about the democratic legitimacy of spatial visions. The Danish National Planning Director Niels Østergård clearly expressed the nation state's support for strategic nodes in the new global urban competition (Østergård, 1998: 3), whereas a Swedish politician expressed the opposite rationale, that is a critique of European growth bananas drawn on the map on the basis of insufficient planning (Nilsson, 1998: 3). The Salamanca seminar, held in October 1998, focused on the urban-rural relationship. One of the strongest critiques of the way the ESDP handles this theme came from the very pro-ESDP oriented German Ministry for Raumordnung, Bauwesen und Städtebau (BMBAU, 1998: 1). However, this is a voice that does not appear in the ESDP. Thus following the seminars, DG XVI published a summary highlighting the general consensus amongst participants on the ESDP's rationale (DG Regional Policy, 1998b).

The question of democracy in the process of institutionalising the ESDP has been raised before in research on European spatial policy (BMBAU, 1998). However, with the advent of the White Paper on EU Governance, the EU explicitly sees an increasing role for the ESDP in promoting better coherence between territorial development at different levels (CEC, 2001a: 13). Faludi and Waterhout note that: 'Most importantly, The Commission, in its White Paper on European Governance, has placed the ESDP at the core of its future efforts to achieve more coherence, this being one of the five "principles of governance" that it wants to pursue' (Faludi and Waterhout, 2002: 174). However, in a critical analysis of this same relationship between the ESDP and the White Paper, Atkinson concludes that: 'For all the ESDP's hopes of balanced and polycentric development these are likely to prove difficult, if not impossible, to achieve, division and competition are more likely outcomes and whether the White Paper and its proposals can adequately cope with such a situation is a moot point' (Atkinson, 2002: 789).

Another dimension of this discussion is its relation with the whole debate on the 'Democratic deficit'. On the one hand, Faludi recognises that experts have been the key players and that legitimacy of the process leading to the ESDP is of a 'technical nature' (Faludi, 2000b: 251). On the other hand, the question of democratic deficit relies on a huge assumption: 'It is that the EU is a polity, or at least in the process of becoming one, along the lines of democratic nation states. There is a powerful argument for saying that this is not the case: there are no European political parties, no European newspapers and no European public' (Faludi and Waterhout, 2002: 26). One could even broaden this sort of argumentation by reference to Weiler's point that there is no European 'demos'. By this is meant that there is no European people that can constitute a democratically elected body (Weiler, 1999). In the last part of the book we will return to some of the wider implications of these issues, as well as their link to issues of territory, belonging and citizenship.

According to Tewdwr-Jones and Williams, the development of the European spatial policy discourse coincides with the general trend from the later 1990s where policy making through legislation is gradually being substituted by the development of mutual support initiatives and incentives (Tewdwr-Jones and Williams, 2001: 22).

In the midst of the many nice words published on new forms of governance these days, we find it worth mentioning that there exists no automatic relationship between the new flexible forms of governance and the basic 'virtues of democracy' in terms of transparency, accountability and participation (Held, 1987). Rather we should strengthen our critical and analytical approach as 'we should recognise that the development of a complex web of negotiations between public, private and NGOs (and individuals) may well actually mean that the decision-making process is less accountable, more opaque and just as exclusive as traditional bureaucratic forms' (Atkinson, 2002: 784).

Practice 4 – a 'window' into the process of territorial transformation: INTERREG as an institutional site

Given the legal status of this policy field, it comes as no surprise that the ESDP focuses especially on the transnational level when it comes to the discussion of possible actions under the rationale of the ESDP (CSD, 1999: 35). It is at this level that we also find the initiatives under the INTERREG fund, activities that since 1996 have proven to be the *de facto* field of implementation of the ESDP rationale and policy, or a 'success story' of European integration (Christiansen and Jørgensen, 1995: 8). Indeed, INTERREG is only a little window into the processes of territorial transformation which are ongoing in the EU (Christiansen and Jørgensen, 1995: 10).

Under INTERREG, possible actions are focused mainly on the transnational level, avoiding friction with member states (CSD, 1999: 35). As we have shown, INTERREG IIc enables cross-border transnational planning initiatives between national and European levels within the context of mega-regional perspectives and visions. In accordance with the evaluation of the importance of the INTERREG initiative, it is further suggested that the Commission and the member states continue the 'project-oriented transnational co-operation' for spatial development, and this preferably within the new INTERREG III initiative that is seen as the test bed for the ESDP (CSD, 1999: 39).

Some analysts have even interpreted the INTERREG programme as being the bottom-up antidote to the relatively clear top-down character of the ESDP, due to its workings at a more tangible project level (Tewdwr-Jones and Williams, 2001: 163). Obviously, the specific projects in INTERREG may be more easily comprehended by regional policy makers and stakeholders. Nevertheless, we would argue that one should be very careful to not think automatically of, for example, the INTERREG as something cut lose from its wider institutional and discursive context of European spatial policy making.

The new (and economically stronger) INTERREG IIIB programme explicitly states that recommendations made in the ESDP must be taken into account, and that the programme especially encourages the drawing up of 'spatial visions' at the transnational level (Tewdwr-Jones and Williams, 2001). In the words of a participant in one of the preparatory meetings, NorVISION is the ESDP translated to the North Sea Region. However, a transboundary planning process such as NorVISION can also be seen as being negotiated between the EU spatial vision, expressed through the ESDP, and those of constituent member states, regions and other partners.

As an example of such an 'institutional site' the NorVISION document proposes a framework for action proposals (VWG, 2000b: 83–89). These 'integrated planning themes' are to be translated into projects, and are followed by an annex of specific IR IIC projects that conform with the NorVISION strategy as well as a number of possible projects identified by the VWG (VWG, 2000b: 92–97).

Elsewhere, analysing the INTERREG programme as it is applied in the Baltic Sea Region (BSR), Jørgensen and Nielsen hold that there has been established a 'transnational space for spatial planning without a superstructure of substantial political contents'. Furthermore this has been, according to Jørgensen and Nielsen, at a relatively technocratic administrative level and leading to an institutional frame for the development of future regional and spatial planning policies (Jørgensen and Nielsen, 1997: 6). These new transnational institutions are far from reflecting the principal players characteristic of national planning (Jørgensen and Nielsen, 1997: 10).

In the short term, the more immediate question this raises is one of implementation. The ESDP concentrates on practical initiatives over which the EU does have power – principally transnational programmes such as INTERREG. The Commission and member states are encouraged to continue 'project-oriented transnational co-operation' for spatial development under a new INTERREG III initiative that is seen as the test bed for the ESDP (CSD, 1999: 39).

Seen as the institutional implementation area of the ESDP process, the INTERREG programme facilitates both a horizontal and a vertical function of policy integration (Figure, 6.2):

> The horizontal function attempts to promote European integration by creating a sense of the regions of Europe, providing them with greater identity and giving financial support for spatial planning initiatives which may help achieve this by promoting greater interaction and practical cooperation. . . . The vertical function attempts to provide the link between the European Spatial Development Perspective at the supranational scale and the planning activities of the local and regional authorities of member states.
>
> (Tewdwr-Jones and Williams, 2001: 30)

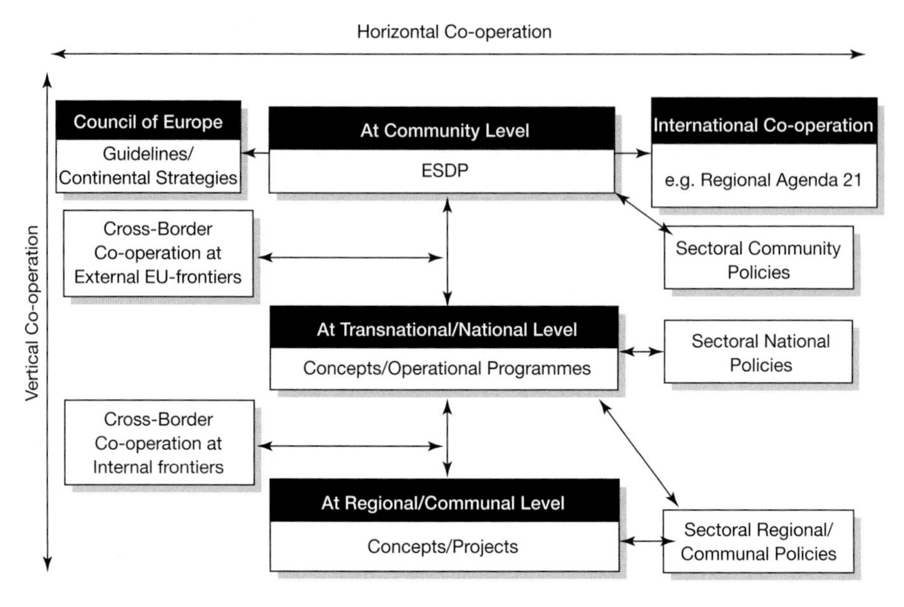

6.2 Ways of co-operation for spatial development.

Source: CSD 1999: 36.

Furthermore, it is at the transnational level that the national planning policies might be reduced to 'sectoral policies'. This seems to be an option, at least if the framework of vertical and horizontal co-operation under the ESDP is considered (CSD, 1999: 36). This might be a premature conclusion on behalf of the national planning policies, but should not be neglected as a long-term vision that comes out of the ESDP rationale. But given the legally non-binding status it is significant that the document has support across the established EU institutions:

> The considerations and application of the ESDP by the European institutions can lead to a greater effectiveness of Community policies. The European Parliament, the Committee of the Regions and the Economic and Social Committee have made statements on the ESDP voicing their support for a regionally more balanced development of the cities and regions in the EU.
>
> (CSD, 1999: 37)

In accordance with the evaluation of the importance of the INTERREG initiative, it is further suggested in the ESDP that the Commission and the member states continue the 'project-oriented transnational co-operation' for spatial development, and this preferably within a new INTERREG III initiative that is seen as the test bed for the ESDP (CSD, 1999: 39).

The Europeanisation of national planning systems

Tensions exist between the new overarching EU spatial policy objectives and those of national planning systems. The ESDP is dependent on a plethora of national systems of land ownership, planning control and building regulations, pursuing separate and potentially exclusive objectives, moving into harmony with the overall spatial strategy. This certainly creates problems in transnational planning situations, and challenges the possibility of constructing an EU planning framework within which these conflicting objectives can be pursued equitably (Williams, 1996a). So the momentum towards EU spatial planning is concerned partly with spatial problems *per se*, but also with resolving conflicting spatial objectives at different levels and in different regions: 'The European Spatial Development Perspective thus represents the most recent stage in a continuing, incremental process of developing a constituency and a legal framework for a distinct European spatial planning policy' (Tewdwr-Jones and Williams, 2001: 47).

A vital dimension of the 'competency issue' is also the question of subsidiarity, or the 'deliciously vague concept' in the words of Weiler (Weiler, 1999: 318). The basic point here is that the principle of subsidiarity is not legally 'activated' by the ESDP as it is outside the Treaty. But indirectly the principle of subsidiarity is built into the Leipzig principles which the ESDP has adhered to throughout the process. Thus the question of subsidiarity, which basically is a question of which level of governance has the power to exercise decisions, is one of ambivalence when it comes to the EU spatial policy discourse:

> The treatment of subsidiarity and the proper roles of the Commission and/or local and regional authorities in spatial policy is rather ambivalent. On the one hand, the political realities of lack of EU competence in spatial policy, plus the political pressures for subsidiarity, are fully recognised, as they are in the political principles of the ESDP. . . . On the other hand, there is an implication that spatial policy coherence cannot be achieved without some direction from the Commission that is enforceable.
>
> (Williams, 1996a: 220)

In between the 'cracks and holes' – the emergence of new governance structures and institutional forms

We now turn to the new institutional forms which have emerged to enable the implementation of the new policy discourse. As we concluded in Chapter 2, the construction of new institutions and governance forms characterising this new EU policy field can best be understood in terms of 'multi-level governance' and 'infranationalism'. Here we will look into the more specific workings of such practices in order to detect the meaning and importance of these activities. We would argue that the new spatial policy discourse, because of its infranational dimension and its affiliation with the multi-level form of governance, is a form of policy making taking place within the 'cracks and holes' of the huge institutional complex that we call the European Union, or the 'network state' in Castells' terminology (Castells, 1998: 310). What this means is that 'European spatial development policy operates within small margins' (Faludi *et al.*, 2000: 126).

Working at these 'margins' then is a dimension of the particular approach termed 'comitology' which the CSD, as key institution in this new complex web, has been affiliated with: 'The CSD can make use of the services of interpreters extended to ordinary comitology committees. In fact the Commission considers the CSD as presently constituted as an anomaly and would prefer it to be reconstituted as a consultative committee' (Faludi *et al.*, 2000: 120).

However, the CSD is not a genuine example of comitology since it was not chaired by the Commission, who only took part in the meetings and provided the secretariat (Faludi and Waterhout, 2002: 50). Working in such an environment meant that the CSD had to create itself and its planning tradition from scratch (Faludi *et a*l., 2000: 127). Furthermore, still according to Faludi, the European spatial planning discourse has materialised within a process going from a situation characterised as an 'anarchic field' to a situation where the ESDP is surrounded by a core planning ('epistemic') community (Faludi, 2000b: 249).

However, it is not only at the European level that the issue of new forms of governance in the wake of the ESDP is actualized. Thus, the informal status has led to a situation of *de facto* European spatial policy making with strong practical implications for both the national and the regional level. Or in the words of Tewdwr-Jones and Williams: 'The impact of informal EU activity in spatial planning has been almost as significant as that which might have existed if the European Union had been awarded formal planning powers' (Tewdwr-Jones and Williams, 2001: 20).

Hajer speaks of a 'transnational discourse coalition' in which there is now a multi-level governance in the shape of shared discursive principles that permeate governance in Europe (Hajer, 2000: 139). The TEN-T in particular and the discourse of 'Europe of flows' in general embody this new governance field:

> The above discussion suggests that in the EU's multi-level system of governance and in the area of spatial planning, the process of European integration produces asymmetrical power shifts. These power shifts from the national level, albeit incremental, are towards the EU and regional levels. . . . Increasingly in the field of European spatial policy, subsidiarity in the three member states examined [Germany, Spain and the UK] is seen as an important component of a system of multi-level governance or cooperative regionalism, which involves Europeanization of the policy process and power shifts to the EU level on the one hand, and decentralization of decision-making and power shifts to sub-national levels of government on the other hand.
>
> (Eser and Konstadakopulos, 2000: 795–796)

Even though the ESDP has *de facto* effects in shaping policy discourses (Davoudi, 1999: 367), it needs to offer a notion of its ability to 'survive'. Thus in the section on the application of the ESDP it is stressed that the ESDP still is legally non-binding, and should therefore be a basis only for voluntary actions and heralding the principle of subsidiarity (CSD, 1999: 35). The more sensitive questions of the formalisation and inclusion of the ESDP into the Treaties of the European Union are not addressed explicitly, but it is proposed that Member states examine the suggestions of the European institutions to formalise both the Ministerial meetings on Spatial Planning and the Committee on Spatial Development, while maintaining the principle of subsidiarity (CSD, 1999: 37). Given the legally non-binding status it is significant that the ESDP has support across the established EU institutions, such as the European Parliament, the Committee of the Regions and the Economic and Social Committee, which all have made statements on the ESDP voicing their support for a regionally more balanced development of the cities and regions in the EU (CSD, 1999: 37).

Is there a system under development?

At the moment, at least it is clear that the ESDP does not have the legal force of the Treaty of European Union. So one finally faces the question of whether there is a 'system' under development. If so, what is the nature of such a 'system'? Taking departure in these windows into practice, we would argue that these questions should be addressed with the utmost care. Obviously such a discussion depends on the notion of 'system' and its definition. As we have illustrated more than once, the informal character of the new European spatial policy discourse is in no way without practical importance and implications. Some analysts thus find reason to speak of a more coherent collection of rationales and institutions, making way for a new 'planning regime': 'At the supranational level, the EU has begun to develop an explicit and integrated spatial planning regime for the first time' (Gleeson, 1998: 221).

Perhaps Gleeson's interpretation is too upbeat in terms of its expectation of an 'explicit and integrated' regime for planning. Nevertheless, we would agree upon the importance of these new practices and institutions. Furthermore, in identifying the 'regime' Gleeson points to four vital elements. The first two are identified as the two directorates responsible for regional policy (Regional Policy DG) and environmental policy (Environment DG). Third, the Committee of the Regions is mentioned, as it lobbied for recommendation on a trans-European airport network. The fourth and final element of the planning regime is the informal 'Council' of planning ministers and its advisory body the CSD (Gleeson, 1998: 222). At the end of her analysis Gleeson contributes to the jigsaw puzzle of reasons behind the emergence of the new regime. These are the global economic environment of competitiveness (externally), an increased need of policy co-ordination (internally), increased environmental consciousness within the EU, the presence of material environmental problems, and finally an awareness of the increase in uneven social development (Gleeson, 1998: 224).

Whilst recognising its weak legal position, the ESDP retains the prospect of developing over time into a mature and legally binding EU policy field. The fact that there is no legal competency for spatial planning in the European Union has been referred to as a situation of 'institutional vacuum' (Faludi *et al.*, 2000: 118). By this is meant that even though it is now recognised that European integration is a 'spatial project' the EU has taken a long time entering the field. Many analysts have argued strongly around this issue of competency as one indicating the real powers of this spatial policy field. However, some draw the conclusion that 'if spatial planning is about strategy, then competency is a non-issue' (Faludi and Waterhout, 2002: xi). The lack of a legal remit for spatial planning powers in the EU has, however, been circumscribed by informality and voluntary co-operation (Tewdwr-Jones and Williams, 2001: 40), pointing once more to the importance of new complex and informal policy webs and institutions.

As we suggested at the beginning of this chapter, the whole issue of formal versus informal should be handled with care. Thus not being in the Treaty certainly does not mean being without power. So speaking of informality one should realise that the 'top-down' EU project has needed to find ways to reproduce itself and bring about 'Europeanisation'. We can discern a quest for formality both in terms of legal competence, and in terms of creating operational capacity (INTERREG, tuning of structural and cohesion funds, etc) and an informal approach. We could argue that the ESDP probably has as much power as the TEN-T to 'apply' itself, though with a much less clear sense of what exactly should be applied! Furthermore, and as a direct consequence of understanding the distinction formal/informal in a more complex sense, it should be acknowledged that some actors may even prefer the informality and non-Treaty status, as being on the margins and in the 'cracks and holes' gives one less public visibility – an often treasured quality to some of the pressure groups behind, for example, the TEN-T.

The significance of the ESDP and INTERREG in shaping the EU policy agenda on transnational planning and policy making could also be witnessed at the conference on *European cities in a global era – urban identities and regional development*, held in Copenhagen in November 2002. Here the 'Copenhagen Charter 2002' was launched as the Danish EU Presidency's contribution to keeping the spatial dimension of EU policy 'hot'. The document stresses the importance of both INTERREG and the ESDP in future work and progresses ten statements that are unlikely to be opposed by many, but will neither have a high value as guiding principles in practical policy making (Ministry of the Environment, 2002) (Box 6.2). The Copenhagen Charter nicely embraces the three guiding themes of our analysis: the environment, the urban and the question of identity. It proclaims that it 'intends to contribute to establishing an agenda that gives the priority to the role of the cities in ensuring continuing effort to achieve balanced development in Europe'. Furthermore, at the conference the Director

Box 6.2 **The Copenhagen Charter's ten statements**

Use the forces of globalisation constructively by assessing the local potential in the global economy and integrating this into strategies for urban and regional development.

Use regional and urban identities as the starting point in adapting to global changes and dynamics by interpreting and registering the characteristics of the physical environment, architecture and the social and cultural capital in the region and its cities.

Develop an integrated perspective on urban and regional policy by promoting awareness of the role of towns and cities in regional development, to promote regional cohesion and polycentric development.

Co-ordinate strategies for urban and regional development and support partnerships between public and private actors.

Develop innovative and sustainable long-term perspectives in which regional identity and cities' potential strengths are linked to regional competencies, creativity and culture.

Use the architectural history of the city and global trends to shape the urban and regional environment, to protect diversity and local identity and to counteract the monotony of the global architectural expression.

View the revitalisation of the city and region as a dynamic process and make use of local customs and new initiatives.

Create diverse and creative living and working environments in all urban districts by including all cultures and potential factors in the development process.

Enhance integration in the entire region to avoid social exclusion by ensuring that everyone has access to sustainable transport, jobs, housing, knowledge, education and social services.

Strengthen opportunities for public participation in the discussion on strategies for urban and regional development and thereby empower local actors by making use of their knowledge about the place and its potential.

Source: Ministry of the Environment 2002

General of Regional Policy DG, Guy Crauser, saw the Copenhagen Charter 2002 as yet another example of integration within EU spatial policy as he 'fully endorsed the goal and spirit' of the Charter and foresaw that it will become 'part of the debate of the future Cohesion policy'.

On the CSD and the 'post-ESDP process'

What has happened since the launching of the ESDP in 1999 is very much characterised by the construction of the new knowledge building institutions (ESPON, SPESP) and the continuation of the transnational planning activities (INTERREG). However, one could also pause to question what has happened with the main institutional driver, the CSD. Under the French Presidency in the summer of 2001 the CSD was substituted with a 'Subcommittee on Spatial and Urban Development' (SUD). This is a subcommittee to the 'Committee of Development and Reconversion of the Regions' (CDCR) – also called the Structural Fund Committee. The status of the SUD is best understood as a commitological 'think tank' with no formal powers from which the Commission, if it so wishes, can draw policy directions. According to civil servants in the Danish central administration, this institutional innovation must be seen in the light of the Commission's wish to attach the European spatial policy field closer to its merits – but also as a symbol of the Commission's wish to 'revitalise' the ESDP in what has now come to be called the 'post-ESDP process'.

An indication of this is the reframing of the spatial policy discourse away from 'spatial planning' or 'spatial policy' towards a new language of 'territorial dimensions' and 'territorial development'. Part of the explanation for this change of vocabulary, according to a Danish planner in the National Planning Department, is to be found in the negative image of planning as an activity associated with 'no development'. Accordingly the Commission (and some member states) see more leverage and scope for political action in the conceptualisation coined around notions of the 'territory' and 'development' as opposed to 'planning' and the 'spatial'. With an eye to the next Structural Funds period (2006–2012) the Commission and the more enthusiastic member states clearly have the agenda of regaining control of the spatial policy discourse by means of continuing the implementation of the ESDP rationale. Or in the words of a Danish civil servant: 'The Commission thought so much of the ESDP that they wanted to tie it to the Structural Funds.' This interest is shown in the fact that the Commission is working towards including the thoughts and rationales in the 3rd Cohesion report. The Commission is among other things basing this on the writings of a new working group to which we now turn.

The 'Mermaid Group' and the 'willing people'

The SUD has had five or six meetings each year since its launch in 2001 and is still an exponent of the informal working mode that characterised its predecessor. Thus it can be pictured as representing the informal planning culture against the more formalistic procedures of the CDCR that mainly recruits from Ministries of Economy or Ministries of Industry.

Members of the SUD met under the Danish EU Presidency in Copenhagen (next to the Little Mermaid) and discussed what may come to be the next ESDP. The meeting was held as an informal meeting where the EU Presidency had invited selected members of the former CSD and the new SUD in their capacity of being professional transnational planners. Thus a group of professionals or 'people of interest' as the invitation dubbed it. The outcome of this meeting was, amongst other things, that a joint writing process has been taken on under the auspices of the 'Mermaid Group' in order to prepare a text for the Commission in the fall of 2003 (if the CDCR approves of SUD's efforts). The self-proclaimed 'willing people' of the Mermaid Group make a striking parallel to the 'roving band of planners' (Faludi, 1997). The main drivers of the voluntary writing process up until now are said mainly to be planners from Holland, Denmark, the UK, Sweden, Greece and Italy. The text that the 'willing people' are now writing is called the *common document* and deals with core issues of the European spatial policy discourse as, for example, with the interpretation of the concept of polycentricity and what is seen as the implementation of the 'urban dimension'.

New words and institutions – but the same underlying rationale

In the understanding of some of the members of the 'Mermaid Group', the whole process of spatial policy articulation has come to a watershed, with the ESDP Tampere Action Programme fulfilled, and with the ESDP as a document attaining the status of an influential reference document, but with a question mark hanging over the future of the ESDP itself. The work of the SUD keeps the policy process going within an informal and comitological setting. Thus the next phase in the discourse of monotopia is marked by new linguistic wrappings (the change from 'spatial policy' to 'territorial dimension'/'territorial development'), new institutional settings and practices (the SUD and the aim to include the common document in the 3rd Cohesion Report), but still with the rationale of offering an arena for policy articulation outside formal EU competency, founded on voluntary interaction and a view of the European Union's territory as based on the seamless flows of goods, services and citizens. In our interpretation this shows persistence and continuity, as new representations and practices carry the basic rationale of the Europe of monotopia.

Concluding remarks

In this chapter we have discussed and explored a number of cases which we see as institutionalising practices of the spatial policy discourse. The first case was that concerning the struggle to prioritise the projects to be dealt with in the trans-European transport network. Second, we addressed the issue of competency, and the insights that emerge from considering this question in relation to both TEN-T and the ESDP. Third, we looked at the process of drafting the ESDP and its importance for the institutionalisation issue. Fourth, we addressed the case of INTERREG as yet another example of the practices that frame the question of a European spatial planning system. From these very different cases of institutional practice we would hold that one lesson would be not to confuse informality and non-Treaty affiliation with EU spatial policies with insignificance. TEN-T and the ESDP stand as vivid examples of spatial policy fields that go beyond the expectations of public representatives in the official governing bodies of the EU, and have shown their capacity to influence well established EU policies such as the Structural Funds.

Though this chapter has deliberately 'stepped back' from the three core themes of the environment, the question of identity and the urban, we would like to make some links in closing. Evidently the mobility policy of the TEN-T seems to be carried by a rationale that at best attaches the environmental concerns for good measure instead of seeking a genuine shift away from environmentally unsound transport solutions. The question of identity as the reflexive understanding of what Europe is about seems to be offered new 'playgrounds' with the new transnational activities within INTERREG. In much the same way, we would argue that the institutional constructions and linkages uncovered in this chapter must be seen as prerequisites for building a monotopic Europe.

As to the question of whether there is in fact a process of shaping a pan-European spatial planning system, there is no simple yes or no answer. Rather we would argue for an understanding of a system-like governance form in the making, albeit without firm and well-institutionalised principles of regulation in place. Questions of subsidiarity and legal nation state frameworks still seem to be major obstacles towards one coherent transnational juridical space.

However, as we will see in the next chapter, the forms of framing and thinking about knowledge forms play a vital role in the discursive articulation processes that may or may not in due time lead to a more formalised planning system.

Chapter 7

Creating new knowledges of Europe

> We should abandon a whole tradition that allows us to imagine that knowledge can exist only where the power relations are suspended and that knowledge can develop only outside its injunctions, its demands and its interests. . . . We should abandon the belief that power makes mad and that, by the same token, the renunciation of power is one of the conditions of knowledge. We should admit rather that power produced knowledge . . . that power and knowledge directly imply one another; that there is no power relation without the correlative constitution of a field of knowledge.
>
> (Foucault, 1979: 27)

> The single market will produce all the expected positive effects to benefit citizens and firms only if it can rely on effective trans-European networks.
>
> (Extract from the Conclusions of the Presidency of the Corfu European Council, 3–4 June 1994, published by the CEC, Brussels)

> (Infrastructure) patterns are far from neutral or value-free, let alone driven uniquely by a 'natural' process of technological change and scientific progress. Mobility itself is one of the arenas in which the struggle for control and power is fought. An important strategic weapon of the powerful in this struggle is the ideology of progress and the legitimising scientific discourse of scientists and engineers.
>
> (Swyngedouw, 1993: 324)

Introduction

The central, contested, but often invisible issue that is played out in the construction of a policy process is: what form of rationality will secure legitimacy? Rationality is defined through the effects of power relations on the creation of structures and frameworks for policy development and decision-making, and through the selection or construction of particular tools of policy analysis which form and reproduce particular knowledges. The point here is that the construction of the planning process is where a particular policy rationality (or multiple rationalities) becomes embedded in practices. It follows, then, that this embedding of rationality in the everyday practices of spatial policy making is shaped by discursive conflict and power struggles.

In accordance with the theoretical framework on discourses we will in this chapter analyse how the institutionalisation of the policy discourse of monotopic European space has required the construction of new knowledge forms and fields of knowledge. These new forms of knowledge, which are generated by new (or refashioned) techniques of spatial analysis, are found to be demarcated by shifting and contested boundaries between what counts as legitimate and illegitimate knowledge. The definition of these boundaries is vital in institutionalising European spatial policy as a 'rational, science-based policy field', and in framing, transforming or excluding certain forms of knowledge, such as radical environmental considerations or indicators of social equity, when they threaten to destabilise smooth policy making by throwing up uncomfortable 'facts'.

The thread running through this chapter links together a series of moments where, in the struggles to shape the policy processes for TEN-T and the ESDP, rationality was redefined in response to such challenges. We follow shifts in the framing of knowledge, from the problem framing of missing infrastructure and missing institutions to the creation of the economic knowledge that would prove the case for constructing TENs, to the need for environmental knowledge to counter the challenges that unacceptable impacts would result. Eventually, with the ESDP's broadening of the spatial agenda, we see a shift towards a spatialised and integrated knowledge of policy impacts.

Several arguments will unfold as we chart shifts over time and across policy arenas in the ways that knowledge was framed first to trigger a policy response, and then to sustain the case for political support and investment in major projects and policy ideas that amount to a fundamental restructuring of the fabric of, and relations within, European space. We follow a rocky trail of debris, as 'knowledge' is hacked and hewn in quite rough ways, into new shapes: from the dramatic problem framing of missing infrastructure and missing institutions; through the convoluted attempts to prove an economic case for the trans-European networks; to the need to integrate strategic environmental concerns following the activities of environmental pressure groups; and finally towards a potentially more holistic field of territorial analysis to accompany the new field of European spatial planning. We will see how tools of analysis have been bent into new shapes to deal with the specific challenges of understanding the possible benefits and negative impacts to Europe of (for example) new motorways and urban patterns. We will encounter the ways in which the new 'knowledge' about these impacts has been used to mask uncertainties over how policies and programmes will affect the 'real world'. And we will then examine how this new knowledge field is being actively reproduced in the implementation of the ESDP. Each of these knowledge forms required a different type of planning tool to instutitionalise it, and it is the examination of the contested nature of these tools that helps us to understand the different ways in which monotopic Europe is being rationalised at the micro-level of policy practice.

Institutionalisation and new tools of analysis

What may be the crucial stage in the process of defining the rationality of the policy process is the selection of particular methods, or techniques, of policy analysis. A key dimension of the institutionalisation of the spatial discourse is therefore the deployment of these tools, providing the knowledge required about the difficult issues of spatial integration, peripherality, and so on, at the heart of the spatial strategy. It has been argued that EU spatial policy cannot exist without 'a solid patrimony of analyses and interpretation referred to the whole of the European territory' (CSD, 1999). In this process, certain forms of knowledge will be deemed appropriate, while others will be seen as less useful or misleading. Creating boundaries of knowledge will be vital in institutionalising European spatial planning as a 'rational, science-based policy field'.

It is through the application of planning tools that the world is analysed, and information gathered by recognised methods which create knowledge, reconstructing and representing a particular version of the world and its problems and opportunities, and thus providing the crucial support for policy and decision making.[1] The importance of selecting one technique rather than another is that each is imbued with its own characteristics: drawing from certain data types and forms, lending itself to certain forms of analysis, and therefore possibly addressing planning policy issues in particular ways. This is an area which is becoming increasingly contested, although it appears that there is little critical work being done in it. The political importance of these techniques has been recognised, for example by Throgmorton (1992), who argued the need to explore the political deployment of policy evaluation tools, and in the specific literature discussing the political nature of evaluation (reviewed, in for example, Karlsson, 1996).

Constructing rationality for the trans-European transport network

First, then, we will analyse in some detail the discursive competition over the construction of rationality in the TEN-T policy process. We will explore how this construction became an arena of competition between discourses – competition over the embedding of particular horizons within the policy process, reinforcing certain patterns of inclusion and exclusion of language, ideas, organisations and people. A struggle which can be understood as a battle over the process by which certain knowledges – the vital basis for rational planning – would be created (or legitimised), which would be the basis for planning a pan-European transport system.

Within the TEN-T policy process, debates have taken place over what methods of decision making are appropriate: the use of micro-level cost-benefit analysis has been strongly argued by economists, assessment of environmental impacts has been demanded by environmentalists, and assessment of wider economic benefits (like jobs created) has been pressed for by politicians (MEPs). Here, different discourses can be seen asserting control over the techniques which could be used in developing policy. The adoption of one technique rather than another shifts the balance of power in the policy process. The type of knowledge which should be used as a basis for 'rational' decision-making has itself become an area of political conflict between economic, social and environmental interests.

Often, the battle over tools of policy analysis is not apparent. Tools are handed down through established policy, practice and tradition and so, within a particular policy process, the selection of tools of analysis may appear to be more of an academic debate than an exercise in power relations. However, what is important about the TEN-T policy process is that selection of methods became a crucial site of opposition. Contrasting approaches were advocated by economic and environmental discourses.

The tools which receive most detailed scrutiny here are cost-benefit analysis (CBA) and Strategic Environmental Assessment (SEA). Studying the heated debate which surrounded the construction of CBA and SEA, and the progress of policy and methodology, reveals a clash of discourses. By analysing this debate, it is possible to shed light on how boundaries of knowledge were being constructed in the policy process. CBA and SEA, analysed here politically rather than technically, can be understood as central fields of conflict in struggles over European space.

Constructing economic knowledge: proving community benefits and smoothing over uncertainties

The lobbying of the ERT, discussed in earlier chapters, was an important factor in the creation of the new policy discourse. Language coined by the ERT is recognisable throughout later documentation, and appears to have been successful in framing the need for TEN-T as a clearly defined and urgent problem, and in shaping the policy response. The policy debate thus became dominated by several key knowledge claims. These related to: the necessity of improved international infrastructure networks for the completion of the single market; the beneficial role of infrastructure in economic development; and the political and economic benefits that would flow from TEN-T. So far, these claims to knowledge had been no more than assertions in the process, based on traditional if poorly understood assumptions in transport planning and economics. Together, however, they constituted a powerful political and economic rationality, which succeeded in raising TEN-T to the top of the European political agenda (recognised by a separate chapter in the Maastricht treaty), and triggering a formal EU policy process.

The acceptance of these knowledge claims was demonstrated by the very high level of lobbying, particularly from regions and other local governments, for the addition of projects to the outline network plans. Very few questioned whether the opening up of their regions by the development of major international corridors would be beneficial for local economies (for example).

However, as the crisis in public investment grew in the 1990s, the question of finance became a serious problem for the TEN-T. There was increasingly a need to demonstrate the economic benefits that might actually be created by the networks. This was thrown into sharp relief when, following ratification of the Maastricht Treaty, TEN-T policy came under the new process of co-decision between Council and Parliament. The European Parliament's first reading of the Commission's TEN proposals took place on 18 May 1995, where the opportunity was taken to criticise the undemocratic nature of the early stages of policy development. The EP demanded a clear identification of the economic benefits that were likely to be created by TEN-T.

In response to this challenge, and to the need to establish legitimacy for continued and increased support for TEN-T, two strategies were pursued by the Commission. The first was to secure the institutionalisation of economic evaluation of international transport movements. The second was to elevate the broader economic imperative of TEN-T to unquestioned status. The effectiveness of these twin strategies will be analysed next.

Institutionalisation of micro-economic evaluation: proving European 'added value'

For the EU to give financial support to the development of the networks, there was a need to prove the overall benefits to the community that could accrue from such investment. This was achieved through methodological innovation in cost-benefit analysis, identifying what has been termed 'Community Benefits'.

CBA has become the main technique in support of infrastructure decision making in member states: 'The convergence of the core countries is seen in a renewed commitment to economic evaluation in investment appraisal and decision-making' (Roy, 1994: 53). Work by the European Centre for Infrastructure Studies (ECIS), analysing CBAs of the flagship Paris-Brussels-Cologne-Amsterdam-London (PBKAL) high-speed rail project, identified a persistent methodological flaw in the evaluation of international infrastructure projects (Roy, 1994). Because CBAs are carried out at the national level, within national boundaries, they ignore the benefits accrued by travellers on international routes outside their country of origin, thereby undervaluing international projects. This finding, welcomed by the European Commission, proved the economic viability of the individual national elements of the PBKAL, and led to the prospect of evaluation of the 'community benefits' for decision making in individual corridors and for the network as a whole.

This might seem a fairly arcane detail, but it becomes increasingly significant as we trace how the debate over these community benefits proceeded. A key problem in the implementation of the TEN-T, discussed in Chapter 6, has been the difficulty of creating an appropriate funding mechanism. Part of this difficulty has been in constructing a rationale that public support (whether from the EU budget or from member states is another debate) for transnational infrastructure projects is justified. Often such projects have been perceived to be very much in the European interest, but have escaped the capacity of the member states' number crunching frameworks to grapple with them. In the light of the urgent focus on implementation created by the EU Transport White Paper and the review of the TEN-T, this question of the calculation of the European added value of transnational projects has now become the key knowledge which will underpin decisions about investment and prioritisation:

> The main obstacle to carrying out infrastructure projects, apart from technical or environmental considerations, remains the difficulty of mobilising capital. The Commission sounded the alarm in this connection in its 1993 White Paper on growth, competitiveness and employment. The suggestion of raising a loan through bonds issued by the Union to help funding has not been followed up. The headache of funding remains. To overcome this problem, not only must public and private funding be equal to the task, but also innovative methods of funding must be applied.
>
> Experience has shown, however, that in some cases, particularly those involving cross-border priority projects such as Lyon–Turin or the future central crossing of the Pyrenees, the present Community contribution rate is not a sufficient incentive to act as a lever to mobilize and coordinate the required investment. It is therefore proposed that this rate should be raised to 20 per cent for 'critical' projects with a high added value for the trans-European network but a low socioeconomic return at national level. A package of this type lies in the time lag between the capital expenditure and the first returns, which come only when the project becomes operational. These first returns do not necessarily mean profits. The most tangible effect of this failure at the financial level has been the lack of interest on the part of private investors to fund transport infrastructure, especially cross-border infrastructures on which profits, often low, are by no means certain.
>
> (CEC, 2001c: 58–59)

Certainly the arguments set out here point to the need to justify a strengthened EU role in financing cross-border infrastructure. However, we can go further into the underlying ambitions of the Commission. The central aim of identifying added value is not only to rationalise a case for EU investment. It is also to play a more political role in asserting the EU's vision over which projects should be prioritised, by itself but also by member states. The shifts from 'community benefits' to 'European added value' to a 'Declaration of European interest' are key steps in shifting the priorities of member states, by attributing a new significance to the projects that the EU views as being particularly important to deliver as part of its vision for TEN-T, but which are seen as less significant by other actors:

> The idea is to concentrate on a primary network made up of the most important infrastructure for international traffic and cohesion on the European continent. In this context the Commission will look at the idea of introducing the concept of declaration of European interest where specific infrastructure is regarded as being of strategic importance to the smooth functioning of the internal market and would help reduce congestion, but is of less interest at national or local level. This mechanism will be designed to assist arbitration to bring the points of view of the various local, national and European players closer together.
>
> (CEC, 2001c)

What is particularly interesting here is the shift from 'analysis' to the underpinning of a new rationality of decision making. The Declaration of European Interest is put forward as a mechanism to assist arbitration between scales, but surely its point must be to strengthen the European view of 'necessary' infrastructure, in an attempt to direct member states' funding towards schemes that they might not otherwise prioritise.

The economic imperative – establishing macro-economic consensus/knowledge

A second key strategy was to secure consensus on the wider economic benefits of TEN-T. It has been noted that all the EU institutions supported TEN-T in principle, because of the perceived causal link between infrastructure investment and economic growth. In particular, the potential for job creation through TEN-T was heavily underlined in the Delors White Paper. Uncertainties about the nature and distribution of benefits have yet to be taken seriously in decision making, in spite of a vigorous debate among policy makers, pressure groups and academics over the extent and direction of economic benefits that actually flow from infrastructure investment (see discussion in Chapter 4) (CEC, 1994a, 2001).

Critical work in establishing a way forwards has been carried out by the European Centre for Infrastructure Studies (ECIS). The existence of ECIS is the result of ERT lobbying. Its role has been described by one international NGO representative as to prove that infrastructure is good for the economy, 'for anyone who cares to question it' (interview). ECIS is funded by the Commission and by industrialists. Work by ECIS highlighted the importance (and contingent nature) of macro-economics:

> The novel element provided by the macroeconomic research is to indicate the degree to which primary transport benefits [of new infrastructure] feed through to

> economy-wide productivity gains. The relevance of macroeconomic research is thus to complement CBA – not indeed by magnifying the benefits but, rather, by demonstrating to decision-makers the significance of those benefits in terms of the national interest in competitiveness.
>
> (Roy, 1994: 5)

The findings of macro-economic evaluation were that the fourteen priority projects would lead to the creation of 700,000 person years of work between 1998 and 2007 (the construction phase), and that the complete TEN-T would generate as much as 3.2 million person years of work over this period. The wider employment benefits would be as much as 4.7 million permanent jobs (CEC, 1996f). However, these evaluations have failed to remove the uncertainties raised in Europe 2000+ about the risks for peripheral regions.

Nevertheless, the twin strategies of developing micro- and macro-economic evaluation at the EU level served to support the case that TEN-T projects would bring a high level of social return for the EU as a whole, and that the overall employment benefits would be very large. A knowledge base was being established, which all the key institutions involved in the policy process could accept. MEPs – the most accountable – could justify their support for TEN-T by the number of jobs that could result.

The proposal by the Federal Trust for a single European infrastructure agency to co-ordinate the future development of the TEN-T suggests the possibility of an even deeper hierarchy in infrastructure planning, and one which would further entrench the single market discourse: 'A principal function of a TENs agency . . . would be to evaluate projects from an overall European point of view, and to harmonise the assessment of potential projects. What is clearly required is a common methodology for network Europe' (Federal Trust High Level Group, 1996). The methodology anticipated is based, unsurprisingly, on economic evaluation. Earlier work by EURET, based on a review of infrastructure appraisal methods in member states, had concluded that there was a need for a common appraisal framework for road schemes in the EU. The basis of this framework would be extended cost-benefit analysis, incorporating economic evaluations of, for example, strategic environmental impacts (Mackie *et al.*, 1994).

We should place this new rationality in the context of recent work by Flyvbjerg *et al.*, who have analysed in detail and across a wide range of big infrastructure projects how the real costs of construction systematically overshoot the costings generated during decision making, which are balanced against the social and economic benefits discussed here. Their analysis of cost overruns in different 'megaprojects', including the case of the Øresund link, concluded that the Øresund coast-to-coast link has had a cost overrun of 26 per cent. (Flyvbjerg *et al.*, 2003:14). Furthermore, there was evidence showing that existing knowledge about the magnitude of costs and the expected cost overrun were withheld from the public:

> For the Øresund link, partial risk analyses were carrried out. In one such analysis, a group of government officials assessed that given historical experience a 50 per cent cost overrun 'cannot be seen as an unrealistic maximum estimate' for the link. . . . Yet, when the Minister of Transport presented the project for ratification in 1991, none of this information was mentioned. Neither the proposed law nor the accompanying comments contained any information about risks or non-viability. When, more than two years later, it became publicly known that such information existed and had been withheld from Parliament, the result was a sharp critique of the Minister of Transport by the Auditor-General of Denmark. . . . The treatment of risk in the Channel Tunnel, Great Belt and Øresund projects has clearly been inadequate.
>
> (Flyvbjerg et al., 2003: 75–76)

Clearly, the political dimensions of evaluation play a critical part in blurring how financial, social, and economic costs are brought together and mediated in decision making.

Environmental knowledge: responding to challenges and reflecting wider uncertainties

How, then, were environmental concerns integrated in the TEN-T policy process? In this section, key events which conditioned the shaping of SEA as an instrument of environmental policy integration are analysed. We focus on the treatment of environmental issues in the development of Policy Guidelines for the trans-European transport network. Through a narrative account, key events are charted by which environmental integration in the TEN-T policy process came to hinge on a single issue – the inclusion of an article on Strategic Environmental Assessment (SEA). This account of the policy process closely parallels the discussion of the struggles over the Christophersen list in the previous chapter. Here, we follow it with an evaluation of the extent to which environmental integration was actually achieved in the policy output. An important aspect of this approach is to explore how, through the actions of the key players, the hegemonic discourses in the EU shape the policy process, and condition the success or failure of environmental integration, which links back to our discussion of ecological modernisation in Chapter 4.

Growing unrest

While policy making was starting to make headway in the early 1990s, environmental NGOs across Europe were slowly beginning to develop a concerted campaign against TEN-T. Targeting the roads bias of the emerging network, and the powerful role of the infrastructure lobby in the decision-making process, campaigns focused on major planned infrastructure projects filling key 'missing links' in environmentally sensitive areas. Critical projects such as the Somport Tunnel, linking France and Spain across the Pyrenees, were targeted. Here, decision making had taken place before TEN-T policy was finalised, and construction work had begun without strategic consideration of environmental impacts and alternatives.

The potential environmental effects were summed up in the following extract from a lobbying document produced jointly by the NGOs Birdlife International, Greenpeace and the European Federation for Transport and the Environment:

> TENs represent an obsolete approach to transport policy, focusing heavily on infrastructure building, at odds with the widely accepted need to focus efforts on demand management. What could have been a major opportunity to direct investment in Europe towards sustainable transport will result in a major programme centred around infrastructure projects. These will damage nature conservation and landscape, contribute significantly to the growth in greenhouse gas emissions from transport, and fuel the growth in demand for transport. It will also jeopardise individual countries' attempts to promote sustainable transport.
>
> (Birdlife International *et al.*, 1996: 9)

The diverse arguments put forward by environmental pressure groups varied from fundamental rejection of single market values, because of their potential environmental impacts, to advocacy for better integration of environmental concerns within the policy process. It was noticeable that the debates and documentation within the policy process followed this latter course. There was little space for expression of positions which were contrary to the basic aims of the EU. The coalition of NGOs campaigning on TEN-T therefore comprised some insider groups, which lobbied for procedural reform, and others which supported massed international direct actions, operating outside the formal policy process, and advocating alternative development paths. However, whilst economic concerns were being strongly integrated into the process, the integration of environmental concerns, through the development of environmental evaluation techniques, did not fare so well. Strategic Environmental Assessment was advocated throughout the process as a means of integrating environmental concerns into the policy process. But it was the specific construction of SEA in the policy process which was to determine its effectiveness.

In late 1993, Environment DG (then Directorate General for Environment, Nuclear Safety and Civil Protection) first proposed that SEA should be carried out for TEN-T. In 1994, the Directorate General for Transport held an expert hearing, which concluded – in spite of the experience with the pilot SEA of the High Speed Rail Network – that there was at that time no established methodology for SEA (Box 7.1). As a result the Commission launched studies on methodology and best practice in SEA. This action served to delay the implementation of SEA, reflecting a tension throughout policy development between advocates of early

Box 7.1 **Strategic Environmental Assessment (SEA)**

Until 2001, EU legislation provided for Environmental Impact Assessment (EIA) only at the project level (EEC Directive 85/337). Critics of EIA identified many constraints to the effectiveness of EIA (see for example Therivel *et al.*, 1992). Major weaknesses include the inability to consider the cumulative impacts of a number of individual projects, and the limited treatment of alternatives to proposed projects. The 2001 EU Directive on Strategic Environmental Assessment (SEA), then, extends the principles of EIA to address the environmental effects of strategic actions, such as plans and programmes (though, significantly, not policies). It is important to stress here the potential nature of SEA as a participative planning process, rather than simply a 'scientific' study (Therivel *et al.*, 1992). Although SEA has been anticipated in various EC policy documents, it is a relatively new process. There is relatively little experience of SEA in the transport sector, and less still which integrates different transport modes (Chadwick, 1996). SEA is generally conceptualised as a cascade: SEA carried out at the policy level provides a context for SEAs at lower levels, ending in project level EIA. The concept of corridor analysis has emerged from the TEN-T/SEA debate, and is generally understood as the comparative study of the environmental impact of different transport options within a particular geographical corridor, which may extend across national boundaries.

application and hands-on development of SEA using best available methods, and advocates of a more cautious approach based on researching and improving methodology before application.

As co-decision progressed, environmental NGOs produced documents arguing the need for SEA of the TEN-T (Bina *et al.*, 1995, Birdlife International *et al.*, 1996). SEA was called for as a combination of EU level analysis of the proposed network, using best available information, followed by corridor analysis for every TEN-T scheme. This 'strong' SEA should 'play a decisive role during implementation and revision of the TENs Guidelines', and corridor analysis should be a condition of EU funding (Birdlife International *et al.*, 1996: 5, 7).

Translating environmental concerns into policy

Interestingly, a Strategic Environmental Assessment pilot study was carried out for the high speed rail (HSR) network in 1992 (Mens en Ruimte, 1993). This study attempted to make a comparative assessment between HSR and competing conventional rail and road networks and key airports. The findings suggested that HSR could help to reduce the environmental impact of long distance travel relative to other modes, although wider policy options were not addressed. Significantly, the study was carried out at an expert level, with no public consultation or dissemination of findings. There was little apparent influence on the decision process for the network. The pilot study showed that SEA is feasible, but that there are both methodological and procedural problems to overcome if SEA is to become an integral part of the planning process. The procedural problems included the extent of binding power of the SEA, in relation to the actions of member states, and decisions on EU financial support (Dom, 1996).

The response by campaigners to such constraints on decision making has ranged from selling off parcels of land in the path of the planned access roads, to long term non-violent direct action. A significant further development was the formation of TENGO, a coalition of international environmental NGOs including Worldwide Fund for Nature, Greenpeace, Friends of the Earth International, Birdlife International, European Federation for Transport and the Environment (T&E), and Action for Solidarity, Equality, Environment and Development (A SEED), to lobby with a stronger voice for improved environmental measures in the TEN-T proposals. However, a constant feature of the policy process was that, although the infrastructure lobby enjoyed a high level of access, environmental organisations were never formally consulted. The Member States were expected by the Commission to represent environmental interests (Frommer, 1992: 10).

Co-decision

In co-decision with the Council, the European Parliament's first reading of the Commission's TEN-T proposals took place on 18 May 1995. The tone of the Parliament's position was set in the report of the EP's Committee of Transport and Tourism (rapporteur Wilhelm Piecyk), which sought to redirect EU transport policy towards transport modes least harmful to the environment, to achieve a 'sensible balance between economy and ecology' in the creation of TEN-T. Here, then, was an explicit attempt to change the culture and language of TEN-T from a simple instrument of the 1992 process, to a more environmentally sensitive instrument of sustainable development.

The Parliament's position centred on the principle that as an EU policy, any EU investment in TEN-T should be conditional on projects satisfying EU environmental objectives. This clearly presented difficult new obstacles in a process which had so far concentrated on removing them. However, in spite of its environmental concern, the overriding aim of the Parliament remained, like the Commission, to complete the single market process. A tension existed between the Parliament's desire to see the economic benefits of TEN-T arrive speedily, and the concern that environmental issues should be properly addressed. The debate was therefore characterised by contradictory references to environmental protection, rapid implementation of TEN-T and advocacy for the inclusion of many new individual projects. The Parliament's pragmatic attitude to environmental integration was put in this way by one MEP:

> You've got to be practical, and our view was, it's better to try and develop an awareness of the environmental issues and build in some safeguards than just say 'oh there's no real attempt to properly plan this, there's no participation, no environmental dimension, its going to be bad for the environment, so we're just against it'. We don't think we would have really achieved much. It may have made us feel better, but wouldn't have achieved much for the environment. So we felt this attempt to be positive and constructive, and try and build in environmental safeguards, was the right approach.
>
> (MEP)

The lobbying activities of environmental NGOs, the presence of the Green Group and the EPLP in the Parliament, and the Parliament's formal involvement through co-decision, were clearly important in bringing environmental concerns to the centre of the policy debate. But, as has been stated, 'despite its newly acquired "pinkish and greenish" tinge, the Parliament remains reasonably receptive to the input of business interests' (Gardner, 1991: 82).[2] In both Parliamentary Readings, during 1995, the Parliament maintained pressure for the adoption of stronger environmental measures. Their proposals included a mix bag of evaluation approaches, clearly reflecting in part the advocacy of environmental NGOs (European Parliament, 1995):

> the requirement to carry out Strategic Environmental Assessment (SEA) of the networks; Further to this is the requirement to carry out a corridor analysis for every project, using cost-benefit analysis, and incorporating environmental considerations; cost-benefit analyses of economic and ecological aspects.

In the meantime, consultations within the Parliament had been carried out by the Committee on Transport and Tourism. In particular, the Committee on the Environment, Public Health and Consumer Protection had adopted a very critical position, pointing out that the Commission's proposals remained biased towards road transport, and stating that SEA should be carried out before the road network and airports were adopted in TEN-T. The Committee's opinion stresses that the emphasis on roads in TEN-T highlights the gap between Commission policy and practice on sustainable development (European Parliament, 1995: 74).

In the Parliament's Second Reading, on 13 December 1995, the Parliament largely maintained its original position, recommending many amendments to the Council's Common Position, and maintaining its demand for SEA. Together, the Parliament's proposals set out a demanding and innovatory series of environmental conditions for new infrastructure, which would exceed the requirements for new infrastructure in most individual member states (for example there was at the time no requirement for SEA in infrastructure planning in the UK). The Commission incorporated an article on SEA in its revised proposal, although the extended use of cost-benefit analysis was not accepted (CEC, 1996b). Here, then, was an explicit attempt to change the culture and language of TEN-T from a simple instrument of the 1992 process, to a more environmentally sensitive instrument of sustainable development.

However, a proposal for economic cost-benefit analysis and a proposal for job creation studies for the regions affected by TEN-T was rejected, on the grounds of subsidiarity: this should be the responsibility of Member States. In contrast, the Council adopted an uncompromising position, rejecting all the Parliament's proposed amendments. The proposed article on SEA was specifically rejected, on the basis that environmental safeguards were already substantially built into the proposals. In the Council's position can be seen the resistance of several member states to handing over decision-making power to the EU on what were regarded as, essentially, national projects. SEA was rapidly becoming a pivotal issue in the policy process, offering real prospects for environmental integration, but also threatening disruption of a major policy initiative. The Council's position was clearly to be a major factor in limiting the weight of SEA. The continued stand-off between the Council and Parliament triggered a formal conciliation process.

The Christophersen list (discussed in detail in Chapter 6) and SEA were both crucial issues in the difficult and heated conciliation process. The conciliation committee finally reached agreement on a renegotiated Common Position on 19 June 1996, which was subsequently adopted by both Council and by Parliament (by 351 votes to 41 with 5 abstentions) as the Policy Guidelines (CEC, 1996c). The Parliament were not entirely happy with the outcome, some MEPs expressing disappointment on the outcome on the environment, others criticising the Council's attitude. However, the Common Position was regarded as a workable compromise, bearing in mind the underlying urgency of implementation: 'we have to be practical; we have to be aware of the need for TENs, in infrastructure terms and in job-creation terms and in getting people and goods moving throughout the European Union' (European Parliament, 1996). The cost of not reaching agreement through conciliation would have been to disrupt the legislative path of TEN-T, leading to a possible delay of several years. This was considered to be unacceptable by all parties, so it was not surprising that the conciliation committee reached agreement.

Evaluating the integration of environmental policy

The final construction of SEA was the result of intense political struggles and difficult compromises. It raises a number of procedural, methodological and practical issues which have been discussed more fully elsewhere (Richardson, 1997). However, the final construction of SEA embedded certain knowledges whilst excluding others, principally because of its weakness in decision making, its non-participative construction and its narrow scope. The TEN-T Policy Guidelines (CEC, 1996c) include network plans for road, rail, inland waterways, airports and combined transport (known as projects of common interest). These are supplemented by new criteria for other potential projects of common interest, and the potential for future interconnections to neighbouring regions. The fourteen Christophersen priority projects are listed in an annex, with the possibility of adding more in a planned 1999 revision (which did not actually take place, but which is partly carried out in the 2001 White Paper). The main environmental articles in the Guidelines are set out in Box 7.2. Several rather general formal policy statements are accompanied by a set of main substantive environmental measures contained in Article 8, Environmental Protection, for implementation at EU and Member State levels. A significant omission from the Guidelines is the Parliament's

Box 7.2 **Environmental articles in the TEN-T Policy Guidelines**

Article 2. Objectives:
'. . . ensuring the sustainable mobility of persons and goods within the area without internal frontiers under the best possible social and safety conditions, while contributing to the attainment of the Community's objectives, particularly in regard to the environment . . . '

Article 5. Priorities:
'. . . the integration of environmental concerns into the design and development of the network', and '. . . optimisation of the capacity and efficiency of existing infrastructure.'

Article 8:
the Commission will develop methodology for Strategic Environmental Assessment of the entire network; the Commission will develop methodology for corridor analysis covering all relevant modes, but without prejudice to the definition of the corridors; the findings of this work to inform the review of Guidelines, to take place before 1 July 1999, and then after every five years. The review to be overseen by both Council and Parliament.

Member States should take environmental protection into account when implementing projects, by implementing the EIA and Habitats Directives.

Source: CEC, 1996b

Box 7.3 **Weaknesses in SEA of the trans-European transport network as adopted in Article 8 of the EU Policy Guidelines**

Procedural issues

Incomplete SEA cascade

Lack of formal power in decision making

Not a participative planning process

Methodological issues

Comparability of data

Scoping excludes land use impacts

Scope only includes Brussels impacts

Modal alternatives unavailable

Implementation issues

SEA not integrated at early stages

Project selection, development and investment run in parallel with debate on SEA methodology

proposal for a quota limit for roads funding, and a quota minimum for rail and inland waterways, to encourage modal shift away from roads.

The issues raised by the final Article are summarised in Box 7.3 and discussed in more detail below.

Procedural issues

The following procedural issues concern how SEA could be integrated into the decision-process for TEN-T.

First, Article 8 does not require mandatory SEA or corridor analysis, emphasising instead the further development of methodology. There is, surprisingly, no formal commitment actually to carry out an SEA of TEN-T. As a result, the weight of the SEA in the decision process is seriously limited. SEA is not linked to EU investment decisions on TEN-T, and will have no power over the actions of member states. It therefore seems that SEA will have little effect on the network plans now adopted, and particularly on the Christophersen projects. The corridor analyses will be also carried out 'without prejudice to the definition of the corridors themselves'.

Second, the cascade approach does not appear to have been fully adopted. At the EU level, the scope of the network SEA appears to be focused on the overall environmental impact, representing SEA at the programme level. There is no mention of policy level SEA, which could evaluate TEN-T against EU environmental objectives, and alongside options for transport demand management, and pricing and regulatory measures set out in the transport White Paper (CEC 1993). Similarly, the cascade does not flow smoothly across the subsidiarity divide – from the EU to the Member State level. Proposals by Parliament to consider environmental impacts at the national level – included in the Commission's amended proposal prior to conciliation – were lost in the conciliation process. This is an important issue because, given the weakness of EU level SEA and corridor analysis, much responsibility for implementation falls back on national frameworks for environmental assessment. Research has indicated that few member states have formal SEA requirements which would meet the needs of an SEA of trans-European transport networks (Chadwick, 1996). Two problems may occur here. First, EU SEA and corridor analysis will require inputs from the national level, where large variations in structures and policies for dealing with environmental issues can be found between respective states. Second, the absence of national level SEA frameworks means that environmental assessment by Member States will generally be restricted to project level EIA. However, project level EIA suffers from several critical weaknesses, which include a frequent fragmentation of application down to very small projects along the length of a corridor; this removes the possibility of strategic analysis of environmental impacts; and a lack of comparison of the impacts of different modal options. Taken together, it would seem that there will be inadequate support from Member States for EU level analysis, and a reliance on EIA frameworks to perform a strategic task for which they have not been designed. This problem is particularly important because most detailed project development, funding and implementation will take place at the national level.

Finally, SEA as described in the Guidelines contains little apparent potential for public participation. The model adopted appears to resemble an analytical tool to be used in closed policy analysis and decision support rather than to facilitate a participative planning process for TEN-T.

Methodological issues

Although the Guidelines require further development of methodology, it is possible at this stage to identify several important methodological issues. SEA methodology has been discussed elsewhere (see, for example, Therivel and Partidario, 1996; Therivel *et al.*, 1992). However, of particular relevance to transport SEA at the European level is the problem of comparability of data between countries, and in particular the lack of transport models for all EU member states. Also, scoping in previous transport SEAs has generally excluded impacts on land use, such as the pressure for development in new locations resulting from infrastructure provision, which is a poorly understood area (Chadwick, 1996).

The Guidelines do not clarify whether the EU level assessments will focus on 'Brussels impacts' (i.e. the purely international elements of the environmental impacts of the network) or on all impacts (i.e. impacts resulting from internal movements). This will hopefully become clear as methodology is developed. However, the parallel debate on the economic evaluation of the EU benefits of TEN-T has taken the former path, so it seems likely that the network SEA will do the same, and focus only on the international elements of movements on the TEN-T. Such a development would strengthen the case for national level SEA, to capture the impacts of these internal movements.

Corridor analysis rests on the principle that there exist modal options for corridors, so that realistic investment alternatives exist between, say, road and rail. However, for many corridors identified in the roads network, there exist no proposed or actual rail options. It is therefore difficult to see how corridor analysis could be used as a widespread tool for encouraging multimodal shift away from roads, as anticipated in the update of the fifth environmental action programme. The separate development of the outline plans for different networks has perhaps masked this problem. Corridor analysis is further weakened by the absence of a requirement to indicate the variant least harmful to the environment (one of the Parliament's rejected proposals).

Implementation issues

The preparation of maps and lists of projects and networks has in practice proceeded in parallel with the debate over the integration of environmental policy measures. The policy process was so tied to the removal of obstacles to implementation that in the 1996 Guidelines network plans were adopted whilst the selection of techniques for planning and evaluation was still unresolved. As a result, by the time SEA is eventually carried out, policy and decision making will be far advanced, and implementation of many prioritised corridors and other network projects will have become irreversible (Bina *et al.*, 1995; Sheate, 1994). Research shows that SEA carried out at a late stage in the policy process does not generally result in policy changes (Chadwick, 1996). In fact, even this debate in co-decision over which projects should be adopted in TEN-T was to some extent being overtaken by events. TEN-T projects were being progressed quickly under separate budget headings, in particular via EU Structural Funds, even before the agreement of a financing regulation in September 1995, which allowed the release of EU funds for the co-financing of feasibility studies, interest subsidies, guarantees and direct grants (Table 7.1).

Since then, EU funding for TEN-T has grown dramatically. The EU budget for 1995–2000 earmarked a total of €1.830 billion for the TEN-T. Alongside

Type of assistance	*Instrument*	*1993–1994*	*1995*
Loans	EIB (1)(2)	4028	3310
Guarantees	EIF (1)(2)	76	85
Grants	Structural Fund (1)(3)	884	115
	Cohesion Fund	1887.5	1107.6
Grants, interest rate subsidies, loan guarantees, co-financing of studies	TEN heading	385	240
	(of which the 14 priority projects)	180	181.05

(1) TEN and TEN related projects.
(2) Signed contracts.
(3) Usually includes appropriations committed, for the 1996–99 period.

Table 7.1 EU financing of trans-European transport networks (million ECU), 1993–1996.

Sources: CEC, 1995, 1996a.

this, the European Regional Development Fund (ERDF) and the Cohesion Fund contributed a total of some €14 billion for projects of common interest in the 'cohesion countries' (Ireland, Spain, Portugal and Greece). In June 1999 the Council of Ministers and European Parliament adopted a new financial regulation which will mean that the RTD budget (including the telecommunications and energy networks) totals €4.6 billion by the year 2006. The transport network's share is expected to be around €4 to 4.2 billion (CEC, 2003a).

Constructing environmental integration

As the environmental impacts of transport have become a key area of EU concern, TEN-T has emerged as a critical area for the integration of environmental policy. Within the policy process, the use of SEA became the central instrument for achieving integration. However, SEA techniques were not simply taken off the shelf by policy analysts, and applied objectively in laboratories. They were constructed in a contested political process, where they became vulnerable to shaping by, and in favour of, particular interests.

The final formulation of Article 8 in the Policy Guidelines fails to establish SEA as either participative planning process or useful analytical tool in strategic decision making, with weaknesses in procedure, methodology and implementation. The gulf between policy rhetoric and practical measure reveals the weakness of this construction of SEA. Its eventual implementation is unlikely to ask basic policy questions, to veto any particularly harmful project, or to move transport in Europe towards sustainability. Furthermore, by failing to enable EU environmental intervention, SEA leaves the powers of environmental jurisdiction and competence largely at the member state level. Quite apart from the problems this raises in achieving EU environmental objectives, the opportunity to use SEA as a tool to achieve broader objectives of sustainable development – creating a more transparent, accountable and participative approach to infrastructure planning – had been missed in the writing of the TEN-T Policy Guidelines.

Since then more work has been done on a methodology for SEA of the TEN-T, but as yet this has not been used in a systematic review of the overall programme. Rather, it is framed for use at a corridor level, and pointing to future decision making rather than to encourage any fundamental rethink of the vision. But now we return to the wider field of EU spatial policy, where these struggles over economic and environmental impacts shape the terrain of a contemporary struggle for knowledge and rationality based on territorial and spatial analysis.

Knowledge building for European spatial planning

A critical aspect of the institutionalisation of the ESDP, which will seriously test the level of harmony between the EU and member states, is the establishment of a new approach to spatial analysis, focusing on (1) urban systems, infrastructures, and natural and cultural heritage, (2) on the spatial impacts of major socio-economic phenomena (e.g. the information society), and (3) on the spatial impacts of sectoral policies.

It is clear that within various policy sectors the selection and use of analytical tools in building policy knowledge has been strongly contested. In the case of TEN-T, for example, we have seen how a heated power struggle ensued over the selection and deployment of evaluation instruments to justify the necessity of new infrastructure projects and address environmental concerns. This analysis leads us to the conclusion that economic criteria will be used to justify EU intervention to enable infrastructure projects to be progressed, whilst environmental knowledge will support decisions rather than carry any binding power. The imposition of these boundaries of knowledge ensures that the economic value of international mobility will be more significant in influencing decision making than the 'value' of environmental impacts. The question then is how such boundaries are metamorphosed into the more integrated work of the ESDP.

It seems likely, then, that knowledge construction within the ESDP process has been and will continue to be subject to similar power struggles. As European spatial planning becomes institutionalised as a rational, scientific policy field, boundaries are being established between valid and invalid, reasonable and unreasonable knowledges. So, for example, in the ESDP, TEN-T are articulated as potentially contributing to environmental benefits. For example the high level of investment in high-speed rail is argued to be a means of encouraging modal shift from air over distances up to 800 km, as well as from road on certain corridors. We know of course that this claim is not based on any overall SEA of TEN-T. The discourse of mobility contained in the ESDP is clearly driven by economic interests. The utopian ideal of frictionless mobility is articulated through the twin aims of increasing accessibility and efficiency, to be implemented through the construction of a trans-continental high-speed network of roads, railways, sea and airports, reaching into every region through local networks. But how is this ideal pinned down to what we can know about movements in European space?

Why knowledge boundaries matter: accessibility

The new policy language of European space has to be rationalised, supported by an elaborate framework of evidence, so that progress towards elusive concepts like 'balanced spatial development' and polycentricity can be measured. The development of the system of spatial analysis within the ESDP framework therefore warrants careful scrutiny, as criteria such as 'spatial integration' and 'peripherality' become subjects for analysis. This is one of the crucial (but difficult to track) steps between rhetoric and institutionalisation, where policy ideas become embedded in new frameworks for compartmentalising our understanding of the world, and articulating or foregrounding certain ways of looking at it. Once we analyse certain movements between certain places as a matter of everyday planning work, and naturally use those measurements to show that these places are more 'integrated' than they used to be, then the reproduction of the core idea that integration requires more movement, which is all central to European progress, is more or less assured.

For example, the question of improving accessibility between regions is likely to be informed by gathering data about inter-regional traffic movements by different modes. The assumption is that more movements will equate with increased accessibility. Assumptions of this type lead the analysis towards a focus on knowledge which supports the underlying rationality of the ESDP, that increasing mobility is 'a good thing', without integrating the complex effects of such movements which are recognised at a rhetorical level. It is in the institutionalisation of the rhetoric, through new practices of generating knowledge, that such differences become clear.

Finding the right tool for the job: towards TIA

The overall prospect is of a dramatic increase in gathering and managing spatial information at the EU level. A central task of the transnational spatial policy community is therefore the creation of a new tool to reproduce the knowledge forms which are within the discourse. The policy debate has focused on a new tool which is being promoted as the one for the job: Territorial Impact Assessment (TIA). TIA is flagged in the ESDP (policy options 29, 42, 52) (Williams *et al.*, 2000). For example, member states are likely to be required to contribute analyses of the territorial effects produced at national level by both EU and national policies (CSD, 1999). From the background papers, it is clear that TIA is a policy driven, normative tool. It is shaped by policies. Williams *et al.*, in reviewing the limited experience across member states to date, point out that TIA is 'a tool for assessing the impact of spatial development against spatial policy objectives or prospects for an area' (Williams *et al.*, 2000). So the policy options set out in the ESDP again start to take on a new importance as they begin to underpin the new approach to analysing future spatial projects. And this is the important point, that the way TIA seems to be developed is for applications for big transnational projects, rather than for a more strategic view of particular regions or spaces (Schindegger, 2001; Williams *et al.*, 2000). Once again, we find the knowledge tools being pushed by the requirements to build big new infrastructure rather than the need for effective spatial planning.

Further consideration probably needs to be given here to how TIA can potentially act as a further weakening of environmental concerns through integration with other issues. The balancing of the environment within an integrated study process potentially masks the ways that trade-offs may take place, whereas strictly environmental studies, it could be argued, generate a clearer sectoral output. Further complications arise with the introduction of SEA, which seems not to have been worked through in the discussion of TIA, at least as far as it has currently progressed. However, almost as an afterthought, Schindegger does note that TIA is itself seen as being important as a means of institutionalising public involvement: 'By the way: in para 186 the TIA is considered as an institutionalised consultation process on matters concerning spatial development' (Schindegger, 2001: 2).

Though it has a long way to go, TIA looks likely to strengthen wider spatial interests in decision making, but in ways that would not obviously resolve any of the difficulties mentioned above in more traditional environmental and economic assessments. It seems that INTERREG will become a key arena for testing the new approach. The ESDP points out that one of the key tasks for INTERREG III will be 'the use of projects for the preparation of investment measures and for the further development of instruments of spatial development, in particular cross-border territorial impact assessments' (cited in Schindegger, 2001).

Concluding remarks: power, knowledge, discourse

The logic of political integration, supported by the rationality of market economics, and the increasing demand for high levels of mobility, has begun to underpin a new pan-European vision of transport and mobility. A vision of a frictionless, shrinking, high-speed, single market Europe, where physical and institutional barriers to movement are removed. This has been supported by the marginalising of environmental knowledge, and the construction of a methodology for policy implementation which will create knowledge, attribute relevance and enfranchise interests which espouse this mobility-oriented approach to European futures.

What forms of knowledge, then, are being constructed through the deployment of the different genres of tools? A major contested area in the TEN-T policy process was the construction of evaluation strategies. A line of cleavage in this struggle opened between the advocates of cost-benefit analysis, and the advocates of strategic environmental assessment. Whilst the case for economic rationality has been put consistently and strongly by many actors in the process, the call for alternative evaluation came from the margins. It was perhaps not surprising that economics was adopted as the appropriate primary discipline to evaluate measures that were designed principally to bring economic benefits. However, our first, inescapable, conclusion is that the idea of frictionless mobility as a community good is inherent in the value base underpinning each of the genres, regardless of their source, or inspiration. Their political shaping ensured this.

In terms of environmental knowledge, a framework for analysis was required to deal with a threat to policy making, but the particular construction of the EU spatial policy process created the effect of successfully assimilating environmental concerns through positive integration. Our analysis shows, however, first the weakness of this construction, but second, and more importantly, to argue that this construction is the product of the hegemonic discourses of the EU itself. The project of TEN-T would not be slowed by SEA.

A range of evaluation tools has emerged with a mix of roles. Macro- and micro-economic evaluation is used to justify EU financial support for individual transport corridors, and to justify the EU's broad support for the TEN-T. Environmental evaluation tools (SEA and corridor analysis) will provide information on the overall impact of the networks, and different modal options at the corridor level. The outcome of a paradigmatic battle appears to have been the elevation of economic evaluation to hegemonic status. Economic criteria will be used to justify EU intervention in projects, whilst environmental knowledge will support decisions rather than carry any binding power. The value of international mobility will be more significant in influencing decision making than the value of 'for example' the impact of constructing new motorways in remote mountain valleys.

Power is also found to be a crucial consideration in the process of evaluation. The hegemony of economics in evaluation would appear to favour the wide range of interests which are likely to benefit most from the construction of the trans-European networks. Concerns about the environmental impacts of the networks are marginalised. The particular methodologies further compound this exclusion of interests. CBA is a technical exercise which does not lend itself to the participation of multiple actors. Its values and workings are not transparent. SEA, alternatively, has the potential for implementation within a participative planning framework. However, in the case of TEN-T, it does not appear that this possibility has been followed – rather SEA, like CBA, is being conceived as a desk exercise. The processes by which these methodologies have been selected and incorporated into the policy framework are opaque, and have not benefited from public participation. The ground rules are being laid down for projects which will be implemented within member states, yet evaluation is not being used in a way

Box 7.4 **Rationalisation effects of the evaluation strategy for TEN-T**

What the evaluation strategy excludes:

any significant risk to projects because of potential environmental/social impacts
scrutiny of primary EU visions/policies/objectives
alternative mobility scenarios/transport options
transparency/participation of many interests

What the evaluation strategy achieves:

support for the vision of international mobility at the heart of the Single Market project
justification for EU investment in TEN-T
enables member states to advance prioritised TEN-T projects, without imposing decisions

which opens up the planning of projects, corridors and networks. It appears that the democratic deficit in infrastructure planning, which we are familiar with at the national level, is being reconstructed at the EU level, and embedded in evaluation strategies (Box 7.4).

It appears that innovations in evaluation in the TEN-T policy process will provide information about the broader environmental impacts of infrastructure development in major international corridors and networks as a whole, but will not create transparent processes of decision making, or broaden the scope of the policy debate. The possibility of any subsequent communicative events having any major impact on policy seems minimal.

We have seen in this chapter that the political and institutional setting of knowledge tools clearly shapes their scope, timing, methodology and, ultimately, their impact. Frameworks for economic and environmental analysis were shaped by the discourses of the single market and political integration, by inter-institutional politics, and by the actions of interest groups. Appreciating their constructed nature helps us to understand the dangers in regarding them simply as rational scientific tools. These attempts to shape and control the evaluation process can be interpreted as struggles over the embedding of particular values, knowledges and power relations. The adoption of particular approaches and techniques in evaluation creates boundaries of inclusion and exclusion of knowledge, which potentially establishes bias in favour of a particular set of interests.

An important dimension in our narrative of power/knowledge is the way that the need for the rationalisation of policy shifted in response to changing political agendas which created risks and uncertainties for policy making. We have seen how new versions of the everyday tools used by planners were constructed so that they could be used to stabilise the policy process in response to the uncertainties – economic, environmental and spatial – of trans-European infrastructure planning and spatial policy making.

The attempt to create an integrated field of spatial policy creates a new force for a spatialised rationality that has several important effects. It pulls together into one analytical framework (TIA) many of the contested issues, which can be seen as an attempt to find a rational settlement of the tensions and conflicts within and across previous knowledge boundaries – particularly between the environmental and the economic in this case. Is this likely to be significant in permanently shifting the way that spatial impacts are understood and integrated into policy making? This is an open question, but we note that the strongest advocates of TIA practice are not calling for the institutionalising of TIA in EU law. This creates an unusual situation, where SEA now has legal force and will be applied in future to all forms of transnational spatial planning activity (at least to plans and programmes), but where the favoured approach within the spatial planning community has no such weight. We seem, then, to be on course for a new unbalanced period in the rationalisation of spatial policy, replacing the previous tensions between environment and economy with a new *frisson* between discrete analysis of these impacts, and the attempt to harmonise them within a new spatial agenda. This seems to reinforce questions about the role of the tools that might perform this complex task – are they attempting to provide better information, or are they (surely) part of a process of ordering and normalizing the field of spatial planning by rationalizing conflicts? A clear problem in the use of similar approaches (such as the use of integrated assessment in the transport sector) has been how conflicts are either represented, buried or traded-off within these tools.

Our detailed examination of knowledge building in the TEN-T policy process therefore allows us to pose a series of questions for the new 'science' of integrated Territorial Impact Assessment. Will the new approach simply re-embed the values of frictionless mobility, as our example of the analysis of cross-border movements as a measure of regional integration illustrates? Will it suppress and conceal how difficult trade-offs between impacts are? Will it increase the prospects for transparent, accountable and participative spatial planning?

Our interpretation is that the new knowledge tools are beginning to provide the required rationalisation of the new discourse of European space: frictionlessness and polycentricity are the new 'given', and analysis is becoming grounded in these new norms of spatial development. The idea of community benefits, once inserted into new tools, legitimises the analysis of transnational activities and the physical intervention that is inevitably triggered by this analysis.

From this perspective, the development of TIA, and the implementation of

SEA, become key areas for future scrutiny. The work of the emerging network of European spatial observatories, as it considers how 'problems' such as accessibility and urban-rural relations should be factored into Territorial Impact Assessment, demands critical attention. This means ensuring that those working in the laboratories within which the new knowledge tools are being bench-tested, are challenged to reflect critically on the core question: is a hegemonic discourse of frictionlessness and polycentricity simply being embedded in the new tools?

We have set out a detailed argument here that the definition of knowledge boundaries has become a vital strategy in institutionalising European spatial planning as a 'rational, science-based policy field', which necessarily excludes destabilising forms of knowledge. Meanwhile, everyday planning at different scales, through the Europeanisation processes we discuss elsewhere in this section, seems likely to be subtly but fundamentally reshaped to reproduce this discourse. Spatial planning will increasingly revolve around these organising, epistemic concepts, shaped by EU high and low politics and by the politics of interest.

Chapter 8

The Europeanisation of spatial planning

> At the beginning of the 1990s, the Øresund Region was located at the periphery of the European Communities. Now, at the end of the 1990s, the situation of the region has changed. It is still, formally, a Danish-Swedish border region, but in the European Union, it is also a region that transcends boundaries, a laboratory for a transnational city construction and a model for European integration.
>
> (City of Copenhagen and City of Malmö, 1999: 16)

> Where else in the world can you choose to spend the evening in an outdoor café in your hometown and be in a world city thirty minutes later? Without a doubt, the Øresund bridge has created new, exciting possibilities.
>
> (Malmö City, 2002)

> European culture is marked by its diversity; diversity of climate, countryside, architecture, language, beliefs, taste and artistic style. . . . But underlying this variety there is an affinity, a family likeness, a common European identity.
>
> (Malmö City, 2002; cited in Morley and Robins, 1995: 76)

Introduction

When a policy language is created, and it becomes institutionalised by the construction of frameworks and measures which spread and apply its core ideas, we are seeing Europeanisation at work. Conceptually, we are talking here partly about the ability of a policy discourse to create the conditions for its own survival and reproduction – the active promulgation of the European project – and partly about the ways that a hegemonic discourse is 'naturally' reproduced through practices which absorb its policy ideas – the passive adoption of the EU spatial policy discourse into policy making across scales and places. In this chapter we will explore these subtle processes of enabling the 'silent development' of a discourse of monotopia across the new multi-level field of spatial policy (Graute, 2000).

Conceptually one can operate with (at least) five different notions of the term Europeanisation. It can be seen as changes in external territorial boundaries (e.g. in the form of enlargement); as the development of institutions of governance at the European level; as central penetration of national and sub-national systems of governance; as exporting European forms of governance beyond the European territory; and finally as a political project aiming at a unified and politically stronger Europe (Olsen, 2001: 3). This chapter seeks to identify how the new spatial policy discourse influences spatial policy making at different scales, and as an expression of an overlapping of some of these different notions of Europeanisation.

We will explore the extent of penetration of policy making in member states using the cases of England and the Scandinavian countries to show how the Europeanisation of spatial policy and planning in Europe is already in the making. We will also analyse Europeanisation within the new transnational governance arenas, in the Øresund cross-border region, and the North Sea Region as this is represented in NorVISION. The chapter focuses on both the standard top-down view of the trickling (or cascading) down of the ESDP into the planning systems in member states and in transnational regions, i.e. the implementation (or 'application') of the ESDP, and the opposing view of the open-house 'opportunity'. We end this discussion with the case of Hamburg, suggesting that one of the future modes of development of European spatial policy may be through a complex nestedness of particular cities and regions within a number of different spatial strategic sites and linkages.

We close the chapter by looking at a very different aspect of Europeanisation: the creation of a new geography textbook, part of the ESDP action programme, which is intended to form the basis of a common education about EU geography for Europe's future citizens.

Implementation in the member states: the institutionalisation of a new discourse

What, then, does Europeanisation mean for spatial policy making and planning in the EU member states? Tensions potentially exist between the emergence of overarching regional spatial policy objectives at different scales, and the individual programmes of national planning systems within them. The existence of many national systems of land ownership, planning control and building regulations, working with separate and potentially exclusive objectives, could be argued as a countermeasure to the single market, which depends on member states and other interests pursuing policies and actions which are in harmony with the overall EU integration project. This certainly creates problems in transnational planning situations, and challenges the possibility of constructing a planning framework within which these conflicting objectives can be pursued equitably (Williams, R.H., 1996a). So, the momentum towards EU spatial planning can be seen to be linked with the need to deal with not only spatial problems, but also with conflicting spatial objectives at different levels and in different regions.

As a further attempt to facilitate the institutionalisation and legitimation of the Europeanisation of spatial policy, the ESDP proposes that member states take into account its policy aims and options in their respective national spatial policies (CSD, 1999: 44):

> The member states also take into consideration the European dimension of spatial development in adjusting national spatial development policies, plans and reports. Here, the requirement for a 'Europeanisation of state, regional, and urban planning' is increasingly evident. In their spatially relevant planning, local and regional government and administrative agencies should, therefore, overcome any insular way of looking at their territory and take into consideration European aspects and inter-dependencies right from the outset.
>
> (CSD, 1999: 45)

This is an 'exercise' that countries such as The Netherlands and Denmark have already progressed quite a long way with (Faludi, 1998; Jensen, 1998). However, such a message has not been universally accepted as a neutral and objective statement, and opens up the question of how divergent interests, agendas and power relations will be played out across scales of policy making.

Needless to say, the Europeanisation of spatial planning will develop differently in the different member states. As part of a 'new regionalism', the subnational scale is where the European agenda is being most actively pursued in England. This is explicitly acknowledged as a new direction within national planning policy guidance:

> Widening the spatial planning scope of RPG is in keeping with the trends elsewhere in Europe. Moreover, both the European Spatial Development Perspective (ESDP) and the Community initiative on transnational cooperation on spatial planning – INTERREG IIC and INTERREG IIIB – programmes will provide a European context for the preparation of RPG. So too, will other European funding regimes, in particular EU Structural Funds.
>
> (DETR, 2000, para 3.1)

This is nicely illustrated in research on local planning in England which reveals a context of Britain simultaneously becoming more integrated in the EU while devolving powers within the state, and where central government is failing to keep up with local government's increasing relationships with other European regions as part of the emerging transnational planning practices (Tewdwr-Jones and Williams, 2001). From case studies of urban and rural planning in Kent, Northamptonshire, Strathclyde, Mid Glamorgan, Leicester and Gwynedd, they conclude that:

> In most of the case study areas there were explicit references in the development plans to: the requirements of particular items of EU legislation; the eligibility of

> particular areas for EU financial assistance; and/or the impact on the local economy of developments in particular EU policies. . . . As well as influencing the general context of development plan preparation, EU membership was found to have influenced the formation of individual policies.
>
> (Tewdwr-Jones and Williams, 2001: 150)

Interestingly in this study the regional and national levels were found not to be as affected by the EU as the local level, with evidence of a general transformation within the 'planning community' towards networking in new transnational settings. The authors end the analysis by regretting the 'dismissive' attitudes within British planning towards European policies – an 'isolated view' which the authors suggest limits the actors' 'capacity for thinking in terms of EU space and spatial relations' (Tewdwr-Jones and Williams, 2001: 162).

What is being pointed to here is the Europeanisation of local planning both through a top-down emphasis on the need to think European when preparing local development plans, but also a more informal exchanging and spreading of ideas through transnational structures and programmes.

Attending a meeting of the North of England Assembly of Local Authorities (NEA) on the INTERREG IIC North Sea Programme[1] illustrated that the motives and rationales that drive the local authorities do have a certain European flavour. Though it has to be admitted that the basic reasoning seemed to be more to do with 'bidding for funds' than about European integration. The whole exercise was very much about how to 'tune in' on the programme by fitting project descriptions to the goals and intentions of INTERREG IIC. At the NEA meeting this was expressed in terms of what one participant called 'using the right EU buzz words'. At this meeting at least, there was apparent consensus about making an application that stressed 'empowerment, sustainability and social and economic cohesion'. The feeling was that this was the necessary vocabulary to use in order to be seriously considered for funding. This is part of a wider trend, where many local and regional authorities are engaged in making their own 'foreign policy' (Williams, 1996a: 250). It is also in accordance with the general 'bypassing the capital' trend that seems to be sweeping European local authorities (Rometsch and Wessels, 1996: 343–346). And finally it is a sign that local authorities work together to construct agreed 'storylines', marketable to external audiences such as the EU (Healey, 1995: 267).

Evidence from cross-border co-operation elsewhere in the EU also suggests that there is a growing practice of Europeanisation of spatial policy and planning across Europe. Thus Schulz (Schulz, 1999) concludes that in the case of the Saar-Lor-Lux-Region co-operation between German, French and Luxembourg:

> The projects are generally well accepted by the local population and reinforce the transborder regional identity of the people. Their contribution to the reduction of the inner borders of the European Union seems exemplary. By establishing networks

> between local authorities, the common motivation and the financial support are used to take advantage of synergy effects and to strengthen the position of these areas in their national and European frameworks. They are the basis for a bottom-up integration as an alternative to the top-down forces executed by European Directives, the Common Market or the Monetary Union.
>
> (Schulz, 1999: 240)

This rather optimistic view of the new regional transborder activities as bottom-up antidotes to centralised European bureaucracy, and solutions to a 'democratic deficit', should be balanced against a more critical perspective, which requires a focus on what sorts of ideas and projects materialise in these new arenas. What seems to be in play, however, is that transnational activity plays a crucial role in the Europeanisation of spatial policy.

The Europeanisation of Nordic planning

As a special case of the Europeanisation of spatial planning we will briefly discuss Böhme's analysis of the implications of EU spatial policy for the Nordic Countries (Böhme, 2002). Taken as a whole the Nordic countries Sweden, Denmark, Finland, Norway and Iceland (the latter two not being EU member states) can be said to constitute a 'planning family' of their own within a wider European planning context (Newman and Thornley, 1996). This means that apart from the obvious closeness of their nation state territories, these states also share (some) similar political, administrative and cultural features influencing their 'ways of doing planning'. From the findings of Böhme we learn that some of the key characteristics of the Nordic countries are their strong position of local self-government and that unitary states counter-balance the strong local levels (Böhme, 2002: 214). On top of these 'constitutional factors' the Nordic countries are also characterised by a political culture of neo-corporatist networks, policy consensus and framework legislation (ibid.). However, there are obviously also differences between the political structures and cultures within the Nordic countries. Böhme draws out some general conclusions on the Nordic countries and their relationship to EU spatial planning (Böhme, 2002: 214–238), which we summarise here:

- The Nordic countries have entered transnational spatial planning exercises with national planning systems not very well equipped for this kind of work (Denmark being the only exception).
- All Nordic Countries (except Iceland) discuss and act on European Spatial development policies.
- There is a lack of conceptual precedence in all countries when it comes to the interpretation of 'spatial planning'.
- National planning as a regular and mandatory activity does not exist except in the case of Denmark.

- In the Nordic EU member states Structural Funds clearly have influenced regional policy.
- There is a considerable congruence of spatial issues discussed at European and Nordic level (although some issues may have different interpretations depending on the scale – polycentricity being one such example).
- Even though the Nordic countries often act in unison, they are deeply divided on issues of European co-operation and formal integration.
- There is a common environmental agenda uniting the understanding of spatial development policies.

Böhme concludes that corporatist decision-making, the widespread reliance on network governance, and the influence of the policy discourse as an informal frame of mind, makes links to the ESDP very evident as an expression of European integration by means of network governance within the Nordic countries (Böhme, 2002: 230–231). This conclusion is clearly also in accordance with our analysis of the INTERREG programme in the North Sea Region, which embraces parts of some of these Nordic Countries.

A 'green room in the European house': the case of Denmark

Böhme identifies the Danish case as one of the most explicit examples of convergence between the EU spatial policy discourse and national planning. During the last decade the Danish government's National Planning Reports have gradually imported the very logic of argument that one finds in the CSD and Commission documents. One of the planning documents that initiated Danish orientation towards European spatial planning was 'Denmark towards the year 2018: the spatial structuring of Denmark in the future Europe' (Ministry of Energy and Environment, 1992): 'the report . . . illustrates the trend towards marketing Denmark in the European context' (Newman and Thornley, 1996: 64). The report holds that if the new possibilities provided by increasing international economic competition are going to be exploited, then the spatial development of Denmark must be seen in an international perspective, as the cities and the urban system must compete to acquire a prominent place on the future map of Europe (Ministry of Energy and Environment, 1992).

From equality to appropriateness – the changing rationale of Danish planning

One major change that must be recognised in relation to the European spatial policy discourse was the 1992 reform of the Danish Planning Act. This was a radical break with the spatial planning traditions within the welfare state. The new Planning Act of 1992 indicates this by focusing on 'appropriate' spatial development in contrast to the former focus on 'equal' spatial development. This shift matches the trend of a growing number of city co-operations, city marketing and inter-urban competition. Among the many implications this shift seems to have, the most important one is probably that the welfare state is put in question:

> This change in the planning law together with the message of 'Denmark Towards the Year 2018' amounts to a significant statement that Denmark is prepared to a more polycentric and market-oriented spatial planning within a larger European context. We see this as a tendential break with the former primarily politically dominated welfare orientation of the Danish territory. The space is gradually being transformed into a space of economics.
>
> (Jensen *et al.*, 1996a: 14)

Why the Planning Act was changed is an important question. At the time of the reform there was very little public debate. This probably owes its explanation to the massive de-regulation and 'slimming' of the public sector that characterised Danish government policy in the 1980s. It has also to do with the understanding of the global territorial changes. Thus the National Planning Agency already stated in their National Planning Report of 1989 that: 'In the opinion of the government the previous objective of equalisation through national planning has been made obsolete by the recent development' (National Planning Report, cited in Jørgensen and Tonboe, 1993: 390). On top of this it should be noted that Denmark is one of the European planning 'families' that responds to the increasing competition by preparing national spatial plans as marketing tools (Newman and Thornley, 1996: 73). This is seen in the case of the plans for the Øresund region, which we shall turn to later in this chapter.

Dealing with the 'fourth level'

The impact of the European spatial policy discourse is perceptible at the level of the local Danish authorities. Asked to comment on the planning situation in Denmark in the mid 1990s, regional planners from the County of Vejle saw it this way:

> With the new planning act of 1992 and its shift of objective from equal to appropriate development it can be questioned whether the regional plan can reach all corners of the county. . . . With the new planning objective, appropriate development, it has become legitimate to let development come about naturally wherever possible, since this is supposed to be of benefit to the weaker areas as well. . . . This might have the effect that the regional plan, instead of being a programme for action is developing more in the direction of a catalogue of visions of long-term goals. . . . This development has legitimised that some decisions are being prepared and/or made between groups not under direct democratic control and with the participation of various interests groups in society who have announced their opinion beforehand. . . . There

> seems to be a tendency towards less openness as soon as industrial policies are involved because of the factor of competition.
>
> (Danish County Planner, in Fosgaard and Jørgensen, 1996: 11–13)

Clear evidence of the influence of the European spatial policy discourse on Danish regional planning is found in this statement from a planner from another Danish County, Viborg County. In the words of the regional planner the European spatial policy level is clearly seen as the 'fourth level' of planning adding to the already existing hierarchical system of state, county and municipal planning:

> The change in the planning act of 1992 from equal to appropriate development will most likely lead to a modification of our urban pattern. But already in our latest regional plan of 1993 we changed our main objective, interpreting the new objective of appropriate development in the direction of positive discrimination of the municipal centres of the weaker areas instead of equal development. . . . Positive discrimination as we practice it now is rather unequal development. . . . But with the advent of EU a fourth level has been introduced and now regional policy is not only about relating to the kingdom at large, but now we must take into consideration the development trends which can be envisaged in our corner of the overarching totality which is Europe.
>
> (Danish County Planner, in Fosgaard and Jørgensen, 1996: 15)

Changes in actual planning practice among the Danish regional authorities are documented here, but also a shift of mind and attitude in the direction of the 'think European' mode of thought. Such thinking should be understood as an important dimension of the Europeanisation of spatial planning, supplementing the Europeanisation taking place at the organisational level.

Denmark and European spatial planning policy – the 1997 National Planning Report

Even though the European orientation of Danish national planning was very explicit with *Denmark towards the year 2018* (Ministry of Energy and Environment 1992), the Danish National Planning Report of 1997 is even more illustrative on these matters. It is clearly the national planning document that lies closest to the EU documents in rationale and style. Furthermore, it is the first national planning report ever to be published in English as well as in Danish, the title being *Denmark and European Spatial Planning Policy.*

The report has a first chapter on the 'challenges' to Danish planning within a territorially changing Europe. The second part contains the development trends within the 'points' (cities), the 'lines' (infrastructure) and the 'planes' (landscape). Then the national planning policy that is proposed in order to deal with these trends is outlined. This is done under the colourful heading 'A green room in the European house'. Finally a chapter on environmental assessment is presented. In line with the developments we analysed in Chapter 5, the document continues the trend of *Denmark towards the year 2018*, with its very widespread use of maps and colourful illustrations.

The overall national planning goals are identical with the goals of European spatial policy discourse in general, and the ESDP in particular: balance in the urban system, environmentally acceptable accessibility and the protection of nature and cultural heritage (Ministry of Environment and Energy, 1997: 5). Spatial planning is seen as having an important role to play in the wider integration process. The territorial changes of Europe are articulated as a move from a Europe of centre and peripheries, to a Europe of 'complex mosaics' (Ministry of Environment and Energy, 1997: 9).

A number of issues are dealt with in the report. Amongst the main ones is the increase in transport which is leading to a 'crowding of the continent'. The many maps suggest that in order to keep the competitive edge of globalised economy, the flows must not be hindered. In this context, Denmark is said to have a fairly high accessibility to the other countries in Europe (Ministry of Environment and Energy, 1997: 31). It is also said that Denmark has a well developed infrastructure and communication between cities.

As a continuation of the previous National Planning Reports, the report states a number of political goals for the urban system. It is stated that all Danish cities have potential in international markets, and that the multiplicity of various specialisations should be considered as an advantage in an age of increasing inter-urban competition. A balanced urban system can be obtained by means of a five-string strategy, focusing on the following themes (Ministry of Environment and Energy, 1997: 55–58):

- Development of city-networks between regional centres and municipality centres;
- Regional centres with increased European orientation;
- The Øresund-region as an international urban region;
- Development in the small towns and rural areas;
- Planned co-operation across borders.

The strategy results in a number of actions to be taken internationally as well as nationally. At the European level, the government will secure the status of the Øresund-region as a European metropolis, work for a diffusion of knowledge of the international strength positions held by Danish regional centres and city-networks, strengthen the focus on the threatened rural areas of Europe, increase Danish participation in the trans-regional plan co-operation in the North Sea and the Baltic Sea regions, continue the co-operation of *Visions and Strategies around the Baltic Sea 2010* and, finally, continue the cross-border regional co-operation with Sweden and Germany (Ministry of Environment and Energy, 1997: 58).

In the National Planning Report from the year 2000 the line of argument and the inspiration from the EU spatial policy discourse is continued. This is at least the case in its general framing of the problems, even though it could be argued that the European profile is rather low (Böhme, 2002: 99). However, this we would rather ascribe to the relatively high profile of the former reports than as evidence of the reduction of the European agenda in Danish spatial planning. At the moment of writing (2003) the Ministry of Environment (as it is now termed) has published a new planning report which reinforces the 'Danish experience' as being one of explicit compliance with the European spatial policy discourse:

> The most distinct case of transferring the ESDP into national policy is Denmark. The national planning reports of 1992 and 1997 clearly combine national and European aims and in the report of 2000 ESDP features can also be identified. . . . Denmark, especially, is an outstanding example of adapting national planning policies to European spatial development policies.
>
> (Böhme, 2002: 222, 225)

This conclusion is furthermore in accordance with the earlier analysis of the convergence between Danish national spatial planning and EU spatial policy discourse made by Jensen and Jørgensen:

> Summing up, the most important trends of the 1990s are: further internationalisation; an explicit adoption of the concepts and rationale behind the emerging new spatial planning agenda of the European Union; and finally the legal confirmation of the change in Danish national spatial planning from equality to differentiation. Not only can we say, therefore, that the rationale of Danish spatial planning has shifted from a 'space of politics' towards a 'space of economics', we can also identify it as a 'spatial policy of difference' and thus in the end as a less equity-oriented ideology of spatial development. . . . As described above, Danish national planning reports have embraced the logic and wordings of the European Spatial Development Perspective. However, the very complex processes of institutionalisation of the EU planning discourse raises questions as to the political legitimacy of planning, in both the EU as a whole as well as in its Member States . . . Danish municipal and regional politicians involved have been quite explicit about planning under INTERREG II C not being subject to Danish requirements for public participation. In this respect it is also interesting to note that, with financial support from INTERREG II C, central government representatives of the Member States concerned have come together to formulate a spatial vision for the NSR (NorVision 1999). . . . As mentioned, the INTERREG programme has played a key role in the institutionalisation and articulation of the ESDP and the European Union discourse. . . . The conclusion is

> thus, that the direction taken by planning within the nation states and the European Union in the near future should be of concern not only to planners; democracy and democratic planning are at issue.
>
> (Jensen and Jørgensen, 2000: 36–39)

Obviously this strong EU spatial planning commitment from Denmark seems to be part of a paradox as Denmark is well known as one of the more reluctant EU member states (at least in some respects). However, this is probably also the key reason why the Danish case has been deeply dependent on the whole informal and non-binding nature of the ESDP programme. Given the reluctant attitude towards European integration (so far at least, considering a new liberal government in office from November 2001), a formal spatial policy with its presumed repercussion on the National Planning Act and Planning System would certainly have been a non-starter in the Danish context. These findings are clearly an interesting example of the Europeanisation of spatial planning. Furthermore, such a picture makes it necessary to revise the strict and simple dichotomy of the important formal fields of 'high politics' versus the equally unimportant spheres of informal 'low politics'. The lessons from this analysis point to the need for new and more subtle concepts for the 'spatialisation of governmental ideas' which we are now witnessing. We shall return to this theme in our closing section.

Region building in the European Union: Case one – the Øresund

Alongside this Europeanisation through variable convergence, the EU's programme of action is focused mainly on the transnational level, avoiding friction with member states (CSD, 1999: 35). In line with the importance of the INTERREG initiative, the Commission and member states are continuing the 'project-oriented transnational co-operation' for spatial development, and this preferably within the new INTERREG III initiative that is seen as the test bed for the ESDP (CSD, 1999: 39). Increasingly, resources allocated through other programmes such as the Structural Funds, will also need to work within the ESDP policy framework.

We now move on to explore Europeanisation in the form of transnational spatial planning that transgresses national borders. By looking into the making of new cross-border co-operation within the European spatial policy area we find another form of Europeanisation.

Twentieth-century Europe has been described as 'a factory of borders' (O'Dowd, 2001: 95), leading to 'trans-frontier regionalism' (O'Dowd, 2001: 100) a phenomenon that INTERREG is an explicit expression of: 'While the EU has encouraged a more consensual and negotiated approach to state borders, border policy continues to be relatively undemocratic with consequences for the EU as a transnational polity' (O'Dowd, 2001: 96).

The notion of nation-state-crossing border regions as 'experimental laboratories' (Maskell and Törnqvist, 1999: 12, O'Dowd, 2001: 101) and 'integration laboratories' (Tangkjær, 2000: 187) has become more widespread in the last few years. This adds to the notion of the European territory as one of many actual changes of which the outcome is far from certain, and where words such as 'experiment', 'risk' and 'vision' are making their way into the vocabulary of official policy documents as well as into the minds of developers and policy makers.

The Øresund region, containing the national capital of Denmark, has for some time been looked upon as the most competitive urban region that the Danish state could support in the global game. Thus we find the Øresund region as one of the high priorities in the Danish National Planning Reports from 1992, 1997 and 2000. According to the 1997 report, a balanced urban system centred on the Øresund region as an international urban region (Tangkjær, 2000: 55–58). Furthermore, there is reason to take note of this region's nestedness within the EU spatial policy discourse, since the 1997 report explicitly adopts and rearticulates the basic rationales of the ESDP (Jensen, 1999). Thus we have gone 'full circle' so to speak.

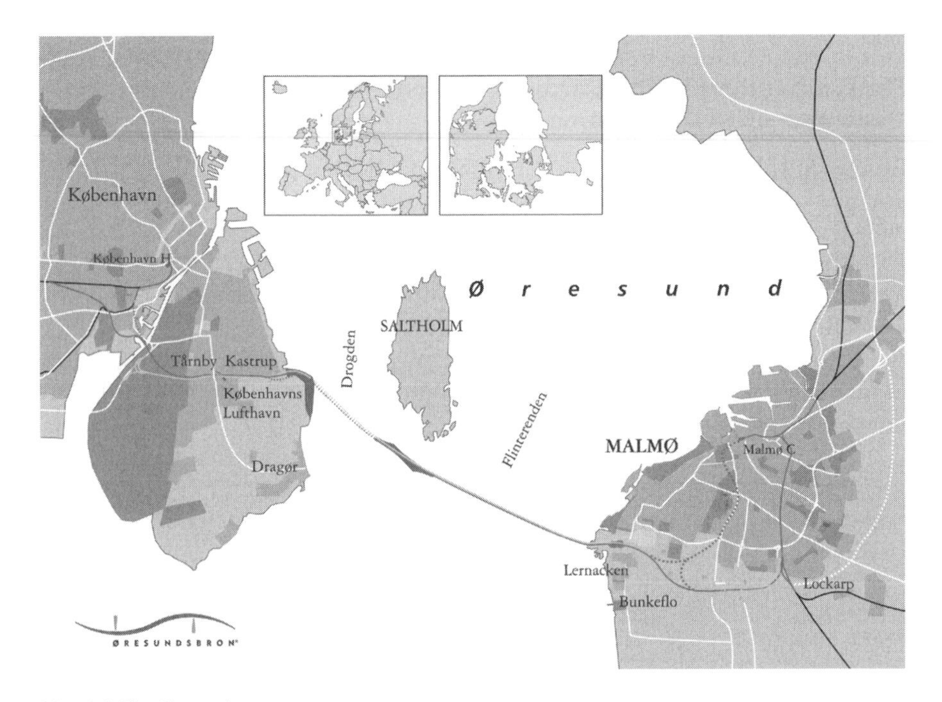

Map 8.1 The Øresund.

Source: Øresundsbro Konsortiet.

The region will include around 3.5 million inhabitants and covers an area of some 21,000 km² (Map 8.1). The Øresund Region comprises Zealand, Lolland-Falster and Bornholm on the Danish side and Skåne, the southernmost part of Sweden. Its core competencies are said to be: provisions, research, medicine, biotechnology, tourism, environmental industry, design and distribution. The most notable dimension of the Øresund region is probably the 16 km long bridge, which opened in July 2000. This fixed link for road and rail is part of the bigger transnational infrastructure project of the TEN-T and the project as such is said to have effects on 'the spatial structure of Europe as a whole' (Williams, 1996a: 176). The road traffic was expected to increase by 17 per cent compared with 2001, to an average of 9,495 vehicles per day.

The development of the Øresund region was supported by INTERREG IIA in the period 1994–1999, and is linked to INTERREG IIIA for the Structural Funds period 2000–2006. A political body termed 'The Øresund Committee' is responsible for co-operation in the Øresund region, containing members from Swedish and Danish Counties and Municipalities in the region. Amongst other activities the Committee administers the European Union's INTERREG programmes. The Committee administers the EU's INTERREG fund, receiving about 100 million Danish kroner between 1994–1999, and 460 million Danish kroner for the 2000–2006 period. Thus the Øresund INTERREG region is but one of the many cross-border regions that have materialised under the EU spatial policy discourse. The INTERREG II programme alongside other EU programmes was influential in engaging political actors:

> The development of Structural Funds policy and related principles contributed to establishing a discourse on the making of the Europe of the Regions, and a little later, on the Europe of Cities . . . the Commission has created a pressure on – or at least, has encouraged – cities and regions to become political actors in Europe.
>
> (Le Galès, 2002: 100)

Furthermore, 'with the initiation of the INTERREG program, the EC Commission became a major actor in cross-border regions' (O'Dowd, 2001: 102). This also seems to be recognised by the Council of European Municipalities and Regions, as they see the Øresund region as being intimately linked to the ESDP:

> A very practical example of polycentric spatial development is the growing Øresund region in Denmark/Sweden and the towns and cities it embraces. This development, stimulated by the new bridge, also has radically useful lessons for cross-border co-operation; there have been proposals for a directly elected council with tax-raising powers.
>
> (O'Dowd, 2001: 1)

The proposal of a directly elected council was probably more of a provocative suggestion, judging by the way it was launched by the Lord Mayor of Copenhagen in the press. However, the ensuing public debate showed that people have at least started to think transnationally about the issue of metropolitan governance in this region, and that the issue raised by the Mayor may serve as a catalyst for such a future debate.

There are other explicit links to the thinking in the ESDP. The Øresund Region has been pointed to as one of the so-called 'global economic integration zones' that is mentioned as a counterpart to the traditional European growth pole: 'Now, there is an indication that two more areas have the potential to become global economic integration zones: the Øresund region and the region of Barcelona' (Faludi and Waterhout, 2002: 156).

The Øresund as a locus of struggle

The Øresund region, with its bridge, has also functioned as an icon of a transnational mobility struggle between industrialists and environmentalists across Europe over alternative economic, spatial and mobility futures:

> A SEED started campaigning against the TEN-T proposals in 1992, concerned both about the environmental impact of road building, and about the globalising impact of the programme: Our position was clear: we were against new motorways, and the TEN-T plans were shaped by and for industrial giants like Volvo, Philips and Fiat (ERT members). All these roads would be used to shift goods back and forward through the regions of Europe and strengthen the grip of TNCs on markets everywhere.
>
> (Environmental lobbyist, pers. comm.)

The origins of the A SEED position can be traced back to campaigns against infrastructure projects in member states which had European dimensions. For example:

> Swedish environmental groups (like Miljoforbundet) campaigning against the Øresund bridge which was part of TEN-T. The campaign against the Øresund bridge all the time hammered on the fact that the bridge was not built for people in Denmark or Sweden but for long distance transport of goods from and to the Internal Market. Alongside this was the work of Belgian NGOs that had been monitoring the activities of the European Round Table of Industrialists in promoting TEN-T. Awareness of the motives behind the infrastructure 'boost' was there all the time. But A SEED's central message was 'No more roads', and arguing linkages between the 12,000 km of new roads proposed in the TEN-T with environmental impacts of transport. Those involved in the A SEED campaign were surprised at the lack of involvement by other NGOs: During the first years of campaigning (mainly through information distribution, action days, letter writing, etc.) we were amazed that the big NGO's kept so quiet and did not do anything against TEN-T.
>
> (Environmental lobbyist, pers. comm.)

Targeting the roads bias of the emerging network, and the powerful role of the infrastructure lobby in the decision-making process, campaigns focused on major planned infrastructure projects filling key 'missing links' in environmentally sensitive areas. Critical transnational projects such as the Øresund link, and the Somport Tunnel, linking France and Spain across the Pyrenees, were targeted. This was done, as we showed in Chapter 7, because the powerful infrastructure lobby promoted the fixed link across Øresund as a critical missing link of iconic status.

However, the advocates of the Øresund region see the region in a rather different light. We will now listen to the voice of the managing director and CEO of A/S Øresundsforbindelse, which is the main contractor for the Øresund bridge. Here the CEO is targeting what he regards as the 'dishonest methods' of the environmentalists:

> The effects of the Øresund link on the environment has been the principal concern for those who have opposed building the bridge. It's my feeling that critics have employed dishonest methods. When it comes right down to it, their opposition is founded on a political concept about what sort of a society we want: one based on economic growth, or one based on stagnation? . . . Seen from an international perspective, the matter is absurd. I have just returned from a trip to South-East Asia and the rape of nature I witnessed there makes the Øresund issue tame by comparison.
>
> (Henning Hummelmose, managing director and CEO of A/S Øresundsforbindelse in the SAS Journal 'Scanorama', July /August 1995)

Interestingly these statements were found in 'speakers corner' of the Scandinavian Airlines journal 'Scanorama', which must be considered to be the voice of yet another pro-region player in the field.

As can clearly be detected, the Øresund region is the locus of a struggle between different powers and interests, and their accompanying knowledge forms – a striking parallel to our analysis of power and knowledge forms in Chapter 7. The themes and issues at stake are, however, not confined to the question of the environment alone, but reach deeper into the normative and political interests in the new power geometry of transformed territorialities and spatial practices. Thus, the CEO relates to the question of the changing power balance between the nation state, the regions and the supra-national level and argues for a new 'spatial fix' (Harvey, 2001), or space-power configuration based on a strategy of strong urban agglomeration growth and concentration as opposed to a rationale of equal growth and re-distribution:

> The general philosophy among politicians has long been to equalise economic growth and try to distribute it throughout the country. I think this has been wrong. No one profits by holding the strong region in check; on the contrary. If strong regions are permitted to grow, the cake to be divided will be that much bigger and growth in

> one region often offers various spin-off developments in others. . . . The development in Europe shows unequivocally that national states and traditional boundaries are becoming less significant. Instead it's the regions that are growing stronger, demanding self-determination and guarding their individuality. I don't think Øresund will be any exception.
>
> (Henning Hummelmose, managing director and CEO of A/S Øresundsforbindelse in the SAS Journal 'Scanorama', July/August 1995)

Here we see a multi-level power struggle, where the Øresund becomes both the iconic focus of a wider struggle as well as the terrain for its local resolution. Actors and issues move across regional, transnational and European arenas in the playing out of this conflict.

Rescaling peripherality

The divergence of interests and rationales behind the stakeholders in the Øresund Region can be traced back in time to the historical conditions of the cities within the region. The Swedish city of Malmö, in particular, has 'suffered' from being defined as periphery within a nation state territory:

> Swedish and Danish political and economic actors have, however, different geographical visions about the future of the Sound. The Danish establishment has, as a primary goal, the enlargement of Copenhagen's hinterland (as a hexagonal hinterland in the central place theory) and at the same time wishes to enhance Copenhagen's position in Northern Europe (with Hamburg and Berlin as main competitors). In Sweden, regional actors (in Scania) see this as an opportunity to take advantage of the Scania's close proximity to Copenhagen and the (eu)ropean heartland. The possibility to strengthen Scania's provincial position in Sweden has also been of significance. Since the 17th century, Scania has felt itself unjustly treated by central powers in Stockholm. The central actors in Sweden hope that the bridge will provide a way for Malmö in particular to emerge from its structural stagnation and revitalise the economy.
>
> (Ek, 1998: 11)

This notion of a Europe of strong city regions shows how ideas about the urban are being reconfigured, in the sense that new socio-spatial referents are offered for the social agents living on each side of the bridge, changing the territorial dimension of identity. The CEO's assessment clearly should be seen as a political statement, nevertheless it strikes a chord with an analysis which points at the changed position of cities and nation states within the European Union:

> The making of the European Union (EU) gives a different meaning to the term 'European Cities', going beyond sociological and geographical analysis. They are

> now part of a polity in the making . . . European cities are not organized solely by the state but, increasingly, in relation to cities and regions in other countries – the horizontal dimension of European institutionalization – and – in relation to Brussels – the vertical, multi-level dimension.
>
> (Le Galès, 2002: 5, 75)

Moreover we would argue that the physical infrastructure of the fixed link acts as a potential symbolic signifier for the attempt to construct not only a transnational mobility region, but also in due time the construction of a new transnational regional identity. Obviously, the everyday life of people in the region has not yet come to such a state of practice and mind. However, if one speaks with people, for example, in Copenhagen about the practical importance and the symbolic meaning of the bridge, one clearly senses that it has turned into a combined practical and symbolic landmark. In an interview for a research project on Transportation and Urban Planning[2] conducted at Aalborg University we thus find the voice of people whose everyday practice relates to the bridge one way or the other:

> I have crossed it [the Bridge]. And even very fast because that seemed fun to do. But otherwise I really find the bridge misplaced. To be honest. I can't understand why at all . . . And it maybe that in one hundred years' time people will make pilgrimages across it because things take time . . . But I cannot understand why people suddenly . . . why people are puzzled by the facts that the Swedes are not crawling over the place and we don't . . . why should we?
>
> (Copenhagen resident interviewed in 2001)

Clearly this statement does not call for optimism about the speedy construction of a new transnational identity. However, it seems to be a rather commonly held perception of the bridge and the region amongst 'ordinary people' on the Danish side of the nation state border. This perhaps underlines that the concerted and deliberate construction of a transnational region requires both physical and socio-cultural approaches. In the words of the City Director of Planning in Copenhagen, we can see how the bridge is intended to fulfil both roles: 'The bridge is needed more as a symbol than for speeding up transportation flows' (quoted in Newman and Thornley, 1996: 238).

The 'good life' on the doorstep – 'the human capital' as a transnational metropolis?

With a vast number of place marketing publications playing a part in the naming and branding of the Øresund Region, and constructing its identity, the creativity of self-labelling seems endless. Thus it has now become official policy to brand the region under the label 'The Human Capital' (Øresund Network AB, 2002). This is explicitly an attempt to add a more human and soft dimension to a project that otherwise might seem to be more about hard infrastructure and cool business. The idea is to articulate a particular 'Øresund Way of Life' (Øresund Network AB, 2002):

> Balance and harmony are keywords for life in the Øresund Region. The people of the Øresund live in one of Northern Europe's fastest growing business areas, while the good life awaits them right on their doorstep. . . . According to an American survey based on 160 countries, Denmark is the best country in the world to live in. Sweden is not far behind in fourth place. The social systems are well developed and take good care of the sick and the old. Crime is limited and unemployment is low. Interest in taking care of the environment is expressed in the unspoilt countryside and in urban development. . . . Accessibility characterizes the Øresund Region. The tailor-made road and rail network blurs the borders and puts the entire region within reach. . . . The quality of working life an leisure activities makes the Øresund Region peerless.
>
> (Øresund Network AB, 2002: 9)

The Øresund Region has been described as a new 'transnational metropolis' and as a model for the 'new Europe without borders' (Berg and Löfgren, 2000). Some see this reaction to the processes of globalisation as a kind of 'regional panic' in which stakeholders and government bodies are busy transforming themselves into competitive global players (Berg and Löfgren, 2000: 8). However, as we saw before, making such a new transnational metropolis is not an expression of concerted consensus. What we find in the case of the Øresund Region is a loosely defined institutional and territorial arena for those players who want in on the global game, or in other words: 'The only thing that actually unites many of the actors is that they agree upon working under the label "the Øresund Region" and that they often share a specific optimistic rhetoric we call Ørespeak' (Berg and Löfgren, 2000: 12).

This corresponds to our analysis of the spatial policy discourse in general, and in the case of the ESDP in particular as it can be understood as an arena for power-struggles over meaning. In many other ways the Øresund region seems to 'fit the picture' of the new spatial policy discourse of monotopic Europe. Thus the institutional arrangement for the region resembles that of the ESDP process as we described earlier: 'The authority structure in the Øresund region can thus be perceived as a black hole which has exercised its gravity on all kinds of political organizations and made various actors and agents rush in to fill it' (Berg and Löfgren, 2000: 63).

This kind of 'open house' strategy (Tangkjær, 2000: 170) furthermore challenges the more rigid notion of top-down versus bottom-up strategy, as it is an illustration of the multiple scales and levels of institutions that all go together in forming the particular place as the Øresund region. Needless to say such a place still has to be comprehended by means of its relations to other places, and flows, as is the point in the 'relational approach' to regional development (Allen *et al.*, 1998).

The creation of a transnational metropolis region such as the Øresund Region within, and with the help of, the EU can thus be said to depend on both material conditions of economic, institutional and physical resources as well as on vision and imagination (Berg and Löfgren, 2000: 19). Furthermore, the linkage of the two nation states in question by the bridge is a very explicit example of the politics of European mobility. In other words a process of 'transnational metropolisation' (Löfgren, 2000: 29), in which we find embedded a particular view of the EU territory and its relation to the urban places (nodes) and the infrastructures connecting them (flows): 'This metropolitanism is immanent in much thinking in Europe since the introduction of the now famous 'Blue Banana' – the industrial/ urban core that runs southeast from the Benelux countries toward Catalonia' (Linde-Laursen, 2000: 155).

In the centre of such a process the mobility rationale behind the Øresund Region comes out very strongly in key metaphors contextualising the region: speed, mobility, flexible and mobile subjects and the bridge as concrete artefact and symbolic connection (Löfgren, 2000: 27) – thus connecting to the cultural grammar of seeing mobility and speed as progressive forces and distinctive for an (upwards) moving urban metropolis. The bridge is thus part of the 'positive narrative of globalisation and European integration' (Löfgren, 2000: 38) as well as an articulation of the quest for increased speed, interaction and movement: 'In the Øresund vision there is not only a cult of speed but a cult of flow. . . . The bridge and the transformed transport infrastructure of motorways, railroads, and airports are part of a vision of zero friction' (Löfgren, 2000: 46–47). This links to the tension (to which we shall return to in Chapter 10) between the 'Europe of Places' versus the 'Europe of Flows', as the Øresund Region thus embodies 'a tension between everyday life of local settings and the larger abstracted space of the transnational' (O'Dell, 2000: 232). Such a tension furthermore bears witness to one of the crucial dilemmas that the European Union faces when it applies this new transnational regionalism in its attempt to fuel the political integration process. Here the functionality of, for example, the Øresund bridge does not stand alone, but rather relates to more visionary forces which envisage the making of a genuine 'identity region', even though the creation of such an identity will take time:

> It took generations to build national identities and establish complex national innovation systems favouring growth and prosperity, including at a regional level. It will take years of hard work to amalgamate two countries' distinctive innovation systems into one, even when most formal barriers have been eroded. It will take even longer for a common cross-border regional identity to form. Only then will the full potential of cross-border synergy begin to materialise.
>
> (Maskell and Törnqvist, 1999: 11)

How such strategies of nested visions and functional/symbolic attachments to regions coincide with the EU's notions of European identity and democracy is an issue to which we shall return in the final part of this book. As mentioned, some analysts have viewed the whole strategy around the Øresund region in terms of an 'open house' strategy. This means that the stakeholders, agents and policy makers playing on this field are engaged in a game characterised by a high degree of uncertainty and with an explicitly experimental status, but also that this new European urban mega-region is open to anyone interested in playing the game of global interurban competition at a transnational level. However, thinking of the Øresund region as a case of such new transnational region building understood as an 'open house' strategy represents a very selective openness which runs the risk of sidestepping democratic processes (Berg *et al.*, 2000: 280).

'Medicon Valley' – on naming the region

The Øresund Region is often pictured as 'Medicon Valley', suggesting an association with one of the most iconic mega-regions of global competitiveness, Silicon Valley. This kind of place promotion practice can obviously be criticised both in terms of being yet another copy of the US knowledge-intensive region and also in terms of who really decides and wants this type of regional development. Having said that, it is worth noting that the notion is furthermore based on a strong regional competency within the field of medical research and business (Clausen, 2000: 54). Moreover the branding of 'Medicon Valley' incorporates all the five dimensions of an alleged successful strategy for global competitive regions (metaphorical richness, geographical positioning, existing local competencies, legitimising analogies and supportive regional agents) (Boye, 2000: 215–216). As always, though, there is scope for a more cautious interpretation:

> Only within fields where a region possesses a strong and distinct scientific base do R&D intensive firms stand a chance of sustained growth and competitiveness. It may therefore be questioned whether it would be reasonable to expect that the Øresund Region could become a European Silicon Valley or a Boston in the 21st Century.
>
> (Maskell and Törnqvist, 1999: 56)

Furthermore, by giving the region a name, and by reciting the name over and over again – in statements, in written texts, at meetings – the presence of the region is acknowledged (Berg, 2000: 77). Here we find a strong parallel to the workings of the discourse of monotopic Europe, as the framing of the urban in terms of global competition and regional knowledge-based industries are certainly common features in both cases. This is part of what has been identified as an important shift in the thinking around regional development in Europe in the 1990s:

> This is a shift of emphasis from immediate support for the lagging and less successful to an acceptance that successful cities and regions hold lessons for all, and will also benefit, eventually, more peripheral areas. The propositions of the new regionalism have a clear affinity with the changing direction of thinking in the European Commission.
>
> (Herrschel and Newman, 2002: 61)

Such 'new regionalism' is part of a wider general transformation from traditional Keynesian-style and welfare-oriented policies towards more city-focused and network-based growth strategies (Herrschel and Newman, 2002: 75): a process within the European Union in which the nation state borders have become increasingly less visible as *loci* for territorial identities (Herrschel and Newman, 2002: 107). This especially being the case in cross-border regions such as the Øresund region.

It is interesting to note that the Øresund Chamber of Commerce, representing business interests in the Danish and Swedish halves of the Øresund region, feels that progress on institutional integration has failed to keep up with the material construction of the bridge. Here we see market stakeholders demanding new transnational regulatory frames and regimes. Specifically, they call for a new 'transnational authority with powers to cut through a raft of legal and practical differences between the two sides. Otherwise there is a risk that the dynamics created by the new bridge will be replaced by stagnation and inertia' (Øresund Chamber of Commerce, 2002). Bent Larsen, Chairman of the Øresund Chamber of Commerce commented: 'We can only take note that the positive effects of the new bridge have yet to materialise. The dynamics of the integration process are coming to a halt' (Øresund Chamber of Commerce, 2002). The key obstacles identified by the Øresund Chamber of Commerce include differential tax regulations, lack of a common currency and the toll fees on the Øresund Bridge.

Hands across the border – the future of the Øresund region

Although marked by some disintegrative forces such as high costs for crossing the fixed link, uncoordinated nation state bureaucratic rules, and lack of an overall political follow-up on the commitment to make the Øresund Region a global player, Mathiessen and Andersson do express a certain optimism concerning the future of the region (Mathiessen and Andersson, 2002). Not least, the ESDP's ideas of polycentricity and further dynamic growth zones as antidotes to the 'Blue Banana' are seen to be in favour of strengthening the Øresund Region (Mathiessen and Andersson, 2002: 82).

Contextualising the Øresund Region within the new transnational European space also means locating it within the TEN-T and as such mapping its relations to other important and highly prioritised links that may materialise in the future. One such link would be the proposed Fehmarn Belt fixed link between Denmark and Germany. In the 2001 Transport White Paper it is suggested that this project should become one of the 'priority TENs' projects, and this is linked to the future development of the Baltic Sea region:

> Fehmarn Belt: The bridge/tunnel crossing the natural barrier of the Fehmarn Belt between Germany and Denmark is a key link which will complete the north–south route connecting Central Europe and the Nordic countries and allow the development of trade between them. This project on the route including the recently opened Øresund fixed link aims to cross the 19 km-wide belt. Completion of this project, which is still at the preliminary study stage, should contribute to the development of the Baltic Sea region.
>
> (Mathiessen and Andersson, 2002: 55)

Concerning the future of the Øresund Region, one should also pay close attention to the expectations in the wake of EU enlargement, which will re-position the Øresund region, thus changing its relative position within the European geography from one of periphery to one of centrality. Having looked into this alleged 'laboratory' of transnational urban development and Europeanisation, we now focus on a case at another spatial scale. Still within the realm of the EU's regional policies, we turn to the North Sea Region.

Region building in the European Union: Case two – the North Sea Region

We have already alluded to the significance of the INTERREG programme in reproducing the new spatial policy discourse. Here we will focus on some of the events within the North Sea Region, where INTERREG is being used to develop new transnational activities between regions bordering this sea, and where the region's spatial vision has been described as the ESDP translated to the North Sea Region. However, a transnational planning process such as this can also be seen as being negotiated between an EU spatial vision and alternative visions of constituent member states, regions and other partners. Here we will examine the final draft of NorVISION, and we will report from a meeting in Aalborg (Denmark) held by the Danish National Planning Department in collaboration with the German consultant PLANCO that had the assignment of preparing the document.

The INTERREG IIC North Sea Programme should be seen not only as the implementation of the ESDP in new institutional settings, but also as a distinct example of the Europeanisation of spatial planning (Moll, 2002:2). Furthermore, Moll suggests that the ESDP and INTERREG embody two distinct planning traditions:

> This suggests that European planning has followed, up to now, two different directions in planning theory: While the ESDP revives the old tradition of rational

> comprehensive planning, taking up the technocratic belief in prognoses and all-embracing concepts from the 1960's and 70's, Interreg IIC reflects the trends of the 1990's towards project-based planning and competition for funding through broadly defined programmes that have no clear future perspective. . . . This means that the transnational INTERREG initiative and the ESDP are, or will be, inter-linked, establishing a form of 'Mixed Scanning'.
>
> (Moll, 2002: 16)

A snapshot: reproducing discourse in Aalborg

One event in the NorVISION process illustrates how the dialectical relation between space of places and space of flows is articulated and shaped by the micro-politics of policy making. At a meeting in Aalborg, in March 2000, partners from across the North Sea Region came together to refine the NorVISION document. Taking our departure in this specific event, we will elaborate on the practice side of discourse analysis.

Several agents and institutions were represented at the Aalborg meeting. Among these were the 'North Sea Region Spatial Vision Working Group' (VWG), a sort of CSD for the NSR. Furthermore, the national and regional planning authorities in Denmark, Germany, Norway (buying herself into the EU funded INTERREG programme, since she is not an EU member), the Netherlands, Sweden and the UK were present. Finally, the head of the INTERREG IIC NSR secretariat in Viborg (Denmark) and the German consultancy were present. These were the agents and institutions directly involved in the NSR NorVISION programme. On top of this list were representatives from academia as well as from neighbouring INTERREG IIC visions – the North West Metropolitan Area and the Baltic Sea Region, altogether thirty-nine people.

The participants gathered in four working groups to discuss the themes of traffic and information technology, environmental protection and energy, rural development and tourism and urban development and participation. In the plenary session one of the main issues discussed was the relationship between rural and urban areas (VWG, 2000a: 1). Two issues in the draft concerned the participants. One was the conceptual framework that created an impression of a very rigid split between rural and urban areas. The other was the debate on the status of the rural areas.

Here, as in many of the ESDP discussions, the issue was urban hegemony over rural peripherality. The minutes of the meeting reflect a divided attitude towards this theme amongst the INTERREG project workers. A representative from Norway coined this issue of urban hegemony in terms of local identity and place bound loyalty, a way of framing that was not only rare at the meeting but also expresses a very interesting way of thinking that might be on its 'way into' these visions. Another theme that was central to the agenda was the question of competition. Several of the workshops reported that their theme needed to be seen in the light of increasing competition amongst cities and regions. However, in accordance with the ESDP this question of competitiveness is articulated within the vocabulary of balanced competitiveness, and competition within co-operation (VWG, 2000a: 2).

Studying the working process and methods used at this meeting it becomes clear that the activity of transnational document writing in practice has as much to do with connecting people and network building as with the more specific wording of the documents. Thus most of the participants were unaware of many of the other projects under this 'umbrella' of a document. From the workshop activity there also seems to be an indication of the character of common language building of the whole exercise. In this way, one can see this form of collaborative spatial vision making as an attempt to construct a vocabulary of spatial issues and problems. Here the connection to the ESDP was very clear, giving the impression of another important function of this 'mother document', namely to facilitate such transnational discussions and articulation processes all over the European Union with an 'adequate' vocabulary and frame of mind. This comes as no surprise when one studies collective articulation processes amongst planners. Certain concepts were seen as the 'magic words', sustainability being such a concept. Not being a word with any specific semantic content, the concept of sustainability was called 'the great word' by one of the planners in the workshop on urban development. As such this is another example of the 'seismographic sensitivity' that the new breed of European spatial planners are developing towards picking the right words and icons of spatial development, an example of one of the skills of the new transnational group of planners (Faludi, 1997). Another example of this sensitivity surfaced in the urban workshop, where a major issue was how to avoid foreclosing options for funding from the future INTERREG IIIB programme. Some participants in the working group expressed fear of the vision document being 'too specific' and project oriented, and thus cutting project participants off from further funding. The working process and the discussions around NorVISION cannot be described as anything but elite oriented and without transparency. This makes the question of democratic validation or any broader public support behind this spatial vision a legitimate concern.

As in many of the other INTERREG programmes the North Sea Region is also the re-producing of the discourse by means of new programmes, institutions and documents. Thus we find that in the new INTERREG IIIB programme for the North Sea Region the NorVISION document is seen as the pre-condition for further integration and aids the 'harmonisation of spatial planning in the NSR' (INTERREG North Sea Region, 2002: 66). The vision is seen to bridge the spheres of the ESDP and the TEN-T and as such articulates the general discourse of monotopic Europe at the transnational level (INTERREG North Sea Region, 2001: iv).

Finally, both the cases of transnational cross-border planning in the Øresund Region and the North Sea Region share the hallmarks of a new breed of 'network-based transnational super regions in Europe':

> The more recent type of cross-border regionalism is the large scale transnational regions sweeping across Europe, held together by mainly informal networks, and showing a distinct absence of clearly defined territoriality. Much of their purpose is about external visibility as a growth region or 'core region' in Europe, and thus a positive image for any territory associated with, or part of, it. Not surprisingly, therefore, a lot of bargaining and politicking has been going on between cities, regions and states on the one side, and the European Commission on the other, to press for inclusion in one of the 'super regions'. Much of Europe has thus been covered by variously themed super regions, mainly based on urban clusters and clearly visible geographic features.
>
> (Herrschel and Newman, 2002: 110)

In terms of the reproduction of policy discourse, another part of the power theme has to do with the planners involved. Put crudely one could say that the prime result of such vision making is that some social agents make interesting contacts and get to travel around. As one participant in the urban workshop coined it: 'the document must facilitate a discussion, and the discussion is the action.' Furthermore, the potential power of the exercise lies in the opportunity for these planners to make NorVISION 'work' in terms of being a fund-directing frame of reference that future applications to the INTERREG programme will have to submit to. It was explicitly articulated by the lead manager of NorVISION (who also acted as the national representative from the Danish National Planning Agency) that the vision is considered to be an input for the INTERREG IIIB programme. NorVISION can be said to be a politically 'weak' document since it is written on the 'outskirts' of the EU's formal structures and prepared by civil servants. However, in terms of timing one has to bear in mind that the NorVISION document will enjoy compensation for this status by the fact that it was presented to the North Sea Commission on 9 June 2000. This forum contains the ministers of the member states, and is an expression of the attempt to export the vision into the formal political system at a very high level and thus to widen its power base. In a draft resolution from this meeting, the North Sea Commission states its positive position towards NorVISION and recommends political councils and authorities at EU, national, regional and local level to take note of the document and implement the concepts where possible in their respective spatial policies (North Sea Commission, 2000). Finally the participants of the NorVISION meeting all agreed on this document being a contribution to a common ideology of increased Europeanisation and political integration. In other words there is a very explicit acceptance among the project partners in this INTERREG programme that this discourse is *de facto* 'working its way into' the European Union.

The new complex nestedness: the case of Hamburg

We shall now turn to an example of the new complex nestedness of particular cities and regions as they engage with a number of different spatial strategic sites and linkages. In other words, we will be dealing with how European spatial planning in the future will be about the merging of (Europeanised) national planning systems with cross border structures.

The Europeanisation of spatial planning surfaces in concrete places, being one locality or city that finds itself nested in a number of different levels and activities of spatial planning. This is, for example, the case in Hamburg, where the city's active engagement in multiple planning activities at many different levels is a showcase of the new situation for urban governance. Hamburg, being part of the 'Pentagon' of growth mentioned in the ESDP, clearly does not restrict itself to being a player at this level. Thus Ache identifies how the city is actively promoted as both global economic integration zone, part of a Euroregion co-operation (STRING), active in an inter-urban network with Berlin, developing a regional strategy (Metropolregion), bidding for the Olympic Games in 2012, as well as extending its city centre by way of converting the harbour districts along the river Elbe (Ache, 2002). Emanating from these six cases of nested planning activities the City of Hamburg operates a mix of strategies ranging from the local to the transnational level. Setting the work of co-ordinating all these activities aside, there still seems to be reason for caution as:

> Actors try to position Hamburg at various spatial and strategic levels. . . . All projects resort to the region as a container of different potentials. . . . All projects work with quite extensive networks between institutions and people. The standard buzz word applies to the strategies. Sustainability comes in the usual triangle of economic growth, social equity and environmental protection. However, it is clear, that on the basis of the current development trend, the environmental aspect is very likely to come last. . . . The problem with dominating economic issues lies in a number of aspects, in particular regarding environmental sustainability. But, it also brings negative effects in another dimension: the regional society and the potentials embedded are mainly seen from a functional perspective – turning the region into a soulless product.
>
> (Ache, 2002: 15–17)

Thus even in the wake of the multiple strategies in which Hamburg is embedded there is a predominant rationale and logic that threatens to flatten out the meaning of Hamburg in a movement similar to the notion of Europe as monotopia.

From case studies published in 1998 on the two cross-border co-operations in Kent–Nord-Pas de Calais (France and UK) and Euroregio Maas–Rhine (Holland, Belgium and Germany), Brown reaches the conclusion that certain limitations in terms of different national regimes of regulation, disagreement about economic development themes, implementation and status of cross-border plans and a lack of co-ordination between public regulation and planning function lead to only a partially successful evaluation of the ESDP and its trickling down:

> Under the rationale for the development of a European spatial planning policy discussed at the beginning [the ESDP], emphasis was placed on the general role of spatial planning in the integration process, as well as the specific contribution that spatial planning is deemed to be able to make towards integrating borders. However, although consideration of the issue in a theoretical context suggested that the benefits ought to be considerable, findings from two different border regions highlighted the limitations of spatial planning in the cross border context.
>
> (Brown, 1998: 13)

At the conference *European Cities in a Global Era – urban identities and regional development* in Copenhagen, November 2002, workshops were held where experiences from a number of INTERREG projects were discussed. The cases spanned the Øresund Region, the Baltic Palette Region project, the North West Europe Region project on New Urban landscapes, the Metrex Transnational European Network, the CADSES region, the Basque Eurocity Bayonne-San Sebastian and the Finnish Gulf.

All cases bore evidence of the importance of the INTERREG programme. It was noted that the nation state control of INTERREG IIC has been lessened in the new and more decentralised INTERREG IIIB. The new INTERREG III programme, according to the Commission's wishes, has two focus points. One is the issue of transnationality, and the other is the issue of concrete implementation. At the level of the INTERREG programme administration this means that the applications for funding new projects under the INTERREG programme must document transnationality as well as their more tangible results at one and the same time (interview with Danish National Planner).

Furthermore, and very much in line with our previous experiences from INTERREG meetings, the planners complained about the bureaucratic procedures and rules governing INTERREG. A couple of particularly interesting points were made by the European Commission representative Rudolf Niessler who stated that in the beginning of its functional life the INTERREG programme was set up to deal with nation state borders as a problem, but today facilitated transnational planning to which the nation state border should now be seen as a window of opportunity. Furthermore, Niessler proclaimed that with the use of INTERREG as a predominant instrument in the deepening of the European integration process, we are on the verge of leaving the context of cohesion policy. This is particularly important in relation to a remark made by a representative of the Danish Forest and Landscape Research Institute who stressed that there is a difference in the goals and rationales of the Structural Funds' welfare policy ('regions lagging behind') and the ESDP's Development Policy ('polycentric regions'). The general lesson here seems to be a growing tension within the spatial policy discourse as to which of the grounding rationales to adhere to: cohesion or growth? This feeds into the present discussion of what to do with the ESDP in relation to the next period of Structural Funds from 2006: include it or dismiss it? Furthermore, such a potential shift in policy rationale from welfare policy to development policy is an explicit expression of the 'new regionalism' (Herrschel and Newman, 2002: 75) within EU spatial policy.

If one were to sum up the INTERREG project experiences of the spatial planners involved in these projects, the main lessons would be: developing transnational networks, communication and a common language that in the end will lead not only to a new 'epistemic community' of transnational spatial planners but also contribute to a furthering of the political integration process in the European Union.

Power of curriculum

A striking example of how the Europeanisation of the new discourse of European space consciously extends beyond the policy structures and practices of spatial planning is found in the French-led initiative to use the ESDP as the foundation for a standard textbook on European geography for secondary schools across Europe (Herrschel and Newman, 2002). In line with attempts across other fields of action to include a 'European dimension' in school books and syllabuses (Shore, 2000: 55), this is a very clear expression of an attempt to shape the minds of social agents by framing a specifically 'European' territorial identity. In a Foucauldian sense, we find a fusion of the powers of 'governmentality' in order to produce future European subjects, by shaping the nascent 'spatial imagination' in the years of childhood. This is an example of the subtle micro processes by which policy discourse can begin to shape our understanding of the world. In its deliberations, the Dutch National Planning Agency clearly sees the 'textbook case' as an important move:

> Often, the first place where people come into contact with the geography of their living environment is the classroom. If some kind of European spatial identity is to emerge, this is the starting point. It was the French who suggested looking at whether, the ESDP could not be translated into geography lessons for further education, a proposal which was welcomed by the other countries. . . . Such initiatives lend themselves well to achieving the ambition of using the ESDP as a building block for the development of a European identity.
>
> (Dutch National Spatial Planning Agency, 2000: 139)

Let us think of the ESDP as a new geographic imagination facilitating the construction of a European identity, complementing the other new symbols of European Union unity: the flag, the hymn, the passports etc. (Hedetoft, 1997: 152–153;

Kohli, 2000: 121). In this sense, then, the underlying discourse of European identity is akin to building an 'imagined community' (Anderson, B., 1991). How might the translation of the ESDP into a geography textbook serve to reinforce this territorial dimension of European identity? One of the contributions to the introductory chapter clearly sets out its mission in this respect:

> Convinced that in order to bring into being the sentiment of a shared responsibility towards our European territory, one must first initiate and develop a common knowledge of it. At Potsdam, I proposed that the actions retained by the 15 and the Commission include the preparation of a book on European geography which could be read in their own language by all young Europeans. I pledged that France would take charge of a draft of this work and offer it to her partners on the occasion of the French Presidency of the Union in the second half of 2000. This first document is merely an outline of what, in the future, could be a European geography manual. It is now for the States themselves to transform it and add to it. . . . I dream that one day young Europeans will learn European geography, their new common territory, in the same way that French youth have learnt – and continue to learn – the geography of their National territory. Already, reading these pages shows what we share with other Europeans: the wealth of an immense diversity of towns, of landscapes, peoples, cultures; the memories of a tumultuous, often painful past; but also a wide-open future, with a project in which together we value our differences by integrating them in the vast European space. . . . The management of the European territory becomes a crossroads of common concepts and shared policies: the Dutch have brought the principle of cohesion, the Scandinavians that of sustainable development, the Germans have contributed the principles of subsidiarity and polycentrism, and the French that of forecasting and long-term consideration. The British have contributed land planning, and the Italians the need to value our public heritage. The French and the Spanish have together inspired the notion and characteristics of European cities in contrast to American cities. . . . It is an attempt to spread mutual knowledge. . . . Perhaps this trial project will be converted into a common geography textbook for young Europeans.
>
> (Preface by J.-L. Guigou, in Bailly and Fremont, 2001: 3-4).

The geography textbook should, according to one Danish national planner, be seen as 'a very good book for students to get a picture of who is going to be my neighbour' (interview, Danish National Planner). This has to do with the governmentality of the European Union, as the spatial imaginaries are not only visions of infrastructure and urban nodes but also building blocks for the construction of a new citizenship of monotopia.

Clearly this is only a preliminary attempt to frame European space; more sophisticated attempts will follow. What is even more interesting, and certainly in line with our analysis and interpretation, is how the Europeanisation of the curriculum is moulded over the model of geography knowledge building that we know from the nation state. Looking further into the textbook we find more explicit ideas of how to shape and institutionalise the Europeanisation of spatial planning:

> More and more, there exists a European zone, multiple, multi-level: at the continental scale of large networks, at the regional level of the production of wealth or of natural and cultural heritage, at the local level of every day living. This space is not only economic, it is social and cultural; it is a territory, which does not replace National or local territories, but which incorporates them. . . . France proposed, amongst these 12 actions [The ESDP Tampere Action Plan], that the Committee for Spatial Development should address young Europeans, who will be, tomorrow, responsible for this European territory. . . . That which unites Europe . . . is a community of problems: those posed by this immense mixing up of populations in a space in the most part open and welcoming to human colonisation; it is the obligation to respond by integrating these multiple identities within a single identity which they overwhelm, without doing away with them. . . . Europe, in both its global and its individual components, cannot be defined by static geographical limits, but only by the very movement of European construction.
>
> (Introduction by J. Peyrony, in Bailey and Fremont, 2001: 5–14)

The crucial point here is the way that the spatial imagination is seen to be part of the new identity that European citizens may build in the future. Furthermore, the organisational dimension of this Europeanisation of geographical knowledge is linked to the institutions of ESPON and SPESP that we described in Chapter 7.

The issue at stake here is to understand how, through subtle, informal and largely unaccountable ways, a policy discourse of monotopic European space can reach beyond the confines of policy making and shape the minds of citizens.

Obviously the Europeanisation of the curriculum means an attempt to control and frame the way the perception of European territory is shaped. Unimportant as it may seem, this however usurps one of the nation state's traditional privileges – shaping the geographical imagination of its citizens. Thus the question of Europeanising the geographical and spatial imagination is both one of identity construction but is also one of contestation and sensitivity:

> For example, EU institutions, including the Council, have taken an interest in the democratic and European dimensions of education, hoping to make young people more conscious of European ideas and of being Europeans. . . . Member states, however, have been reluctant to give the Union authority to shape the institutional framework for education and socialization. Control over educational institutions . . . is a sensitive issue exactly because it is closely linked to national and sub-national identities.
>
> (Olsen, 2001: 11)

These questions will gain even more weight with the enlargement of the European Union. Here this sort of thinking could work as a stimulus to the new real or imagined geographies of Europe. In this process such representations of space and their accompanying transnational institution- and network-building might function as a vehicle for further European integration. This acknowledges the critical potential that lies within any effort to de-construct the notions and conceptions of space within the minds of planners and policy makers, or in the words of Healey:

> Place conceptions, if memorable, may be much more effective in sustaining reference frameworks in active use, and encouraging the clustering of new intellectual and social capital around what has already been built up. . . . Efforts in 'imagining places' and strategic visioning may thus play an important role, not merely in mobilising attention and knowledge resources, but in structuring practices, in translating new discourses into routinely performed practices.
>
> (Healey, 2002: 21)

These glimpses of the future direction of geography education across Europe bear witness to the way that the Europeanisation of spatial planning transcends the political and technical issues of transnational spatial planning practices as seen from Europe. It is an effort that stretches into the domain of deeper political integration within the European Union, and connects squarely with questions of public legitimacy. Here we certainly enter into the domain of territorial identity, in whatever sophisticated disguise we find it.

Concluding remarks

In this chapter we have explored different dimensions of the Europeanisation of spatial planning. We have examined INTERREG cross-border co-operation as an example of the transgression of the nation state borders in a general attempt to further European integration processes. Furthermore, critical concerns are raised that these regions and interactions carry the underlying rationales of an environmentally unsustainable growth strategy. Finally one must ask the question of '*qui bono?*' or 'who benefits?' This leads to investigations into whether such cross-border regions are the expression of the people living in those very regions, as well as to questions of territorial identification and belonging.

Thus the Europeanisation of spatial policy, as it is firmly expressed in the cross-border lessons of the last decade, goes to show how mixed rationales and different outcomes of the policy process merge at various spatial scales and with the inputs from various stakeholders. Finally, however, the Europeanisation of spatial planning as we find it in the new transnational spatial policy spaces so far seem to be devoid of the participation of civil society representatives, NGOs and other voices that (potentially at least) could contest the democratic legitimacy of those new spatial practices:

> Cross-border secretariats consisting of administrative and technical personnel may be set up to propose or implement particular objects. . . . Their importance, however, illustrates the bias towards bureaucracy and technocracy in trans-frontier regions. Electoral constituencies do not span borders limiting democratic involvement of elected representatives in cross-border networks. Instead, cross-border regions involve a series of flexible strategic alliances between loyal political, administrative and business elites. To this extent they are *fora* for limited forms of participatory democracy.
>
> (O'Dowd, 2001: 104)

Despite the rather critical edge to O'Dowd's analysis it is recognized that the new EU-supported brand of transfrontier regionalism could potentially help underpin 'a form of European multiculturalism which favors free choice of identity, multiple affiliations and dynamic group formation' (O'Dowd, 2001: 106). Whether such progressive outcomes are to be expected is not easy to say; however, we would remain sceptical regarding that dimension. So far we would recognise the Europeanisation of spatial planning as a predominantly interesting example of how policy fields become institutionalised:

> The ESDP . . . represents above all how European spatial planning has made itself an institution by itself, in spite of the original shortcomings in the Treaties. More than its 'policy aims', its development process and the related 'informal' constitution of a European Council of Ministers for Spatial Planning are one of the greatest demonstrations of how the concrete needs of a community can trigger institutional changes in practice and, with the possibility of giving real shape to Europe's 'economic and social cohesion' (one of the fundamental principles after the Single Act), show how deep the aspirations of the European Community to become a Union are.
>
> (Rivolin, 2002: 12)

Summing up, we would point to the fact that the local practices where the Europeanisation of spatial policy and planning take place become the vehicles for the contestation and reconfiguration of the basic themes within the European spatial policy discourse. From the convergence of national spatial planning to the cross-border 'laboratories' of European integration within the realm of the INTERREG programme, we find a growing awareness of a common European territory. Working with modes of thought that transgress borders, and operating within new transnational institutional settings, seems to take the notion of monotopic Europe into its next phase of grounding and expanding. But these themes are being re-contextualised within diverse practical settings in spatial planning ranging from the nation state level, as in the case of Denmark, to the multiple transnational planning 'experiments' covering the wider territory of the EU. Here there seems to be the opportunity to open up critical debate on the meaning of the new transnational spatialities (and mobilities), to ask questions about the implications for places, cities, citizens, travel, life and identity, and to press for critical and inclusive debate.

We close this chapter by briefly returning to our core themes. We have seen cases of Europeanisation taking place in different ways. As transnational institutional creation, as penetration of national planning, as reproduction of a top-down political project, but also as the creation of new spaces and potentials for the content of Europeanisation – for the policy ideas at stake – to be reconstructed and contested, at different scales and in diverse institutional settings.

The environmental theme surfaces in the policy language of national policy documents (e.g. the English and the Danish cases), and is also vividly present as a contested theme in the Øresund region and in NorVISION. We find the urban theme articulated around the notions of new transnational metropolitan experiments such as the Øresund region, but also as a contested spatial scale of NorVISION. The theme of territorial identity underlies all the cases we have explored. However, this is nowhere more subtly manifested than in the case of the ESDP geography textbook. Such an example of the 'power of curriculum' illustrates dramatically the Europeanisation of the spatial imaginary, and the transmission of a new frame for territorial belonging.

9.1 Resistance to TEN-T.

Source: A SEED campaign literature.

Part Four

Power, Rationalities and Knowledge

This synthesis of the book's critical investigation into the making of European space focuses on the power-rationalities underlying the new spatial policy discourse. First, we draw together the threads of our argument that the new policy discourse of monotopia is predominantly based on a rationality of mobility, accessibility, connectivity and global competitive flows – a *Europe of flows*, articulated against a competing notion of a *Europe of places*. Then we continue the unpacking of the underlying rationalities, exploring the risks to a Europe of places posed by monotopia. We do this by exploring how the central objectives of spatial policy, relating to growth, equity and the environment, are riven by internal contradictions. The empirical examples clearly illustrate not only the internal incoherence between these objectives, but also their contested nature. Here we draw together these consistencies and inconsistencies marking the new field of European spatial policy, and examine the implications for two dimensions of European space: the environment and the urban. Finally, the potential broader significance of the policy discourse is re-addressed. We conclude that the outcomes of these new contested, multi-level spatial policy processes reflect the increasing importance of mobility and competition, with consequent threats to spatial justice, but that alternative paths and opportunities for resistance do exist.

Chapter 9

A Europe of flows

Creating the preconditions for monotopia

To remain stationary in these times of change, when all the world is on the move, would be a crime.

(Thomas Cook, 1854, quoted in Lash and Urry, 1995: 262)

The policy discourse of Europe of Flows operates from the commitment to the creation of a 'level playing field' which explains why the eradication of barriers is among its central concerns. This is quite distinct from the familiar concern of planners for the preservation of spatial diversity or the value of hierarchy.

(Hajer, 2000: 142)

For business purposes . . . the boundaries that separate one nation from another are no more real than the equator. They are merely convenient demarcations of ethnic, linguistic and cultural entities. They do not define business requirements or consumer needs.

(IBM, quoted in Morley and Robins, 1995: 10)

TEN is for no good use in relation to the ESDP. . . . TEN looks at Europe . . . 'where do we have congestion? . . . and where we have congestion we will enlarge to have more room for the congestion . . . it will just increase congestion . . . ESDP and TEN are contradictory'.

(Interview, Danish National Planner)

Introduction: European power-rationalities of space and mobility

In this chapter we begin to draw together our analytical threads by specifying the power-rationalities at work within the new monotopic mode of framing European space. We will focus in particular on the representation and remaking of European space as a Europe of flows, which we will argue is a necessary precondition for the creation of a monotopic Europe.

Here we draw again on the cultural sociology of space (discussed in Chapter 3), and in particular its capacity for dealing with the practices and symbolic meanings of the socio-spatial relation. In particular we will use the thinking of Hajer and Castells to analyse the power-rationalities underpinning the new field of European spatial policy. To do this we need to flesh out our basic proposition that this field of activity is currently overwhelmingly shaped by a monotopic discourse coined around notions of a Europe of flows.

The spatial visions being created across the new transnational policy spaces can be seen as a new language of urban problems (Boyer, 1983: 4) and as an example of the 'power to name' (Harvey, 1996: 264). To better understand these visions, it is helpful to analyse the power-rationalities that shape them. There is no single rationality or privileged sense of reason, but rather multiple forms of power-rationality that seek to govern and legitimise social actions and practice. Furthermore, we need to understand the linkage of language forms, practices, institutions and power-rationalities. Thus it is important not to understand this emergence of an EU spatial policy framework as a purely comprehensive scientific rational process. 'It bends to an agenda, and to forces, which contest the future path of development of Europe, and so is likely to have at its core the currently hegemonic ideologies of the single market and political integration, but will also reflect other debates about cohesion and environment' (Dabinett and Richardson, 1999: 228).

Thus European spatial planning, given shape through spatial policy processes at different transnational scales, is conceptualised as being implicitly normative and ideological – about politics and power as much as about technical/rational planning. It seems important, then, to investigate how particular power-rationalities, embedded in particular discourses, contest the ideas, languages, knowledges and practices taking shape in these new processes.

For example, questions of nested places at various spatial scales imply that cities, regions and nation states are renegotiating their relations and status within the socio-spatial processes of globalisation. This complex concept must in our interpretation be seen as a dialectic process of time-space compression, uneven geographical development and local-global interaction (Castells, 1996; Harvey, 1996, 2000).

The rationales of the different manifestations of the European spatial policy discourse are expressed in their own specific vocabularies, and are transformed into social reality through the actions of social agents within particular institutional settings. The ESDP for example is articulated in terms of 'polycentric spatial development' and 'balanced competitiveness' by senior EU officials and politicians through the institutions of the Committee on Spatial Development, the informal ministerial meetings and the Commission. The spatial discourse frames knowledge and reality in a particular way which becomes 'installed' as the 'natural way' of perceiving European space. The scope of this new spatial logic is illustrated by the plan for the ESDP to become the backbone for a new textbook in geography for secondary schools, which we discussed in the previous chapter. Furthermore, the action programme on EU spatial policy makes references to the CEMAT Guiding

Principles being used as basis for geography teaching in secondary schools. This is paralleled by an apparently instrumental emphasis on the importance of participation of young people in the new spatial planning processes: 'The involvement of the younger generation in the planning process increases the chances of interesting the public in the long-term planning of their home region and in efficient and innovative participation. This is essential in gaining wider acceptance of the "European idea"' (CEMAT, 2000: 20). These are clear expressions of how such discourses attempt to frame the minds of social agents, in terms of creating a specific 'European' spatial thinking. Furthermore, it is an example of the micro processes within which such discursive powers also operate. Thus the ESDP policy discourse might be understood as a new geographical imagination that complements the other new symbols of European Union (as opposed to European) unity – the flag, the hymn, the passports etc. The aim is to gain hegemonic status for its core rationale. Examining the spatial policy discourse that is articulated in the ESDP, it becomes clear that the relations between these nested rationalities are by no means fixed. Rather, the process, and the ESDP document itself, reflects the balance between plural competing 'power rationalities'. Thus the ESDP's spatial policy discourse can be seen as an arena for playing out different and contested views of European space.

Relating these conclusions to the institutional analysis of governance that Weiler performs, one might say that these discursive practices are so far being articulated and put to work in the rather 'dark places' of the EU's institutional framework. By this we mean that the ESDP and the NorVISION are articulated in what we described earlier as the 'cracks and holes' of the EU institutional complex (Weiler, 1999).

Perhaps living a 'silent existence' on the outskirts of the institutional framework makes it possible to gain some internal coherence before being put to the more serious test of public scrutiny. The CEMAT vision is characterised by being prepared within an even more diverse discursive arena, and within the less well developed and rapidly growing institutional framework of the Council of Europe. Its status is thus even more marginal than that of the ESDP, and its need to address such an array of interests must compromise the prospects for application. This raises concerns for the democratic perspectives of these new forms of planning, not least when it is considered that these 'paper visions' are already *de facto* impacting on policy and programme decisions and networking.

Analysing the vision documents one clearly get the impression of a new knowledge field in the making. The concept of 'infographics' that we analysed in Chapter 5, for example, indicates a conscious and deliberate framing of knowledge that challenges more 'realistic' spatial representations based on scientific rationality. Infographic framing can be seen as a powerful rhetorical and creative way of reproducing the discourse through new forms of spatial representation. Through such devices, the new spatial discourse gives top priority to propositions that place cities as growth motors in an increasingly globalised world. The multiple references to the questions of identity, multiplicity and otherness appear merely as a legitimising vocabulary, and are not articulated in these visual representations.

The construction of new spatial visions at different spatial scales can be understood as a consequence of the repositioning of the nation state, as new regional formations pursue strategies of increasing their coherence in a globalised economy. As the traditional position of the nation state is challenged, spatial visions with associated power-rationalities emerge at different scales, recasting regional spaces across the European continent.

Space of places/space of flows

Following Castells (1996), we find the dichotomy between 'space of places' and 'space of flows' a useful way of understanding the complex dynamics of globalisation: as a dialectical struggle between two incompatible 'spatial logics' or rationalities. In line with the work of, for example, Hajer (2000) and Urry (2000), Castells finds the mobility aspects of globalisation of increasing significance. The essence of this conceptualisation is a dialectical tension between the historically rooted local spatial organisation of human experience (the space of places) versus the global flow of goods, signs, people and electronic impulses (the space of flows):

> **The space of flows is the material organization of time-sharing social practices that work through flows**. By flows I understand purposeful, repetitive, programmable sequences of exchange and interaction between physically disjointed positions held by social actors in the economic, political, and symbolic structures of society. . . . The overwhelming majority of people, in advanced and traditional societies alike, live in places, and so they perceive their space as place-based. **A place is a locale whose form, function and meaning are self-contained within the boundaries of physical contiguity**.
>
> (Castells, 1996: 142, 423 emphasis in the original)

According to Castells' analysis, the relationship between the space of places and the space of flows is not predetermined in its outcome. This is important: Castell's conceptualisation does not a-priori favour one or the other of these logics. It becomes an empirical question how this simultaneous globalisation and localisation is played out in the specific environments studied, in our case the nested visions and spatial representations of Europe which bear on this tension. A tension that, according to Castells, is the hallmark of our time (Castells, 1996: 428). In his later work, Castells has drawn attention to the ways in which grassroots movements and NGOs are finding new and alternative modes of action within the network society. Thus Castells speaks of 'grassrooting the space of flows' as an indication of a potential empowering of global civil society. The main point here is that even within the spaces of flows we find counter-actions and resistance practices against the prevailing dominance of global capital. Such counter-practices could be described by an underlying rationale of a 'will to friction'. In line with Foucault, we find this spatial dialectics to be an expression of contested spatiality: 'So, the geography of the new history will not be made, after all, of the separation between places and flows, but out of the interface between places and flows and between cultures and social interests, both in the space of flows and in the space of places' (Castells, 1999: 302). In his analysis of European policy discourses, Maarten Hajer has built on Castells' work and coined the notion of a 'Europe of flows', within which the following characteristics can be identified (Hajer, 2000: 138–139):

1. market integration;
2. global competition;
3. the EU as both 'enabling state' and 'welfare state';
4. infrastructure as the primary policy instrument;
5. enhancing mobility and connectivity;
6. identifying 'missing links' of infrastructure;
7. a vocabulary of 'modernist commitments' – that is a belief in integration, distribution, management and control;
8. 'ecological modernization';
9. anticipation of more international transport demands.

In a policy discourse of a Europe of flows, regions and cities will increasingly present their visions as being repositioned and connected to the spatiality of flows. In this sense the competitive element lies in the options for 'connectivity' and accessibility as much as in sheer mobility.

In the remainder of this chapter, will we argue that the Europe of flows has come to underpin the new discourse of spatial policy. In the next chapter, we will explore the implications for Europe as a space of places. As we showed in Chapter 3, mobility and spatial practices in general are intrinsically related to power-rationalities of contested interest, and to power plays, in terms of spatial policy discourses seeking hegemony. Thus we will now explore in more detail how these power-laden tensions of spaces and flows surface within the European spatial policy discourse. We will argue that the EU spatial policy discourse, with its twin key issues of polycentricity and infrastructure networks, is a classic manifestation of the embedded tensions between mobility/flow versus nodes/places.

Missing links and mixed rationalities – on the flow/place distinction in the TEN-T

As we have shown, spatial visions at different spatial scales are only one dimension of the new spatial policy discourse. Thus these discursive practices must be placed in the context of the power-rationalities underpinning the infrastructure networks of TEN-T (Box 9.1). We would argue that this particular dimension of the

Box 9.1 TEN-T policy discourse: fragmented, marginalised and excluded policy rationalities

TEN-T Policy Rationalities

TEN-T a cornerstone of EU integration
TEN-T crucial for EU global competitiveness and the single market
TEN-T will result in evenly distributed economic benefits
TEN-T part of a sustainable transport strategy for the EU
TEN-T's high speed networks, corridors and nodes integral to the EU spatial vision
Expert knowledge allows proper treatment of impacts and benefits
TEN-T is in the public interest
The EU has no power over infrastructure decision-making
The EU should part-finance TEN-T
Environmental risks adequately addressed
Implementation is a priority
EU institutions in harmony on expediting TEN-T
SEA allows environmental integration into policy process
SEA not necessary in initial policy development
SEA can (and will) show whether TEN-T is sustainable

Marginalised rationalities

Pork barrelling: lobbying replaces network planning
Weak construction of SEA
Uncertainty over possible economic impacts
TEN-T could result in negative economic impacts on the periphery
TEN-T could result in negative environmental impacts
TEN-T is roads biased
Inter-institutional conflicts could stop the process

Excluded rationalities

Local knowledges and protests
Single Market 'a bad thing'
TEN-T threatens cultural homogenisation
Infrastructure consuming space
Striation of local spaces
Risk of homogenisation of culture

Source: Richardson, 2000b

discourse crucially frames a notion of mobility and flows that conditions and shapes the nested visions of European space.

The framing of 'missing links' in trans-European infrastructure, discussed previously, strongly illustrates the point. A central part of the spatial representation that articulates the need for these new links was the powerful notion of 'shrinking Europe', expressed through the graphic depiction of travel time between key centres. Urban areas will become 'closer' to each other, in the manner advocated by the ERT, and strikingly illustrated in the Commission document Europe 2000+ (CEC, 1994a). At the same time there is a new risk, of a finer grain pattern of physical exclusion emerging in the shadows and on the margins of the new high speed corridors and polynodal spatiality of European space (Vickerman *et al.*, 1995). Academics have attempted to interpret the new spatial relations that would result:

> Growth will be concentrated in corridors of good communications and at peripheral urban locations where it is cost effective to link in with both the transport and information networks. Peripheral areas may still remain isolated and separate from the new infrastructure as access costs and capacity requirements may make the installation costs of the new networks uneconomic and the costs of using the system too high . . . the most attractive locations in Europe are likely to be those where the transport and infrastructure networks link in with other factors such as a skilled labour force, a high quality environment and the availability of low cost land. . . . International airports, high-speed rail stations, and major motorway intersections could all provide the sites of maximum accessibility which would minimise location and transport costs . . . . Where more than two of these factors actually work together, then a major Euro-hub would develop.
>
> (Banister *et al.*, 1995a: xiii–xiv)

Alongside the economic and environmental effects of TEN-T, which are themselves bound up in uncertainty, as previously discussed, there are other possible effects of TEN-T which have so far fallen completely outside the policy process. Perhaps the most significant of these is any consideration of the social impacts of the new opportunities for mobility afforded by the TEN-T. New patterns of socio-economic exclusion seem likely to result from changing spatial relations, although these are barely touched on in the policy debate. Questions about accessibility beyond the reductionist economic analysis are beyond the scope of the TEN-T policy process, and even the ESDP.

The other, slightly more abstract, effect seems to be the fuelling of a network of resistance at the European level, of a counter-discourse which challenges the single market development model. Furthermore, connecting the underlying rationale of the TEN-T project to the 'Europe of Flows' means to comprehend 'the wider project of selectively integrating Europe's "glocal": infrastructures to support economic integration' (Graham and Marvin, 2001: 367).

Ultimately, European space is being reconstructed by the outcome of the struggle between these conflicting strategies of development. As TEN-T removes national boundaries physically, reinforcing the new strategy of inclusion in Europe, it simultaneously creates new patterns of exclusion, both inside Europe, and between Europe and its neighbours. The conditions of possibility of the hegemonic discourse of development require the efficient planning and implementation of TEN-T.

In the TEN-T policy process, then, the importance of broader discourses of European integration, the single market and the environment cannot be denied. Ingrained in the culture of the key EU institutions, they fundamentally shaped the nature of the policy process, and consequently the nature of the emerging policy discourse. And it is this new discourse which is crucial to our argument: that through a contested policy process, we have not only come to a decision about a physical programme for European infrastructure, we have created a new discourse which is not only about infrastructure, but also about mobility, economic and political union, environment. And this discourse is articulated in a number of ways: not only new ways of thinking about mobility in Europe, but also in new language and practice. It is the practices, the ways in which the discourse constructs and reconstructs itself, that need special attention. In understanding policy making, it is crucial to identify how policy is articulated not just through language but through practice. In the case of TEN-T we have argued in this book that new practices have been born which will serve to consolidate further the rationality of the single market and political integration, even though their material effects remain uncertain:

> TENS might have a strong institutional position but this is not accounted for by supporting scientific evidence. It is highly questionable whether the transformation of a 'patchwork' into a 'network', the filling of the 'missing links' and the development of an integrated 'multi-modal' transport network using the 'telematic' technologies will actually help achieve the goals set out in the Treaty of Maastricht.
>
> (Hajer, 2000: 137)

The Øresund: creating a new place of flows

As we showed in Chapter 8, the Øresund Region is centrally placed within the new geography of Europe as it resolves one of the critical 'missing links'. The rationale behind the construction of the fixed link across the sound between Denmark and Sweden is firmly embedded within the notion of the borderless and frictionless space of European integration that is the discourse of monotopic Europe. This is in other words an example of the physical and spatial dimension of the single market. Furthermore, we would argue that the forging of links between the two cities of Copenhagen and Malmö, and the creation of a new transnational region, was driven by the rationale of the Europe of flows. Obviously a 'new place' has also been created, but characteristically for the logics of the Europe of flows, the activities of place-making in the Øresund Region have been criticised for being undemocratic and elitist, and thus for being out of contact with the lived spaces of everyday life (Berg and Löfgren, 2000: 280). In the words of O'Dell there exists a tension between 'the everyday life of local settings and the larger abstracted space of the transnational' (O'Dell, 2000: 232). Löfgren even goes as far as stating that the Øresund vision is an expression of 'the cult of flow' (Löfgren, 2000: 46). Further evidence of the Øresund region's embodiment of the Europe of flows is found in its predominantly urban bias, as it focuses on the new activity of 'transnational metropolitanization' (Löfgren, 2000: 29). Indeed, the identity, and the very condition of possibility of the Øresund region lies in the construction of state of the art transport infrastructure – a megaproject: 'The Øresund Link is currently best seen as a grand social experiment in cross-national and cross-cultural integration via transport infrastructure development. Such experiments are rare' (Flyvbjerg *et al.*, 2003: 70).

It is the idea and reality of cross-border movement made possible by the bridge that brings the region to life. As a trans-European missing link (now complete), the Øresund stands as a flagship of the trans-European priority transport projects. This physical linkage of Scandinavia to the rest of the EU, through the construction of the bridge, creates the perfect symbol of how modern infrastructure binds the new European space, and shows how significant the potential for mobility continues to be to the European project.

This is a clear example of the politics of scale and mobility discussed in Chapter 3. The new transnational metropolitan mobility region in the making can be seen as an EU supported attempt to 'up-scale' the urban flows and practices in the Danish and Swedish regions. As mentioned this sort of transnational spatial policymaking challenges the nation state hegemony. This politicised rescaling of mobility patterns reshapes regional transport movements and networks – for example by creating new opportunities for living and commuting to work between Sweden and Denmark – and simultaneously reshapes Scandinavia's internal links, by enabling the Nordic triangle (and hence seamlessly linking the capitals of Norway, Sweden, and Denmark). At the same time it creates a step change in transport links between Scandinavia and western Europe, by making possible continuous high-speed road and rail movement between the EU's core and its northern periphery.

In terms of the political sociology of mobility, we clearly see different dynamics of movement between spaces across transport infrastructure, the frictionless desire in the nodal spaces of infrastructure networks, and the consumption of space by infrastructure. The underlying rationality in the discourse of monotopia clearly contains particular constructions of these spatialities, whilst marginalising or excluding other constructions.

Concluding remarks

In this chapter, we have drawn together our analysis of the different dimensions of European spatial policy discourse, and considered the implications for European spatial planning. Each process we examined has been the result of a convergence of actors at different spatial scales, operating informally in almost every case. None of the processes is formally required, or has legal force. All rely on co-operation and leverage. Across these new European spatial planning processes, operating at very different scales, it is possible to see the emergence of a new discourse of European space. Within the new discourse a particular language is emerging, with core concepts such as polycentricity, cohesion, balanced competitiveness and accessibility, which have particular meanings within these contexts. Although each of the processes is contested, and the policy documents reflect tensions, there is a striking harmony in the rhetoric of each vision. The way language is used, with terms such as 'balanced competitiveness' being very open to interpretation, allows these differences to be masked.

The struggles over the new discourse of European space have played out a conflict between Europe as a space of places and Europe as a space of flows. Our overwhelming conclusion is that the underlying rationales of the new imagined spaces of the TEN-T, NorVISION, the ESDP and the CEMAT Guiding Principles (among others) establish and reproduce the hegemony of the Europe of flows.

In excavating the rationalities underlying the new spatial policy discourse, the dialectical relations between the space of places and space of flows are mapped onto the European spatial policy field. The policy discourse of monotopia is predominantly found to be based on a rationality of mobility, accessibility, connectivity and global competitive flows, bearing the strong imprint of the Europe of flows articulated against a competing notion of a Europe of places. A rationality of frictionless mobility, rehearsed in the TEN-T policy process, and in the major arenas of European integration, has become a natural way of framing the current 'weaknesses' in European space, forcefully (but subtly) setting the agenda for future action. Spatial policy is found to be driven by this preoccupation with mobility. Interventions in mobility, more than anything else, are seen as offering solutions to the major contemporary spatial dilemmas facing the EU. By representing and remaking European space as a space of frictionless mobility, the foundations for the construction of a monotopia are put in place.

Our analysis suggests that as the discourse of the Europe of flows is articulated and embedded in practice, its 'other' is marginalised. The hegemony of the Europe of flows can only be understood as a mobility-, competition- and growth-oriented discourse that derives its distinctive identity in opposition to a Europe of places. In other words the dialectical tension between the two 'spatial logics' is represented in a distinct way in order to draw out the rationale for perceiving European spatiality in terms of flows and mobility rather than its opposite. Ascribing hegemony to the Europe of flows by coining and representing European spatiality in the vocabulary of flows is an act of 'naturalising' the increased urge to be a key player in global economic competition. Overall the 'Europe of flows' discourse enhances and legitimises the notion of a multi-speed Europe in which different 'Europes' are superimposed on one another (Hajer, 2000: 14). Furthermore, this notion clearly contradicts the idea that infrastructure enables balanced development.

However, our narrative of a hegemonic discourse of a Europe of monotopia should not only be understood as a totalising discourse based upon a political scaling of mobilities and flows. Although these dimensions have been foregrounded here, other dimensions of the cultural sociology of space open up alternative paths and possibilities for resistance, grounded in an understanding of the significance of a Europe of places. The critical question then becomes whether the idea of a Europe of places is actually helpful in creating spaces of resistance against the hegemonic monotopic discourse. In the next chapter we explore in more detail the implications of these threats to a Europe of places, and in the final chapter we go on to discuss these questions of identity, democracy and ultimately the possibility of resistance.

Chapter 10

Dimensions of monotopia

Exploring the 'magic triangle'

> Political leadership is essential: Strong political commitment will be needed to make the changes required for sustainable development. While sustainable development will undoubtedly benefit society overall, difficult trade-offs between conflicting interests will have to be made. We must face up to these trade-offs openly and honestly. Changes to policy must be made in a fair and balanced way, but narrow sectional interests must not be allowed to prevail over the well-being of society as a whole.
>
> (CEC, 2001b: 4–5)

> STRENGTHENING ITS EXTERNAL BORDERS: The European Council welcomes the various recent initiatives in this area and in particular the Commission communication entitled 'Towards integrated management of the external borders of the Member States of the European Union', the feasibility study carried out under Italy's leadership concerning the establishment of a European border police force, taking account of the intention expressed by the Commission to continue examining the advisability and feasibility of such a police force, and the study concerning police and border security, carried out by three Member States under the OISIN cooperation programme.
>
> (European Council, 2002)

> Overall there is an increasing contradiction between rights, which are universal, uniform and globally defined, and social identities, which are particularistic and territorially specified.
>
> (Urry, 2000: 166)

Introduction

The next step in our analysis of the European spatial policy discourse is to draw together the consistencies and inconsistencies of the discursive practices surrounding the formation of the new policy discourse of monotopic Europe. In this chapter, then, we take the unpacking of the underlying rationalities further, and explore the risks to a Europe of places posed by monotopia. We do this by exploring how the central objectives of spatial policy, relating to growth, equity and the environment (forming the 'magic' policy triangle of sustainable spatial development, which serves as the guiding light of European spatial policy), are riven by internal contradictions. The empirical examples clearly illustrate not only the internal incoherence between these objectives, but also their contested nature as divergent social actors and institutions compete to determine the meaning and conditioning effects of European spatial policy discourses. Here we draw together these consistencies and inconsistencies of the discursive practices which form the new field of European spatial planning, and examine the implications for two dimensions of European space: the environment and the urban.

We will argue that in spite of internal tensions, a growth rationale, driven by the overall policy and politics of the EU, has gained primacy, at the expense of alternative understandings of European environment and society. A field of discursive practice now avoids the intrusion of potentially destabilising challenges to the policy discourse (e.g. alternative discourses which seek to resist the homogenisation of culture or community, or which argue that local environments 'matter'). We conclude that the outcomes of the new contested, multi-level processes of making a monotopic European space reflect the increasing importance of mobility, with consequent repercussions for the environment and the urban.

By unpacking the underlying rationalities further we identify the tensions and contradictions evolved around the three central objectives – growth, equity and environment – which form the 'magic' policy triangle (Eser, 1997) that serves as the guiding light of European spatial planning (Figure 10.1). Furthermore, we will argue that the themes of the environment, the urban and territorial identity all relate to this triangle of policy reasoning. Evidently the issue of sustainable development is to be found both in the policy triangle and as one of the carrying themes of the discourse of monotopic Europe. The urban theme is to be found in relation to the notion of growth as it surfaces in the view of cities as driving economic motors and polycentric nodes in a global network. The policy goal of cohesion is then to be seen as intimately linked to the question of territorial identity. This is so because the imagined community of monotopic Europe needs cohesion as its vehicle for the idea of a level and coherent playing field in order to carry forward the message of 'one Europe'. This amounts to thinking about cohesion in terms of sharing growth, environment and space.

As we have seen, the new policy discourse constructs and reproduces (across an intertextual field) a set of spatial ideas, articulated in a common vocabulary of symbols and visions. The institutionalisation of this discourse has established a framework which is beginning to direct EU measures, as well as those at national and regional level, towards a concerted set of spatial objectives. Our analysis suggests that, although the discourse clearly attempts to articulate a coherent monotopic policy discourse, its rhetorical statements have left unresolved the tensions which have bedevilled EU policy across the various sectors the ESDP attempts to integrate. This is illustrated, for example, in the way that uncertainties

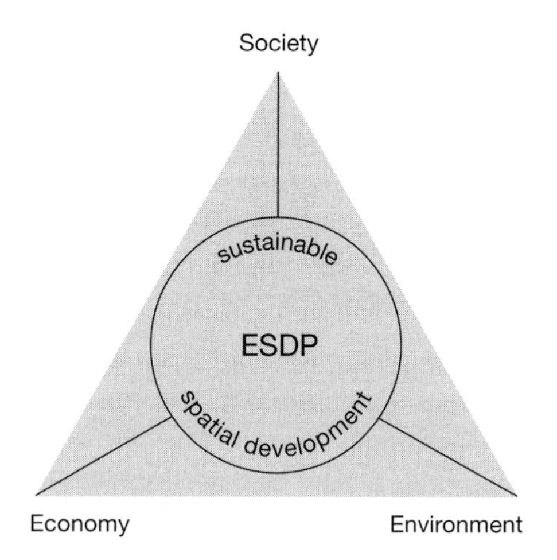

10.1 The Magic Triangle.

Source: CSD, 1999: 10.

about uneven development, and their relationship to infrastructure investment, have been masked in the handling of 'accessibility' in the ESDP's policies. In spite of the construction of a metaphorical golden policy triangle, promising balanced and harmonious spatial development, the economic imperatives of the single market and monetary union prevail.

Furthermore, the case studies clearly illustrate not only the internal incoherence between these objectives, but also their contested nature as divergent social actors and institutions compete to determine the meaning and conditioning effects of European spatial policy discourses.

This chapter counterpoints the discussion of the magic triangle (as the normative ideal) with a more critical discussion of the cultural and social implications of the issues discussed earlier in this book. The construction of new rationalities of space must be seen as part of the terrain of this increasingly fierce competition between newly constituted regional entities. Within these emerging spatial rationalities, a critical issue will be the mediation of the three elements – growth-ecology-equity. That is to say that the rationality of each spatial vision will contain, implicitly or explicitly, a specific combination of these three spheres.

Sustainability and economic growth: the urban dimension

First of all, the ESDP can be read as an explicit growth-oriented strategy coined around the urban as polycentric growth poles. In the words of Davoudi, the ESDP's notion of balanced development is primarily driven by the discourse of economic competitiveness, i.e. the strengthening of the EU's economic position in the global market (Davoudi, 1999: 368). The whole business of creating the

ESDP is to express a 'shared vision of the European territory' (CSD, 1998a: 3). Its *raison d'être* is expressed as an intervention in development characterised by competition between regions and cities in order to secure a better balance between competition and co-operation. This has to be done in order to safeguard what has been described as an 'optimum level of competitiveness' (CSD, 1998a: 2). Thus the document advocates a new scale of spatial planning and as such a new 'vision' of the European Union's territory. In other words, the ESDP can be interpreted as an attempt to address the dual process of internal diversification and the external pressure of global competition.

In common with the other processes of European spatial vision making that we have analysed, the rationale of NorVISION is coined within the vocabulary of 'balanced competitiveness' and 'polycentrism'. However, our reading of the ESDP suggests caution here, given the multiple contradictions within these discourses (Richardson and Jensen, 2000). As mentioned above there are good reasons to interpret the ESDP as mainly a rhetorical and funding device that seeks to optimise the urban growth areas. But this does not seem to be the case to the same extent with the NorVISION project. One could stipulate that the more concrete and specific this spatial vision thinking becomes, the more and not less will the rural areas or smaller cities gain in weight, at least in the more sparsely populated areas of the European Union. Obviously, such a conclusion should be made with utmost caution, but it seems to be an instructive hypothesis to explore in future research. Like the ESDP, NorVISION uses the rhetorical device of the growth-ecology-equity policy triangle. However, the relationship is not as clear cut as within the ESDP, perhaps due to the fact that there is a more realistic scope for a vision framed outside a strict urban agglomeration logic. By this we mean that the spatial context for NorVISION differs from that of the ESDP. Tensions between rural periphery and urban centrality can be found in this vision, marking a contradiction between two competing rationales. The possibility which is contested here is of a future North Sea space which is less completely shaped by a rationale of urban agglomeration, and is more sensitive to peripherality and rurality.

As to how the rationality underlying this vision is shaped by power relations, and in turn conditions the possibility of actions across scales and arenas of planning, one must think in terms of the document's primary capacity to develop links, networks and communication between planners in different countries. Thus a vital part of its rationale is to encourage transnational exchanges within the national territories nested within the larger territory of the European Union – and beyond this limit with the participation of Norway in the programme. Thus, 'breaking with' the nation state oriented spatial thinking seems to be one of the prime targets of NorVISION, as well as with the above mentioned visions in general. This can in general be seen as a rationale embedded within a discourse of European unity. The question therefore arises: who gains and who loses in this new 'game of vision making'? Obviously one can only stipulate a potential answer to this question since we are dealing with a discourse in the making. However preliminary our conclusion on this question might be, it seems crucial to acknowledge that framing exercises such as NorVISION are by no means neutral affairs.

Like NorVISION, the CEMAT Guiding Principles initially appear to promote a rationality which is less urban-biased than the ESDP, with a stronger focus on rural and peripheral regions, and with cohesion as its core objective. However, the dominant rationality again centres on a model of economic growth reliant on balanced competitiveness as a primary strategy for securing cohesion. The related spatial vision is of a polycentric urban system, with high-quality regional transport networks connecting towns and cities with each other, and feeding high-speed long-distance corridors. The place of agricultural peripheral regions is clearly significant, but problematic within this vision. The apparent tension between economic restructuring towards a globalised economy, and the support of employment in 'backward' regions is left unresolved. So a rationality which embraces core concepts such as endogenous regional development appears to be present, but weaker in expression.

Loss of place

The constructions of space in the monotopic discourse raise many concerns for the treatment of places, in the shift to a new European regional political economy where cities and regions become the principal units of implementation of the ESDP's policies. Peripheral rural regions will be classified according to whether they show structural weaknesses. It is intended that this process of spatial distinction will be carried out at administrative levels from regional to European. This is where the ESDP begins to bite, as it establishes a framework which can direct EU measures, as well as those at national and regional level, within a concerted set of spatial objectives which its authors believe have already been successfully framed. Such spatial distinctions should therefore have implications for all measures carried out under the new umbrella of spatial policy, influencing EU programmes and governmental actions at other levels. So the different institutions of government and other bodies at these different levels will clearly have interests in the outcome of spatial analyses and subsequent decision making. Regional authorities, for example, will have a great deal at stake in establishing a case for peripherality or structural weakness. So the precise construction of methods of spatial analysis, and their deployment, will be important. The success of development paths in different regions may rely on such spatial distinctions which may increasingly regulate the allocation of resources.

What interests will be excluded or marginalised along the way? In the loss of a fine-grain focus and the shift towards a regional emphasis, the voice of local communities in both peripheral and more urbanised regions seems to be a distant one. The ESDP is all but silent on the issue of social exclusion. The distinctive interests of regions, such as the Nordic states discussed above, also seem not to fit the emerging strategy.

Sustainability: the environmental dimension

The question of an environmentally sustainable approach to spatial development is a very explicit corner-stone of monotopic Europe. This is made clear by the numerous cross-references and intertextual links between the policy documents concerning the environment and spatial policy. As we have seen, across sectors and scales of European spatial policy, the 'good word' of sustainability has been applied with great persistence. Furthermore, the traces of ecological thinking spread out into other policy documents, but still with clear references to the new spatial policy discourse. For example we find in the Commission's sustainable development strategy (see extract in Box 10.1), clear endorsements of the ESDP (see third headline objective), as well as the strong articulation of frictionless mobility. In the document we detect an overall shift towards a TIA type approach, and a cross-sectoral emphasis. However, there also clear statements reminiscent of the industrialists' lobbying vocabulary of, for example, missing links.

Box 10.1 **Extracts from the EU Sustainable Development Strategy**

Improve the transport system and land-use management

Headline objectives

Decouple transport growth significantly from growth in Gross Domestic Product in order to reduce congestion and other negative side-effects of transport.

Bring about a shift in transport use from road to rail, water and public passenger transport so that the share of road transport in 2010 is no greater than in 1998 (the most recent year for which data are available)

Promote more balanced regional development by reducing disparities in economic activity and maintaining the viability of rural and urban communities, as recommended by the European Spatial Development Perspective.

Measures at EU level

The Commission will propose in 2002 a framework for transport charges to ensure that by 2005, prices for different modes of transport, including air, reflect their costs to society.

continued

Implement in 2003 a framework ensuring through the use of intelligent transport systems the interoperability of payment systems for road transport; promote further technological progress enabling the introduction of road pricing.

Give priority to infrastructure investment for public transport and for railways, inland waterways, short sea shipping and intermodal operations. In particular, the Commission will propose in 2001, for adoption in 2003, a revision of the guidelines for the Transeuropean transport networks, and will promote, in the mid-term review of the Structural Fund programmes, a marked reduction in the share of finance given to road transport.

Improve transport systems by addressing missing transport links, developing open markets and co-operation at EU level (e.g. railway liberalisation, air traffic systems). European Single Sky to be operational by 2004.

Promote teleworking by accelerating investments in next generation communications infrastructure and services.

In 2001, start the implementation of the European Spatial Planning Observatory Network (ESPON) in order to define a set of territorial indicators to analyse the regional impacts of Community policies.

Assess the coherence of the zoning of different Community policies, taking account of their objectives (e.g. NATURA 2000, less-favoured agricultural areas, areas eligible under the Structural Funds or for State Aids).

Diversify income sources in rural areas, including by increasing the proportion of Common Agricultural Policy funds directed to rural development.

Source: CEC, 2001b

In earlier chapters, we have seen how in the EU, the powerful discourses of the single market and political integration are deeply ingrained in the culture of the key EU institutions, conditioning the possibilities of the policy process, shaping the problems that need to be solved, the methods to be used in their analysis, and the solutions that can be considered. We showed how, in the case of TEN-T policy making, a powerful conditioning effect successfully assimilated environmental concerns by not only creating a suitable policy rhetoric, but constructing a process which, at first sight, appeared to allow positive integration. In our analysis, we attempted to show first the weakness of this construction, but second, and more importantly, that this construction is the product of the hegemonic discourse of the EU itself. Sustainability has become allied to frictionless mobility.

In its 2001 White Paper on transport, the Commission declares in stark terms its inability to break with the culture of mobility due to the principle of subsidiarity. This challenge is however sidestepped by concentrating on breaking the link between economic and transport growth:

> This is the context in which we have to consider the option of gradually breaking the link between economic growth and transport growth, on which the White Paper is based. . . . A simplistic solution would be to order a reduction in the mobility of persons and goods and impose a redistribution between modes. However, this is unrealistic as the Community has neither the power nor the means to set limits on traffic in cities or on the roads or to impose combined transport for goods. To give just one example of the subsidiarity problems, it must be remembered that several Member States contest the very principle of a general Community-wide ban to keep heavy goods vehicles off the roads at weekends. Moreover, dirigiste measures would urgently require unanimous harmonisation of fuel taxes, but just a few months ago the Member States took diverging paths on taxation in response to the surge in oil prices.
>
> (CEC, 2001c: 14–15)

> The revised Community guidelines on the trans-European network must form part of an environmentally sustainable policy which, as the Gothenburg European Council underlined, should 'tackle rising levels of congestion and encourage the use of environment-friendly modes of transport'.
>
> (CEC, 2001c: 50)

The seemingly overwhelming problem of this inability to counter the culture of mobility as it is articulated with references to the principle of subsidiarity is avoided by building an alternative form of legitimacy by explicitly acknowledging links between transport intensity and economic growth and targeting this more abstract set of relations. One example of this reoriented thinking is to be found in the conclusions from the Goteberg European Council, where the following goals are set out (European Council, 2001):

> S24. To achieve better policy coordination in the Union, the European Council:
> will at its annual Spring meetings give policy guidance, as necessary, to promote sustainable development in the Union;
> invites the Union institutions to improve internal policy coordination between different sectors. The horizontal preparation of the Sustainable Development Strategy will be coordinated by the General Affairs Council;
> notes that the Commission will include in its action plan for better regulation to be presented to the Laeken European Council mechanisms to ensure that all major policy proposals include a sustainability impact assessment covering their potential economic, social and environmental consequences.
> [. . .]

S29. A sustainable transport policy should tackle rising volumes of traffic and levels of congestion, noise and pollution and encourage the use of environment-friendly modes of transport as well as the full internalisation of social and environmental costs. Action is needed to bring about a significant decoupling of transport growth and GDP growth, in particular by a shift from road to rail, water and public passenger transport. To achieve this, the European Council:
invites the European Parliament and the Council to adopt by 2003 revised guidelines for trans-European transport networks on the basis of a forthcoming Commission proposal, with a view to giving priority, where appropriate, to infrastructure investment for public transport and for railways, inland waterways, short sea shipping, intermodal operations and effective interconnection;
notes that the Commission will propose a framework to ensure that by 2004 the price of using different modes of transport better reflects costs to society (European Council, 2001).

Ecological modernisation

The analysis presented in the previous chapters suggests that ecological modernisation in the EU is taking a different form to the institutional approach anticipated by Gouldson and Murphy (Gouldson and Murphy, 1996). It is not just the lack of strategic capacity, caused by the resistance of member states, that limits the possibility for environmental integration. It is the very nature of EU discourse, reproduced in every EU institution, that conditions and sets limits to institutional learning. The discourse of ecological modernisation in the EU may be closer to Hajer's more pessimistic concept of institutional problem: 'Behind the official rhetoric of ecological modernisation one can discern the silhouette of technocracy in a new disguise that stands in the way of implementing "real solutions" for what are very "real problems"' (Hajer, 1996: 253).

If this is the case, then the prognosis for environmental integration in EU policy is poor as long as we rely on the EU institutions to 'learn' how to deliver it. However, Hajer also offers a more positive way forwards, introducing the alternative concept of ecological modernisation as cultural politics. Here, the relations between environment and development in EU policy can be understood as the product of cultural politics: environmental problems are constructed through the adoption of certain metaphors, categorisations, techniques of analysis, 'making certain framings of reality seem plausible and closing off certain possible future scenarios while making other scenarios "thinkable"' (Hajer, 1996: 257). From this starting point, cultural politics offers new opportunities to unmask and challenge these discursive practices, problematising the problems and challenging unchallenged assumptions. Hajer advocates a clear role for academics in this activity: 'they have to help to open the black boxes of society, technology and nature' (Hajer, 1996: 259). In following this line of academic inquiry, Hajer notes the relevance of Michel Foucault's post-structuralist analyses of how discourses construct and condition social 'reality'. This book may be read as an exploration of this type of critical analysis. A fundamental challenge for ecological modernisation in the EU is to make space for alternative discourses which extend the boundaries of what is 'thinkable', and hence what is possible. Unless this occurs, it seems likely that the construction of policy tools like SEA, and the framing of policy problems in ways that avoid the hardest challenges, will continue to protect the interests of existing hegemonies. Whether the EU institutions have the will or the capacity to make this space remains to be seen.

Sharing space and growth: territorial identity and cohesion

Beneath the questions we have already addressed about relations between growth, ecology and equity, lies the question of how to imagine a European territorially-based identity and unity. Even though the rationales underlying the ESDP might be seen as mutually incompatible, here the general discourse is inescapably one of building a European identity. This is certainly not a coherent rationale, since it also contains the idea of a 'Europe of difference'. So speaking about building identity does not necessarily mean cultural homogenization. Rather, there is an inbuilt tension between imagining Europe as the homogenous cultural denominator on the one hand, and acknowledging 'identity as diversity' on the other (Dutch National Spatial Planning Agency, 2000: 7).

In contrast to the explicitness of the theme of mobility in the ESDP, revealing the discourse of identity requires more interpretation. However, we shall propose to understand the ESDP as more than a strategic spatial policy discourse focusing on the frictionless functionality of the EU territory. In our reading and interpretation of this phenomenon the ESDP can also be seen as an arena for re-articulating the notion of 'Europeanness'. In John Urry's words: 'The development of a possible "European identity" cannot be discussed without considering how massive patterns of short-term mobility may be transforming dominant social identities' (Urry, 1995: 169).

The basic rationale of the argument is simply that mobility leads to increasing levels of social and economic interaction, which leads to cohesion that again (potentially) leads to an imagined community and a sense of a shared territorial identity.

> Transnational policy discourses frame various social and physical realities, make some futures more conceivable while others are suggested to be irrelevant. They come with a particular idea of rational action and present particular 'identity-offers'. To correct the dominance of one structured way of seeing strategic spatial development of Europe would benefit if alternative identity offers would be made available in one central form. But this is not an institutional reality.
>
> (Hajer, 2000: 142)

The relationship between the cool policies of territorial and spatial intervention may seem to belong to another world than the emotional and subjective theme of territorial identity. Nevertheless, we will argue for a broader perspective, understanding the shaping of the European spatial policy discourse as but one dimension of 'bringing Europe together':

> To the extent that in our times supranational organizations are replacing the organizational form of the nation state, the question arises whether the collective identity has accordingly changed its character. . . . Symbols are the essentials of integration. They are particulary necessary when the number of citizens to be integrated is so large that a direct experience of participation processes is not assured.
> (Göhler, 1996: 14–15)

Thus, we would contend, even though there may not be a fixed notion of European identity, the European spatial policy discourse must be understood as a contribution to it. In a sense it becomes an arena for identification as it 'pictures' Europe or offers a representation of Europe: 'Social identities emerge out of imagined communities, out of particular structures of feeling that bind together three elements; space, time and memory, often in part in opposition to an imagined "other" such as a neighbouring country' (Urry, 1995: 166).

Even though this book is based on research that has as its basic value to be of a critical nature (should social science be anything else?), the uncovering of the link between the European spatial policy discourse and the larger project of building a European identity is not an expression of a 'conspiracy theory' or a notion of a 'sinister plot'. Rather this is based upon not only critical social theory and our own interpretation of the policy processes, but also statements from key actors involved in the making of the European spatial policy discourse. In other words, these policies are also about positioning oneself: 'Too often, Europeanization is seen as a zero-sum game, as if all that matters is minimizing the impact of European regulations . . . and maximizing the receipt of European funds. However, Europeanization is also about new perspectives, about better being able to position oneself in European space' (Faludi and Waterhout, 2002: 179). These themes and questions will be taken up again in the final chapter.

Concluding remarks

We find numerous tensions and contradictions between different rationalities within the discourse of monotopic Europe. One such tension is between economic growth and ecological/environmental sustainability. Another is found between economic growth and the question of social equity. A third is the tension between the urban and the rural – often articulated in the vocabulary of the centre-periphery dualism (Richardson, 2000a). A fourth tension can be found at another level, namely the overall conflict between the EU as an agricultural policy unit and this new urban discourse. Such tensions and conflicts get mediated as a hegemonic discourse is shaped. This hegemonic rationale is coined around the term 'balanced competitiveness' and the supporting concepts of polycentricity and accessibility (see also Richardson and Jensen, 2000). In other words, one could conceive of the tensions as 'problems' and the hegemonic discourse as the 'solution' (however fragile, contradictory or uncertain).

Summing up, we would argue that the urban, the environment and the question of territorial identity all are dimensions of the monotopic Europe coined around a specific notion of mobility as zero friction. Furthermore we see the magic triangle of economy, environment and equity as intimately related to and underpinning the imagined community of one seamless territory.

Chapter 11

Conclusion

Making European space?

I think that the central issue of philosophy and critical thought since the eighteenth century has always been, still is, and will, I hope, remain the question: What is this Reason that we use? What are its historical effects? What are its limits, and what are its dangers? How can we exist as rational beings, fortunately committed to practising a rationality that is unfortunately criss-crossed by intrinsic dangers? . . . This is the situation that we are in and that we must combat. If intellectuals in general are to have a function, if critical thought itself has a function, and, even more specifically, if philosophy has a function within critical thought, it is precisely to accept this sort of spiral, this sort of revolving door of rationality that refers us to its necessity, to its indispensability, and at the same time, to its intrinsic dangers.

(Michel Foucault in Rabinow, 1991: 239)

European integration requires not only new governmental structures and physical infrastructure links but also new mental maps and removal of Cartesian inhibitions. It is necessary for policy-makers to learn to think European, and for educators to develop the capacity for this mode of thinking in their students. . . . The next generations of spatial planners may be brought up on the story of EMU, the Blue Banana and the Bunch of Grapes!

(Williams, 1996a: 265)

The conceptual perception in everyday man is something which eventually will change over time. . . . I don't think that my generation will start doing it. . . . I see it not necessarily as something terrible. . . . I will not stop being a Dane, and my son will not stop being a Dane. . . . To have this knowledge that a person in Portugal is just as much a European as I am is much the same as saying 'I am an American whether I come from New York or Los Angeles' . . . we are part of the same territory.

(Interview, Danish National Planner)

Introduction

In the previous chapters, we have explored the construction in policy space of a discourse of monotopic Europe. A Europe where utopian qualities of frictionless mobility and balanced competitiveness are balanced against dystopic tensions and fractures of interest and outcome between winners and losers. The discourse walks a fine tightrope in order to sustain its compelling argument for the reordering of European space. A Europe that survives on its ability to deliver growth and prosperity beyond its economic heart has necessarily grappled with the spatialisation of its future. This making of European space is, as we have seen, played out in discursive struggle, in which competing positions lead to claims (and counter-claims), which lead in turn to the construction of new (contested) fields of knowledge and policy agendas which need to be communicated in new ways. In this final chapter we will try to give some sense of where this may lead: for the policy makers working in this new field; for future European citizens and the territories they inhabit; and for the spaces and places of a monotopic Europe.

The shaping of European spatial policy is clearly happening in a fragile and uncertain way. However, there is no doubt that the implementation of the ESDP is moving ahead quickly, for example through the action programme agreed at the meeting between spatial planning ministers in Tampere, Finland (Tampere Ministerial, 1999). A new discourse is shaping practice across scales and sectors throughout Europe. But what are the implications for places and citizens as this new discourse increasingly shapes our thoughts and space?

The concern at the heart of this final discussion is that EU spatial policy is being reproduced in ways that naturalise the idea of monotopia, and promulgate uncritical acceptance of its core values. It is our clear conviction that critical analysis which begins to reveal the risks and dangers of this simultaneous shaping of thought and space, creates an alternative space within which the boundaries and possibilities for thoughts about alternatives and about resistances can emerge.

Here, we begin to explore what could happen within that space. We discuss critical aspects of the contested institutionalisation of a monotopic discourse of European space, and explore what can be done in the face of the hegemony of monotopia. We do this by first reflecting on the broader theoretical context within which our analysis sits, and then returning to the policy domain, to raise some fundamental questions about the reproduction and future legitimacy of the policy field. From this platform, we open up a discussion about what can be done – what are the possibilities for engagement? We explore the issues for democratic legitimacy of the attempts to impose a monotopic vision of Europe and reflect on the possibilities for new resistance counter-understandings of place in the face of monotopia; and note how citizens may develop multiple loyalties. *Inter alia*, we address the question of the prospects for achieving spatial justice in a monotopic Europe.

A contribution to planning theory?

Coming to the end of our narrative of Europe of monotopia we pause to reflect on this work's relation to the state of the art in planning theory. As a first reservation we could not, and will not, claim to have aimed for a strictly theoretical contribution. We had a story to tell from the empirical 'battlefields' of EU spatial policy making. Having said this, we would suggest that our contribution still has something to add theoretically as well.

The first dimension of this contribution is to show how thinking spatially about spatial policy and planning processes can be conceptualised and carried out. We think of this piece of research as a fruitful way of framing the importance of a spatial imagination. Fusing a critical geographical and sociological imagination to policy analysis opens up a new perspective for understanding the real world practices of politics. From our analysis, the possibility of a theoretical and analytical perspective framed by the cultural sociology of space and a discourse framework hinges on perceiving how the spatiality of social life is played out in a dialectical tension between material practices and symbolic meanings at scales from the body to the global. Furthermore, we would argue not only for a *spatialisation* of planning theory but also for a *mobilisation* in the sense of underlining the importance of understanding the socio-spatial relation in terms of mobilities, movements and processes.

Second, we would argue for the particular perspective on discourse and discourse analysis we have applied in this research. We would especially advocate the broadening of a Foucauldian inspired perspective to include more explicitly the institutional level of policy analysis. What ensues in the policy debate is therefore seen to be conditioned, in that the permissible knowledges, statements, actions, etc., are already institutionalised. As a result, the transparently communicative stages in policy making take place after the critical decisions have been made. Furthermore, this early conditioning takes place not through formal, transparent or obvious processes of debate, but in ways that are contested, but outside and before the policy debate begins. Within this context a spatial policy discourse seeking to direct or produce new spatial practices works by means of constructing and reproducing new language uses and other practices expressing specific power-rationalities.

Third, and finally, we would highlight the critical perspective focusing on the contested nature of all political articulation processes. Thus we acknowledge the point of departure to be dissent and conflict rather than pre-established consensus. This perspective certainly lends itself to a meta-theoretical reflection on policy research, as the critical perspective in our understanding should be the hallmark of social science. Furthermore this perspective carries with it a research ethic. By this we mean a call upon the researcher either to operate in a reflexive way at a critical distance from the study object (our research strategy in this work) or to engage in a more applied, but similarly reflective and critical manner with the study field.

Drawing together these dimensions, we have attempted to set out a way of researching a complex policy process that can open up a multi-level analysis of relations between power and space. This analysis leads us, inevitably, to a question at the heart of conceptual debates in planning: so, what do we do then, once we have begun to develop a critique and found uncomfortable things? We do not seek to resolve this question here. Rather, our intention is to set out some thoughts that may contribute to a wider debate about what can or 'should' be done in the face of a risky policy hegemony, to move towards the idea of reflexive critique and engagement, which we believe can provide a useful basis for action.

The unbearable lightness of European spatial policy?

A first step in considering what to do is to reflect on what the new spatial policy means, whether it matters and how. This hinges on the questions of competency, informality and legitimacy, as the discourse claims to be articulated on the basis of a democratic context.

We have argued that the spatial discourse expresses a power-rationality of monotopia. Rather than adopting the ESDP's traditional instrumental view of rationality, which frames knowledge that connects means and goals, our aim is instead to encourage deeper reflection on the more general epistemological problem of planning and policy making: on what counts as knowledge. We speak of rationalities in the plural in order to recognise that the human ability to comprehend its environment can be expressed through different forms of knowledge and rationality – what Leonie Sandercock describes as an 'epistemology of multiplicity' (Sandercock, 1998). We have argued that certain types of environmental knowledge have been excluded from the ESDP's framework of knowledge and rationality, 'everyday life-oriented ways of knowing' certainly find no place within this quasi-scientific discourse.

Furthermore we are in line with the Foucault-inspired analysis of Bent Flyvbjerg, which insists on comprehending the dialectical relation between power and rationality. That is to say that not only can rationality define what to do in terms of 'survey before plan', but that the reverse can also be the case, where 'power defines rationality' (Flyvbjerg, 1998). Relating this to the ESDP means that not only is there a 'rational' agenda on more efficient political integration but also 'room' for framing what counts as rational. Furthermore it would be in line with Foucault and Flyvbjerg to suggest that one should not seek a single institution or agent which 'carries' the power of the spatial discourse, but rather to understand power as multiple and heterogeneous relations of agenda settings (Foucault, 1990).

The ESDP process can be seen as in a phase of becoming. Even though we have argued that the emerging spatial discourse is characterised by a specific configuration of rationality and knowledge, this does not mean that the field is closed or predetermined. There remain many opportunities for 'investments' in the shifting 'discursive territory'. As a strategic planning document the ESDP can be seen as a battlefield for the agents that know of its existence and have been allowed onto the field.

The institutionalisation of the new discourse of a monotopic European space is likely to prove difficult. The vision of dramatic socio-spatial reconfiguration is likely to be increasingly contested with the translation of policy outputs into implemented measures. We have simply illustrated some of the dimensions of this looming struggle. Experience of the sectors which the ESDP process attempts to integrate underscores the importance of such power relations over implementation. The over-riding question facing this policy field is which direction it should now take (or will be allowed to take) in terms of EU competence: should the EU formally take on the role it is already performing 'without competence'?

However, difficult questions of democracy and public knowledge about the ESDP, and about the 'lower levels' of transnational planning and co-operation have been left untouched in these discussions (Jørgensen and Nielsen, 1997). Furthermore, the institutionalisation of such spatial policies, in order to be effective, seems to be in need of some sort of federal arrangement and institutional backing:

> Its (apparently only seemingly) technical nature notwithstanding, spatial planning activities at national, regional and local levels have typically been facing more protest, strife and conflict than perhaps more consequential regional development activities. This probably has a lot to do with the almost metaphysical (some would say primitive and arcane) emotions attached to the territory. . . . There cannot be much doubt that it is this protective attitude towards the national territory which lies behind the many provisos and escape clauses with which the European Spatial Development Perspective most likely will be provided. A supranational territory seems an impossibility in the absence of some minimum of federal elements. So far, however, federation seems to be a word non grata in official EU contexts. Nonetheless, we shall argue that it is such supranational institutions which the Commission, together with the informal ministerial meetings and aided by the CSD, is indirectly trying to construct through the attempt to link together spatial planning and regional policy with the help of the financial instrument Interreg IIC, the planning instrument of ESDP, and emerging new territorial 'polities', namely transnational regions.
>
> (Jørgensen and Nielsen, 1997: 314–315)

Other researchers argue that insufficient attention is given to the competitive position of Europe in a global economy. It is necessary to enable economic core areas to fulfill their role as the power house of European economy (Zonneveld and Faludi, 1996: 58). These researchers advocate a spatial development strategy of centrality and hierarchy, and thus also of a Europe of variable speeds when it comes to planning (Zonneveld and Faludi, 1996: 59). This might be the case for reasons of smoother implementation, but not necessarily when seen in the light of a socially legitimate basis for planning. Thus questions of the normative basis, social legitimacy and democratisation of planning are still on the agenda.

So what to do, then?

From this analysis, a basis for action begins to emerge, which has implications for all actors across the multi-scale processes of European policy.

The first requirement for action is that, in the face of complex and informal policy making processes which are interlinked across multiple scales, the single necessary basis for action must be the possibility of multi-level reflexive critique and engagement. It can no longer be adequate to understand regional policy in isolation, or to analyse bottom-up public involvement in local decision making, when issues are being dealt with that take shape and reach deadlock or resolution across a complex multi-level field.

This raises enormous challenges. Not least, how do you manage, as a single actor (perhaps a single citizen), to critically engage with multiple levels of activity, and move reflexively towards a new form of action? We do not pretend that this can be easily done, but we see in this point a recognition of the ways that certain interests (such as the infrastructure lobby and certain environmental movements) now operate, and a need for many actors to reflect on their current modes of operation. The question of what to do with Europe, of how you counter a European idea you feel is wrong, depends on this.

This is more than a question of analysis. It reaches deeper into a question of the nature of identity. For multi-level engagement to be possible, it requires a first move towards multiple levels of identity, which is then translated to a new capacity for multiple levels of action and engagement. This applies just as well to those inside and those outside the policy process. Such a form of engagement could make it possible to (re)introduce ideas which have been marginalised or excluded, that have become unthinkable within the policy process. Perhaps what we are calling for is a concerted attempt to make a space for the 'will to friction' as an alternative to frictionlessness.

The possibilities for action are of course different for politicians, planners and policy makers, interest groups representatives, academics and for citizens. As Flyvbjerg has powerfully argued, there are different responsibilities and possibilities for action, and this is where reflexivity is needed (Flyvbjerg, 1998). We move towards our discussion of a possible basis for this multi-level reflexive engagement by setting out some pointers for those inside and outside the spatial policy process.

Internal possibilities for action

The detailed analysis set out in this book suggests a need for reflexivity with regard to the design and operation of the institutions and practices of EU spatial policy making. This includes in particular the ways of working within the new transnational policy spaces, such as mega-regions. It calls for a rethinking of the ways that tools (such as cost-benefit analysis and strategic environmental assessment) are used, and in particular that the contingent nature of the core ideas which are reproduced within these tools is understood. The values which should be brought into this rethinking include transparency and legitimacy, but also wider values which relate to the costs, to the winners and losers, to what is at stake in reproducing certain visions and ideas.

Such issues should be debated more openly than they currently are, and we would suggest that the European Parliament provides an potential arena for debate on the meaning and significance of spatial ideas within the European project. However, alongside such public debate there is a need for subtler forms of action, by those working within and close to policy making.

A fundamental challenge for this type of engagement is that the ideas raised, and the proposals for action that flow from their consideration, are likely to be controversial within everyday policy-making environments. This calls for subtlety and strategic reflexivity. To shift the agenda, to open up room for new and challenging ways of thinking may be achieved by formal institutional means, but we should remember how much policy work is informal, and reflect on how much is achieved by informal working.

Our message to the 'roving band of planners'

This leads to an idea of reflexive critique and engagement which we feel is particularly relevant to actors within transnational policy processes. They need to work increasingly in a way which questions the hegemony at the heart of the European project. They need to understand how a monotopia can be reproduced across policy spaces, and how minds and actions are subtly shaped so that once highly controversial ideas become natural, and alternatives become unthinkable. This means understanding the relations between discourse and the ways they are institutionalised: how policy ideas get formed and reproduced. In particular, this suggests not becoming too uncritical about what can be delivered by institutional innovation, or over-trusting in the nature of such institutions. It means taking care to understand the ideas that underpin emerging spatial policy – with their possibilities as well as their limits and dangers. Furthering the project of European spatial policy must be understood as more than Europeanisation by institutional design. Its discursive dimensions must also be taken into account, so that creation of new institutional forms, arenas and processes does not simply reproduce the currently hegemonic discourse of monotopia. In part this means ensuring that new institutional forms are designed in ways which leave open possibilities for dialogue, for the introduction of new ideas. They need to be participative, transparent and accountable.

This also applies to academics whose work can be located on different sides of the fuzzy boundaries between critical research and analysis for policy making. Reflexive critical engagement needs to be supported by the research community. European spatial policy processes are already attracting the interest of planning academics. We suggest the need for further critical research, possibly using the discourse analytic approach utilised here, which would complement the more applied research currently being pursued (see Box 11.1). Such critical research, of the type reported here, seems likely to provide challenging and possibly uncomfortable critiques on the creation of new spatial policy discourses, but is a necessary adjunct to the future development of the policy field. Alongside discourse analytic research, there is scope for sociological research which explores the potential effects of the new policy discourse on social conditions in different localities across Europe. For example, John Gray has powerfully illustrated how such connections may be explored using ethnographic research (Gray, 2000).

External possibilities for action

EU spatial policy, as we have seen, is made in the shadows of the EU institutions. What is paramount is that European spatial policy ideas become the stuff of public interest and debate. Here one evident difficulty has been the lack of European public space(s) within which citizens and civil society can deliberate on possible future shapes and logics of European space. Furthermore, there are many different roles in making such a debate possible, but these include the need for academics to help push back the boundaries of thought and possibilities for action. They also include the need for pressure groups to operate in ways that can engage a broad public (once again across scales and places). And they include the need for politicians to ask public questions about these issues and for professionals to recognise that the citizens have a capacity to understand and react to complex issues, so that they may feel inspired to introduce such ideas into more local/regional policy processes.

And it is possible to make a difference. We have mentioned that proposals for new road building through the Vallée d'Aspes in the Pyrenees attracted organised and prolonged resistance from local communities and international environmental NGOs. The 2001 Transport White Paper shifts away from road building across the Pyrenees, proposing to add a new trans-Pyreneean heavy rail freight line to the TEN-T instead: 'The Commission is proposing in the revision of the guidelines for the trans-European network the inclusion of a major project for a high-capacity rail crossing in the Pyrenees (Annex III), the route being left to the interested countries to agree' (CEC, 2001c: 55). It continues: 'It will also be necessary to rethink the question of a future road link through the Pyrenees which, for reasons connected with environmental impact, cost and acceptance by local residents, should ensure that piggyback transport is adopted as of right'(CEC, 2001c: 55). Things can be changed, but here a great deal of activity brought a result that, in a wider perspective, failed to dent the momentum of the

Box 11.1 **The need for further research**

1 While this book begins to inform such a critique, analysis is needed of the future development of spatial policy ideas at the EU level and within member states (particularly in the south of Europe and in the new member states and accession countries), to enhance understanding of the overall process. This work should squarely address the power dynamics within and between European and national policy arenas.
2 Monitoring and analysis of the process of spatial convergence between programmes operating across the different sectors. A crucial element of such research should be analysis of the effects of power struggles over the process of spatial integration within each of these sectors, and within the ESDP process overall. The implementation of the ESDP strategy and specific policies through the use of structural funds, INTERREG, the TEN-T program and other measures to provide regional infrastructure networks, are some examples.
3 Closer analysis of the relations between the emerging EU spatial discourse and those of particular member states, regions and cities. In the current implementation phase, the ESDP is seen as providing a policy framework for structural policies, for national and regional planning documents, and for the co-ordination of sectoral policies in member states. The central question is whether the ESDP will facilitate convergence between spatial strategies at different levels and in different places. What struggles over localities are taking place within different regions across the EU, and what is the place of localities in debates about development within peripheral and urbanised regions? For example could the structural funds be focused on regional infrastructure networks in peripheral regions? How will member states planning systems respond to the new spatial discourse? And what are the implications for the accession countries?
4 Discourse analytics would also be useful in providing explanatory power as the rhetoric of a new policy language is institutionalised through the development of a new system of spatial analysis. The policy knowledge and rationality of European spatial policy need careful scrutiny if hegemonic trends are to be exposed, and the marginalising of difficult or 'other' knowledge is to be revealed. Crucially, how are localities, and mobilities, being subsumed into new frameworks and techniques of spatial analysis of peripheral or urban regions?

overall spatial project. At least, it indicates that hegemonies are not impregnable. But as in the local context of national and local policy making, the connection must be made between the particular project in question and the more general issues of value, rationality and power which are being played out.

Democracy, participation and citizenship

Such questions lead us to the themes and questions of democracy and resistance, which we turn to next, as they reveal the possibilities of exclusion, silence, ambivalence, difference and conflict in the final outcome of these complex policy processes. Significantly, by reminding us that there are winners and losers in spatial policy making, and that policy making is always contested, we can develop further our discussion of the possibility of alternatives and resistance to monotopic Europe.

It is clear that practice in policy making across the arenas of European spatial policy making reflect the wider crisis of democracy in the EU. The general problem of the lack of democratic legitimacy of EU decision making is reproduced and even amplified in the informal, infranational nature of much of the work of spatial policy making, and the non-constitutional nature of many of the new cross-border and trans-European institutions that have been established. This, then, is one of the most important questions for the future development of this policy field: while questions of competency remain, how can EU spatial policy develop as a field of action which can attain high standards of legitimacy, transparency and accountability?

As we have shown throughout, policy making for European spatial planning, from the TEN-T to the ESDP, provides anything but exemplary cases of participatory and transparent European democracy in action. In making this claim, it is important to bear in mind the nature of 'democracy' being adhered to. Certainly, the policy discourse clearly demonstrates a claim to legitimacy based on the democratic nature of its construction. However, we have found many cases of elitist and semi-closed policy and decision making.

In reflecting on these difficulties, we should first review the claims made about the democratic nature of the ESDP process. Democratic validation of the ESDP was clearly espoused by the Commission when early drafts were published (CSD, 1999: 13), with consecutive drafts stating that the citizens of Europe should be included in the process (CSD, 1997), and that 'wide public support' is a precondition for effective implementation (CSD, 1998a: 72). However, though the ESDP claims itself to be the result of 'a Europe-wide process of public debate' (CSD, 1999: 12), the consultation process has in fact been more exclusive, concentrating on professional, political and corporate elites within the member states (Williams, 1999). The final document shifts towards a more practical stance: voluntary co-operation between relevant authorities is the crucial precondition for further progress. For strategic as well as for democratic reasons, the question of the social legitimacy of European spatial planning is therefore raised, but with less clarity over precisely how legitimacy will be attained. The question for implementation is how the principle of subsidiarity can be applied to deliver citizen participation in a process which remains steadfastly opaque and apparently academic to the outside observer.

There are difficult unresolved issues here: will the ESDP – as both planning framework and strategic spatial vision – institutionalise a spatial discourse capable of delivering spatial justice within the EU (at what cost to those outside it?)? Or will the discourse of monotopic Europe preclude such possibilities?

The issues of democracy and citizenship are obviously not to be seen as a finished project in terms of European integration. Alongside the lack of a common mother tongue and the lack of a public arena or sphere for democratic discussion (Habermas, 1996; Morley and Robins, 1995; Shore, 2000; Weiler, 1999), Weiler and Morley and Robins point to a vacuum of citizenship, the absence of a 'people' from which democratic legitimacy can flow, due to deficiencies in the political culture of Europe:

> Citizenship is not only about the politics of public authority. It is also about the social reality of peoplehood and the identity of the polity. Citizens constitute the *demos* of the polity. . . . Simply put, if there is no *demos*, there can be no democracy'.
>
> (Weiler, 1999: 337 emphasis in original)

> The European Community has so far failed to develop an adequate political culture or a basis for European citizenship. Questions of identity and of citizenship have become dissociated.
>
> (Morley and Robins, 1995: 19)

Certainly, as we have discussed throughout, the EU seeks to construct a common identity, of which the territorial dimension is highly significant. Part of this process is clearly to create a form of citizenship, and here lie problems. Citizenship creates subjects of government since it is both a 'way of ordering people as well as being an "identity-marker"' (Shore, 2000: 71):

> European citizenship is not so much a discourse of rights as a discourse of power. It is a political technology for making the EU more visible to its newly constituted subjects. . . . Its function is to generate a new category of European subjectivity and thereby enables the new European state to communicate directly with its citizens.
>
> (Shore, 2000: 83)

Obviously one needs to be very careful not to reproduce the nation state model as the only model for democracy in terms of nationalist belongings. Having said this it seems evident that any polity marketing itself as a democratic entity needs to think carefully about the question of legitimacy. Thus at the end of the day there must be an answer to who is going to decide policies on behalf of whom? And how can the loyalty of those governed be manufactured and maintained? In the analysis of Weiler, democracy and identity are linked via this question of 'multiple loyalties', which we will return to below. These are clear challenges to politicians, policy makers and institutional designers. However, in the absence of European democracy, what options are left to those who are in the shadow of European spatial policy? And crucially, can spatial justice be secured in a monotopic Europe?

Towards a progressive sense of place/spaces of resistance

The question is, then, what could be done in the face of monotopic Europe? And further, is there a future for the local, the peripheral and for (new) places of friction spread across the European territory? Is there scope for 'spaces of resistance' to the overarching notion of monotopia?

Shore identifies the 'agents of European consciousness' and sees these as forces and objects through which knowledge of the European Union is embodied (Shore, 2000: 26). Such 'agents' can thus both be human agents, artifacts, bodies, institutions, policies and representations that serve as an instrument for promotion and acceptance of the 'European idea':

> What is interesting here, however, is the way that EU officials have appropriated core sociological concepts such as 'culture', 'identity', 'social cohesion' and 'collective consciousness' as mobilising metaphors for building 'European culture', 'European identity' and 'European consciousness'.
>
> (Shore, 2000: 25)

This affinity with sociological thought as an expression of the bureaucracy's need for a new vocabulary can be taken further by looking into how the general political imaginary operates on the notions of unity and coherence, and thus finally a particular way of framing European identity:

> What kind of identity for Europe? The language of official Euro-culture is significant: it is the language of cohesion, community, unity, integration, security. . . . European identity is imagined in terms of an idealised wholeness and plenitude.
>
> (Morley and Robins, 1995: 23)

The political project is thus to articulate a progressive sense of place, that takes departure in a spatial logic based on the 'places of difference' (Sennett, 1990: 125) and the 'space of places' (Castells, 1996: 428). Thus this perspective is an expression of particularism and localism, whose biggest political challenge lies in avoiding an identity of exclusion. In its extreme form this spatial logic is a utopia of autonomous, self-sustaining localities.

As the making of identities uses materials from history, geography, biology, institutions, collective memory and personal fantasies, power apparatuses and religious revelations (Castells, 1997: 7) its constitution obviously reveals a contested field for political action. Or in the words of Chantal Mouffe: 'What we commonly call "cultural identity" is both the scene and the object of political struggles' (Mouffe, 1994: 110).

However, if the European spatial policy discourse is part of the effort to picture European unity and identity, one might ask what sort of identity? Castells operates with three forms and origins of identity building (Castells, 1997: 8):

- legitimising identity;
- resistance identity;
- project identity.

Legitimising identity generates a civil society in the Gramscian sense of the word. That means a set of organisations, institutions and structured social actors that reproduce the identity that rationalises the sources of structure domination. Resistance identity leads to the formation of communities, and is perhaps the most important type of identity-building today. It generates a defensive, and often exclusionary, identity (i.e. neo-tribes or gated communities). Project identity produces subjects, understood as the collective social actor through which individuals reach holistic meaning in their experience.

Some analysts are quite dismissive of the potential for developing a European identity due to the situation of more or less permanent flux in the vital elements of its building blocks: 'The prerequisite for a specific socio-spatial consciousness and identity are weak in Europe, since both the territorial, symbolic and institutional shapes of this entity are unclear' (Paasi, 2001: 21). However, according to Castells it is not as much a question of whether a European identity can be constructed as on what premises:

> If meaning is linked to identity, and if identity remains exclusively national, regional or local, European integration may not last beyond the limits of a common market, parallel to free-trade zones constituted in other areas of the world. European unification in a long-term perspective, requires European Identity. . . . So, by and large, there is no European identity. But it could be built, not in contradiction, but complementary to national, regional, and local identities.
>
> (Castells, 1998: 332–333)

The interesting question here is, then, how these more general notions of identity and territory link to the European spatial policy discourse. In other words, is this nurturing resistance identity or project identity?

According to the cultural sociology of space, social agents invest meaning in localities as well as relating emotionally to space and place. One must thus recognise that the historical and temporal dimension cannot be ignored. This means that new identities are always based on the heritage from past and present identities (Massey, 1995: 286). Thus, one should not imagine the relation between identity and place as dislocated from the history of socio-spatial practice. On the other hand, there lies a huge political challenge in working out how to recognise the meaning and importance of place, without articulating 'regressive' and exclusionary 'Blut und Boden' discourses. The question is: is it possible to articulate a 'progressive sense of place' and not a self-referentially, closed and defensive sense of place? In the words of Doreen Massey: 'There is a need to face up to – rather than simply deny – people's need for attachment of some sort, whether through a place or anything else. . . . The question is how to hold on to that notion of geographical difference, of uniqueness, even of rootedness if people want that, without it being reactionary' (Massey, 1991: 319).

Thus the question is really what sort of geographical imagination and European identity the European spatial policy discourse is nurturing? Evidently, this is not an easy question to answer in a simple mode but it seems that the European Union has the character of 'legitimising identity' rather than 'project identity' in Castells' terminology, even though it may seek to represent itself in the latter rather than the former sense. However, the issue of picturing Europe as a self-sufficient and closed space fencing off the 'unpleasant Other' could lead to a more outspoken strategy of 'resistance identity' within the European project. It is in other words a question of how to handle multiple loyalties.

Towards multiple loyalties?

The tension of spatial logics calls for an investigation into the socio-spatial identification processes when we look at the European Union in general, and at its spatial planning policy in particular. A way of dealing with this theme is by examining the before-mentioned 'no-demos thesis'. According to this, there is no European 'Volk' (people), and thus not any traditional territory-identity relation within the Community (Weiler *et al.*, 1995: 6). The question is whether to seek (or invent) an organic and authentic form of European 'demos', or to understand 'demos' in non-organic civic terms (Weiler *et al.*, 1995: 12). The latter 'supra-national' conception of the European project implies a 'double identity' of nation-state identity and European identity and therefore also a notion of 'multiple loyalties' (Weiler *et al.*, 1995: 19):

> Redefinitions of spatial concepts have been important elements in the current discourse on Europe, often linked with ideas of identity. Europe is experiencing a dramatic change in its institutionalization: territorial shapes are being sought, symbols are under construction and institutions are in the making at all spatial scales.
>
> (Paasi, 2001: 25)

Some argue that if we are to see the emergence of a democratic and empowering European Union, we must leave the idea of a 'European fatherland' and replace this notion with that of a public sphere of disparate communities (Tassin, 1995: 189). So the way to a more democratic European development, is seen to come about by means of a 'de-territorialisation of politics'. By this is meant a vision of democracy where citizenship is separated from nationality and place, and is instead founded on participation in the political institutions and philosophical principles of Europe. This idea of decoupling the territorial and spatial from the political is a 'solution' that is opposite both to the notion of a 'United States of Europe' and to the notion of a 'Europe of regions'. It is a notion of a 'dual citizenship', with emphasis on the 'universal' side of citizenship, instead of the territorial place-oriented side ('dual identity'). It is a notion of a 'performative citizenship' contrasting both the nation state and the EU, and instead finding its frame of reference in constructed identities beyond the nation state, such as Black Atlantic Culture, Greenpeace, the idea of the Islamic nation or the feminist movement (Albrow, 1996: 201). A 'Europe of Heimats', to borrow an expression from Morley and Robins, will imply particularistic and localistic identities, combined with 'universal' identities. To be European can thus be said to imply a threefold spatial identity concept: that of continent, nation and region. Being a European is about managing some amalgam of these different scales of identity (Morley and Robins, 1995: 20). A rather voluntaristic interpretation of this situation would say that social actors must establish 'invented communities' by means of an increased 'aesthetic reflexivity' and thus actively decide which communities they will 'throw themselves into' (Lash and Urry, 1994: 316). However, the problems of mobilising political legitimacy for place-bound identities, whether they are of the international labour movement (Harvey, 1989: 303), the ecological grassroots or the citizens of the European Union, are the same. This points to the problem of how to construct a political identity within a socio-spatial unit with the size and geographical dispersion of the expanding European Union. In other words: 'Is it possible, from a spatial perspective, to contribute to the gradual creation of a broadly based European cultural identity? The idea is bold, but not illusory' (Dutch National Spatial Planning Agency, 2000: 137).

In one interpretation, a de-coupling of sovereignty and territoriality, and thus the emergence of major non-national and post-national social formations could be an indication of a new way of thinking of sovereignty and territoriality (Appadurai, 1996: 42). The changing socio-spatial relations from the local to the global result in two challenges to the 'post-national' order. On the one hand, the production of locality challenges the order of the nation state. On the other hand, human motion in the context of changing nation states encourages the emergence of translocalities, e.g. border zones, tourist zones, Free Trade Zones, refugee camps, migrant hostels and neighbourhoods of exiles and guest workers (Appadurai, 1996: 42). The very essence of international competitive capitalism contributes to these new translocalities, where the social interactions and normative bonds are crossing the borders of the nation states. In this process of socio-spatial transformation, a divergence exists between the national rights of citizens versus a broader set of post-national geographic processes. The core of this process is a conflict where national space becomes differently valorised for the state and for its citizens (Appadurai, 1996: 46). For many citizens, the 'territorial referents of civic loyalty' are increasingly divided among different spatial horizons: work loyalties, residential loyalties, and religious loyalties may create disjunct registers of affiliation (Appadurai, 1996: 47). This is essential to the basic discussion of identification and loyalty not only towards the nation states, but also in the case of 'Project Europe'. On the global 'market for loyalties' new forms of social interaction, loyalty and interests are emerging, as it becomes clear that the states are the only players in the global scene that really need the notion of territorially based sovereignty (Appadurai, 1996: 49). Thus, according to Appadurai, the traditional thinking of the relation between humans, territoriality and identity must be re-addressed. This might be through a process of 'de-territorialisation' and 're-territorialisation' grounded on an imaginary of local autonomy instead of a national imaginary (Appadurai, 1996: 54–55). However, the question is how far such loyalties can be 'stretched'. The problem is, of course, that such processes of re-thinking and re-claiming the territorial can just as easily be thought of in terms of exclusive nationalism and ethnocentric policies:

> Discourses of the soil tend to flourish in all sorts of populist movements, both local and transnational, while discourses of territory tend to characterize border conflicts and international law. Loyalty often leads individuals to identify with transnational cartographies, while the appeals of citizenship attach them to territorial states.
>
> (Appadurai, 1996: 57)

Thus proponents of this de-territorialised notion of politics advocate a choice of 'cosmopolitanism' in their rejection of Herder's Volksgeist, and advocacy for Montesquieu's Esprit Général (Kristeva, 1993: 16, 33). Such advocacy is then, among other things, articulated in the vocabulary of 'new forms of citizenship, based on the active realisation of multiple identities' (Christiansen and Jørgensen, 1995: 19). Even though the proponents of de-territorialisation and socio-spatial homogenisation have been thoroughly referred to above, it will remain no secret that we find these notions of socio-spatial transformation processes too simple-minded and idealistic. At the end of the day, it is a question of how social agents relate to the territorial entity of the European Union in terms of social identification, but also in terms of social legitimate basis of decision making. This is vital in relation to the concept of spatial planning and policy, at least if it is considered important that the EU citizens share the visions of the EU institutions.

Prospects for spatial justice: a new battle for Europe?

Striking a 'utopian realist' chord of political thought we would agree with Harvey on the need for some 'solution' to questions of socio-spatial identification and power that provides a meaningful basis for political action: 'Somewhere between the vulgar essentialist view and the potentially infinite fluidity of multiple and shifting identifications there has to be sufficient permanence established (however contingent) to give direction (for a time and in a place) to political action' (Harvey, 1996: 357).

From Harvey's attempt to nuance the question of from where to participate, and from where to draw the energies for territorial identities, the ground is set for a questioning of from where to think a space and identity of resistance. From where can a counter-view of the monotopic vision of Europe be articulated, let alone launched? Clearly answers must lie within the civil society and the deliberations around what to do with this place called Europe. Furthermore, they cannot be simply read off from this particular analysis of European spatial policy making. However, we would argue that NGOs and other agents of civil society might need to turn their attention to these new policies in order more completely to picture the vision of monotopic Europe. From this acknowledgement the next step would include thoughts about alternative mobility rationales, questioning the need to build capacity for even more traffic in the arteries of the European infrastructure network. Taken from that, issues of what sort of political strategies for European cities would benefit their inhabitants would emerge. Here, for example, a problematisation of more prestigious and iconic conference and office buildings as part of the endless reproduction of entrepreneurial strategies would be timely: leading to the discussion of what sort of territory the EU should develop into.

These questions need to be articulated in public spheres and political forums across Europe. Furthermore, there should be no doubt about the strength of the institutions and networks supporting the vision of monotopic Europe, leading us to the conclusion of a rather gloomy outlook for spatial justice. The question of spatial justice does not carry with it evidence which points to this prospect as having a very bright future. Spaces of resistance and modes of resistance need to be established. By this we mean articulation of counter-visions and practices that would allow the places and spaces not included in the monotopic notion of Europe. Spatial justice will be a battle for Europe as we are entering a contested space of both material practices and symbolic meanings attached to the European territory.

From our discussion we do not imply that there is a simple and linear read-out of the 'new identities' of monotopic Europe and its Others. Rather, we would suggest there is a field of articulation within which different identity conceptualisations are prone to stand up against each other. Needless to say exclusionary territorial identities of resistance in the sense that Castells describes them are not the way forward towards spatial justice. So the kind of identity that could offer an alternative to the monotopic discourse of Europe would need to be at the same time locally and globally oriented. Locally in the sense that regional ways of relating and acting are appreciated without excluding 'Others'. Globally in the sense that the interrelationship with other places needs to be recognised, as well as the fact that, for example, environmental problems will need a global-local dialectical approach to be properly handled.

The question is whether the discourse of monotopia is at all capable of providing an open field of articulation in terms of a new spatial imagination based upon a democratic basis, or whether European spatial policy is rather to be characterised by an 'unbearable lightness'. A 'lightness' that offers opportunities for those agents and institutions that have the resources and powers to play the new game.

Monotopia: is that all there is then?

The idea of monotopic Europe, then, raises a complex debate that requires reflections and contributions from many academic fields. It intertwines questions about constructions of identity, mobility and the nature of our inhabited spaces. It requires a focus on the work of policy making, but bears in mind that this work has implications for people and places, and attempts to hold these implications in the analysis.

We have shown how the discourse of monotopia seeks to re-order EU space by redefining the way that this space is imagined and understood, by creating a new language and knowledge base for communicating about it, which is reproduced across a multi-level intertextual field, by building new institutional frameworks across borders to implement these new ways of organising space, and instilling this thinking into existing planning systems. It works in subtle ways, including the shaping of our future educational horizons, and in less subtle ways by funding the construction of new international high-speed transport infrastructure. It therefore reaches beyond 'planning' into many areas of European cultural and economic activity.

But we have also attempted to explore why it is so difficult to resist this currently hegemonic discourse, and we have begun to identify some of the starting points for resistance. Mapping out the critical moments in the construction and institutionalisation of the new discourse helps to do this by showing the key areas of activity, which may be contested in new ways.

Whether the spatial discourse articulated in the ESDP will be institutionalised will be decided by conflicts such as those discussed above. There is all to play for. One way forwards could be for the Nordic and accession countries (and possibly southern member states) to shape the institutionalisation of the discourse with a more nuanced policy approach to places and peripherality. However, the risk is that divergent regional positions will not be able to achieve this, and that the core/urban hegemony in the EU spatial policy will prevail. If this happens the survival of locally constructed places in Europe appears unlikely as anything other than rundown backward spaces, or exotic and 'authentic' communities.

From our forays into European spatial policy, we have illustrated how socio-spatial relations, seen from the perspective of a combined framework of a cultural sociology of space and discourse analysis, can reveal the relations between the languages, practices and power-rationalities of policy discourses. Thus the words, images and languages used to represent and frame European space reflect particular spatial symbolic meanings and representations. Furthermore, such representations of space are a reflection of contemporary material globalisation processes which create the incentive for the European Union to facilitate action in new policy fields such as transnational planning, and policy making. Ultimately, such spatial policy discourses carry a (not necessarily coherent) mix of rationalities. Three competing rationalities of economic competitiveness and mobility, environmental sustainability and social equity surface in the ESDP, and the first of these is found to be dominant. Furthermore, one could also interpret these new spatial policy discourses as contributing to a general discourse of European integration through the implicit notions of European community and identity.

The discourse of monotopia creates the conditions for a new set of spatial practices which are shaping European space, whilst at the same time creating a new system of meaning about that space – based on the language and ideas of urbanisation and hyper-mobility and polycentricity.

We hope that the contribution of this book will be received as a critical call to arms. Its message is not Eurosceptic, it is about the need to engage with the politics of making European space as vigorously as we have become used to contesting the future of local places (in fact, these increasingly become inseparable concepts). We have pointed to many ways in which the practices which give shape to the new policy field are weak, and this may encourage some to think about how institutional forms, policy processes, planning instruments, modes of working, can be reconsidered. However, we hope that our analysis shows that this cannot be done as an 'empty' exercise. It is these particular practices that have reproduced a particular policy discourse. They have in many subtle ways been designed precisely to do this. So we cannot ignore the content of the policy discourse, and debate institutional reform in a manner removed from the substantive issues of European space. We hope that readers will feel inspired to reflect on how Europe might be, and to move from this reflection to consider what could be done to make this Europe more thinkable, or attainable. Rather than allowing a single discourse to dominate every corner of spatial thought across Europe, how can policy spaces be created which do provide opportunities for other ways of understanding space and mobility?

So whether one is a regional, national or European politician, policy maker or planner, whether one is a representative of a particular NGO, or an EU citizen, we hope this research will encourage reflection about the state of knowledge about these new policy processes and to what extent the processes themselves are played out in a transparent and open manner. We conclude that the material spaces that the new policy discourse of monotopic Europe is creating should be of concern to all.

Annex 1

Abbreviations

CBA	Cost-benefit analysis
CEC	Comission of the European Communities
CEMAT	Conférence Européenne des Ministres pour Aménagement du Territoire
CDCR	Committee of Development and Reconversion of the Region
CSD	Committee for Spatial Development
DETR	Department of the Environment, Transport and the Regions
ECIS	European Centre for Infrastructure Studies
EP	European Parliament
ERT	European Round Table of Industrialists
EPLP	European Parliamentary Labour Party
ESDP	European Spatial Development Perspective
ESPON	European Study Programme Observatory Network
EU	European Union
MEP	Member of the European Parliament
MoE	Ministry of the Environment
MWG	Motorway Working Group
NGO	Non-Governmental Organisation
NSR	North Sea Region
NWE	North West Europe
NWMA	North West Metropolitan Area
RPG	Regional Planning Guidance
SEA	Strategic Environmental Assessment
SPESP	European Study Programme on European Spatial Planning
SUD	Subcommittee on Spatial and Urban Development
TEN-T	Trans-European Transport Network
TIA	Territorial Impact Assessment
TINA	Transport Infrastructure Needs Assessment
VWG	Vision Working Group

Annex 2

Interviewees and other information sources

Our findings are informed by wide ranging discussions with policy makers and researchers, and exhaustive analysis of policy documents and other literature. In addition, a number of interviews, carried out in 1996, provided the basis for analysis of the policy processes, which has been supplemented by further interviews in 2003. Interviews took place in Brussels, Copenhagen, Den Haag, Berlin, Rotterdam, London, and Sandy (Bedfordshire). We have noted the position of the interviewee at the time we interviewed them.

MEPs and Parliamentary Aides

Anita Pollack, MEP, Member of the EP Environment Committee and delegate to the conciliation process.

Brian Simpson, MEP, member of the European Parliament Transport Committee.

Mark Watts, MEP, member of the European Parliament Transport Committee, European Parliamentary Labour Party transport spokesperson.

Paul Beekmanns, Aide to the Green Group of the European Parliament.

Environmental and transport lobbyists

Gijs Kuneman, Director, European Federation for Transport and the Environment.

Olivia Bina, Senior Policy Officer, Royal Society for the Protection of Birds (RSPB) and Birdlife International.

Roger Higman, Transport Campaigner, Friends of the Earth UK.

Olivier Hoedeman, Action for Solidarity, Equality, Environment and Development (A SEED), campaigner on trans-European networks and ERT.

European Commission officials

Chris Boyd, cabinet member for Commissioner Kinnock, former cabinet member of Commission President Delors, in charge of economic and monetary affairs.

Alfonso Gonzalez Finat, DGVII Directorate General for Transport, Unit A/3 – Networks and infrastructures: projects. Responsible for implementation of TEN-T projects.

Mr J. H. Rees, European Commission, DG VII Directorate General for Transport, Unit A/2 – Networks and infrastructures: strategy. Responsible for development of TEN-T policy.
Henning Arp, DGXI Directorate General for Environment, Nuclear Safety and Civil Protection, Directorate B: Integration Policy and Environmental Instruments. Responsibility for transport policy.
Dr. Kevin Bradley, DGXI, Directorate General for Environment, Nuclear Safety and Civil Protection, European Commission.
Ann Dom, Auxiliaire, DGXI, Directorate General for Environment, Nuclear Safety and Civil Protection, European Commission.

Other Brussels bureaucrats

Norbert Schobel, Director, Committee for the Regions (COR).
Martin Jones, UK Government Permanent Representation in Brussels (UKREP).
Mateu Turro, European Investment Bank.

National spatial planners and transport planners

Derek Martin, member of the CSD and Co-ordinator of International Affairs at the Dutch National Spatial Planning Agency, September 1996.
Peder Baltzer Nielsen (Head of Division), Danish Ministry of Environment, April 2003.
Flemming Thornæs (Civil Servant), Danish Ministry of Environment, and member of the Interreg IIC North Sea Region Programme Monitoring Committee, interviewed in Copenhagen, April 2003.
Simon Evans, Highways Policy and Programme Division, UK Department of Transport, official responsible for Trans-European Road Network (TERN) policy in the UK.
Mike Hayward, UK Government Office, North West Region.

Others interviewed

Wolfgang Hager, Director, European Centre for Infrastructure Studies (ECIS), Rotterdam.
Lawrence Harrell, European Centre for Infrastructure Studies (ECIS), Rotterdam.

Meetings attended as observer

Meeting of environmental activists campaigning against TENs. Vitoria, Spain.
Meetings of the European Parliament's Transport and Environment Committees in Brussels, 1996.

Meeting of the North of England Assembly of Local Authorities (NEA) in Sunderland on the INTERREG IIC North Sea Programme, 5 March 1997.
Meeting on the North Sea Programme held by the Danish National Planning Department and the German consultant PLANCO, Aalborg, 2-3 March 2000.
Meeting on the North Sea Interreg IIIB Directoria 2001, Aalborg 20 June 2001.

Notes

Chapter 1

1 The 1996 Policy Guidelines set out a trans-European transport network (TEN-T) of road, rail, inland waterways, airports and combined transport infrastructure. The individual components of the network are known as *projects of common interest*, or *specific projects.* The focus of this book on transport networks excludes other trans-European Networks for energy, social infrastructure and telecommunications. The term TEN is also in common use as a generic reference to the networks. We also make reference to TERN, the trans-European roads network, which was developed separately in the early stages of policy development.

Chapter 2

1 Relations with other European Commissioners were not so good. Carlo Ripa di Meana resigned from the post of Environment Commissioner in June 1992, following a turbulent period in which environmental policy was increasingly marginalised (Endo, 1999). The relative strengths and weaknesses of the Directorates responsible for transport and the environment during the critical early stages of the TEN-T process would profoundly affect the character of environmental integration.

Chapter 4

1 See Faludi and Waterhout (2002) *The Making of the European Spatial Planning Development Perspective: No masterplan* for an insightful and detailed account of the ESDP's drafting.

2 Final Declaration of the Second Summit of the Council of Europe, Strasbourg, 10–11 October 1997, Heads of State and Governments of the Member States.

Chapter 5

1 EP working document on TEN-T, September 1994, cited in Doherty and Hoedeman, 1995.

2 As an illustration of how this particular metaphor has stuck in the minds of European politicians we will make a small contribution to the increasing number of 'folk

narratives' about the Blue Banana. Supervising a student project, one of this book's authors read a number of interview transcripts conducted by the students in question. One was particularly interesting, as it was with the former Danish Minister of the Environment (and planning). In an interview he explained very frankly how his civil servants had shown him a map of Europe picturing the development banana going to the 'wrong side' of Denmark. And the minister said: 'If you see something like that, it is your obligation to straighten up that banana.'

3 The Study Programme (SPESP) is set up as a Pilot Action under ERDF ('Structural Fund') Article 10.

Chapter 7

1 Transport infrastructure planning has become increasingly concerned with the legitimacy of its decision processes. A new realism has emerged, a result of increasing environmental concern and the dramatic reduction of public investment in transport infrastructure through financial as well as regulatory and institutional changes (Goodwin *et al.*, 1991). Correspondingly, the process of transport planning has been critically reviewed in the light of this changing context: 'Transportation planning is no longer a "fixed route" planning, but is increasingly characterised by the need for flexible and visionary policy strategies and decision processes in an uncertain environment' (Nijkamp and Blaas, 1994: 3). A significant factor has been the retreat from public support, and a belief in competition and entrepreneurship. A decade ago, infrastructure planning could be understood as a mechanism for ensuring 'the greatest welfare for the greatest number of people (Button and Pinfield, 1991, cited in Nijkamp and Blaas, 1994: 3). It has now become an art of conflict resolution (Nijkamp and Blaas, 1994: 3). A result has been a shift in scope and methodology in the process.

Within this debate Nijkamp has called for a democratisation of the decision process, and a diminution of the gap between technically sophisticated techniques and their relevance in planning: 'well focussed decision support and evaluation systems can help to restore the balance by providing a framework for looking at both positive and negative aspects of mobility, and for assessing its value in relation to social life and human well-being in changing industrial societies' (p. 11). A further element is the inaccuracy of much evaluation work: 'Transport impact analysis and evaluation is fraught with multiple problems, as the assessment of the spatial-economic consequences of new transport systems is a far from easy task' (p. 13).

2 The Parliament's effectiveness in the TEN-T process may have been limited by several further factors. First its inexperience in handling the powers it acquired in the new co-decision process, and second the lack of technical capacity to engage in the often highly technical policy debates.

Chapter 8

1 The meeting took place on 5 March 1997 in Sunderland.
2 The research program Transportation and Urban Planning was financed by the now abolished Danish Transportation Council, with additional internal funding from Aalborg University. The research work started in 1998 and was completed in 2003. The citation quoted here is from the Greater Copenhagen research report on the relationship between the urban structure of the city and everyday life transportation.

References

Ache, P. (2002) 'Hamburg: planning strategies in a corner of the "pentagon"' *XVI AESOP Congress*, Volos, Greece.

Albertsen, N. and Diken, B. (2001) 'Mobility, justification, and the city', *Nordic Journal of Architectural Research* 14(1): 13–24.

Albrow, M. (1996) *The Global Age: State and society beyond modernity*, Cambridge: Polity Press.

Allen, J., Massey, D. and Cochrane, A. (1998) *Rethinking the Region*, London: Routledge.

Andersen, S.S. and Eliassen, K.A. (1993) *Making Policy in Europe: The Europeification of national policy making*, London: Sage.

Anderson, B. (1991) *Imagined Communities: Reflections on the origin and spread of nationalism*, London: Verso.

Anderson, J. (1996) 'The shifting stage of politics: new medieval and postmodern territorialities?' *Environment and Planning D, Society and Space* 14(2): 133-153.

Appadurai, A. (1996) 'Sovereignty without territoriality: notes for a postnational geography', in P. Yeager (ed.) *The Geography of Identity*, pp. 40–58, Ann Arbor: University of Michigan Press.

Atkinson, R. (2002) 'The White Paper on European Governance: implications for urban policy', *European Planning Studies* 10(6): 781–792.

Augé, M. (1995) *Non-places: Introduction to an anthropology of supermodernity*, London: Verso.

Bail, A. (1993) 'The importance of environmental compatibility', *EC Commission's White Paper on future development of the common transport policy*, Brussels: EEB.

Bailly, A. and Fremont, A. (eds) (2001) *Europe and its States: A geography*, Paris: La Documentation Francaise.

Ball, R.M. (1995) *Local Authorities and Regional Policy in the UK: Attitudes, representations and the local economy*, London: Paul Chapman Publishing Ltd.

Banister, D., Capello, R. and Nijkamp, P. (1995a) *European Transport and Communications Networks: Policy evolution and change*, Chichester: John Wiley and Sons.

—— (1995b) 'European Transport and Communications: lessons for the future', in B.D., C.R. and N.P. (eds) *European Transport and Communications Networks: Policy evolution and change*, pp. 333–342, Chichester: John Wiley and Sons.

Bastrup-Birk, H. and Doucet, P. (1997) 'European spatial planning from the heart', *Built Environment* 23(4): 307–314.

Beauregard, R.A. (1995) 'If only the city could speak: the politics of representation', in H. Liggett and D.C. Perry (eds) *Spatial Practices: Critical explorations in social/ spatial theory*, pp. 59–80, London: Sage.

Begg, I. (1989) 'The regional dimension of the 1992 Proposals', *Regional Studies* 23(4): 368–376.

Bengs, C. (2002) 'Introduction', in C. Bengs (ed.) *Facing ESPON*, Vol. 2002: 1, pp. 7–24, Stockholm: NordREGIO.

Berg, P.O. (2000) 'Dreaming up a region? Strategic management as invocation', in P.O. Berg, A. Linde-Laursen and O. Löfgren (eds) *Invoking a Transnational Metropolis: The making of the Øresund Region*, pp. 55–94, Lund: Studentlitteratur.

Berg, P.O., Linde-Laursen, A. and Löfgren, O. (eds) (2000) *Invoking a Transnational Metropolis: The making of the Øresund Region*, Lund: Studentlitteratur.

Berg, P.O. and Löfgren, O. (2000) 'Studying the birth of a transnational region', in P.O. Berg, A. Linde-Laursen and O. Löfgren (eds) *Invoking a Transnational Metropolis: The making of the Øresund Region*, pp. 7–26, Lund: Studentlitteratur.

Bina, O., Briggs, B. and Bunting, G. (1995) *The Impact of Trans-European Networks on Nature Conservation: A pilot project*, Sandy, Bedfordshire: Birdlife International.

Birdlife International, Greenpeace and European Federation for Transport and the Environment (1996) *Strategic Environmental Assessment and Corridor Analysis of the Trans-European Transport Network: A position paper*, Sandy, Bedfordshire: RSPB.

BMBAU (1998) 'German delegation to the Transnational Seminar on the ESDP: For a new Urban-Rural partnership on 15 & 16 October 1998', *Transnational Seminar on the ESDP: For a new Urban-Rural partnership on 15 & 16 October 1998*, Salamanca: Bundesministerium für Raumordnung, Bauwesen und Städtebau.

Böhme, K. (1998) 'Northern impressions of the ESDP', in C. Bengs and K. Böhme (eds) *The Progress of European Spatial Planning*, pp. 77–86, Stockholm.

—— (1999a) 'Interdependencies of spatial planning in and for Europe', Bergen, Norway: XIII AESOP Congress, 7–11 July 1999.

—— (1999b) 'A Northern view on the ESDP', *North* 9 (4/5): 1, 31–34.

—— (2002) 'Nordic echoes of European spatial planning', *Nordregio*, Stockholm.

Boye, P. (2000) 'Competing with concepts: the conception of an industrial platform', in P.O. Berg, A. Linde-Laursen and O. Löfgren (eds) *Invoking a Transnational Metropolis: The making of the Øresund Region*, pp. 211–230, Lund: Studentlitteratur.

Boyer, M.C. (1983) *Dreaming the Rational City: The myth of American city planning*, Cambridge, Mass.: MIT Press.

Brenner, N. (1998) 'Between fixity and motion: accumulation, territorial organization and the historical geography of spatial scales', *Environment and Planning D, Society and Space* 16(4): 459–481.

Brown, C. (1998) 'Planning for an integrated Europe: lessons from the border regions', Aveiro, Portugal: XII AESOP Congress, 22–25 July, 1998.

Brunet, R. (1989) 'Les villes Européennes, report to DATAR', Paris: RECLUS, La Documentation Francaise.

CADSES (2000) *Vision Planet. Strategies for Integrated Spatial Development of the Central European Danubian and Adriatic Area. Guidelines and Policy Proposals.*

Casey, E.S. (1996) *The Fate of Place: A philosophical history*, Berkeley: University of California Press.

Castells, M. (1996) *The Information Age: Economy, society and culture, vol. I: The rise of the network society*, Oxford: Blackwell.

—— (1997) *The Information Age: Economy, society and culture, vol. II: The power of identity*, Oxford: Blackwell.

—— (1998) *The Information Age: Economy, society and culture, vol. III: End of Millennium*, Oxford: Blackwell.

—— (1999) 'Grassrooting the space of flows', *Urban Geography* 20(4): 294–302

CEC (1990) 'The European high speed train network', Brussels: CEC.

—— (1991) 'Europe 2000: outlook for the development of the Community's territory', Luxembourg: Office for Official Publications of the European Communities.

—— (1992) 'Trans-European Networks: towards a master plan for the road network and road traffic, Motorway Working Group Report to DGVII', Brussels: CEC.

—— (1993) 'White Paper on growth, competitiveness and employment: the challenges and ways forward into the 21st Century', Luxembourg: Office for Official Publications of the European Communities.

—— (1994a) 'Europe 2000+: co-operation for European territorial development', Luxembourg: Office for Official Publications of the European Communities.

—— (1994b) 'Growth, competitiveness and employment. White Paper follow up: interim report on trans-European networks. Bulletin of the European Union, Supplement 2/94: 46–102', Vol. Supplement 2/94, Brussels: CEC.

—— (1994c) 'Trans-European Networks: Europe on the move', Brussels: CEC.

—— (1995) 'Progress on Trans-European Networks: Commission Report to the Madrid European Council, CSE (95) 571', Brussels: CEC.

—— (1996a) 'Commission Press Release, IP/96/401, 8.5.96', Brussels: CEC.

—— (1996b) 'Commission proposal for a European Parliament and Council decision on the review of the European Community programme of policy and action in relation to the environment and sustainable development "Towards sustainability", COM(95) 647', Brussels: CEC.

—— (1996c) 'Decision No. 1692/96/EC of the European Parliament and of the Council of 23 July 1996 on Community guidelines for the development of the trans-European transport network. OJ L228 vol. 391', Brussels: CEC.

—— (1996d) 'Opinion of the Commission on the European Parliament's amendments to the Council's common position regarding the proposal for a European Parliament and Council Decisions on Community Guidelines for the Development of the Trans-European Transport Network, COM(96) 16 final, 94/0098 (COD)', Brussels: CEC.

—— (1996e) 'Towards sustainability: Progress report from the Commission on the implementation of the European Community programme of policy and action in relation to the environment and sustainable development, COM(95) 624 final. 10.1.96', Brussels: CEC.

—— (1996f) 'Trans-European Networks, 1996 Annual Report, Communication from the

Commission to the European Council, the Council and the European Parliament, COM(96) 645 final, 6.12.96', Brussels: CEC.
—— (1997) 'The EU Compendium of Spatial Planning Systems and Policies', Luxembourg: Office for Official Publications of the European Communities.
—— (2001a) 'European Governance: a White Paper, COM (2001) 428', Brussels: CEC.
—— (2001b) 'A Sustainable Europe for a Better World: a European Union Strategy for Sustainable Development. Commission proposal to the Gothenburg European Council. COM(2001)264 final', Brussels: CEC.
—— (2001c) 'White Paper. European Transport Policy for 2010: time to decide. COM (2001) 0370', Luxembourg: Office for Official Publications of the European Communities.
—— (2003a) 'A few budget figures – TEN-T funding and achievements. <http://europa.eu.int/comm/transport/themes/network/english/hp-en/bfin/tn16 en.html> accessed 2 June 2003'.
—— (2003b) 'Revision of the Trans-European Transport Networks "TEN-T" Community Guidelines. Trans-European networks the way ahead', Brussels: CEC.
Cecchini, P. (1988) *The Benefits of a Single Market*, Aldershot: Wildwood House.
CEMAT (1999) 'Guiding principles for sustainable spatial development of the European continent: preparatory document', Strasbourg: Council of Europe.
—— (2000) 'Guiding principles for sustainable spatial development of the European continent. Adopted at the 12th Session of the European Conference of Ministers responsible for Regional Planning on 7–8 September 2000, Hanover', Strasbourg: Council of Europe.
Chadwick, N. (1996) 'Strategic environmental assessment of transport infrastructure – the state of the art', European Transport Forum.
Chapman, M. (2000) 'Planning, Europe and the twenty-first century', in P. Allmendinger and M. Chapman (eds) *Planning beyond 2000*, pp. 205–222, Chichester: Wiley.
Christiansen, T. and Jørgensen, K.E. (1995) *Towards the Third Category of Space: Conceptualizing the changing nature of borders in Western Europe*, Århus: Institut for Statskundskab.
City of Copenhagen and City of Malmö (1999) *Our New Region*, Copenhagen and Malmö: City of Copenhagen and City of Malmö.
Clausen, O.B. (2000) *Øresundsregionen*, Frederikshavn: DAFOLO.
CoR (1997) 'Draft opinion of the Committee of the Regions on INTERREG IIC Community Initiative and the potential role for local and regional authorities, 7 May 1997', Brussels: CdR 108/97.
Council of Europe (1983) 'European Regional/Spatial Planning Charter (the Torremolinos Charter)', Strasbourg: European Conference of Ministers Responsible for Regional Planning (CEMAT).
CSD (1994) 'Principles for a European Spatial Development Policy. Leipzig, 4 October 1994', CSD.
—— (1996) 'Spatial planning: discussion document on spatial planning presented by the Italian Presidency for the Ministerial Meeting on Regional Policy and Spatial Planning, May 1996', Venice: CSD.

—— (1997) 'European Spatial Development Perspective – First Official Draft, Presented at the Informal Meeting of Ministers Responsible for Spatial Planning of the Member States of the European Union, Noordwijk, June 1997', CSD.

—— (1998a) 'European Spatial Development Perspective – Complete Draft, Presented at the Informal Meeting of Ministers Responsible for Spatial Planning of the Member States of the European Union, Glasgow, June 8 1998', CSD.

—— (1998b) 'Note for the CSD. Subject: Study programme (1998–99) on European Spatial Planning to be carried out by a network of specialized institutions (ERDF art. 10). A3/PM/29.1.98', Brussels: DG XVI.

—— (1999) 'European Spatial Development Perspective – Towards Balanced and Sustainable Development of the Territory of the EU, Presented at the Informal Meeting of Ministers Responsible for Spatial Planning of the Member States of the European Union, Potsdam May 10/11 1999', Committee for Spatial Development.

Dabinett, G. and Richardson, T. (1999) 'The European Spatial Approach: the role of power and knowledge in strategic planning and policy evaluation', *Evaluation* 5(2): 220–237.

Davies, H.W.E. (1994) 'Towards a European planning system?' *Planning Practice and Research* 9(1): 63–69.

Davoudi, S. (1999) 'Making sense of the ESDP', *Town and Country Planning* 68(12): 367–369.

De Gaulle, C. (1971) 'A concert of European states', in F.B. Nelsen and A.C.G. Stubb (eds) *The European Union: Readings on the theory and practice of European integration* (1998), pp. 27–44, 2nd edition, London: Macmillan.

Deleuze, G. and Guattari, F. (1988) *A Thousand Plateaus: Capitalism and schizophrenia*, London: Athlone Press.

Delors, J. (1989) 'A Necessary Union: speech given at College of Europe, Bruges, Belgium', in F.B. Nelsen and A.C.G. Stubb (eds) *The European Union: Readings on the theory and practice of European integration* (1998), pp. 55–68, 2nd edition, London: Macmillan.

Dematteis, G. (2000) 'Spatial images of European urbanisation', in A. Bagnasco and P. LeGalés (eds) *Cities in contemporary Europe*, pp. 48–73, Cambridge: Cambridge University Press.

DETR (2000) 'Planning Policy Guidance Note 11: Regional Planning', London: HMSO.

DG Regional Policy (1998a) 'Conference on the European Spatial Development Perspective. Programme for the transnational seminar on the ESDP', Berlin: European Commission, DG XVI.

—— (1998b) 'Report on the Contribution of the Transnational Seminars to the improvement of the European Spatial Development Perspective, November 1998', Brussels: CEC, DGX VI.

DG TREN (2000) 'Single European Sky: Report of the High-Level Group', Luxembourg: Eur-OP.

Diken, B. (1998) *Strangers, Ambivalence and Social Theory*, Aldershot: Ashgate.

Doherty, A. and Hoedeman, O. (1995) 'TEN green battles', *New Statesman and Society*, 10 March 1995.
Dom, A. (1996) 'SEA of the trans-European transport network', in R. Therivel and R. Partidario (eds) *The practice of Strategic Environmental Assessment*, London: Earthscan.
Doucet, P. (2002) 'Transnational planning in the wake of the ESDP: the Northwest experience', in A. Faludi (ed.) *European Spatial Planning*, pp. 59–79, Cambridge, Massachusetts: Lincoln Institute of Land Policy.
Dutch National Spatial Planning Agency (2000) 'Spatial perspectives in Europe', The Hague: Ministry of Housing, Spatial Planning and the Environment.
Dyrberg, T.B. (1997) *The Circular Structure of Power: Politics, identity, community*, London: Verso.
Ek, R. (1998) 'The Öresund Region as a geographical vision', Paper for Nordic doctoral course: urban and regional change in Europe: economic and political restructuring in contemporary Europe, University of Oslo.
Endo, K. (1999) *The Presidency of the European Commission under Jacques Delors: The politics of shared leadership*, Basingstoke: Macmillan.
ERT (1984) *Missing Links*, Brussels: ERT.
—— (1991a) *Reshaping Europe*, Brussels: ERT.
—— (1991b) *Missing Networks: A European challenge. Proposals for the renewal of Europe's infrastructure*, Brussels: ERT.
Eser, T.W. (1997) 'The implementation of the European spatial development policy: potential or burden?' Trier.
Eser, T.W. and Konstadakopulos, D. (2000) 'Power shifts in the European Union? The case of spatial planning', *European Spatial Planning* 8(6): 783–798.
European Council (1994) 'Extract from the Conclusions of the Presidency of the Corfu European Council, June 1994', Brussels: CEC.
—— (2001) 'Presidency Conclusions, Goteborg European Council', Brussels: CEC.
—— (2002) 'Presidency Conclusions, Seville European Council, 21–22 June 2002', Brussels: CEC.
European Investment Bank (1994) *EIB papers no. 23*, a series of papers on the relations between infrastructure investment and economic growth. Luxembourg: EIB.
European Parliament (1995) 'Recommendation for second reading on the common position established by the Council with a view to the adoption of a European Parliament and Council Decision on Community guidelines for the development of the transEuropean transport network. C4–0423/95 – 94/0098 (COD). Committee on Transport and Tourism', Brussels: CEC.
—— (1996) 'Minutes of the European Parliament. Sitting of 17.7.96, provisional edition', Brussels: CEC.
Faludi, A. (1996) 'Framing with images', *Environment and Planning B: Planning and Design* 23: 93–108.
—— (1997) 'A roving band of planners', *Built Environment* 23(4): 281–287.
—— (1998) 'Polynucleated metropolitan regions in Northwest Europe', *European Planning Studies* 6(4): 365–377.

—— (1999) 'The European Spatial Planning Development Perspective: what next?' Bergen, AESOP XIII Congress, 7–11 July 1999.
—— (2000a) 'The application of the European Spatial Development Perspective: evidence from the North West Metropolitan Area', Brno: XIV AESOP Congress, July 18–23.
—— (2000b) 'Strategic planning in Europe: institutional aspects', in W. Salet and A. Faludi (eds) *The Revival of Strategic Spatial Planning*, pp. 243–258, Amsterdam: Royal Netherlands Academy of Arts and Sciences.
—— (2001) 'The application of the European Spatial Development Perspective: evidence from the North-West Metropolitan Area', *European Planning Studies* 9(5): 667–679
Faludi, A. and Waterhout, B. (2002) *The Making of the European Spatial Development Perspective: No masterplan*, London: Routledge.
Faludi, A., Zonneweld, W. and Waterhout, B. (2000) 'The Committee on Spatial Development: formulating a spatial perspective in an institutional vacuum', in T. Christiansen and E. Kirchner (eds) *Committee Governance in the European Union*, pp. 117–185, Manchester: Manchester University Press.
Federal Trust High Level Group (1996) *Private Partnerships and Public Networks in Europe*, London: Federal Trust.
Fischler, R. (1995) 'Strategy and history in professional practice: planning as world making', in H. Liggett and D.C. Perry (eds) *Spatial Practices*, pp. 13–58, Thousand Oaks: Sage.
Flynn, T. (1993) 'Foucault's mapping of history', in G. Gutting (ed.) *The Cambridge Companion to Foucault*, pp. 28–46, Cambridge: Cambridge University Press.
Flyvbjerg, B. (1998) *Rationality and Power: Democracy in practice*, Chicago: University of Chicago Press.
—— (2001) *Making Social Science Matter: Why social inquiry fails and how it can succeed again*, Cambridge: Cambridge University Press.
Flyvbjerg, B., Bruzelius, N. and Rothengatter, W. (2003) *Megaprojects and Risk: An anatomy of power*, Cambridge: Cambridge University Press.
Flyvbjerg, B. and Richardson, T. (2002) 'In search of the dark side of planning theory', in P. Allmendinger and M. Tewdwr-Jones (eds) *Planning Futures: New Directions for Planning Theory*, pp. 44–62, London: Routledge.
Fosgaard, M. and Jørgensen, I. (1996) 'Recent tropisms of regionalization – as observed in Denmark', Exeter: European Urban and Regional Studies Conference. A changing Europe in a changing world: urban and regional Issues, 11–14 April 1996.
Foucault, M. (1969) *The Archaeology of Knowledge*, London: Routledge.
—— (1979) *Discipline and Punish: The birth of the prison*, New York: Vintage.
—— (1989) 'Space, knowledge, power', in S. Lotringer (ed.) *Foucault Live: Collected interviews 1961–1984*, pp. 335–347, New York: Semiotext(e).
—— (1990) *The History of Sexuality, volume 1: An introduction*, London: Penguin.
Frommer, R. (1992) 'The European Commission view', *European Transport: The environmental challenge, Proceedings of a seminar presented by the European Environmental Bureau*, pp. 4–11, Brussels: EEB.
Gardner, J. (1991) *Effective Lobbying in the European Community*, Deventer: Kluwer.

Giannakourou, G. (1996) 'Towards a European spatial planning policy: theoretical dilemmas and institutional implications', *European Planning Studies* 4(5): 595–613.

Gleeson, B. (1998) 'The resurgence of spatial planning in Europe', *Urban Policy and Research* 16(3): 219–225.

Göhler, G. (1996) 'Institutions in political theory: lessons for European integration', in D. Rometsch and K. Wessels (eds) *The European Union and Member States Towards Institutional Fusion?*, pp. 1–19, Manchester: Manchester University Press.

Goodwin, P., Hallett, S., Kenny, F and Stokes, G. (1991) *Transport: The new realism*, Report no. 624, University of Oxford, Transport Studies Unit.

Gottdeiner, M. (1995) *Postmodern Semiotics: Material culture and the forms of postmodern life*, Oxford: Blackwell.

Gouldson, A. and Murphy, J. (1996) 'Ecological modernisation and the European Union', *Geoforum* 27(1): 11–21.

Graham, S. and Marvin, S. (2001) *Splintering Urbanism: Networked infrastructures, technological mobilities and the urban condition*, London: Routledge.

Grahl, T. and Teague, P. (1990) *1992: the Big Market: The future of the European Community*, London: Lawrence and Wishart.

Graute, U. (2002) 'Kooperation in der Europäischen raumentwicklung [Co-operation in European spatial development policy]. IÖR Chriften. Band 37', Dresden: IÖR.

Gray, J. (2000) 'The Common Agricultural Policy and the re-invention of the rural in the European Community', *Sociologia Ruralis* 40(1): 30–52.

Greenwood, J., Grote, J.R. and Ronit, K. (1992) *Organised Interests and the European Community*, London: Sage.

Habermas, J. (1996) 'Citizenship and national identity', in J. Habermas (ed.) *Between Facts and Norms: Contributions to a discourse theory of law and democracy*, pp. 491–515, Cambridge: Polity Press.

Hajer, M.A. (1995) *The Politics of Environmental Discourse: Ecological modernization and the policy process*, Oxford: Clarendon.

—— (1996) 'Ecological modernisation as cultural politics', in S. Lash, B. Szerszynski and B. Wynne (eds) *Risk, Enviroment and Modernity: Towards a new ecology*, pp. 246–268, London: Sage.

—— (1999) 'Zero-friction society: the cultural politics of urban design', *Urban Design Quarterly* 71: 29–34.

—— (2000) 'Transnational networks as transnational policy discourse: some observations on the politics of spatial development in Europe', in A. Faludi and W. Salet (eds) *The Revival of Strategic Planning*, Dordrecht: Kluwer.

Harley, J.B. (1996) 'Deconstructing the map', in J. Agnew *et al.* (eds) *Human Geography. An essential reader*, pp. 422–443, Oxford: Blackwell.

Harvey, D. (1982) *Limits to Capital*, Oxford: Blackwell.

—— (1985) 'The geo-politics of capitalism', in D. Gregory and J. Urry (eds) *Social Relations and Spatial Structures*, pp. 128–163, London: Macmillan.

—— (1989) *The Condition of Postmodernity: An inquiry into the origins of cultural change*, Oxford: Blackwell.

—— (1996) *Justice, Nature and the Geography of Difference*, Oxford: Blackwell.

—— (2000) *Spaces of Hope*, Edinburgh: Edinburgh University Press.

—— (2001) *Spaces of Capital: Towards a critical geography*, Edinburgh: Edinburgh University Press.

Healey, P. (1995) 'Discourses of integration: making frameworks for democratic urban planning', in P. Healey *et al.* (eds) *Managing Cities: The new urban context*, pp. 251–272, Chichester: John Wiley and Sons.

—— (2002) 'Spatial planning as a mediator for regional governance – conceptions of place in the formation of regional governance capacity', in D. Fürst and K. Knieling (eds) *Regional Governance: New modes of self-government in the European Community*, vol. 2, pp. 13–26, Hanover: Akademie für Raumforshcung und Landesplanung.

Hedetoft, U. (1997) 'The cultural semiotics of European identity: between national sentiment and the transnational perspective', in A. Landau and R. Withman (eds) *Rethinking the European Union: Institutions, interests and identities*, pp. 147–171, London: Macmillan.

Held, D. (1987) *Models of Democracy*, Oxford: Polity Press.

Herrschel, T. and Newman, P. (2002) *Governance of Europe's City Regions. Planning, Policy and Politics*, London: Routledge.

INTERREG North Sea Region (2001) 'Community Initiative Programme', Viborg: Interreg IIIB North Sea Region.

—— (2002) 'Programme Complement', Viborg: Interreg IIIB North Sea Region.

Janelle, D.G. (1969) 'Spatial reorganisation: a model and concept', *Annals of the Association of American Geographers* 58: 348-364.

Jensen, O.B. (1997) *Discourse Analysis and Socio-spatial Tansformation Processes: A theoretical framework for analysing spatial planning*, Newcastle upon Tyne: Department of Town and Country Planning, University of Newcastle upon Tyne.

—— (1998) 'Polycentrisk balance eller hierarkisk konkurrence? – Byerne og det Globale i Danmarks og EU's planlægnings diskurser', København: Konference om Storbyens Forvandlinger og Kortlægninger, Kunstakademiets Arkitektskole, Center for Tværfaglige Urbane Studier, 25–26 maj 1998.

—— (1999) 'At ville noget med rummet – diskurs & rationalitet i Danmarks og den Europæiske Unions planlægning af byernes rumlige udvikling [Re-thinking the Urban Systems – Discourse & Rationality in Danish and European Union Spatial Planning]' *Institut for Samfundsudvikling & Planlægning*, Aalborg: Aalborg.

Jensen, O. B. and Jørgensen, I. (2000) 'Danish planning: the long shadow of Europe', *Built Environment* 26(1): 31–40.

Jensen, O. B., Jørgensen, I. and Nielsen, J. (1996a) 'INTERREG IIC – a loophole for transnational planning', *NordRevy* (5/6): 13–19.

—— (1996b) 'Progess of INTERREG IIC', *NordRevy* December: 25–26.

—— (1998) 'What has love got to do with it?', in C. Bengs and K. Böhme (eds) *The Progress of European Spatial Planning*, Stockholm: Nordregio, pp. 11–24.

Jørgensen, I. and Nielsen, J. (1997) 'Institutional innovations and implications of transnational planning cooperation: the gestation of the Baltic Sea Region by the European

Union. A research agenda under development', Nijmegen: AESOP International Congress, 28–31 May 1997.

—— (1998) 'Spatial development and planning between "high" and "low" politics: Interrreg IIC in the Baltic Sea Region', in L. Hedegaard and B. Lindström (eds) *The NEBI Yearbook 1998: North European and Baltic Sea integration*, pp. 309–322, Berlin: Springer-Verlag.

Jørgensen, I. and Tonboe, J.C. (1993) 'Space and welfare: the EC and the eclipse of the Scandinavian model', in T.P. Boje and S.E.O. Hort (eds) *Scandinavia in a New Europe*, pp. 365–400, Oslo: Scandinavia University Press.

Karlsson, O. (1996) 'A critical dialogue in evaluation', *Evaluation* 2(4): 405–416

Kohli, M. (2000) 'The battlegrounds of European identity', *European Societies* 2(2): 113–137.

Koolhaas, R. (1995) S, M, L, XL, New York: The Monticelli Press.

Kristeva, J. (1993) *Nations without Nationalism*, New York: Columbia University Press.

Kunzmann, K.R. (1996) 'Euro-megalopolis or themepark Europe? Scenarios for European spatial development', *International Planning Studies* 1(2): 143–163.

Kunzmann, K.R. and Wegener, M. (1991) 'The pattern of urbanisation in Western Europe 1960–1990, Berichte aus dem Institut für Raumplanung 28', Dortmund: Institut für Raumplanung, Universität Dortmund.

Laclau, E. and Mouffe, C. (1985) *Hegemony and Socialist Strategy: Towards a radical democratic politics*, London: Verso.

Lakoff, G. and Johnson, M. (1980) *Metaphors We Live By*, Chicago: University of Chicago Press.

Lash, S. and Urry, J. (1994) *Economies of Signs and Space*, London: Sage.

Latour, B. (1990) 'Drawing things together', in M. Lynch and S. Wodgar (eds) *Representation in Scientific Practice*, pp. 19–68, Cambridge, MA: MIT Press.

Le Galès (2002) *European Cities: Social conflicts and governance*, Oxford: Oxford University Press.

Lefebvre, H. (1974/1991) *The Production of Space*, Oxford: Blackwell.

Linde-Laursen, A. (2000) 'Bordering improvisations: centuries of identity politics', in P.O. Berg, A. Linde-Laursen and O. Löfgren (eds) *Invoking a Transnational Metropolis: The making of the Øresund Region*, pp. 137–163, Lund: Studentlitteratur.

Liniado, M. (1996) *Car Culture and Countryside Change*, Cirencester: The National Trust.

Löfgren, O. (2000) 'Moving metaphors', in P.O. Berg, A. Linde-Laursen and O. Löfgren (eds) *Invoking a Transnational Metropolis: The making of the Øresund Region*, pp. 27–53, Lund: Studentlitteratur.

Low, M. (1997) 'Representation unbound: globalization and democracy', in K.R. Cox (ed) *Spaces of Globalization: Reasserting the power of the local*, pp. 240–280, New York: Guilford Press.

Lyon, D. (1993) 'An electronic panopticon? A sociological critique of surveillance theory', *Sociological Review* 41(4): 653–678.

Mackie, P.J., Palmer, A., Pearman, A.D., Watson, S.M. and Whelan, G.A. (1994) *Cost-benefit and Multi-criteria Analysis for New Road Construction: Final report, consultancy report for the European Commission Directorate General for Transport*, DOC EURET/385/94 R&D Unit, DGVII, Brussels: CEC.

Malmö City (2002) 'Malmö.com: living and projects'.

Marks, G., Hooge, L. and Blank, K. (1996) 'European integration from the 1980s: state-centric v multi-level governance', in F.B. Nelsen and A.C.G. Stubb (eds) *The European Union: Readings on the theory and practice of European integration (1998)*, pp. 273–293, 2nd edition, London: Macmillan.

Marks, J. (1995) 'A new image of thought', *New Formations*: 66–76.

Maskell, P. and Törnqvist, G. (1999) *Building a Cross-border Learning Region: Emergence of the North European Øresund Region*, Copenhagen: Copenhagen Business school Press.

Masser, I., Svidén, O. and Wegener, M. (1992) *The Geography of Europe's Futures*, London: Belhaven Press.

Massey, D. (1991) 'A global sense of place', in T. Burnes and D. Gregory (eds) *Readings in Human Geography: The poetics and politics of inquiry (1997)*, pp. 315–323, London: Arnold.

—— (1995) 'Thinking radical democracy spatially', *Environment and Planning D: Society and Space* 13(3): 283–289.

Mathiessen, C.W. and Andersson, Å.E. (2002) 'Øresundsområdet: Det regionale udviklingsprojekt – status og forslag [The Øresund Area: The Regional development project – status and proposals]', Malmö: South Swedish Chamber of Industry and Commerce.

Mens en Ruimte (1993) 'The European high speed train network: Environmental Impact Assessment, report to the Commission of the European Communities', Brussels: CEC.

Miller, P. and Rose, N. (1993) 'Governing economic life', in M. Gane and T. Johnson (eds) *Foucault's New Domains*, London: Routledge.

Ministers for Spatial Planning and Development (1994) 'Visions and strategies around the Baltic Sea 2010: towards a framework for spatial development in the Baltic Sea Region', Tallinn: Third Conference of Ministers for Spatial Planning and Development.

Ministry of Energy and Environment (1992) 'Denmark towards the year 2018: the spatial structuring of Denmark in the future Europe', Copenhagen.

Ministry of Environment and Energy (1997) 'Denmark and European Spatial Planning Policy: National Planning Report for Denmark', Copenhagen: Ministry for Environment and Energy.

Ministry of the Environment (2002) 'Copenhagen Charter 2002: a statement on the occasion of the Danish Presidency', Copenhagen: Ministry of the Environment.

Moll, M. (2002) 'Interreg IIC North Sea Programme – Successful transnational planning?' Dortmund: Dortmund.

Mønnesland, J. (1995) 'Regional development in the Nordic Periphery', in H. Eskelinen and F. Snickars (eds) *Competitive European Peripheries*, pp. 131–150, Berlin: Springer Verlag.

Monnet, J. (1962) 'A ferment of change', in F.B. Nelsen and A.C.G. Stubb (eds) *The*

European Union: Readings on the theory and practice of European integration (1998), pp. 19–26, 2nd edition, London: Macmillan.

—— (1976) *Mémoires*, Paris: Rayard.

More, T. (1561) *Utopia*, Copenhagen: Fremad.

Morley, D. and Robins, K. (1995) *Spaces of Identity: Global media, electronic landscapes and cultural boundaries*, London: Routledge?

Mouffe, C. (1994) 'For a politics of nomadic identity', in G. Robertson, M. Marsh, L. Ticker, J. Bird, B. Curtis and T. Putnam (eds) *Traveller's Tales: Narratives of home and displacement*, pp. 105–113, London: Routledge.

Newman, P. and Thornley, A. (1996) *Urban Planning in Europe: International competition, national systems and planning projects*, London: Routledge.

Nijkamp, P. and Blaas, E. (1994) *Impact assessment and evaluation in Transport Planning*, London: Kluwer.

Nilsson, J. (1998) 'Tal i Lille, Frankrike, speech for the transnational seminar on the ESDP, Lille, June 22–23 1998'.

North Sea Commission (2000) 'Draft Resolution concerning NorVISION. A spatial perspective for the North Sea Region', North Sea Commission.

Nugent, N. (1999) *The Government and Politics of the European Union*, 4th edition, London: Macmillan.

NWMA Spatial Vision Group (2000) 'A spatial vision for Northwest Europe: building co-operation', The Hague: Ministry of Housing, Spatial Planning and the Environment.

O'Dell, T. (2000) 'Traversing the transnational', in P.O. Berg, A. Linde-Laursen and O. Löfgren (eds) *Invoking a Transnational Metropolis: The making of the Øresund Region*, pp. 231–253, Lund: Studentlitteratur.

O'Dowd, L. (2001) 'State borders, border regions and the construction of European identity', in M. Kohli and M. Novak (eds) *Will Europe Work? Integration, employment and social order*, pp. 95–110, London: Routledge.

Olsen, J.P. (2001) 'The many faces of Europeanization', ARENA Working Papers.

Øresund Chamber of Commerce (2002) 'Renewed call for Øresund integration', Vol. 2002: Øresund Identity Network.

Øresund Network AB (2002) 'The Øresund Region', Malmö: Øresund Network AB.

Østergård, N. (1998) 'Note concerning urban systems', Lille: Transnational seminar on the ESDP, 22–23 June 1998.

Oswald, E. (1998) 'Die Zukunft gestalten: Das Europäische Raumentwicklungskonzept – Auf dem Weg zu einer gesamteuropäischen Politikstrategie', Der Konferenz Berlin 27–28 April, Bundesminister für Raumordnung, Bauwesen und Städtebau.

Paasi, A. (2001) 'Europe as a social process and discourse: considerations of place, boundaries and identity', *European Urban and Regional Studies* 8(1): 7–28.

Padoa-Schioppa, T. (1987) *Efficiency, Stability and Equity: A strategy for the evaluation of the economic system of the European Community*, London: Oxford University Press.

Pavlich, G. (1995) 'Contemplating a postmodern sociology: genealogy, limits and critique', *Sociological Review* 43: 548-572.

Pedersen, O.K. (ed.) (1994) *Demokratiets lette tilstand – syv beslutningstagere om Danmark og fremtid (The lightness of democracy)*, Copenhagen: Spektrum.

Perry, D.C. (1995) 'Making space: planning as a mode of thought', in H. Liggett and D.C. Perry (eds) *Spatial Practices: Critical explorations in social/spatial theory*, pp. 209–241, London: Sage.

Philo, C. (1987) *The Same and Other: On geographies, madness and outsiders*, Loughborough: Loughborough University, Department of Geography.

Rabinow, P. (ed.) (1991) *The Foucault Reader*, London: Penguin.

Richardson, J. (ed.) (1996) *European Union: Power and policy making*, London: Routledge.

Richardson, T. (1995) 'Trans-European Networks: good news or bad for peripheral regions?' *Proceedings of seminar A, pan-European transport issues*, pp. 99–110, Warwick: 23rd European Transport Forum.

—— (1996) 'Foucauldian discourse: power and truth in the policy process', *European Planning Studies* 4(2): 279–292.

—— (1997) 'The Trans-European transport network: environmental policy integration in the European Union', Journal of European Urban and Regional Studies 4(4): 333-346.

—— (2000a) 'Discourses of rurality in European spatial policy: the European spatial development perspective', *Sociologia Ruralis* 40(1): 53–71.

—— (2000b) 'Environmental integration in infrastructure planning: a Foucauldian discourse analysis of the trans-European transport network', *Urban and Regional Studies*, Sheffield: Sheffield Hallam University.

Richardson, T. and Jensen, O.B. (2000) 'Discourses of mobility and polycentric development: a contested view of European spatial planning', *European Planning Studies* 8(4): 503–520.

—— (2001) 'Framing European mobility and identity – on the construction of spatial policy discourses in the European Union', *2001 A Space Odyssey – Spatiality and Social Relations in the 21st Century*, Roskilde University's Field Station, Holbæk, Denmark.

—— (2003) 'Linking discourse and space: towards a cultural sociology of space in analysing spatial policy discourses', *Urban Studies* 40(1): 7–22.

Rigney, D. (2001) *The Metaphorical Society: an invitation to social theory*, Lanham: Rowman & Littlefield.

Rivolin, U.J. (2002) 'Shaping European spatial planning: how Italy's experience can contributes', *XVI AESOP Congress*, Volos, Greece.

Rometsch, D. and Wessels, K. (eds) (1996) *The European Union and its Member States: Towards institutional fusion?* Manchester: Manchester University Press.

Roy, R. (1994) *Investment in Transport Infrastructure: The recovery in Europe*, Rotterdam: European Centre for Infrastructure Studies (ECIS).

Royal Commission on Environmental Pollution (1994) *Transport and the Environment*, Eighteenth Report, London: HMSO.

Ruggie, J.G. (1993) 'Territoriality and beyond: problematizing modernity in international relations', *International Organization* 47(1): 139–174

Rumford, C. (2002) *The European Union: A political sociology*, Oxford: Blackwells.
Rusca, R. (1998) 'The development of a European spatial planning policy', in C. Bengs and K. Böhme (eds) *The Progress of European Spatial Planning. Nordregio 1*, pp. 35–48.
Sandercock, L. (1998) *Towards Cosmopolis: Planning for multicultural cities*, Chichester: Wiley.
Sayer, A. (2000) *Realism and Social Science*, London: Sage.
Schindegger, F. (2001) 'Prospects for further work on TIA. Paper presented at conference on TIA', Louvain-la-Neuve: Austrian Institute for Regional Studies and Spatial Planning.
Schulz, C. (1999) 'City-networking and bottom-up development by transborder cooperation: the influence of local authorities in the Saar-Lor-Lux-Region', in H. Knippenberg and J. Markusse (eds) *Nationalising and Denationalising European Border Regions 1800–2000*, pp. 223–240, Dordrecht: Kluwer.
Schumann, R. (1950) 'The Schumann Declaration', in A.C.G. Stubb (ed.) *The European Union: Readings on the Theory and Practice of European Integration (1998)*, pp. 13–14, 2nd edition, London: Macmillan.
Scott, J. (1995) *Development Dilemmas in the European Community*, Buckingham: Open University Press.
Sennett, R. (1990) *The Conscience of the Eye: The design and social life of cities*, London: Faber & Faber.
Shaw, D. and Sykes, O. (2001) 'Delivering the European Spatial Development Perspective, Draft Final Report', Liverpool: The University of Liverpool.
Sheate, W. (1994) 'Hearing of experts: Strategic Environmental Assessment of the Trans-European Networks for Transport, 28.6.1994'.
Shields, R. (1991) *Places on the Margin: Alternative geographies of modernity*, London: Routledge.
Shore, C. (2000) *Building Europe: The cultural politics of European integration*, London: Routledge.
Sibley, D. (1995) *Geographies of Exclusion: Society and difference in the West*, London: Routledge.
Smith, N. (1993) 'Homeless/global: scaling places', in J. Bird, B. Curtis, T. Putnam, G. Robertson and L. Tickner (eds) *Mapping the Futures: Local cultures, global change*, pp. 87–119, London: Routledge.
Soja, E.W. (1996) *Thirdspace: Journeys to Los Angeles and other real-and-imagined places*, Oxford: Blackwell.
—— (1997) 'Planning in/for postmodernity', in G. Benko and U. Strohmayer (eds) *Space and Social Theory: Interpreting modernity and postmodernity*, pp. 236–249, Oxford: Blackwell.
—— (2000) *Postmetropolis: Critical studies of cities and regions*, Oxford: Blackwell.
SPESP (2000) 'Study Programme on European Spatial Planning, Draft Final Report 3 March 2000'.
Spinelli, A. and Rossi, E. (1941) 'The Ventotene Manifest', in F.B. Nelsen and A.C.G.

Stubb (eds) *The European Union: Readings on the theory and practice of European integration* (1998), pp. 3–6, 2nd edition, London: Macmillan.

Standing Advisory Committee on Trunk Road Assessment (SACTRA) (1999) *Transport and the Economy.* Report to the UK Government's Department of the Environment, Transport and the Regions. London: HMSO.

Steering Group (1963) 'Traffic in towns: a study of the long term problems of traffic in urban areas. Report of the Steering Group and Working Group appointed by the Minister of Transport', London: HMSO.

Swyngedouw, E. (1993) 'Communication, mobility and the struggle for power over space', in G. Giannopoulos and A. Gillespie (eds) *Transport and Communications Innovation in Europe*, pp. 305–325, London/New York: Belhaven Press.

Tampere Ministerial (1999) 'Informal Meeting of EU Ministers Responsible for Spatial Planning and Urban/Regional Policy of the European Union,' Tampere, Saarijärvi: Gummerus Printing.

Tangkjær, C. (2000) 'Øresund as an open house strategy by invitation', in P.O. Berg, A. Linde-Laursen and O. Löfgren (eds) *Invoking a Transnational Metropolis: The making of the Øresund Region*, pp. 165–190, Lund: Studentlitteratur.

Tassin, E. (1995) 'Europe: a political community?' in C. Mouffe (ed.) *Dimensions of Radical Democracy: Pluralism, citizenship, community*, pp. 169–192, London: Verso.

Tewdwr-Jones, M. and Williams, R.H. (2001) *The European Dimension of British Planning*, London: Routledge.

Thatcher, M. (1988) 'A family of nations. Speech given at College of Europe, Bruges, Belgium', in F.B. Nelsen and A.C.G. Stubb (eds) *The European Union: Readings on the theory and practice of European integration* (1998), pp. 49–54, 2nd edition, London: Macmillan.

Therborn, G. (1995) *European Modernity and Beyond. The Trajectory of European Societies 1945–2000*, London: Sage.

Therivel, R. and Partidario, R. (1996) *The Practice of Strategic Environmental Assessment*, London: Earthscan.

Therivel, R., Wilson, E., Thompson, S., Heaney, D. and Pritchard, D. (1992) *Strategic Environmental Assessment*, London: Earthscan.

Throgmorton, J. (1992) 'Planning as persuasive story telling about the future: negotiating an electric power rate settlement in Illinois', *Journal of Planning Education and Research* 12: 17–31.

Urry, J. (1995) *Consuming Places*, London: Routledge.

—— (2000) *Sociology beyond Societies: Mobilities for the twenty-first century*, London: Routledge.

Veggeland, N. (1996) *Regionens Europa. Innføring i teori og praksis*, Oslo: Spartacus Forlag AS.

Vickerman, R., Spiekermann, K. and Wegener, M. (1995) 'Accessibility and Economic Development in Europe', Espinho: ESF/EC Euroconference on European Transport and Communication Networks: Policies on European Networks, 17–23 April.

Vigar, G. (2001) *The Politics of Mobility: Transport, the Environment and public policy*, London: Spon Press.

Virilio, P. (1997) *Open Sky*, London: Verso.

VWG (2000a) 'NorVISION: A Spatial Perspective for the North Sea Region (NSR). Minutes from the 7th workshop meeting with INTERREG IIC project leaders and researchers from the NSR', Aalborg, Denmark.

—— (2000b) 'NorVISION: a spatial perspective for the North Sea Region (NSR). Vision Working Group with representatives from spatial planning offices from the participating countries and regions', Essen, Germany: PLANCO Consulting GmbH.

Wæver, O. (1997) 'Concepts of security', *Institute of Political Science*, Copenhagen: Copenhagen University.

Waterhout, B. (2001) 'Polycentric development: what's behind it?' *Lincoln Institute Conference on European Spatial Planning*, Cambridge, MA.

Weber, M. (1978) *Economy and Society*, Berkeley: University of California Press.

Weiler, J.H.H. (1999) *The Constitution of Europe: 'Do the new clothes have an Emperor?' and other essays on European integration*, Cambridge: Cambridge University Press.

Weiler, J.H.H., Haltern, U. and Mayer, F. (1995) 'European democracy and its critique', in J. Hayward (ed.) *The crisis of representation in Europe*, pp. 4–40, London: Frank Cass.

Wessels, W. (1996) 'Institutions of the EU-system: models of explanation', in D. Rometsch and K. Wessels (eds) *The European Union and Member States: Towards Institutional fusion?*, pp. 20–36, Manchester: Manchester University Press.

Wessels, W. and Rometsch, D. (1996) 'Conclusion: European Union and national institutions', in D. Rometsch and K. Wessels (eds) *The European Union and its Member States: Towards institutional fusion?*, pp. 328–365, Manchester: Manchester University Press.

Whitelegg, J. (1992) *Sustainable transport: The case for Europe*, London: Belhaven Press.

Wiehler, F. and Stumm, T. (1995) 'The powers of regional and local authorities and their role in the European Union', *European Planning Studies* 3(2): 227–250.

Williams, R. (1993) *Blue Bananas, Grapes and Golden Triangles: Spatial planning for an integrated Europe*, Newcastle: Department of Town and Country Planning, University of Newcastle Upon Tyne.

—— (1996a) *European Union: Spatial policy and planning*, London: Paul Chapman Publishing.

—— (1996b) 'Networks and networks in European space', University of Newcastle: The 50th Anniversary Conference: Shaping Places. Conceptions and Directions for Spatial Planning, Department of Town and Country Planning, 25–27 October 1996.

—— (1999) 'Research networking and expert participation in EU policy making', Bergen: The AESOP XIII Congress, 7–11 July 1999.

—— (2000) 'Constructing the European Spatial Development Perspective – for whom?' *European Planning Studies* 8(3): 357–365

Williams, R. and Jørgensen, I. (1998) 'Europe of the regions and the regions of Europe:

the challenge of transnational spatial planning', Paper for XII AESOP Congress: Planning, Professionals and Public Expectations, Aveiro, Portugal, 22–25 July, 1998.

Williams, R., Connolly, P. and Healy, A. (2000) 'Territorial Impact Assessment: a scoping study. Final draft submission to the Committee on Spatial Development', Newcastle: ESPRIN Study Team.

Wilson, E. (1992) *The Sphinx in the City: Urban life, the control of disorder, and women*, Los Angeles: University of California Press.

Wood, D. (1993) *The Power of Maps*, London: Routledge.

Zonneveld, W. and Faludi, A. (1996) 'Cohesion versus competitive position: a new direction for European spatial planning', Toronto: The ACSP-AESOP Joint International Congress, 24–28 July, 1996.

Zukin, S. (1998) 'From Coney Island to Las Vegas in the urban imaginary: discursive practices of growth and decline', *Urban Affairs Review* 33(5): 627–654.

Index